'HOLY WAR' AGAINST SOUTH AFRICA'

How the Vatican and various Protestant institutions supported South Africa's Communist revolution....and why

Shaun Willcock

© Copyright 2003   Shaun Willcock

The right of Shaun Willcock to be identified as the author of this work has been asserted in accordance with the Copyright, Designs and Patents Act 1988.

All rights reserved. No reproduction, copy or transmission of this publication may be made without written permission. No paragraph of this publication may be reproduced, copied or transmitted save with the written permission or in accordance with the provisions of the Copyright Act 1956 (as amended). Any person who does any unauthorised act in relation to this publication may be liable to criminal prosecution and civil claims for damage.

Cromwell Publishers 405 Kings Road London SW10 0BB

Website: www.CromwellPublishers.co.uk

E-mail: Info@CromwellPublishers.co.uk

ISBN 1-903930-04-9

First Edition 1996 Published by Contending for the Faith Ministries, in association with Bible Based Ministries

Second Edition 2003 Published by Cromwell Publishers

DEDICATION

To my wife, Stacey,
Who, with me, lived through these momentous
And tragic times.
Together we watched and prayed.

FOREWORD

This is an extremely important book; indeed, it is vital for a correct understanding of what has in recent years occurred in South Africa.

For those who are unhappy spectators from afar, and have for many years been suspicious of the *political correctness* emanating from the world's media on the subject of South Africa, this book is essential and fascinating reading. Its contents are the fruit of expertise, highly intelligent, thoroughly researched – and written by one who is a close observer of the scene, within the country, and from a Christian and biblical perspective.

In it *political correctness* is swept aside, and instead is exposed the wicked political and ecclesiastical intrigue and corruption behind the façade that the media presents. Men made famous throughout the world by this presentation – Archbishop Tutu, Nelson Mandela, etc – are seen for what they *really* are, and with quotations to prove it.

In fact, from his extensive research Shaun Willcock reveals numerous alarming facts, not least that 'a Marxist dictatorship has risen from the ruins of a once-prosperous South Africa', and that many parts of the country are 'descending into the Dark Ages, from which they had partially emerged with the coming of Protestant missionaries and the subsequent dissemination of the Gospel of Christ'.

I cannot recommend this book too highly, and praise God that at last we have trustworthy information about the South African tragedy upon which all fair-minded people can rely.

Dr Peter Trumper
Vocal Protestants' International Fellowship

CONTENTS

Introduction

PART ONE

1. 1652: Three Small Ships

2. Christ's Great Commission

3. Diaz and Da Gama

4. Jan van Riebeeck and the Dutch Settlement of the Cape

5. Britain Takes Control

6. Religious Toleration and the Arrival of Missionaries

7. Missionary Expansion and the 1820 Settlers

8. The Great Trek

9. British Colonies and Boer Republics

10. Racial Turmoil: Britons, Boers, and the Black Races

11. The Progress of Popery

12. The Conspirators

13. The Conspirators Against South Africa

PART TWO

14. The Victory of Afrikaner Nationalism

15. Apartheid

16. The ANC Banned and Mandela Imprisoned

17. The Vatican, the WCC, and "Liberation Theology"

18. Why South Africa was Targeted

19. The Conflict Escalates, and ANC/"Church" Cooperation Increases

20. The Early 1980's: Roman Catholic Support for the ANC

21. 1983: The SACC Thoroughly Exposed

22. 1985: Massive Intensification of "Church" Involvement in the Revolution

23. 1985: "Evangelicals" Join the Radicals; the Call for Sanctions

24. 1986: Further Intensification of Ecclesiastical Evil

25. 1987: "The Armed Struggle is a Theological Duty!"

26. 1988: When "Standing for the Truth" Meant Supporting Terror

27. 1989: The "Pastoral Plan", Protest Marches, and "Progressive Christians"

28. 1990: Unleashing the Bear

29. 1991: "Reaping a Whirlwind the Churches helped to Sow"

30. 1992: US Pressure, NP Retreat, ANC Advance

31. 1992: "Pray for the Downfall of the Sinister Government!"

32. 1992: The "Declaration on Religious Rights and Responsibilities"

33. 1992: Providing Martyrs for the Cause

34. 1993: Ecclesiastical Eulogies for a Communist They Equated with Christ

35. 1993: "Kill the Pastor, Kill the Church!"

36. 1993: The ANC Effectively in Power Prior to the Election

37. 1994: Eliminating the Opponents of ANC Rule

38. 1994: The "Churches" Prepare for the Election

39. 1994: An Election Neither Free Nor Fair

40. 1994: Inauguration Day

41. What Has This Book Shown?

42. The Christian's Duties

INTRODUCTION

In April 1994, after decades in which South Africa was literally torn apart by a Red revolution of horrifying proportions, the Communist-controlled African National Congress came to power in this great land. The Marxist murderers and other assorted criminals who jubilantly hailed the dawn of a "New South Africa" had bombed and burned, shot and stabbed their way to power, leaving in their wake tens of thousands of people dead, brutally exterminated in the name of "liberation". In order to achieve their goals, they had to clamber over a veritable mountain of corpses, a mountain of their making.

The issue of South Africa became one around which the entire world united, as it had never united before. The world acted in concert to destroy it. This book sets forth a major reason for this unprecedented global focus: the ambitions of the Vatican, operating through powerful political channels that, on the surface, would appear to have no connections with the Vatican or the Roman Catholic religion at all. The world, however, can be a strange place, and full of surprises; for one thing, Roman Catholicism is a political as well as a religious system, with a centuries-old lust for total world domination, and no scruples whatsoever about how to achieve it; for another thing, political rulers will enter into the most unlikely alliances in order to achieve their own ambitions. And they are well aware of the power of religion to move men, even entire populations. One religion in particular, immensely influential on a truly global scale: Roman Catholicism, now holding sway over almost one out of every five people on earth.

This book documents the immense role played by the Roman Catholic system, that religio-political institution pretending to be a Christian church, in the South African revolution. But it was not alone in this. The Papal system, the Mother of Harlots and Abominations (Rev.17:5), was the mastermind, certainly; but its religious daughters, those supposedly "Protestant" institutions affiliated with the South African Council of Churches and the World Council of Churches, were also deeply involved in supporting the revolution, and their diabolical involvement is amply documented here. This book emphasises the undeniable fact that the revolution would never have succeeded were it not for the enthusiastic, active and sustained support of these religious institutions, which, in the name of Christ, blasphemously threw their weight behind the Communist revolutionaries; so that it can be said, without fear of contradiction, that in a very real sense this was a religious revolution. A revolution waged as much with terribly distorted interpretations of the Bible as with bullets. A revolution directed as much by those paying allegiance to the Vatican, and to Geneva, as to Moscow.

Wicked men, falsely claiming to be Christians, through the centuries have done many terrible deeds. But our own twentieth century is replete with examples of religious barbarity. In the first four years of the last decade of the twentieth century, over 50 000 people were killed, in South Africa, by savage revolutionaries urged on, every step of the way, by Roman Catholic and Protestant religious leaders. To many, this may seem unbelievable. Yet it is all too horrifyingly true, as the accumulated evidence of many years makes plain. The book pulls no punches, and the author makes no apology for this. Religious institutions brought untold suffering to the peoples of South Africa, and the truth must be told, in order to rip away the mask of piety and holiness which they wear with such hypocrisy and effrontery. Multitudes are deceived by them. The author urges every reader to look to Jesus Christ, the holy, harmless, undefiled, spotless Son of the living God; and where those who claim to be his followers do not bear his image, they should be shunned for the deceivers that they are.

Part One is a brief history of South Africa, from its beginnings until 1910. This section gives important background information, and examines the subject from a biblical perspective, tracing the hand of God in the affairs of this country, and analysing the various events in the light of the Lord's sovereign purposes for nations and individuals. Part One, then, gives the historical backdrop to Part Two.

Part Two is concerned with South Africa from 1910 (the year of the Union) onwards; its primary focus being the part played by the Vatican, and various Protestant institutions, in the Communist revolution which for so many years engulfed this country, and which was finally victorious.

What is written in these pages reveals that the Papal Harlot, that centuries-old enemy of the truth, remains what she ever has been, and ever will be; and that, in our day, Protestant institutions, daughters of the Harlot, have imbibed her fanatical belief that the end justifies the means - even if those means include terrorism, revolution, untold suffering and bloodshed.

The author has also been at pains to show that the true and living God, the God of the Bible, is in absolute and sovereign control of all events, great and small, that occur on this earth. His purposes are being accomplished. Nothing is by chance, nothing is by accident. And the knowledge of this glorious truth ought to be of immense comfort and encouragement to the true Christian, whether he lives in South Africa or in some other part of the world. For of this the author is certain: we live in momentous times. Behind the scenes, great plans are being set in motion by wicked men. Only in Christ is there peace. Only the true Christian can lift his eyes, as it were, to heaven, and see the Almighty God, the Lord of heaven and earth, upon his throne, in absolute control of all events. And only to the true children of God did the Lord Jesus Christ speak those lovely words: "In the world ye shall have tribulation: but be of good cheer; I have overcome the world" (Jn.16:33).

Shaun Willcock 1994

SOUTH AFRICAN LAMENT

Africa! Even the very word itself
Seems filled with adventure and mystery.
What terrible and tragic tales could be told
Of its savage and bloody history.

An African sunset no man can forget,
Who has stood and watched such a sight;
But for Africa, sunset has come all too soon:
Alas! It's already the night.
For many long centuries, its peoples were bound
In darkness of heathenism;
And though, it is true, Gospel freedom's been preached,
Today Gospel light is so dim.

Across its vast plains much blood has been shed
As power-mad tyrants have raged;
Hideous has been the cruelty shown
To both the young babe and the sage.
From earliest times, chiefs and witchdoctors sought
To control both by force and by fear;
And then foreign tyrants brought a new doctrine in -
A Red burden for Africa to bear.

Country by country, the continent collapsed,
Until only one country was left;
The strongest of all, it would not give in,
Until it was of friends bereft.
South Africa! Land upon which the Lord
Bestowed such rich blessings indeed!
From your shores the Gospel diffused to the north -
Safe haven for that precious seed!

But now my heart breaks as I watch your demise;
You too, dear country? You too?
Will you follow the way of the lands to the north?
Will murderers rule over you?

Will your people continue to bleed and to die?
They looked for Utopia, but followed a lie.

I am a son of the Dark Continent;
I was born here, and here I was raised;
And I love its raw beauty, the bush and the plains,
Where the elephant and antelope graze.
How carefree the days of my childhood were!
What wonders I loved to behold
In this beautiful land of mountains and hills,
Of vast fields of green and of gold.
But will young boys explore, as I used to do,
And as I so love to do still?
Or is this land's beauty now hid from the eyes
Of children who've learned how to kill?

Oh, you will not learn, unteachable men!
A heaven on earth's a dream, a fool's goal;
And what will it profit a man if he gain
The whole world, and lose his own soul?

Written by the present author on 11 August 1992, just less than two years before the Communist forces came to power.

PART ONE

CHAPTER ONE   1652: THREE SMALL SHIPS

On the 6th of April, in the year 1652, three small sailing ships cast anchor in a beautiful bay, called Table Bay, at the Cape of Good Hope, almost at the southernmost tip of the continent of Africa.

The three small ships were the "Goede Hoop" (Good Hope), the "Drommedaris", and the "Reiger". They had set sail from Holland some four months before, bound for this very spot.

The man in command of the expedition was a surgeon named Jan van Riebeeck. As he and his men sailed into Table Bay, they gazed upon one of the most beautiful sights in the world: a great, flat-topped mountain brooded over the lovely natural bay. It is a sight that has lost none of its thrill with the passing of the centuries. Table Mountain, with its famous "tablecloth" of white cloud, is spectacular indeed. Truly, "the fairest Cape we saw in the whole circumference of the earth," as Sir Francis Drake was later to declare.

As van Riebeeck and his men stepped ashore, the continent of Africa stretching before them, history was made. That landing was destined, in the purposes of a sovereign God, to be the beginning of a new European settlement, which would ultimately result in the formation of one of the greatest countries in the world; and, more importantly, in the diffusion of the Gospel of the Lord Jesus Christ to the wild heathen nations of the interior.

In 1652, three small ships cast anchor in a beautiful bay.

This was God's time. An event, a moment, of truly eternal significance for those ordained to eternal life in nations at that time still unknown to the rest of the world, dwelling in the darkness of heathenism.

But before proceeding, we must travel still further back in time.

CHAPTER TWO   CHRIST'S GREAT COMMISSION

Almost two thousand years ago, the Son of the living God, Jesus Christ, about to ascend back to his Father in heaven, said to his little band of disciples, "All power is given unto me in heaven and in earth. Go ye therefore, and teach all nations, baptizing them in the name of the Father, and of the Son, and of the Holy Ghost: teaching them to observe all things whatsoever I have commanded you: and, lo, I am with you alway, even unto the end of the world" (Matt.28:19,20).

"Go ye into all the world, and preach the gospel to every creature" (Mk.16:15).

We read in Luke's Gospel, that he "said unto them, Thus it is written, and thus it behoved Christ to suffer, and to rise from the dead the third day: and that repentance and remission of sins should be preached in his name among all nations, beginning at Jerusalem" (Lk.24:46,47).

Luke also records these words of the Lord Jesus at that time: "ye shall be witnesses unto me both in Jerusalem, and in all Judea, and in Samaria, and unto the uttermost part of the earth" (Acts 1:8).

And God's Word says, "And they went forth, and preached every where" (Mk.16:20).

In obedience to their Lord's command, his disciples carried the Gospel into the world. It was proclaimed in Jerusalem (Acts 2); in Judea and Samaria (Acts 8); and to the Gentile world under the dominion of the mighty Roman Emperor (Acts 10-28). The apostles and evangelists worked tirelessly to spread the Gospel far and wide.

And God, in his all-wise providence, had raised up the Roman Empire, with its astoundingly efficient army, its brilliant administration, its excellent road system, for just such a time as this. There were other reasons as well, of course; but the Almighty God had decreed that the first missionaries of the Gospel of his Son would live at such a time, and *make use of* the Empire for the propagation of the Gospel.

Greek was the language of the Empire; and this meant that, almost wherever the apostles and evangelists went, they were understood when they preached the Gospel. They did not need to spend time learning various languages. The excellent Roman transportation system enabled the missionaries to disperse across the Empire with relative ease.

Thus did the Lord so order events that the Gospel of Christ was spread throughout Europe, the Middle East, and North Africa.

But in time, he who "removeth kings, and setteth up kings" (Dan.2:21), and who "doeth according to his will in the army of heaven, and among the inhabitants of the earth" (Dan.4:35), pulled down that great Roman Empire, as he had pulled down other great empires before it. As a monstrous, counterfeit "church" system rose in power and ruled from the seat of the old emperors in Rome (Dan.7:23-25), the *true* Church of Jesus Christ "fled into the wilderness" (Rev.12:6). The Dark Ages descended upon Europe. Only a small remnant remained who were faithful to the true God, and would not bow the knee to the papal Baal sitting on the seven hills. From the Alps, Waldensian believers kept the torch of the Gospel burning in a Europe darkened by superstition and priestcraft. Missionaries sowed the seed of the Gospel throughout the continent.

But what about the *uttermost parts* of the earth? What about "the regions beyond" (2 Cor.10:16)? The regions beyond Europe?

The Lord, who gave the command to "go into all the world", was preparing the way - just as he had prepared the way for his Gospel to penetrate the utmost bounds of Europe in the days of the Roman Empire.

For it must be remembered that large parts of the earth's surface were *entirely unknown* to the faithful Christian witnesses who lived during the Dark Ages. The Americas, most of Africa, and most of Asia, were unknown, at that time, to the peoples of Europe! First, then, it was necessary for horizons to be broadened; for the maps to be enlarged; for new lands to be discovered! Only when they were known to exist, could Christian missionaries carry the precious Gospel to them.

First, therefore, there had to be an "Age of Discovery". And God, who controls all events, great and small, that occur on this earth, raised up certain nations, and certain *men* from those nations, to venture out into unknown seas, to push beyond the boundaries of the then-known world.

CHAPTER THREE

DIAZ AND DA GAMA

Today, there are those who are indignant that world history is so often viewed from the European perspective. Why, for example (they ask), do the history books say that Christopher Columbus "discovered" America? There were entire nations living throughout that continent! People who had been there for centuries!

Each nation has its history, of course; and it is perfectly true that the heroes of the "Age of Discovery" were discoverers on behalf of *European* nations. They were the first *Europeans* to discover lands that had previously been unknown to Europeans - but not to the peoples already living there.

Yet, from the *biblical* perspective, Europe is vitally important, and the discoveries made by men on behalf of European nations are vitally important. *Not* because the Europeans are better people, in themselves, than anyone else; no, *all* men, of whatsoever nation, are sinners in the eyes of the Lord (Rom.3:9-19,22,23). But Europe is important to world history, from the biblical perspective, because, in the all-wise providence of God, certain nations of Europe were to experience great spiritual awakenings, in which multitudes were saved from their sins, finding peace with God through the Lord Jesus Christ. This ultimately resulted in the Gospel of Jesus Christ being taken, by missionaries from Europe, to "the uttermost part of the earth".

God predestined the greatness of certain European empires, which, like the old Roman Empire, would be beneficial to the missionaries of Christ. In this we see his power and absolute dominion over the affairs of men.

Those empires, like the old Roman Empire, have come and gone. They appeared on the stage of history for a time, and then they faded, as all empires the world has ever known have done, and must do. But they served a purpose in the eternal purposes of God. "Behold, the nations are as a drop of a bucket, and are counted [by God] as the small dust of the balance" (Isa.40:15); "All nations before him are as nothing; and they are counted to him less than nothing, and vanity" (vs.17). As he raised up mighty Pharaoh for a purpose (Rom.9:17), so he raised up certain European nations for a time, to fulfil his divine will.

And so we find that, even before the great spiritual awakenings in Europe, God raised up European empires, and men within them in whose hearts burned the desire to discover and to explore new lands. Once discovered, the ambassadors of Christ could go in with their glad tidings.

Our interest, at this time, is South Africa.

When the Ottoman Turks conquered Asia Minor, capturing Constantinople in 1453, the land route to the Far East was no longer accessible to Western Europe. If a *sea* route could be discovered, the problem would be solved. And Portugal wanted to solve it.

There was, however, another motive behind Portugal's desire to find a sea route to the Indies: religion. Portugal was (like almost all of Europe in the fifteenth century) a Roman Catholic country. And the Papacy desired to use Portugal to conquer new lands for the Roman Catholic religion.

In 1415, the Portuguese began to capture parts of the African coast. They were constantly sailing further south. African slaves were brought to Portugal by the thousands. In the year 1471, the Portuguese seamen crossed the equator.

In August 1487, King John II of Portugal dispatched Bartholomew Diaz on an expedition. Diaz, with three ships, moved down the west coast of Africa. He rounded the southernmost tip of the Dark Continent, and landed at Algoa Bay. On an islet which he called "Ilheo da Santa Cruz" he erected a stone "padroes", or cross, which he dedicated to the Roman Catholic "saint", Gregory; and it was there, too, that the Roman Catholic mass was said for the first time on South African soil.[1]

Although Diaz wanted to press on for the Indies, his men did not. He reluctantly turned back - and on the homeward voyage, in May

---

[1] *The Catholic Church in South Africa*, by William Eric Brown, pg.1. Burns and Oates Ltd., London. 1960.

1488, he discovered the Cape Peninsula. This was named "Cabo Tormentoso", the Cape of Storms. It was also called "Cabo da Boa Esperanza", the Cape of Good Hope; because although Diaz had failed to reach the Indies, the next expedition would hopefully succeed.

His voyage had revealed the southernmost extension of the Dark Continent.

Then came Vasco da Gama.

King Manoel I of Portugal, John's successor, wasted no time in dispatching an expedition to reach the Indies by sea; to succeed where Diaz had failed. The man he chose to command the expedition was a high-ranking soldier named Vasco da Gama.

Da Gama set sail in July 1497, with four ships. The holds of his ships contained stone "padroes"; and he was on a *mission,* not just a voyage of discovery. For the king had told him that his voyage was *primarily* to spread the "Christian" faith (i.e. the Roman Catholic faith); only secondarily, to find a sea route to the East![2] Da Gama took an oath that he would carry "the Faith" wherever he went; and spent the night before setting sail at prayer, in the chapel of "Our Lady of Bethlehem".

The next morning, there was a High Mass, a candle-procession, and prescribed chants. Da Gama and his men knelt to receive a "general absolution", and to hear a bull from the pope read to them, in which the pope granted a "plenary indulgence" to any who might die on the voyage.[3]

Clearly, both Portugal and the Vatican were hoping for great things from this voyage.

Although the Lord God raised up these explorers to chart the coast of Africa, yet in his sovereign purpose, South Africa was not to be settled by Roman Catholics. How different the history of South Africa would have been, if this had happened! But the Lord had decreed otherwise. They were to discover, but not to possess. True believers have cause to thank God that the heavy heel of Rome did not grind South Africa underfoot from the very beginning of its European

---

[2] `The Catholic Church in South Africa, pg.2.`
[3] `The Catholic Church in South Africa, pg.2.`

colonisation! For this powerful politico-religious institution, although professing to be the "one true Church of Christ", is in reality the greatest *counterfeit* the world has ever seen.

Eventually, Rome's power would be felt in South Africa, but not for a long, long time. The Lord decreed otherwise. Some from every southern African nation will have cause to bless God for eternity that he did so (Rev.7:9,10).

It was certainly Rome's plan to use da Gama to propagate the Roman Catholic faith. Christians can look deeper, and discern Satan's plan to enchain more peoples to the feet of the pope and the idols of Romanism.
But let us follow da Gama's voyage.
His expedition left Portugal on 8 July 1497. On the 22nd November, he rounded the Cape, anchoring in Mossel Bay on the 25th November. There the ships remained for two weeks, and then continued their voyage. On the 25th December 1497, da Gama passed the coast that he named "Tierra de Natal" in honour of Christmas. Natal was destined, in the years to come, to become one of the four provinces of South Africa.

In May 1498, da Gama arrived in India. And he reached Portugal again, bearing spices, in September 1499, having lost 115 out of 170 of his company on the voyage. The sea route to the East had been discovered, and in the process, southern Africa had become known to European navigators. Soon the Portuguese ruled the Indian Ocean.

A Roman Catholic "church" building was built at Mossel Bay in 1501. But the Cape was just a station to the Portuguese, not a settlement.

The first viceroy of Portuguese India, D. Francisco de Almeida, was killed, along with 64 of his men, by Hottentots on the shores of Table Bay in 1510. Thereafter Portuguese sailors steered clear of the Cape.[4] The town of Mozambique, on the East African coast, became the main Portuguese port in Africa, from which ships set sail for

---

[4] *The Making of South Africa*, by M.S. Geen, pg.4. Maskew Miller Ltd., Cape Town. Third Edition 1961.

Europe.

As noted before, the hand of the Almighty can be seen in the providential manner in which the Cape of Good Hope, although discovered by the Portuguese, was not settled by them. If it had been, they would have brought the Roman Catholic religion, with its priests and pagan superstitions, to the black tribes of South Africa. Romish missionaries were to come eventually to these shores; but not in such a way that the country could be converted into a Roman Catholic one.

All that it would have taken, was for da Gama, or others, to have discovered the value of the Cape as a supply-point and resting-place for Portuguese ships on the way to the East. Instead, after de Almeida and his men were killed on Table Bay's shores, the Portuguese left the Cape alone. Truly the Lord, who oversees all events, prevented it.

In 1546, the Dominicans established themselves on the Zambesi River; and in 1560, Portuguese Jesuits initiated missionary activity at Luanda and on the Zambesi.[5] Roman Catholic missionaries, particularly the Jesuits, were extremely zealous; and it was only the divine will that prevented them from landing at the Cape and penetrating the interior of South Africa, or from crossing overland into South Africa from the Portuguese settlements on the east and west coasts. It was in the eternal purpose of God to make South Africa a country in which the Gospel could be freely proclaimed; and from which it could be carried to the countries to its north.

And so it is that we arrive at the year 1652, when those three small Dutch ships, under the command of Jan van Riebeeck, anchored in Table Bay.

---

[5] *The Catholic Church in South Africa*, pg.3.

CHAPTER FOUR

JAN VAN RIEBEECK AND THE DUTCH SETTLEMENT OF THE CAPE

In the sixteenth century, the Spanish and Portuguese sea power declined, and the Dutch sea power grew.

The Portuguese throne had passed to King Philip II of Spain, in the second half of the sixteenth century. In 1581, Philip II closed Lisbon harbour to the Dutch, who were now forced to sail to the East themselves. This they did, very successfully. The Dutch East India Company was formed in 1602, and it broke the Portuguese monopoly of trade with the East. It became very powerful indeed. The Dutch sailed to China, Japan, and Siam; explored parts of the Australian and New Zealand coasts; discovered the Fiji Islands; occupied Mauritius and St. Helena and most of Ceylon. For all practical purposes, the Company served the Dutch government, and extended its empire.

Both Dutch and English ships had anchored in Table Bay before 1652, but no settlement had been established. In 1647 a Dutch East India Company ship, the "Haarlem", was wrecked there; and its crew had to live there for over a year. When they returned to Holland, two of them gave such a report of the place that the Company decided to establish itself there; and Jan van Riebeeck, who was a ship's surgeon with the fleet that rescued the men, also spoke well of the bay and its climate. Van Riebeeck was given the task of heading the expedition of 80 men. In April 1652, his three ships arrived in Table Bay, and the Cape of Good Hope fell under Dutch control. European settlers had arrived: the Cape Colony had begun.

Most significant of all, was that van Riebeeck was a Dutch Protestant. In the sixteenth century, the Protestant Reformation had occurred in Europe. The Bible was translated into a number of European languages; the Holy Spirit brought conviction of sin, and the saving knowledge of Jesus Christ, to many through the Word of God; and the Papacy, which for a thousand years had enslaved Europe, suffered great loss. Vast numbers cast off the shackles of Rome.

In the Netherlands, the doctrines of John Calvin came to dominate the northern provinces. In 1581, the Low Countries were divided: the northern provinces of Holland and Zeeland divided from the south. The Dutch Republic was formed, and was Calvinistic. Belgium, in the south, was Roman Catholic.

This is not to say that all in the Dutch Republic were Christians! By no means. Not everything about Calvinistic theology is biblical, including the awful concept of a "State Church", which is nowhere taught in the New Testament. One of its deadly dangers is that it leads many to think that they are Christians merely because they were born to parents of, and baptized into, a particular religion. Nevertheless, there is much in that system of doctrine known as "Calvinism" that is biblical: that God, from all eternity, elected some of mankind to salvation in Jesus Christ (Jn.17:2,6; Acts 13:48; Rom.9; Eph.1; etc.); that Christ died for the elect (Acts 20:28; Eph.5:25; Jn.10:11,15, etc.); that those for whom he died, are in God's appointed time regenerated by the Holy Spirit (Rom.8:30, etc.), and thereby enabled to repent of their sins, and believe in Jesus Christ; and are justified by faith in Christ alone (Rom.4, etc.). Such, in essence, is the Gospel of the grace of God. It is true, not because Calvin happened to teach it, but because it is the truth of the Word of God. And there were many, in Holland and elsewhere, who were saved by God's grace, through faith.

Furthermore, Protestants had a *deep aversion* to the Roman Catholic religion. They recognised, in the Papacy, the fulfilment of the biblical prophecies of the Antichrist (2 Thess.2, etc.). Romanism was proclaimed, rightly, to be the "Great Whore" of biblical prophecy (Rev.17), to be shunned by all Christians.

The great God saw to it that the coming of the Dutch to the Cape (instead of the Portuguese or some other Roman Catholic nation) opened up southern Africa to the Gospel of Christ, as shall be seen - even though the Dutch themselves were, for the most part, Protestants but not true Christians. This, too, shall be seen with more clarity later on.

The arrival of the Dutch at the Cape did not immediately result in missionary work being undertaken among the savage black tribes of southern Africa. In the Lord's will, other matters had to be taken care of first.

Apart from the Bushmen and the Hottentots, there were no African tribes as far south as the Cape of Good Hope. In fact (and this has been conveniently "forgotten" in the modern political climate), the Bantu tribes were, like the Europeans, comparative *newcomers* to southern Africa as well![6]

The Bushmen were a small, yellow-skinned race, nomads who lived by hunting, and who had been pushed south by the larger, more powerful Bantu tribes.

The Hottentots were larger than the Bushmen, and were pastoralists. The Dutch settlers soon came into contact with them. Naturally, both Hottentots and Bushmen were utterly pagan, and desperately in need of the Gospel of Christ.

In 1658, van Riebeeck introduced large numbers of slaves to the Cape. They were blacks from the west African coast; and later, from 1667, slaves were brought from Asia. Thus the Cape settlement soon came to consist of Dutch Europeans, Hottentots, and African and Asian slaves.

The Dutch Protestants saw nothing wrong with owning slaves. God's Word, however, gives clear commands as to how Christian masters are to *treat* their servants (e.g. Philemon vss.15-18; Eph.6:9; Col.4:1; 1 Tim.6:1,2; etc.); and tragically - precisely because the Dutch settlers were (although Protestants) not for the most part true Christians - their slaves were not always treated well. Let it be said again: the coming of the Protestant Dutch to the Cape opened the door for the Gospel of Jesus Christ to penetrate southern Africa; but this in no way implies that all the Dutch, or even the majority of them, were Christians. Politically, their settlement of the Cape was, in the long run, advantageous to the spread of the Gospel; but it was not, as a general rule, the Dutch who carried the Gospel to the heathen nations of southern Africa.

As was stated previously, one of the great tragedies of the Reformation was that it did not do away with the Roman Catholic notion of a "State Church": the notion that all those born within a certain territory, and being baptized as infants into the state-protected religion, were "Christians". This caused much confusion (and still does wherever this doctrine is held): for on the one hand, true Christians

---

[6] *The Making of South Africa*, pg.12.

within these Protestant institutions were preaching that salvation is by God's grace through faith alone; and on the other hand, some of the institutions themselves officially proclaimed the utterly false, heretical doctrine of "baptismal regeneration". By the grace of God, there were those who were enabled to see the truth, and trust in the merits of Christ alone for their eternal salvation; but tragically, the majority were deceived into trusting in human works.

The Dutch inevitably came into conflict with the Hottentots and the Bushmen. Fighting continued until 1677, when the Dutch united with the Hottentots to attack the Bushmen. The Hottentots were now disappearing from the stage of history. Some clans had moved further inland; others were disintegrating. In addition, the terrible European diseases, such as smallpox, were decimating them.

Many of the Hottentots intermarried with the Dutch settlers and with the imported slaves; and the Hottentot identity began to disappear. Their intermingling resulted in the emergence, at the Cape, of the "Cape Coloured" people.

As for the little Bushmen, who found both Europeans and Hottentots to be against them, they were tragically reduced in numbers, and found refuge only in the Kalahari Desert and in South West Africa, where their few descendants are still found today.

The Dutch Reformed denomination was the Cape's "State Church", and no other denomination was officially tolerated until the late 1700's. While this was disadvantageous to the spreading of the Gospel, it did mean that the *Roman Catholic* institution was unable to send its Jesuits or other missionaries to the Cape, either. In this way the Lord held back the plans of the Papacy.

Roman Catholic priests were excluded from Table Bay from the moment the intensely Protestant Dutch took possession of it in 1652. Those settlers were only too well aware of the evil workings of Romanism. The vile atrocities of that institution were too well known. Oh, for that same knowledge amongst Protestants today!

As early as 1660, a French Roman Catholic bishop, who was shipwrecked in Table Bay, was forbidden to say mass!

In 1688, six Jesuits were permitted to land, but only because they were astronomers as well. However, they had to live on their ships, and were forbidden to say mass.

According to their own writings, there were quite a number of Roman Catholics at the Cape. The Jesuits left this record:

"Although we were engaged in observations day and night, they were not our only occupation. Hardly had we taken possession of our new observatory when the Catholics of this Colony, who are fairly numerous, got to hear of it and showed very great interest They drew their rosaries and medals from their necks to show us that they were Catholics Those who spoke French, Latin, Spanish and Portuguese made their confession. We visited the sick in their houses and in hospital. It was all we could do to console them in so short a time, seeing that they were not allowed to come on board to hear Mass, nor were we allowed to say it on shore."[7]

Evidently, then, some of the settlers were Papists, although the vast majority were Protestants. Those who were Papists were not permitted to have priests of their religion at the Cape Colony.

While religious liberty is the best course a government can pursue, it being the work of the Holy Spirit to convict men of sin and of false religion and draw them to Christ, and not any government's duty to make one denomination the "State Church"; yet it *is* the government's duty to protect its citizens from those who are dangerous to the well-being of society. The Roman Catholic institution in general, and the *Jesuits* in particular, are dangerous to the well-being of any society, as history has proved; and the government of the Cape Colony cannot be faulted for refusing to permit the Jesuits to conduct their "religious" work. Let anyone who doubts this, ponder carefully the words of the American president, Abraham Lincoln, who was assassinated by a man under orders from the Jesuits.[8] Lincoln said:

"Till lately, I was in favour of the unlimited liberty of conscience as our constitution gives it to the Roman Catholics. But now, it seems to me that, sooner or later, the people will be forced to put a restriction

---

[7] *The Catholic Church in South Africa*, pg.4.
[8] *Rome's Responsibility for the Assassination of Abraham Lincoln*, by Brig. Gen. Thomas M. Harris. Williams Publishing Company, Pittsburg. 1897.

to that clause towards the Papists. Is it not an act of folly to give absolute liberty of conscience to a set of men who are publicly sworn to cut our throats the very day they have their opportunity for doing it? Is it right to give the privilege of citizenship to men who are the sworn and public enemies of our constitution, our laws, our liberties, and our lives?

"The very moment that Popery assumed the right of life and death on a citizen of France, Spain, Germany, England, or the United States, it assumed to be the power, the government of France, Spain, England, Germany, and the United States. Those States then committed a suicidal act by allowing Popery to put a foot on their territory with the privilege of citizenship. The power of life and death is the *supreme power,* and two *supreme powers* cannot exist on the same territory without *anarchy,* riots, bloodshed, and civil wars without end. When Popery will give up the power of life and death which it proclaims on its own divine power, in all its theological books and canon laws, then, and then alone, it can be tolerated and can receive the privileges of citizenship in a free country.

"Is it not an absurdity to give to a man a thing which he has sworn to hate, curse, and destroy? And does not the Church of Rome hate, curse, and destroy liberty of conscience whenever she can do it safely? I am for liberty of conscience in its noblest, broadest, highest sense. But I cannot give liberty of conscience to the Pope and to his followers, the Papists, so long as they tell me, through all their councils, theologians, and canon laws, that their conscience orders them to burn my wife, strangle my children, and cut my throat when they find their opportunity!"[9]

That the Jesuits are the most dangerous society of men in the history of the world, is amply borne out by their vile history.[10]

The Protestant settlers at the Cape Colony knew, only too well, of the evil dangers of permitting the Papal religion to gain any foothold at the Cape.

---

[9] *50 Years in the Church of Rome,* by Charles Chiniquy, pg.503. The Protestant Literature Depository, London. 1886.
[10] *The Secret History of the Jesuits,* by Edmond Paris. Chick Publications, Chino, California. Translated from the French 1975.

At *precisely* the same time in history, the settlers in the New World were doing the same thing! For example, in the Massachusetts Bay Colony, in 1647, it was *law* that no Jesuit was permitted into the colony.[11]

Today the cry would be: "That's discrimination! It's unjust!" But the point is this: these laws against the Jesuits were passed because the Jesuits were dangerous to society, a menace to law and order, a threat to the public peace! The freedom to practice one's religion is one thing; but when certain members of a religion use their religious freedom to cause wars, topple governments, etc., that is quite another thing!

As recently as 1975, as the Communist revolution was engulfing Rhodesia, this author's country of birth, Senator Desmond Lardner-Burke, speaking in the Senate, said: "The Roman Catholic church in Rhodesia is playing a major role in promoting Marxist Communism among the blacks, and the government is looking seriously at the possibility of declaring this church an illegal organisation."[12] It was not done. If it had not been the year 1975, but, say, the year 1675 or 1775, it *would* have been done, and the country would have been the safer for it.

In the century after the Reformation, the government of the Cape settlement refused to allow Roman Catholic priests to work at the Cape. That law would, much later, be changed; and South Africa has suffered the consequences in modern times.

Under Simon van der Stel, who arrived in 1679, the Cape settlement began to develop into a proper colony. The directors of the Dutch East India Company sent out both Dutch and German settlers to the Cape.

Having decided to encourage colonisation, the Dutch faced a problem: they wanted *Protestant* immigrants of Dutch or German extraction - but the Cape was not yet a very attractive place for

---

[11]*Records of the Governor and Company of the Massachusetts Bay in New England,* Vol.III, pgs.112, 193, edited by Nathaniel B. Shurtleff. Printed, by order of the Legislature, by William White, 1853.
[12]Quoted in *1521,* No.8, 1990-1. Published by the Vocal Protestants' International Fellowship, Clwyd, Britain. Peter Trumper, editor.

prospective settlers. In 1685, however, an event was to occur, far away in France, which was to have a profound effect on the European colonisation of the Cape; and again we can see that the sovereign hand of God was at work, according to his determinate counsel and foreknowledge.

The Reformation in the sixteenth century touched France as well. As early as 1533, the king began a persecution against "heretics" (i.e. Protestants), sanctioned by the pope. It was a terrible persecution, and thousands died. Yet by 1547, Protestant congregations were to be found all over France.

By 1559, there were seventy-two organised Reformed Churches in France.[13] Pastors for these congregations were sent from Geneva.[14] The congregations met in secret, and changed meeting-places often. Yet their growth was rapid. That year, a national synod was held in Paris, at which it was decided to organise a Presbyterian denomination. A Confession of Faith was agreed upon.

Later, the name "Huguenot" was applied to these people.

So rapid was their growth, that by 1561 it was claimed that there were 2150 Protestant churches in France.[15]

The Jesuits began to take root in France in 1551, penetrating the Court. They worked to destroy Protestantism. The Inquisition, too, was established in France to wipe out "heresy", in 1557.

Throughout this period, until the year 1598, the Protestants suffered terrible persecutions. Thousands upon thousands died. Wars were fought between the Papists and the Protestants. Then, in 1598, the king, by an edict known as the Edict of Nantes, made Calvinism a tolerated religion in France.[16]

The Jesuits, however, never accepted the Edict of Nantes, and continued to wage a secret war against the Protestants.[17] In 1685, Louis XIV *revoked* the edict - making Roman Catholicism the only

---

[13] *The Great Reformation,* by R. Tudor Jones, pgs.150,151. Inter-Varsity Press. 1985.
[14] *The Pilgrim Church,* by E.H. Broadbent, pg.228. Pickering and Inglis Ltd., London. 1989.
[15] *The Great Reformation,* pgs.150-151.
[16] *The Reformation of the Sixteenth Century,* by Roland H. Bainton, pgs.171,172. Beacon Press, Boston. 1985.
[17] *The Secret History of the Jesuits,* chapter six.

permitted religion in France. Open persecution broke out against the Huguenots, and some 400 000 fled France, and went to Geneva, Germany, England, America, and the Netherlands.

Now see the hand of God in the history of the Cape Colony: at *precisely* the time when the Dutch were wanting Protestant settlers for the Cape, the population of the Netherlands began to swell with Huguenot refugees from France: industrious, hard-working, and Protestant.

The Dutch initiated a large immigration scheme. Huguenots were offered a free passage to the Cape, a grant of land, and the loan of farming equipment. As a result, in 1688 and 1689, some 200 French Huguenots arrived at the Cape. These new immigrants were settled among the Dutch farmers, to facilitate their assimilation. Although they were Calvinistic Protestants like the Dutch, France was at war with Holland and Britain, and van der Stel was taking no chances. He repressed the French language and nationality. Dutch was the only medium of instruction in public schools.

Very soon, as a result of this policy, the Huguenots were *absorbed* into the Dutch population. Their French language began to disappear; they intermarried with the Dutch; etc. The fact that they were Calvinists like the Dutch helped a great deal. Thus, by the end of the seventeenth century, the "Afrikaner" was beginning to emerge: European in origin, but no longer distinctly Dutch, or German, or French. Rather, a son of Africa; a new white nation forged at the tip of the Dark Continent.

By 1700, it was decided that the Cape population would increase on its own, and so Company-sponsored Huguenot immigration ceased. A staunchly-Protestant colony was established at the Cape of Good Hope. It consisted of people who were well aware of the terrible nature of the Papal religion; indeed, the French Huguenot settlers had experienced first-hand its persecuting power. They were wresting an existence out of the South African soil, far away from their homeland in France, precisely because of the sufferings they and their fathers had endured at the hands of the Jesuits and the Inquisition. Providentially, the revocation of the Edict of Nantes had resulted in the strengthening of the Protestant population at the Cape.

The Lord was laying the foundation, at the tip of Africa, necessary for the propagation of the Gospel to the black tribes with whom the whites would eventually come into contact. The foundation was being laid for a mighty and prosperous country.

CHAPTER FIVE

BRITAIN TAKES CONTROL

Increasingly, the farmers on the frontier of the Cape Colony pushed further into the interior. Inevitably, they were engaged in skirmishes with the Bushmen, and at times the Hottentots.

At this time, and indeed until the year 1780, the Dutch Reformed denomination was the Cape's "State Church", and no other denomination was officially tolerated. As has already been mentioned, this ensured that the Roman Catholic institution could not enter southern Africa; but it also meant that missionary work was virtually non-existent during this period. The colonists were not in favour of missionary activity. This again serves to illustrate the point that has been made before, that while the colonists were Protestants, the majority of them gave no evidence of being true Christians.

Certainly, however, this was all in the Lord's predestined will. In the fullness of time, missionary work would commence; first, the groundwork had to be laid. The true Gospel was not yet being taken to the black tribes, but the *false* "gospel" was not being taken to them, either.

The Moravian Brethren, a Protestant group based in Bohemia and Germany, sent a missionary to work among the Hottentots, which he did from 1737 to 1744. But, due to the opposition of Dutch Reformed ministers, and of the colonists, he had to return to Europe.[18]

As for missionary work among the slave population at the Cape, this had virtually ceased. And the treatment of slaves had worsened.

And all the time, the frontier was expanding....

By 1775, the frontier had been pushed, by the cattle farmers, to the Fish River. Here they came into contact, and conflict, with the Xhosa nation, which had migrated southward to the Fish River. Governor van Plettenberg persuaded two Xhosa chiefs to agree to the lower Fish River being the border between the two, blacks and whites. Yet this, predictably, did not prevent clashes between them. Black and white had met; and South African history entered a new era. In the

---

[18] *The Making of South Africa*, pg.28.

providence of God, the meeting had to occur: the southward-migrating Bantu had to come into contact with the northward-migrating Afrikaners. For the coming of the European to the shores of South Africa, and the coming of the Bantu from the north to the south, was *decreed* by an all-wise and all-powerful God, that the Bantu nations would hear of the One who came to redeem sinners; "for there is none other name under heaven given among men, whereby [men] must be saved", than the name of Jesus Christ (Acts 4:12).

But what movements of peoples, and what wars, had to occur, that these things could be accomplished!

Both the Boers (the word means "farmers") and the Xhosas were livestock farmers. No wonder there was conflict! It has always been so, as the Scriptures themselves testify (Gen.13:1-9). The Boers had the advantage because they possessed firearms and horses.

The type of Afrikaner that this hard life on the frontier was producing came to be known as the "trekboer": tough, nomadic, independent. Religious too - the Bible, and particularly the Old Testament, was read avidly and reverently; but sadly, very often misinterpreted to justify the Boers in all that they did. Religious, yes - but few were genuinely regenerated souls.

What of the blacks they were coming into conflict with? What were their religious beliefs?

Witchcraft and the worship of their ancestors were the predominant aspects of the religious systems of the black tribes. Consequently, *fear* was a daily companion. The witchdoctor was all-powerful. Ritual murders were carried out, often to secure human body-parts for witchcraft purposes. The prince of darkness ruled over the black nations of Africa. Generation after generation lived and died in this terrible spiritual night.

God, whose Word declares that all nations must hear the Gospel of his dear Son, predestined the meeting of white and black at the Fish River. Southern Africa had to be opened up by the Europeans, that the way would be opened for the missionaries later.

In 1779, the First Frontier War between Boers and Xhosas began: the first of a series of wars that would be fought for a century. The Xhosas were formidable, but in 1781 the war ended when the Boers drove them back across the Fish River.

In that year, too, a French fleet, in the wake of a sea battle with a British fleet that had been bound for the Cape in order to capture it for Britain, sailed into Cape waters and occupied the Cape Colony, which remained in French hands until 1784. Meanwhile, Dutch shipping was in decline, and the days of Dutch East India Company dominance of the Cape were numbered. Times were changing. The great God, who "changeth the times and the seasons", and who "removeth kings, and setteth up kings" (Dan.2:21), was controlling events that would profoundly influence the Cape Colony, and open the next chapter in South Africa's history.

From 1789 to 1793, the Second Frontier War was fought. Dissatisfaction with Company rule was rife amongst the Boers, for various reasons; and in 1795 the burghers, who refused to submit to Company rule any longer, set up a provisional government. Thus the wide area occupied by the trekboers no longer answered to the Company.

In June 1795, a British fleet landed at the Cape, and in September of that year the Cape Colony came under British rule. After almost one and a half centuries, the Dutch control of the Cape was over. Such is the transitory nature of all earthly empires. They rise, they prosper, and they fall. Monarchs boast of their great might and dominion; but the time comes when the divine decree goes forth - "The kingdom is departed from thee" (Dan.4:29-31) - for of a truth "the *most High ruleth* in the kingdom of men, and giveth it to whomsoever he will" (Dan.4:32). Only *his* "dominion is an everlasting dominion, and *his* kingdom is from generation to generation: and all the inhabitants of the earth are reputed as nothing: and he doeth according to his will in the army of heaven, and among the inhabitants of the earth: and none can stay his hand, or say unto him, What doest thou?" (Dan.4:34,35). "The powers that be are ordained of God" (Rom.13:1), and remain in power until they have fulfilled God's purposes; and then they are removed, and other powers take their place. For almost a century and a half, the Dutch were masters of the Cape; then Britain was permitted, by the sovereign Lord, to gain control. And the time would come when the sun would set on the great British Empire as well, as it had on all empires before it.

CHAPTER SIX

RELIGIOUS TOLERATION AND THE ARRIVAL OF MISSIONARIES

By late 1796, the British conquest of the entire Cape Colony was complete. British rule was essential, in the purposes of God, for the further penetration of the European into the interior; for the autocratic rule of the British would finally drive the Boers to embark on the Great Trek northwards.

In 1799, the Boers at Graaf-Reneit revolted, but the uprising was put down. Then, the Third Frontier War was fought, between 1799 and 1803.

In 1802, when Britain and France signed a treaty of peace, one of the terms of the treaty was that the Cape would be placed under the rule of the Batavian Republic; and this occurred in 1803. It was to be a very short rule - the British took over again in 1806 - but significant to our present study for one reason: the principle of *religious toleration* was recognised.

As has been pointed out already in this book, during the reign of the Dutch East India Company, the Dutch Reformed denomination was the "Established Church", a branch of the government itself in fact, and no other denomination was tolerated at the Cape. This had the effect of preventing zealous Romish missionaries from spreading their poison, but it also meant that biblical mission work by true Christians was not carried out either. Only in the late 1700's was another religious denomination - the Lutheran - given permission to hold public services, etc. Then, when the British took over, the Cape Malay community was given permission to hold public services.

When the Colony came under the Batavian Republic, J.A. de Mist became the Commissioner-General. He and the Governor established a Hottentot reserve near Fort Frederick at Bethelsdorp; and a missionary of the London Missionary Society, J.T. van der Kemp, was placed in charge of it. They also supported the work of the Moravian Mission at Genadendal. No longer was the Dutch Reformed institution the only officially-tolerated denomination.

On 25 July 1804, de Mist published an ordinance promising religious toleration at the Cape. The document declared that "all Religious associations which for the furtherance of virtue and good conduct respect a Supreme Being" would henceforth enjoy equal protection under the law.

The Roman Catholic institution wasted no time. *Immediately,* three Romish priests arrived from Holland; and in 1805, a priest was appointed as prefect apostolic.[19]

From the Christian perspective, was this ordinance a good thing?

Inasmuch as it is not the place of the civil government to dictate on religious matters, it was good; for civil authorities are to maintain law and order in society (Rom.13:1-7; 1 Pet.2:13,14): it is not their function to control churches. True Christianity is not to be extended by the secular powers, or to be controlled by them. The Gospel is to advance by "the foolishness of preaching" (1 Cor.1:21), and by that alone. As the hearts of men and women are opened to attend to the Gospel (Acts 16:14), so the Church grows; and *not* by a government legislating in its favour.

Yet it was seen, in chapter four, that the Roman Catholic religio-political system in general, and the Jesuit Order in particular, are *dangerous* to the well-being of society, as history so amply testifies. And, as the American president, Abraham Lincoln (himself assassinated on Jesuit orders), said, religious tolerance should not be given to a religious institution that is a threat to the peace and well-being of society. And therefore, inasmuch as this ordinance granted the Roman Catholic institution the same freedoms as other religious institutions, it was *not* a good thing. An enormously powerful, despotic religio-political system, committed to the enslavement of all peoples and countries, by fair means or foul, to the Roman pope, and responsible for the massacre of untold millions through the centuries, was now able to legally work in South Africa.

It is a pity the Commissioner did not see that the wording of his ordinance was sufficient to *forbid* the coming of priests of Rome to the shores of South Africa; for the words of the ordinance were, "all Religious associations *which for the furtherance of virtue and good*

---

[19] `The Catholic Church in South Africa`, pg.6.

conduct respect a Supreme Being". The Papal system has *never* furthered virtue or good conduct! It has furthered all manner of evils wherever it has taken root. "A corrupt tree bringeth forth evil fruit" (Matt.7:17).

In January 1806, 63 British ships, carrying an army of almost 7000, sailed into Table Bay. The force was under the command of General Sir David Baird. Cape Town surrendered to the British.

Baird was a Scottish Presbyterian. All things Papist were (rightly) viewed with deep suspicion by Scottish Presbyterians, and Baird lost no time in expelling the three priests who had come to the Cape when de Mist had granted religious toleration almost two years before.[20]

In 1814, the Cape, which had been under British control by conquest, became Britain's by treaty.

In February 1818, a Benedictine bishop, Edward Bede Slater, was appointed Vicar Apostolic of the Cape. The British government, however, refused him permission to go. He did stop in at Cape Town for three weeks on his way to Madagascar and Mauritius in 1820, and he left a priest named Scully in charge there. In 1822, a foundation stone was laid for a Roman Catholic "church" building in Cape Town.[21]

From 1820, the British government had been prepared to pay an annual stipend to fund a Roman Catholic chaplain at the Cape. And this was done. As Lord Somerset, Governor of the Cape, declared in 1817, "all religious denominations are not only tolerated but entitled to equal privileges in the Colony according to the fundamental laws of the Batavian Republic, guaranteed to the inhabitants by the capitulation."[22]

The British authorities, then, simply followed the lead of the short-lived Batavian government of the Cape in the matter of religious tolerance, even paying an annual stipend to the priest who served the Roman Catholic community at the Cape (under Batavian rule, only ministers of the Dutch Reformed institution received salaries from the

---

[20] *The Catholic Church in South Africa*, pg.6.
[21] *The Catholic Church in South Africa*, pgs.6,7.
[22] *The Catholic Church in South Africa*, pg.10.

government, even though religious toleration was exercised).[23] The Roman Catholic institution now had a foothold on South African soil. Its sinister influence would be felt more and more in the years ahead.

Let us now consider two of the *blessings* that God, in his sovereignty, bestowed upon South Africa through the British control of the Cape.

The first was that missionaries began to arrive in Cape Town, and began work in the colony. The eighteenth century witnessed the Evangelical Awakening in Britain. The Holy Spirit moved with mighty saving power across that land, and multitudes pressed into the kingdom of God. George Whitefield was the chief instrument, in the Lord's hands, in this Awakening, and his clear and powerful voice was heard by countless souls as he preached the Gospel of the grace of God. But not only Whitefield: other men, too, were the instruments of Jehovah in this mighty spiritual work.

The Awakening touched all classes of society; and its effects were felt in all aspects of the life of the nation. Good works flow from genuine saving faith (Jas.2:14-26; Eph.2:10), and the Awakening resulted in many such works. The desire to propagate the Gospel of Jesus Christ to the ends of the earth, in obedience to his great commission, burned in the hearts of many godly men (Matt.28:19,20; Acts 1:8). Consequently, this period saw the birth of various missionary societies: the London Missionary Society, the Baptist Missionary Society, the Scottish Missionary Society, etc. It was not long before missionaries were being sent out to the Cape to work among the Hottentots, slaves, and others. In the will of God, the time had now come for the Gospel of his dear Son to be taken to the inhabitants of southern Africa who had never before heard it. The way had been prepared: the fullness of time had come.

Not all the missionaries, of course, were men of God. But amongst them there were those who were called, both by grace to Christ, and to the work of the ministry; and for this, all Christians will rejoice. Light began to dawn upon the heathen nations of South Africa.

The second blessing which came to South Africa with the British

---

[23] *The Making of South Africa*, pg.50.

control of the Cape was temporal in nature, but a fruit of that spiritual Awakening Britain had enjoyed: the abolition of slavery. The Awakening had aroused the consciences of many, even of those who were not themselves brought to a saving knowledge of Christ. Such is the effect of the Gospel when the Holy Spirit does such a great work as was done during that period. And thus those who are not called by grace, yet benefit from some of the external, temporal results of a great spiritual awakening, when the Lord is pleased to grant it.

As pointed out in an earlier chapter, the New Testament recognises the reality of the institution of slavery; but it lays down very specific instructions as to how Christian masters are to treat their servants. This is not to say that slavery is a good thing: the heart of unregenerate man is so sinful, so desperately wicked, that, when once a man has power over another man, the natural tendency of the unregenerate is to exercise cruelty. Christian masters are commanded to be fair, just, and kind to their slaves; but nowhere does the New Testament say that slavery is a good thing. It declares that *liberty* is a better state than slavery (1 Cor.7:20-24).

Slavery, as practiced by the European powers, was a dreadful thing. The barbarities of the slave trade were numerous and terrible. And, rightly, there was a desire in the hearts of good men to see the practice abolished. This desire was to greatly affect the Cape Colony.

The abolition of slavery at the Cape played an important part in adding to the resentment that the Boers felt towards the British authorities; and this resentment finally culminated in the Great Trek of the Boers. Even this event was according to the determinate counsel of God, for thereby the *interior* of South Africa was opened up, and settled, by the whites. And this was necessary, in order that the Gospel of Christ could penetrate to the farthest corners of South Africa. And beyond.

CHAPTER SEVEN

MISSIONARY EXPANSION AND THE 1820 SETTLERS

The coming of Evangelical missionaries to the Cape Colony was to have a profound effect on the history of South Africa. As was pointed out in the last chapter, the abolition of slavery was to a large extent the fruit of the Evangelical Awakening. And so the British control of the Cape not only proved beneficial to the propagation of the Gospel among the tribes already known to the white settlers, but also, because of the abolition of slavery and other things, was to cause the Great Trek of the Boers, which opened up *new* areas of southern Africa, and thus was ultimately of benefit to the propagation of the Gospel.

The London Missionary Society began sending missionaries to the Cape, the first arriving in 1799. One group began work among the Xhosas, but in 1800 they withdrew due to difficulties. Another group tried to work among the Bushmen, but found it easier to work among the Hottentots.[24]

The missionaries were hated by many of the Boers because they exposed their mistreatment of servants. They were of the opinion that they could treat their servants harshly whenever they deemed it necessary. The missionaries' accusations caused the government to investigate, and this was deeply resented by the Boers. A tragic commentary on the so-called "Christianity" of many of these colonists!

As the years passed, increasing numbers of missionaries arrived. By 1815, representatives of a number of societies were at work. The London Missionary Society (LMS) was working mainly among the Griquas by that year; but in addition, the chief of the Bechuanas invited the LMS to work among his people (Bechuanaland is now called Botswana); and a mission station was established there in 1820.[25]

Not all the missionary societies were truly evangelical, nor were all

---

[24] *History of the Church in Africa*, by Jonathan Hildebrandt, pgs.82,83. Africa Christian Press, Ghana. Third Revised Edition 1990.
[25] *History of the Church in Africa*, pgs.82-86.

the missionaries themselves true Christians. The "gospel" proclaimed by some was not the true Gospel of Jesus Christ. Yet, by the grace of God, there were those who *did* proclaim the Gospel, and many now in heaven have cause to rejoice for their faithful ministries.

Nor did most of those missionaries follow the New Testament teaching on the establishment of local churches, church order, etc. Most were representatives of denominational or interdenominational societies; and most held to incorrect, unscriptural views of baptism and other matters. This is to be regretted; however, all true Christians will rejoice whenever the Gospel is faithfully proclaimed, and the fundamental doctrines of the Christian faith are taught. It is regrettable that, since their inception, most of the Protestant bodies have demonstrated a great lack of conformity to New Testament principles and practices in such matters as church autonomy (practicing denominationalism instead of holding to the independence of each local church), baptism (practicing paedobaptism instead of the baptism of believers only by immersion), etc. While rejoicing for the fact that the Lord has had many dear and godly saints within some of these bodies, believers seeking only to follow the simple New Testament plan will naturally be disappointed that, along with the faithful proclamation of the Gospel, those zealous, devoted servants of the Lord within those institutions did not also obey the next part of the Lord's great commission, and baptize the converts by immersion (Matt.28:19,20).

Be that as it may, the Gospel of Christ, proclaimed by fallible men (as it has always been, and always will be), was beginning to penetrate into southern Africa! Tribes which for long centuries had lived in the darkness of heathenism, worshipping devils and committing all manner of evils, were, one by one, beginning to hear the glad tidings of the One who came to save sinners. It was slow work - painfully slow. It was laborious and beset with numerous difficulties. Every Christian can have nothing but praise for those pioneering evangelists who sought, with all their hearts, to take Christ's message to pagan tribes. If today's modern professing Christians, with luxuries at their fingertips, could be found even half as faithful and zealous as those brave men, how wonderful it would be! Many today, with far more scriptural notions of matters of church order, etc., will not hear, on that great day, the "Well done!" which those men will hear (Matt.25:21).

John Philip, superintendent of the LMS' work in southern Africa, was the driving force behind an ordinance (Ordinance 50), issued in July 1828, which gave the Hottentots and "all free persons of colour" the same legal and civil rights as the Europeans. This was good in that it made whites and coloureds equal; but unfortunately it increased vagrancy. And this ordinance, therefore, was one of the principal causes of the Great Trek.

Let us now briefly consider the emancipation of the slaves. In the wake of the Evangelical Awakening in Britain, a number of politicians came together to form what was called the "Clapham Sect". They were deeply involved in the establishment of the Church Missionary Society in 1799, as well as the British and Foreign Bible Society. And they worked tirelessly for the abolition of slavery. William Wilberforce was one of them. By 1807, they had succeeded in seeing to it that a bill was passed abolishing slave-trading from January 1, 1808. Then, on August 29, 1833, the Abolition of Slavery Bill became law. Slavery was abolished throughout the British Empire.

In the Cape, the colonists had been expecting the abolition of slavery, but what particularly angered them was that many suffered serious financial losses.

In the words of the English historian, Lecky, the crusade against slavery by England "may probably be regarded as among the three or four perfectly virtuous pages comprised in the history of nations".[26] And it was a fruit of the mighty spiritual awakening that England had enjoyed in the late eighteenth century.

In the distant Cape Colony, it caused many Boers to resent British rule, and to begin the Great Trek.

From the beginning of the nineteenth century, whites and blacks continued to clash on the eastern frontier of the Cape Colony; and it was proposed that 6000 settlers should be brought from Britain and settled on the frontier. The Frontier Wars between Boers and Xhosas were frequent and violent. In 1819, Grahamstown was attacked by some 10 000 Xhosas, but the garrison of 300 defended it successfully.

---

[26] *The Making of South Africa*, pg.65.

1000 Xhosas were killed, and three defenders.

Finally, it was decided that the settlement of British emigrants on the eastern frontier was a good idea, for security reasons. They would serve as a barrier between the Xhosas and the Cape settlement. In Britain itself, many were willing to emigrate, because of hard economic conditions in their mother country, as a result of the Industrial Revolution.

So, in 1819, the British Parliament voted to financially assist those who would organise groups of emigrants to the Cape. Each emigrant was offered a free passage with provisions, and 100 acres. From thousands of applicants, 60 parties were formed, totalling over 3600 people, of whom over 1400 were adult males. 21 ships transported these new settlers to the Cape. They arrived in 1820, and by October they were settled along the frontier.

But oh! how different conditions were from what they had imagined, or been led to believe! The hardships they faced were innumerable. Left to fend for themselves, in a new and hostile land, they struggled to eke a living out of the soil. Their wheat crop was ravaged by rust for three consecutive seasons. Floods swept the area in 1823. Many gave up and moved to the towns, so that by the end of that year there were only 1800 left on the frontier.

Gradually, as government laws improved the situation, the settlers began to succeed. They traded with the Xhosas, raised sheep and cattle, and hunted big game. But the British Government did not finance such a scheme again; and so settlers continued to sail from Britain for the United States, Canada, Australia, and New Zealand, but not for South Africa.

The 1820 settlers played an important part in the history of South Africa. In addition to the Dutch, French, and German colonists, English settlers had now entered the South African story. The Lord was working out his divine purpose.

The wars between the settlers and the Xhosas continued. The Xhosas were under pressure from tribes to the north, who were fleeing south as a result of the wars of Shaka, king of the Zulus. Shaka, a military genius but a bloodthirsty tyrant, was decimating the tribes of the interior. Panic-stricken, these tribes scattered, and this exerted pressure on the Xhosas, who in turn came into increasing conflict with the white settlers.

The Sixth Frontier War was fought in the years 1834 and 1835. 12000 Xhosa warriors swept into the Colony, destroying some 400 farms, killing 100 Europeans and Hottentots, and capturing livestock. The British troops retaliated, and were victorious.

We are now on the eve of the Great Trek: the next great event in the opening up of South Africa to the Europeans, with the consequent spread of the Gospel to other pagan tribes. On earth, men make decisions, form plans, and put them into action; but the great God has predestined all that transpires, from the movement of mighty armies (Jer.4:6,7) to the flight of little sparrows (Matt.10:29). The history of South Africa reveals this well.

CHAPTER EIGHT

THE GREAT TREK

By the 1830's, many of the Boer settlers on the frontiers of the Cape Colony were restless, frustrated, and dissatisfied. Their gaze was frequently turning towards the interior. For various reasons, they wanted to migrate away from the Cape Colony: the vagrancy problem; the making of coloureds equal to whites by Ordinance 50; the Emancipation Act of 1833; the constant invasions of the Xhosas; stricter government control over land; the drought at the time; and their feeling that missionaries had portrayed them in an unfair manner - these were some of the factors which led to the Great Trek.

The Boers, as stated previously, were deeply religious, and firmly committed to their denominations, primarily the Dutch Reformed denomination; but sadly, they had imbibed fully the false doctrine, held by many calling themselves Christians, that a *race* could be Christian merely by its children being baptized into the so-called "Christian faith" of that race. "Christianity" had thus come to be identified with a *nationality* (although of course, this was not *authentic* Christianity). Such was an outcome of the false, "State Church" concept, which the bodies formed at the time of the Reformation had retained from Roman Catholicism.

This false doctrine was the *very opposite* of the true Christian doctrine, that a person, even if born to Christian parents, is NOT a Christian because of it, but must himself be regenerated by the Holy Spirit, in order to enter the kingdom of God. It was the *very opposite* of the true Christian doctrine that only those who are brought, by God's grace, to repentance and faith in Christ, are to be baptized. It was the *very opposite* of the true Christian doctrine that the Church of Christ is NOT one and the same with a particular nation, but that the Church is composed of all, from *every* race, who are saved by grace through faith, and ONLY of them - it is a *new* nation (1 Pet.2:9), made up of saved souls from *all* nations.

Anna Steenkamp, a niece of the Boer leader, Piet Retief, put it this way in 1876: "The shameful and unjust proceedings with reference to the freedom of our slaves; and yet it is not so much their freedom which drove us to such lengths, as their being placed on an equal footing with Christians, contrary to the laws of God, and the natural distinction of race and colour, so that it was intolerable for any decent Christian to bow down beneath such a yoke; wherefore we rather withdrew in order thus to preserve our doctrines in purity".[27]

That well sums up this false doctrine within certain religious bodies. Those religious Boers saw, in the Old Testament, that God had a *nation,* the nation of Israel, which was separate from all the heathen nations around it; that its children were forbidden to intermarry with the children of other nations; etc. And the Boers viewed the Church in the same light: the Church, to them, was one and the same with a nation (the Boers), and it was to live separate from all other nations. They possessed an Old Testament outlook that was by no means in accordance with the teachings of the New Testament. Calling themselves Christians, they sought to live by Old Testament principles concerning a "National Religion". This was their error.

The New Testament is to be the principal rule of faith and practice for Christians; and the Old Testament must be interpreted in the light of the New. The true Church is the "Israel of God" of the New Testament (Gal.5:16). Christians are to learn from the Old Testament, for example, that God's people are to live *separate* from the sins of the unbelievers around them. But, as Christians are those whom the Lord has called from *all* nations, they are to be separate, while yet dwelling in the midst of this wicked world. Surrounded on all sides by wicked men, they are to "shine as lights in the world" (Phil.2:15), "*not of* the world", though living in it (Jn.17:14-16). This truth the Boers had not comprehended. One of the greatest failures of the Reformation was that it did not destroy the false Papal notion of a "National Church". And in the Boers, this notion was present to a marked degree. As Anna Steenkamp's words show, the Boers had failed to understand that, *in Christ,* "There is neither Jew nor Greek, there is neither bond nor free, there is neither male nor female: for ye are all one in Christ Jesus" (Gal.3:28). In Christ, distinctions of race, colour, and class fall away; there are only "saints". A converted black man is one with a converted white man. A converted slave is one with a converted freeman. *And,*

---

[27] The Making of South Africa pg 91.

furthermore, an *un*converted white man is as lost, as dead in sins, as hell-bound, as any unconverted black man; it matters not that the white was born to Christian parents, or "baptized" as an infant! He is no more a true Christian than the most pagan black man. One of the greatest tragedies of the South African situation has been the fruit that has sprung from this completely unchristian notion.

And yet it cannot be denied that the Lord used the Great Trek! Not because they were God's special people, as they thought - this was a complete fallacy; but because the interior had to be opened up, and these remarkable, tough, independent, brave people were the instruments in his hands to do it. The desire to be free, to be their own masters, burned within these frontiersmen. The unknown beckoned - and in 1835 the first party of Boers rose to the challenge, and began to trek.

The Great Trek must rank as one of the greatest events in South African history. Facing great hardships, the trekboers penetrated the interior, their ox-wagons carrying their families and possessions, as they drove their herds and flocks before them. They crossed great rivers and mountain ranges, and faced savage tribes. Yet they pressed on, into the areas which later came to be known as Natal and the Transvaal.

They were not the first whites to enter these areas. For years, hunters, traders, and some missionaries had been penetrating the interior. Missionaries were working among some tribes - notably the Griquas and Basuto. The London Missionary Society had representatives working among the former, and the Paris Evangelical Society among the latter. In Natal, Anglican missionaries, and missionaries from America, were at work.

However, it was the Trekboers who formed the first proper white settlements in the interior.

They found large sections of the interior were almost devoid of humans, due to the terrible decimation wrought by Shaka, king of the Zulus. Entire black tribes had been destroyed or dispersed.

The Trekboers under the leadership of Johannes Janse van Rensburg were wiped out by the Bantu near the Limpopo River. Those under Louis Trichardt, suffering greatly from disease, reached the

Portuguese town of Lorenzo Marques, on the east African coast, from where they were taken by ship to Port Natal (Durban). The party under Andries Potgieter and Sarel Cilliers came into contact with the warlike Matabele, under their chief Mzilikazi, a formidable tyrant who could put 20 000 disciplined warriors into the field. Potgieter organised a "laager": 50 wagons tied together in a circle. There were only 40 men, plus women and children; and the Matabele army attacked in October 1836.

The Matabele had short stabbing-spears called assegais; but the Boers were armed with guns, and also had horses. As the women helped load the guns, the Boers rode out to meet the Matabele warriors, firing as they went, then returned to the laager. They succeeded in driving off the Matabele, but lost two men, and their livestock were captured. A friendly black chief, Moroka, among whose people a Wesleyan missionary was working, provided oxen for them.

The party under Gerrit Maritz joined Potgieter's party, and in 1837, 100 Boers, 40 Griquas and 60 Baralong attacked the Matabele, killing 400, and capturing 7000 head of cattle.

By now the trekboer party under Potgieter and Maritz had swelled to about 1000 whites, plus coloured servants. Also in 1837, Piet Retief's party of 400 joined them, and he soon became the Governor of the Trekboers. Treaties were formed with a number of black chiefs. Later that same year, Piet Uys' party of 100 joined the main body. But differences between the leaders caused a split, and Retief headed for Natal.

Port Natal was a British settlement. Retief visited Dingane, the brother of Shaka, who had become Zulu king in 1828 when Shaka was killed. Retief's purpose in visiting him was to acquire land for the Boers. He did not go as an invader into Zulu territory, but approached the king with his request. Dingane promised him some land, on condition that he would recover some cattle which a chief named Sekonyela had stolen from Dingane. Hearing of the promise of land, nearly 1000 Trekboers moved down into Natal.

The other Trekboer party under Potgieter and Uys, meanwhile, had moved north into what later came to be called the Transvaal, after they, with a force of 130 men, had attacked the Matabele and defeated them, causing the Matabele to migrate further north, beyond the Limpopo.

Piet Retief recovered Dingane's cattle for him, and then went to see him. His deputation consisted of 70 white volunteers and 30 coloureds. Unknown to Retief, he and his men were going to their deaths.

Dingane put on a good show of friendship. An agreement was signed, which ceded a certain territory to the Boers. But suddenly Dingane shouted, "Kill the wizards!" His men pounced on the Boers, who had been persuaded to leave their guns outside, and they were clubbed and speared to death. Retief had to watch his men being killed, including his own son, before he was murdered as well.

Some days later, the Zulu armies swept down on the Boer encampments, and hundreds of men, women and children were killed.

Other battles followed. Piet Uys and his son were killed in one of them, and Potgieter led his followers into the territory north of the Vaal River.

In late November 1838, Andries Pretorius led a force of 500 trekkers, and some English settlers from Natal, against Dingane. On December 9, these religious Trekkers made a vow that, if they were victorious against the Zulus, they would forever celebrate the day of victory as a day of thanksgiving, "to the honour of God". Forming a laager on the banks of a river, they were attacked, on December 16, by wave after wave of Zulu warriors. Although vastly outnumbered, the superior weapons of the whites won the day. When the Zulu hordes finally fled, 3000 lay dead around the laager, but not one Trekker had been killed. The river flowed with blood, and was named Blood River. December 16, the anniversary of the Battle of Blood River, was thenceforth a sacred day to the Boers. They believed that God had been on their side, and had enabled them to be victorious.

The Battle of Blood River marked the turning point of the Great Trek. From the Cape Colony, more people started to migrate to the new Boer territories, so that, by the end of 1839, white settlements were permanently established in the areas that would later form the three South African provinces of Natal, the Transvaal, and the Orange Free State (the Cape Province being the fourth).

The Great Trek was an important milestone in the history of South Africa. Negatively, it added to the problems between whites and blacks, for white rule was established over black tribes, and land that had belonged to blacks was now owned by whites. Positively, in opening up the interior to white settlement, it promoted the development of southern Africa, assisted further missionary expansion, and brought a measure of peace to areas of regular tribal warfare.

Again it is possible to discern the hand of the Lord in these events, guiding the destinies of nations, that his Word might be heard by tribes upon whom its light had never shone. It was a violent period, as much of South African history has been. But such wickedness flows from the sinful heart of man, as it has ever done since Adam's fall. God is not the author of sin; but even sinful men do his bidding, even unknowingly (2 Sam.16:5-11); and so he is seen to be in absolute control of all things.

Joseph's brethren sinned terribly when they sold him into slavery; but Joseph said, "But as for you, ye thought evil against me; but God meant it unto good" (Gen.50:20). This did not excuse their sin - man's accountability is not excused by God's sovereignty - but it reveals that the Lord brings good to pass, even out of men's sinful deeds. Though he does not cause them to sin, and they will be punished for their sins, yet he so orders all events that even their sinful acts are made to serve his divine purposes. This is powerfully taught in Isa.10:5-15. The Lord says, "O Assyrian, the rod of mine anger, and the staff in their hand is mine indignation....I will send him against an hypocritical nation ."(vss.5,6). The Lord sent the wicked Assyrians against his people, to chastise them. "Howbeit he meaneth not so, neither doth his heart think so; but it is in his heart to destroy and cut off nations not a few" (vs.7). The Assyrian king planned this campaign in his own wicked heart; yet, unknown to him, the Lord, though not the author of his sin, had determined to use him to achieve his purposes. In vs.12 it says, "Wherefore it shall come to pass, that when the Lord hath performed his whole work upon mount Zion and on Jerusalem, I will punish the fruit of the stout heart of the king of Assyria, and the glory of his high looks." Although the sovereign Lord *used* the king of Assyria to chastise his people, the king would in turn be punished *himself!* For what he did was very sinful.

Let the reader bear these things in mind

CHAPTER NINE

BRITISH COLONIES AND BOER REPUBLICS

At this point, it is necessary to examine the missionary expansion during this period of the first half of the nineteenth century.

As was explained in an earlier chapter, the great spiritual Awakening in Britain in the eighteenth century had a phenomenal effect on mission work. Various societies sprung up, the first being the Baptist Missionary Society, started by William Carey in 1792. Others were the London Missionary Society (1795), the Scottish Missionary Society (1796), etc.

Missionary societies are not strictly scriptural: according to the New Testament, the local church is to send out, and support, the evangelist who takes the Gospel to new areas. But the Lord has used his devoted servants, even though, on matters of church order and practice, they did not all have a clear understanding (and which of his children has a perfect understanding of all things?); and Christians have much reason to rejoice for the good work done by his servants who were affiliated to missionary societies.

By 1840, there were 85 Protestant mission stations in South Africa, run by various bodies. Of course, as stated previously, the "gospel" preached by some of these men was not the true Gospel of Christ, for some of the societies and denominations represented, though "Protestant", were not truly Christian. Yet there were also faithful servants of the Lord at work among the wild and heathen nations of southern Africa.

The LMS was represented in the Cape Colony, Kaffraria, Griqualand, Namaqualand (all today parts of South Africa), and Bechuanaland. Representatives of the Glasgow Missionary Society were at work in Kaffraria; those of the Paris Society were in the Cape, Basutoland (the present-day country of Lesotho), and Bechuanaland; etc.[28]

The Vatican, alas, had wasted no time in dispatching Romish priests to the Cape, once it had become possible to do so, under British

---

[28] *History of the Church in Africa*, pgs.80-86.

rule, as was seen in a previous chapter. By 1838, there were some 700 Roman Catholics living at the Cape Colony, and a Romish school was opened in Cape Town in that year. In 1839, the Romish bishop began planning to build a cathedral, and he begged funds from Protestants as well as Papists; and also petitioned the civil government to make a grant! He received the money.

By 1841, the Roman Catholic population of the Cape Colony had increased to about 2500.[29]

Yet at this stage, Romish missionary work among black tribes had not begun in earnest; priestly activity was confined to the Cape Colony. This was the Lord's doing, for Protestant missionaries were already advancing into the interior, as was seen. In this way, South Africa was prevented from becoming a Roman Catholic country, and it became a safe haven for the Gospel of Christ.

It will be seen a little further on, however, that much harm *was* done by Papal missionaries, once they started reaching out to the black tribes; and their influence *today* is very strong.

But for now, let us continue tracing developments in South Africa.

In 1839, the town of Pietermaritzburg was established, and so the Republic of Natal was created, in the area which Dingane had ceded to Piet Retief. Mpande, brother of Dingane, allied himself and 17 000 followers with the settlers in Pietermaritzburg. When Dingane was killed in 1840, Andries Pretorius made Mpande king of the Zulus. The Republic of Natal took real control of the Zulu nation; Mpande was really a vassal of it.

The British government, however, which controlled the Cape Colony, was in favour of annexing Natal, for various reasons: Natal, it was believed, had coal deposits which the British wanted; a Wesleyan missionary working among the Pondo tribe appealed to the Cape Governor for protection for the Pondos when the Natal settlers attacked the Bhaca, neighbours to the Pondos, whom the Boers suspected of stealing cattle; in Cape Town, Port Elizabeth, and Grahamstown, businessmen were concerned that their trade with the interior might suffer, as American and Dutch trading ships visited Port

---

[29] *The Catholic Church in South Africa*, pg.34.

Natal every so often, and so the Cape Governor was being urged by Cape businessmen to intervene in Natal; etc.

Consequently, in 1842, the Governor sent forces to Natal. The British camp at Fort Victoria was besieged by the Boers; and Dick King and his Zulu servant, Ndongeni, undertook the 600-mile journey to Grahamstown for help which has gone down as one of the great heroic feats in South African history. British forces were sent to raise the siege, and were successful. In May 1843, Natal was annexed; and in 1845 it became a dependency of the Cape Colony.

To the north, the Trekkers came into conflict with Griquas, Basuto, and other tribes. The situation was very complicated, and skirmishes took place; but finally, in February 1848, Sir Harry Smith, Cape Governor and High Commissioner, proclaimed British sovereignty over the territory between the Orange and Vaal Rivers. This was the Orange River Sovereignty.

In the Transvaal, the Trekboers ruled. Their law stated that blacks were not permitted to live near white towns to the detriment of the inhabitants, unless the "Volksraad" (meaning "People's Council") permitted it. Racial segregation was thus the policy even then. Slavery was forbidden, but nevertheless many Boers kept slaves.

In January 1852, a convention of British and Boers was held at the Sand River. The British recognised the independence of the Transvaal, and the Boers agreed not to allow slavery in the territory.

In the Orange River Sovereignty, the British clashed with Moshoeshoe, king of the Basuto nation, a powerful monarch. By this time, Britain was wanting to withdraw from the Orange River Sovereignty: it was expensive to rule because of the Basuto, and it was in any case unprofitable. A convention between British and Boers was held at Bloemfontein in February 1854, and the Orange Free State Republic came into being, governed by the Boers. They agreed not to permit slavery, as those in the Transvaal had also done. The Dutch Reformed denomination was made the "State Church".

By the year 1854, then, the situation was as follows: the Cape Colony and Natal (which received many British emigrants during this time) were under Britain, and the Transvaal and Orange Free State were under the Boers.

It is possible to see the Lord's hand in this: a vast territory was now under European control, which served to ensure much peace between once-warring black tribes, while at the same time opening up all of southern Africa to development; and in addition, the way into the north was now much easier for Christian missionaries, who could take God's Word from the Cape in the south, through the territories of Natal, the Orange Free State, the Transvaal - and *beyond,* into the very heart of Africa itself. The way was prepared by he who governs the motions of the heavenly bodies and the movements of nations. Africa - the Dark Continent - was to receive the Light. "The dark places of the earth are full of the habitations of cruelty" (Psa.74:20); but as it was written of the lands of Zabulon and Nephthalim, so it would be true of Africa, that "the people which sat in darkness saw great light" (Matt.4:15,16). For Christ, "the light of the world" (Jn.8:12), was to be preached "to them which sat in the region and shadow of death" (Matt.4:16).

CHAPTER TEN

RACIAL TURMOIL: BRITONS, BOERS, AND THE BLACK RACES

It became difficult to rule Natal from the Cape Colony, and so in 1856 it became a separate Crown Colony. The settler population in Natal continued to grow between 1858 and 1864.

Theophilus Shepstone, who was firstly Diplomatic Agent and then Secretary for Native Affairs in the period 1845-1877, was responsible for improving the lot of both whites and blacks in Natal. He believed in racial segregation, but not in racial repression. He created eight reserves, with a total area of a million acres, and in these reserves the black chiefs were permitted to rule according to their traditional system, under the supervision of magistrates and police. It was his desire to enable the blacks to progress, but separately from the whites. We shall examine, at a later stage in this book, the whole policy of "separate development" in South Africa; for now, let it suffice to say that Shepstone realised that the white and black nations, being so radically different in culture, language, etc., etc., could not possibly be peacefully integrated at that stage. Such a policy is heavily criticised today; but the critics fail to take the stark reality of the situation into consideration. The fact that in later years it was abused does not alter the original intention. It is highly questionable whether any other policy could have been followed at the time. Shepstone was dealing with two extremely different groups of people: the white settlers, and the Zulus, the latter only beginning to emerge out of barbarism, through the work of the missionaries.

Shepstone faced opposition to his policy from the Lieutenant-Governor, Benjamin Pine, who felt that the reserves were too large, and also from the colonists, who complained that the reserves were preventing black labour from coming to their farms. Here we see a fundamental problem in the attitude of the whites: they liked the policy of separate development, but they also wanted the cheaper labour force the blacks provided! It must be one or the other - something the whites never grasped. If they wanted the black labour, they would have to accept integration. This was a chief reason for the failure of the separate development policy, and the cause of much misery and discontent, as huge shanty-towns of black labourers developed on the outskirts of major white cities. The blacks were allowed to work for the whites, but not to enjoy the benefits the whites enjoyed. This was a wicked and stupid attitude.

Then there were the Asians. A sugar-cane industry had begun in Natal, and labour was needed. Indian labourers were imported from India to work on the sugar-farms. From 1860 to about 1865, some 6500 Indians arrived in Natal. They were brought to serve white interests, but were regarded by the whites in a bad light. These matters served to add to the problems.

Meanwhile, in the area of the Transvaal, the Boers adopted a constitution in 1856, and revised it in 1858. The Transvaal was named the South African Republic, Pretoria became the seat of its government, and the Dutch Reformed denomination became the "State Church".

From the outset, this Boer republic was beset with problems. Some areas declared virtual independence, and the Basuto tribe was a serious threat. There was civil war between rival parties in the territory.

The Boers' attitude to the black people was stated in Article 9 of the constitution. It said: "The people desire to permit no equality between coloured people [i.e. blacks] and the white inhabitants, either in Church or State". Such was the so-called "Christianity" of the Boers. But this is not the teaching of the New Testament. In the true Church of the living God, all who are born again are one in Christ. "There is neither Jew nor Greek, there is neither bond nor free, there is neither male nor female: for ye are all one in Christ Jesus" (Gal.3:28). Whatever the policy of the state may be, the true Church will not make a distinction between races. The unconverted are to be barred from membership, regardless of their race; but those who are converted, and baptized, are to be received, regardless of race. But the theology of the Dutch Reformed denomination ran contrary to this. The unscriptural practice of infant-baptism, and the false notion that the white Boers were somehow special in God's sight, and therefore superior to the blacks, produced this attitude in their hearts.

At the same time as these things were occurring in Natal and the Transvaal, there was tension between the Boers of the other republic - the Orange Free State - and the Basuto nation. And also, in 1857, what came to be known as the National Suicide of the Xhosas, the tribe bordering the Cape Colony's eastern frontier, occurred.

This terrible and tragic event is a vivid example of the effect of witchcraft on a black nation. There are those today who will stop at nothing to convince the world that the coming of the white man to South Africa resulted in nothing but misery. The truth, however, is that the heathen darkness in which the black tribes lived was degrading and cruel; and the preaching of the Gospel by white missionaries was instrumental, under the sovereignty of God, in improving the lot of the black nations in general, in all aspects of life.

In 1856, a sixteen-year-old Xhosa girl, Nongquase, and her uncle, a well-known witchdoctor named Mhlakaza, led the Xhosa Paramount Chief, Kreli, and the entire Xhosa nation to believe that spirits of the dead had visited them, and told them that they had come to drive the white man into the sea. They insisted, however, that firstly, all the cattle of the Xhosa nation had to be slaughtered, and all the corn had to be destroyed. They "prophesied" that, once this was done, the sun would rise blood-red, and stand still at midday. The great Xhosa warriors of the past would live again, and a hurricane would sweep the whites into the sea. This would occur on the 18th of February 1857. The "prophecy" also declared that then, new cattle and corn would be miraculously provided, everyone would be healthy, rich, and happy, and even the old people would become young again.

This incredible prediction was *believed* by Chief Kreli and the entire nation. For a year, cattle were slaughtered, despite the attempts of Cape Government officials and missionaries to dissuade the Xhosas from carrying out this deed. By February 18, 1857, 85% of the cattle - an estimated 400 000 - had been slaughtered, and the grain destroyed.

On February 18, the nation waited. Widows sat beside their husbands' graves; old women waited to be made young again; cattle-pens were left open, to receive the new cattle; and all eyes were lifted skyward.

As the sun sank, as usual, in the west, the Xhosa nation realised their predicament; "A wail of utter despair swept the country from the Bashee to the Great Fish River".[30] The nation began to starve to death. Many resorted to cannibalism, even eating their own children. In the territory of British Kaffraria, the population dropped from 104 721 to 37 229. And if it were not for the fact that whites had gathered supplies of food to distribute among the blacks, the situation would have been even worse.

Such was the power of witchcraft over the Xhosa people. It resulted in the might of the Xhosa army being broken for at least twenty years; in the expansion of white settlers into the territory of British Kaffraria, so largely depopulated; and in some 30 000 Xhosas pouring into the Cape Colony and providing a cheap labour force. 6000 whites were settled in the depopulated area. Industrial schools and hospitals were established, in order to *counteract* the influence of the witchdoctors over the Xhosas.

How foolish are those, today, who argue that Christian missionaries are a nuisance, and even a threat to the wild nations they seek to reach with the Gospel! "Leave them alone!" the cry is often heard. "They're happy as they are." No; apart from the *eternal* consequences for those who live and die in heathenism, the plain fact is that the *temporal* conditions of those who dwell in such heathenism are terrible indeed. Wherever the true Gospel of the Lord Jesus Christ has been proclaimed, and believed, it has resulted, in addition to the eternal salvation of souls, in the *upliftment* of people in all aspects of life.

The tension between the Orange Free State and Basutoland finally erupted into war, in 1858. It is known as the First Basuto War. The black tribes, particularly the Basuto and the Zulus, were a major threat to the whites scattered throughout South Africa, and Sir George Grey, the British High Commissioner at the Cape, was convinced that a *federal* government, uniting the European nations of southern Africa, was the best solution to the problems of the region. The Orange Free

---

[30] *The Aida Parker Newsletter,* Issue No.156, August 1992. Published by Aida Parker Newsletter (Pty) Ltd., Johannesburg.

State was not against this. The British Government, however, was opposed to exercising any authority over the two Boer republics, and so nothing happened at the time.

This was a period of much racial turmoil in southern Africa. The Zulus were a very real threat to Natal and the Transvaal, and the Second Basuto War broke out in 1865 between the Orange Free State and Basutoland. Moshoeshoe, king of the Basuto, but now an old man, requested the British authorities to annex Basutoland. In 1868 the High Commissioner did so.

It was the best thing that could have been done, under the circumstances. The Orange Free State did not have the necessary might to govern Basutoland; and, as the Boer authorities had planned to take the land away from the Basuto if they had been victorious, this would have resulted in Basuto refugees pouring into Natal and the Cape Colony, causing even further problems. In 1871, Basutoland came under Cape control.

At this time, too, there was a complicated dispute between the two Boer republics over the diamond fields that had been discovered. Finally these fields were annexed by the Cape Colony, and thus Griqualand West came under British control; and the Boer republics were united in their opposition to Britain.

Naturally, the discovery of diamonds had far-reaching consequences. Immigrants from Britain, the British colonies, Germany, France, the USA, and other countries, poured into Griqualand West. The town of Kimberley mushroomed. Blacks came to the diggings in large numbers, increasing white-black tensions and greatly damaging black tribal and family life. The entire social structure of the black races began to undergo a transformation.

Of course, the discovery of diamonds did wonders for the South African economy, and this, in turn, resulted in the further development and industrialisation of the sub-continent, with roads, railways, trade and commerce expanding.

Britain, by now, was very enthusiastic about the concept of federalism for South Africa, for a number of reasons: it would go a long way in making South Africa self-governing; the Zulu threat to the Natal colony was very real; the Boer republics had many problems of their own; the peace among the diamond-diggers of Kimberley was a very uneasy one; there were economic advantages to federalism; and also, there was the danger of powers like Germany becoming involved in South Africa.

There were, however, other reasons - sinister ones - why Britain was anxious to organise the races of South Africa into a federation, and later into a unitary state. There were secret, international forces at work in Europe, which were casting their eyes towards South Africa, and the fantastic wealth that was beginning to be discovered there. It was at this stage that the history of South Africa became intertwined with these sinister forces; forces which have brought great misery and bloodshed to all the races of this beautiful country during the century that has passed since then. And, insofar as they have affected the history of South Africa, an examination of them is vital.

But first, a brief look at the progress of the Gospel.

In southern Africa, Christian mission work had been expanding. In 1850, Protestant missionaries penetrated Zululand. Various Protestant missions established themselves in South Africa, and nowhere else in Africa had Christianity made greater progress than in South Africa by 1880. The progress of Roman Catholic missions was mercifully slow at the time.[31]

From South Africa, missionaries pushed northwards. In 1859, they moved into the area that became known as Southern Rhodesia, and established a mission station. In 1878, the London Missionary Society entered Northern Rhodesia. In both Northern and Southern Rhodesia, various mission societies soon established themselves, schools and hospitals were opened, and the Scriptures were translated.[32] By no means were all of these societies, or all of the individual missionaries who were members of them, soundly scriptural. But there were nevertheless faithful men, called by God's grace, who spread the Gospel of Jesus Christ.

The Dark Continent was receiving the Light! And the settlement of South Africa by Europeans had prepared the way for it. More than any other part of Africa, South Africa before the beginning of the twentieth

---

[31] *History of the Church in Africa*, pgs.174-6.
[32] *History of the Church in Africa*, pgs.176-179.

century had enjoyed the blessings of Christianity; and the Gospel had penetrated northwards, deep into Central Africa. The sovereign Lord had directed all these events in accordance with His great will.

CHAPTER ELEVEN

THE PROGRESS OF POPERY

While the Christian message was penetrating deeper and deeper into Africa, and into all corners of South Africa in particular, what of Popery? Though its progress was not rapid at first, yet its adherents increased, especially (to begin with) in the Cape Colony.

In 1850, a Romish bishop, Devereux, founded a weekly newspaper called the *Cape Colonist*. It was published at Grahamstown. Devereux used his paper chiefly to answer attacks on Roman Catholicism. In 1842 he noted in his diary that the Protestants tried to stop the Coloured population from coming to hear him: "they tell all sorts of stories about the Catholic religion," he wrote.[33] Consequently, he devoted space in the *Colonist* to carrying Roman Catholic answers to the "stories of St. Bartholomew, the inquisition, and the gunpowder plot, and to the scurrilities of the Maria Monk type".[34]

Rome has always had those who have sought to defend the undefendable: The St. Bartholomew's Massacre in 1572, in which tens of thousands of Protestant Huguenots were brutally killed by Roman Catholics, urged on by their priests, in France; the Inquisition, which for hundreds of years was one of Rome's primary instruments to destroy "heresy" (i.e. Protestantism, etc.) by all kinds of barbaric means; and the Gunpowder Plot in England, when Romanists, under the direction of the Jesuits, sought to blow up King James. These things are facts of history. They cannot be denied or justified. They show the depth of the hatred and intolerance of Rome for all who differ with her.

As for Maria Monk, she was a nun who escaped from a convent, and told the shocking story of what she had seen and experienced in the convent, in the 1800's.[35] Her story was never disproved, and many others were also set free from the horrors of cloistered convent life, and published their testimonies. Naturally enough, Popery suffered as

---

[33] *The Catholic Church in South Africa*, pg.42.
[34] *The Catholic Church in South Africa*, pg.52.
[35] *The Awful Disclosures of Maria Monk*, published by Howe and Bates, New York. 1836.

a result of these revelations, and sought by every possible means, fair and foul, to destroy the witnesses' credibility. As Protestants in South Africa received these testimonies as well, it is not surprising that Devereux, in his paper, sought to "refute" the charges.

Meanwhile, Romish priests in South Africa were seeking to advance their religion by public lectures. A priest named James O'Haire lectured on the Romish doctrine of the temporal power of the Papacy at Fraserburg and Victoria West, and large numbers went to hear him. In 1866, Roman Catholic bishop Grimley wrote to O'Haire: "Don't pitch into the Protestants....You don't know this Colony yet. Keep to your moral discourses, win the Protestants by the beauty of your morality".[36] He also wrote: "Our grand principle must be never to compromise an iota of our faith, yet never give unnecessary offence".[37]

The reason for Grimley's advice was that, in a non-Romanist land like South Africa, Popery had to proceed with caution. In places where it does not have the power, it has ever been Rome's method to use the "gentle" approach, the "appealing" approach, in proselytism. Where it has the power to use harsher means, it does not hesitate to do so; but in South Africa, it was not in a position to throw its weight around.

As Grimley and O'Haire delivered lectures in various cities and towns, the secular press reported that a considerable number of Protestants went to hear them. When Grimley preached at the opening of O'Haire's "church" building at Malmesbury, the *Advertiser and Mail* of 30th September 1865 declared: "Protestants of every denomination attended both at the opening and evening services", listening "with delight and edification."[38]

Already, by the middle of the nineteenth century, evangelical Protestantism worldwide was in decline; and the situation was to worsen as the century drew to a close. This would be one reason for the numbers of Protestants who attended these services. There were still considerable numbers who were well aware of the evils of Popery, but not as in previous centuries, when the great majority of Protestants had no doubt whatsoever of its true nature. Of course, in the 1800's (as

---

[36] *The Catholic Church in South Africa*, pg.76.
[37] *The Catholic Church in South Africa*, pg.76.
[38] *The Catholic Church in South Africa*, pg.77.

in all ages), those *calling* themselves "Protestants", and *professing* to be Christians, were more numerous than those who were *true* Christians, regenerated by the Holy Spirit.

In their lectures, these two servants of the Roman pope were careful to speak in such a way as would *attract* Protestants, not repel them; although they hinted strongly that the Roman Catholic religion was the "Church" to which all men should belong.[39]

By the early 1870's, mainly as a result of emigration to America and New Zealand, the Roman Catholic population in South Africa had dropped considerably. But with the discovery of diamonds and then gold, new centres of population grew up at Kimberley and on the Witwatersrand, and the Papist population, along with all others, increased. By 1891, Romanists numbered 2.4% of the population. This was not by any means a high figure, and Romanists have never been a large percentage of the population in South Africa, but history shows that the Papal institution has at times been able to exert an influence on a country out of all proportion to its numbers within that country. And South Africa in modern times has been no exception, as shall be seen.

In 1875, Romish bishop Ricards, Vicar Apostolic of the Eastern District of the Cape Colony, visited Europe, and persuaded the provincial of the *Jesuits* in England to take over St. Aidan's College as a school, and also to send two Dutch Jesuits to run the mission at Graaf-Reniet. As pointed out previously in this book, the introduction of the sinister Jesuits into any country spells trouble for that country.

As a result of the Romish bishop's visit to Europe, other Romish missionaries also came to South Africa. Dominican nuns arrived from Germany, and were established at King William's Town. Their school attracted Protestants as well as Papists. It was given a state grant in 1879. The nuns opened two other schools, one of them for black children, and with Jesuit assistance they started an industrial school for blacks in 1891.

In 1883, they had a school in East London, and in 1894 a convent (and later a school for Coloureds) at Graaf-Reniet. They spread to

---

[39] *The Catholic Church in South Africa*, pgs.78-81.

Potchefstroom in the Transvaal, and Oakford in Natal, in 1889.[40]

It had been Ricards' plan to "evangelize" the blacks in his vicariate for the Roman Catholic faith. He thought the Trappist monks would be best suited to the task, for they would teach agriculture, and dispose the blacks to the Papal "gospel" by so doing. In 1879, he again went to Europe, and the French Trappists agreed to establish themselves in South Africa. Arriving in Dunbrody in 1880, they moved to Mariannhill in Natal in 1882, to work among the Zulus.[41]

Also in 1879, the Jesuits were sent to the territory of the Zambesi River. The Dominican nuns established themselves in Mashonaland. The Jesuits also took over the Dunbrody scheme left by the Trappists when the latter went to Natal. They also started schools in Keiland, along with the Dominican nuns.[42]

For centuries the Cape Colony, and the rest of South Africa, had been spared the ill-effects of Roman Catholic evangelistic efforts. This was the Lord's doing, as it meant that the heathen black tribes of the country heard the Gospel of Christ before they heard the corrupt, false "gospel" of Rome. This was a blessing to South Africa, and ensured that it never became a Roman Catholic country, but a safe haven for the Gospel instead, and a base for its dissemination to other parts of the world.

But it was not the Lord's will to *entirely* prevent the Roman Catholic religion from establishing itself in South Africa. By 1876, Ricards was able to write that although the Cape had been Britain's "pet Protestant colony" forty years before, Roman Catholic institutions were now respected throughout the Cape.[43] Rome had done its work well.

Before the 1860's, education in South Africa was provided largely by private individuals and institutions, notably church denominations. Only in the 1860's did the government become deeply involved in education, although government schools had existed before this.

---

[40] *The Catholic Church in South Africa*, pgs.101-103.
[41] *The Catholic Church in South Africa*, pgs.104-106,108,120.
[42] *The Catholic Church in South Africa*, pgs.111,112,120,123.
[43] *The Catholic Church in South Africa*, pg.112.

In 1839, when a government Director of Education was appointed at the Cape, the government offered 50% grants to all church schools which would accept certain conditions, such as that *only* the Bible would be used for daily religious instruction. Naturally, the Papal institution refused, and did so for twenty years.

Then, in 1859, Romish bishop Grimley asked the Superintendent of Education if, by the "Scriptures", the law meant *any* version, even the Douay version (the Roman Catholic version); and the Superintendent replied that this version could be used. Grimley asked if teachers could offer doctrinal explanations of what was read, and the Superintendent replied that they could. The result: Roman Catholic schools received a grant, by privilege; and they were permitted to interpret the Bible according to Romish doctrine - although they were not allowed to impose their doctrine on Protestant pupils. So, in the Cape, separate classes in religion were given to Papists and Protestants at Romish schools, the syllabus for Protestant children being submitted to the Director of Education.[44]

Thus Romish schools received government funds, and were permitted to keep Protestant pupils. Of course, Rome denied that it proselytized the Protestant children.

Romish schools grew and spread throughout South Africa. The Marist Brothers, the Jesuits, the Salesians, the Dominican nuns - all were deeply involved in education by the end of the nineteenth century. Other teaching orders were the Holy Family, Holy Cross and Loreto nuns, and the Oblates of Mary Immaculate. At a still later stage, the Irish Christian Brothers, the De La Salle Brothers, the Brothers of Charity, and the Sisters of Mercy, were to arrive.[45]

The importance of education, as controlled by the Roman Catholic institution, must not be underestimated. The education of impressionable children, when in the hands of unscrupulous agents of the papal prince in Italy, is the most powerful means of moulding future generations in precisely the way desired by the teachers. That the education of thousands of children was in the hands of various Roman Catholic religious orders in South Africa in the latter half of the nineteenth century boded ill for the future. It matters not that the

---

[44] *The Catholic Church in South Africa*, pgs.125-131.
[45] *The Catholic Church in South Africa*, pgs.133-135.

number of Romish schools was not large, compared with other schools; as pointed out earlier, the Papal religious system has often exerted an influence out of all proportion to its size. By the late 1800's, many Roman Catholic laymen had risen to prominent public positions in South Africa.[46]

Romish missionaries zealously propagated their religion amongst the black tribes of South Africa. In 1854, two priests arrived in Pietermaritzburg, and the following year they began work among the Zulus. The Zulus, however, did not readily adopt Romanism, and progress was slow.[47] The arrival of the Trappists at Mariannhill, however, advanced the work among them.

The Basuto proved to be far more sympathetic to the Papal religion. With the support of the king, Moshoeshoe, a mission was opened in Basutoland in 1862; and by 1875, there were 500 Roman Catholic Basuto. The number continued to rise rapidly, and today Lesotho (formerly Basutoland) is a predominantly Roman Catholic country.

In the Boer republics, Romanism faced difficulties, due to the staunch traditional Protestantism of the Afrikaners. In the second half of the 1800's, accounts appeared frequently in the republics (as in other parts of South Africa and indeed the world) of the debauchery and sadism that occurred in monasteries, convents, etc. Romanists tried to get the Dutch Reformed denomination and others to believe that these accounts were merely slanders circulated by the "Protestant underworld", but without much success. The Boers were too well-acquainted with the sufferings of their forefathers at the hands of Rome, and the evidence in favour of the accounts of the sinful goings-on in Papal institutions was too ample, for them to believe the Romish attempts at explaining it all away. In the somewhat more liberal, more English Cape Colony, many Protestants may have been taken with the lectures of priests of Rome, etc., but the Boers would have none of it. Their Protestantism may have contained much that was unscriptural, as pointed out elsewhere in this book, but on the true nature of Romanism

---

[46] *The Catholic Church in South Africa*, pgs.86-90.
[47] *The Catholic Church in South Africa*, pgs.204-207.

they were clear. A Transvaal paper called priests and nuns "emissaries of Satan", "liars, murderers, and doers of everything that is abominable". High officials of the Dutch Reformed denomination encouraged the dissemination of books and pamphlets that painted Rome in her true colours. The Romish leaders complained that "the average rank and file of that Church [the Dutch Reformed] are animated by a narrow-minded, scandal-mongering, persecuting spirit."[48] Considering the history of Romanism, that accusation is utterly hypocritical! The plain truth is that, in the Boer republics, the deep awareness of the people of their history caused them to *abhor* Popery. The "Christianity" of the majority of them may have been nothing more than mere form; but their deep distrust of everything Papal was to the advantage of their republics. It is a great pity that Britain, which was to come to control the Boer republics, had not retained such a distrust, having, it appears, forgotten its own struggles with Popery in previous centuries.

And yet, even the Boer republics eventually changed their attitudes, at least officially. A Romish school was opened in the Orange Free State in 1877, and President Brand even sent a niece to be educated there. Freedom of worship had been forbidden to Roman Catholics, but this was finally obtained by a bishop, assisted by some Portuguese officials who were on a mission to the republic.

In 1870, in the Transvaal, the law which made the saying of mass illegal was repealed.[49] As late as 1880, however, in the Orange Free State, the law excluding Papists from all government positions was re-enacted.[50]

The increase in the numbers of Roman Catholics, and the gradual relaxation of the laws regarding the Papal religion, were to have far-reaching effects in this beautiful land.

---

[48] *The Catholic Church in South Africa*, pgs.182-183.
[49] *The Catholic Church in South Africa*, pg.272.
[50] *The Catholic Church in South Africa*, pg.173.

CHAPTER TWELVE

THE CONSPIRATORS

It has been seen that Britain, especially after the discovery of diamonds and gold in South Africa, was anxious to impose a federal system on the entire country; and reference was made to sinister, international forces at work in Europe, whose ambitions certainly extended to South Africa. To these we must now turn.

Events of history, from the human perspective, must either be the result of a series of accidents and coincidences, or the result of deliberate schemes of men with agendas of their own. For the Christian, only the latter can be true. He knows that history is the outworking, in time, of God's sovereign will for this earth, and that nothing is by chance or mistake. All events, great and small, occur in accordance with the divine will. This does not mean he approves of them all, but it means that none could occur outside of his will.

As the Christian looks at the Bible, he finds that the Lord raises up men, both good and evil, to fulfil his purposes. Again, this does not mean that evil deeds are excused - men are accountable for their sins, and he will by no means clear the guilty - but none could rise to positions of power and influence unless the Lord had ordained it: "the powers that be are ordained of God" (Rom.13:1).

To evil Pharaoh, who so persecuted the children of Israel, the Lord said, "Even for this same purpose have I raised thee up, that I might shew my power in thee, and that my name might be declared throughout all the earth" (Rom.9:17; Exod.9:16). Pharaoh's sin was his own, but his coming upon the stage of history at that time was of the Lord, for the Lord's own purposes. And so it is of all rulers.

This being so, the Christian can never view historical events as mere accidents and coincidences! He knows that there is a God in heaven, who does according to his will on earth. And furthermore, he sees from the Bible that, the heart of man being corrupt, and full of ambition and lust and greed, there are those who, from positions of influence and power, seek to enslave other men, and even masses of people, to themselves, or their religions, or their ideologies. And thus schemes and plots are laid, and at times come to fruition, if God so wills it. Wars do not just happen; they are *made* to happen. Countries do not just find themselves invaded for no reason; powerful men *plan* these things, for their own gains. The Lord has his purposes in permitting these plots, and the men who carry them out have their purposes for doing so, never realising that they, like Pharaoh of old, have been "raised up" at that time, and in that place, by the One who rules over heaven and earth, and they shall bear their own iniquity.

The world is not where it is today, by accident. Powerful men, and even more powerful spiritual forces, have been (and are) at work. South Africa has played a major part in their plans.

The Christian also knows that Satan is at work, as well. *His* purpose, as always, is to attempt to destroy the Church of the living God (Matt.16:18). Political and religious forces are the devil's instruments, which he uses to try to destroy the Church, and to prevent the preaching of the Gospel of Christ. South Africa was a haven for the Gospel, and for Christians. While the devil seeks to prevent the preaching of the Gospel everywhere, he naturally is particularly desirous of seeing it stamped out in those places where it has been most favourably received.

And so there are three levels to keep in mind. Men, because of their depraved natures, lust after power and wealth, and in order to get these things, they plot, and make war, and kill, and enslave. In doing so, they serve the interests of Satan, who seeks to use them against the saints of God. And behind it all, there is the purpose of the Most High himself: using these miserable creatures for his own wise ends, to fulfil prophecy, to purify his true Church (Dan.11:32-36), etc.

As far back in history as the time of the building of the tower of Babel, men have sought to have a world government and a world religion, in opposition to God (Gen.11:1-9). The Lord has never permitted their schemes to succeed, but this has not prevented them from trying. In the early centuries of the Christian era, the devil's masterpiece gradually arose: a massive, wealthy, powerful, counterfeit "church" system that came to be known as the "Roman Catholic Church". It grew and grew in strength, persecuting the saints of God (Rev.17:6), controlling kings and emperors and dictators (Rev.17:2), becoming the most powerful religio-political institution in the world.

The ages-old desire of the Roman Catholic institution has been for absolute world domination. To this end, it has sent out its emissaries to the far corners of the world, subjugated governments and countries by any and all means, fair and foul, and viciously persecuted all opponents.[51]

In AD 774, the "Donation of Constantine" made its appearance. This clever forgery (for that is certainly what it was) was said to be the Roman Emperor Constantine's donation, to the "Catholic Church", of the entire territory of the Roman Empire, and also of all lands to the west and beyond. It placed the popes above all earthly rulers.[52]

The Roman pope, Innocent IV, in an encyclical published in 1245, promoted the idea that the pope, in accepting the "Donation of Constantine", showed thereby that he had sovereign dominion over the *whole world*.[53] Claiming that all islands belonged by right to the Papacy, the next step was to claim that all newly-discovered lands, or lands *yet to be* discovered, belonged to the popes as well! This had hugely-significant consequences when Columbus discovered the Americas in 1492. One year later the pope, Alexander VI, issued a document in which he *granted* all lands yet to be discovered to his subject, the king of Spain! In other words, he acted as if he *owned the world* - even those parts of it that were unknown to Europe at that time. Later, another pope, Leo, did the same thing, granting to the king of Portugal permission to possess the kingdoms and islands of the Far East, including those not yet known or discovered.[54]

That the pope owns all the world has been boldly proclaimed by popes and their theologians through the centuries since then. Bellarmine, a cardinal, declared: "the Supreme Pontiff, by divine right, has the fullest powers over the whole world" ('Opera', Tom.I: 'De Romano Pontefice'); Gregory IX declared: "Constantine....wished that the Vicar of Christ and Prince of Apostles .should also possess the

---

[51] See, for example, the famous work, *Foxe's Book of Martyrs*; as well as other historical works, *The Secret History of the Jesuits*, etc.
[52] *The Vatican Billions*, by Avro Manhattan, pgs.32,33. Chick Publications, Chino, California. 1983.
[53] *The Vatican Billions*, pg.42.
[54] *The Vatican Billions*, pgs.49,50.

government of corporeal things in the whole world" (Pope Gregory to the Emperor Frederick II, October 1236);[55] etc.

When the New World was discovered, Alexander VI, in his document addressed to the King of Spain, "granted" him the lands, and revealed the motivation behind the discoverers' voyages: "to the intent to bring the inhabitants.....to profess the Catholic Faith...."[56] The Vatican's primary desire was (and remains) world domination: a world in subjection to the Roman pontiff.

Just how expansive was the pope's "grant" to the Spanish king? Here are the words of the document: "We do give, grant and assign to you, your heirs and successors, all the firm Lands and Islands found or to be found, discovered or to be discovered, towards the West and South, drawing a Line from the Pole Arctic to the Pole Antarctic (that is) from the North to the South...."[57]

Just a few years after Columbus discovered America, Vasco da Gama, the Portuguese explorer and a good Roman Catholic, sailed round the coast of South Africa, on a mission that had, as part of its goal, the spreading of the Roman Catholic faith. Before him, Bartholomew Diaz had reached the southern extremities of Africa, discovering the Cape Peninsula for Portugal and Europe in 1488 (see chapter three). The Lord did not permit the Papal power to control southern Africa; but certainly the Roman pope wanted to!

The popes of Rome had at least three good reasons (in their minds) for wanting to own South Africa. Firstly, they claimed ownership of the entire world anyway, and "their" explorers, Diaz and da Gama, had discovered it; secondly, when it fell into Protestant hands (first the Dutch and then the British), this would have angered the Vatican, especially when the proselytizing activities of Romish priests were forbidden; and thirdly, when at a still later date diamonds and gold were discovered, the Papacy's lust would have increased even more.

South Africa - ruled by a non-Papist power, fabulously wealthy, and with a population generally opposed to all things Papal - had to be conquered. And the ones to do it would be internationalist conspirators

---

[55] *The Vatican Billions*, pgs.88,89.
[56] *The Vatican Billions*, pg.90.
[57] *The Vatican Billions*, pg.92.

who, knowingly or not, served the interests of the Vatican.

It must first be shown that, in fact, there *is* an international network, seeking world domination, and ultimately serving the long-term interests of the Vatican, knowingly or unknowingly; and then, how this network has worked unceasingly for the destruction of South Africa, and its subjugation to the one-world schemes of these shadowy figures.

That there *are* powerful forces working for world domination - Communistic, Masonic, Islamic, etc. - many researchers have realised. And details about the plans of these conspirators have been published from time to time. All too often, however, researchers, having unearthed many solid facts about these institutions, religious systems, and ideologies, fail to take into account the biblical and historical reality that there is a religio-political system with its headquarters in Rome, far more powerful than all the others, and often pulling the strings behind the scenes in ways not even perceived. Regrettably a large number of professing Christians are either ignorant of, or deliberately ignore, this biblical and historical reality. When seeking to view world events from a sound biblical and historical perspective, believers must keep in mind that "all roads lead to Rome". In his prophetic Word, the Lord has clearly drawn the attention of his people to *one* institution: and that is the Roman Catholic institution. This evil system is dealt with, by the Holy Spirit, in the prophecies of Daniel; of Matthew 24 and similar passages in the other Gospels; of 2 Thessalonians 2; of 1 John; and of the book of Revelation. It is without doubt the Lord's will that Christians, in seeking to understand historical and contemporary events in the light of prophetic Scripture, focus their attention on the city of *Rome,* on the religio-political monstrosity that has its headquarters there, and that dares to masquerade as the bride of Christ when in truth it is a harlot (see Rev.17). Other religious and political systems, as well as various individuals, have had, and have now, plans for world domination; but the Lord has *told* us where the real heart of all conspiracy lies, and it is sinful to neglect the revelation of his Word. This is not to say that other systems are not a great threat to the Church of Christ: many of them are, and for this reason must be warned against. But to understand the *source,* the real *centre,* of intrigue and conspiracy, we must look to Rome. The Holy Spirit has said, in effect - "There! Look to the city on seven hills (Rev.17:9)! *There* is the great deceiver of the nations (Rev.17:2)! *There* is the source of political and economic and (above all) religious woe (Rev.18:3,4,5)!"

Let us now proceed.

The Spanish "Illuminati" was a secret society, known as the "Alumbrados". Ignatius Loyola, a Spanish Roman Catholic, was tried by an ecclesiastical commission, in 1527, for alleged sympathy with this organisation.[58] Some years later, this same individual founded the so-called "Society of Jesus": the *Jesuit Order.* And the Jesuits became the most powerful Roman Catholic order in the world.[59] We have looked at the Jesuits to some extent in earlier chapters. They are fanatically devoted to placing the entire world under the feet of the pontiff of Rome.

The evidence points to the fact that, at a very early stage, the Spanish Illuminati came under the control of the Jesuits. According to the Encyclopaedia Britannica, "the Alumbrados came especially from....Jesuits";[60] and it "was organised along Jesuit lines and kept internal discipline and a system of mutual surveillance based on that model".[61]

Researchers almost invariably point to Adam Weishaupt, a Jew, as the founder of the Illuminati, in 1776. But they do not probe deep enough (or, if they do, they deliberately gloss over certain facts). He established the Illuminati in *Bavaria;* but as the evidence given above reveals, the Illuminati existed long before 1776. It has many branches; and the term itself can be very broad in meaning, covering all those involved in the internationalist conspiracy, and not merely a single, specific order of men. Certainly Weishaupt established such an order in Bavaria, and there is no reason to doubt that the Illuminati, as an order, still exists; but in addition, the *spirit* of Illuminism permeates many secret societies and organisations, interlocking and very

---

[58] *Occult Theocracy,* by Lady Queenborough, pg.307. The Christian Book Club of America, Hawthorne, California. 1980.
[59] See *The Secret History of the Jesuits.*
[60] *Encyclopaedia Britannica,* Vol I, pg.692.
[61] *Encyclopaedia Britannica,*Vol.XI, pg.1096.

complex, and all working for the same goals. And in the shadows, behind the Illuminati, are the Jesuits. Not only do we see them controlling the Illuminati of Spain in the sixteenth century, but they *created* Weishaupt's Illuminati Order in the eighteenth century. The facts, extremely important, are these:

Weishaupt was professor of canon law at Ingolstadt University in Bavaria. What is the significance? This: Ingolstadt was a *Jesuit* university, and a centre of the Jesuit Counter-Reformation![62] And Weishaupt was a trained Jesuit, a professor at this Jesuit university! The Encyclopaedia Britannica says that he was "a former Jesuit".[63] But no *former* Jesuit would have been able to continue his professorship at a Jesuit university! The Britannica reveals much, but one has to look deeper. The fingerprints of the Jesuits can be seen all over the creation of the Illuminati. Weishaupt would not have been a *former* Jesuit, but a Jesuit in good standing. It serves the purposes of the Jesuits if people are convinced that he was a former Jesuit, who founded the Illuminati. For then they will not come to the conclusion that the Illuminati was founded and controlled by the Jesuits. The Jesuits, of course, would not want this fact known. But the evidence reveals it to be so.

The goal of the Illuminati is world control (and this is the Jesuits' goal): control through politics, economics, religion, etc.

There is not a vast amount of detail available on all the behind-the-scenes intrigues of the Jesuit-controlled Illuminati and its plots for world domination; nor, for that matter, is there a vast amount of detail available on the various other organizations that played, and still play, a role. But we do not need to have every single detail, or be perfectly certain of every step they took towards the goal. It is sufficient to know that world domination has always been Rome's goal, and that it has created various organizations to achieve that goal. Every now and then, a fact or two comes to light, which enables us to see behind the curtain a little; but we cannot expect to have, and nor do we need, every single conspiratorial detail. The results of their intrigues are more important to us than the details regarding the intrigues themselves. We find that there is a plan, spawned by Rome; that the

---

[62] *Encyclopaedia Britannica*, Vol.XII, pgs.250,251.
[63] *Encyclopaedia Britannica*, Vol XI, pg.1096.

Jesuits in particular, and other Papal emissaries in general, are deeply involved; and every now and then, a detail or two comes to light, which provides further confirmation of this.

Let us turn our attention to Communism. Communism did not just arise spontaneously. The Illuminati was behind it. John Robison, a Scottish Protestant and professor at the University of Edinburgh, stated, as far back as 1798 in his work, *Proofs of a Conspiracy,* that Weishaupt's Illuminati planned to abolish all ordered government, inheritance, private property, patriotism, family, and religion - the very principles found in Communism.[64] According to one researcher,[65] who, it appears, like many others, unearthed some truth but did not see to the *root* of it all - the Papacy - the Illuminati in the 1850's were told of a plan to form an *Internationale,* to be called "Communist". Its purpose would be to frighten the world into accepting the plans for a world government. Other researchers concur with this.[66] Two men, Engels and Marx, were financed, by the Illuminati, to write *Das Kapital* and the *Communist Manifesto.*[67] The *Communist Manifesto* was based on *Weishaupt's* ideas.[68]

In 1864, Marx founded the *Internationael,* for gaining world control, just as the Illuminati wanted. International Communism was funded by the financiers who supported the Illuminati.[69] Such evidence as exists, then, points to the fact that Communism was a creation of the Illuminati. And since the Illuminati was under the control of the Jesuits, Communism was a daughter of the Roman Catholic institution.

Further details of the Vatican/Illuminati connection with

---

[64] *Understanding the New World Order,* by Roy Livesey, pgs.48,49,78. New Wine Press, Chichester, England. 1989.
[65] *The Illuminati-CFR* (tape), by Myron Fagan. See *Understanding the New Age,* by Roy Livesey, pgs.165,183. New Wine Press, Chichester, England. 1986.
[66] See, for example, *The Plot Against South Africa,* by Klaus Vaqué, pg.61. Varama Publishers, Pretoria. 1989.
[67] *Understanding the New Age,* pg.184.
[68] *The Plot Against South Africa,* pg.63.
[69] *The Plot Against South Africa,* pg.63.

Communism are available. For example, when Lenin returned to Russia from exile, in a sealed train, this was arranged by the German High Command - and the German government at that time was intensely loyal to the Papacy. Trotsky, Lenin's co-conspirator, was financed by Jacob Schiff, senior partner in Kuhn, Loeb and Co. And other powerful financiers supported the Bolsheviks as well,[70] including one Lord Alfred Milner, who paid over 21 million roubles towards the financing of the Russian revolution. Milner was at one time the leader of the secret Round Table organisation, which was supported by the house of Rothschild. His name will soon resurface in connection with South Africa.

These international bankers (Schiff, Warburg, Morgan, Rockefeller, Rothschild) had connections with the Illuminati, and thus (whether all of them were fully aware of it or not) were being manipulated by the Jesuits. The house of Rothschild had been lending money to the Vatican since 1831.[71]

For Rome, there were at least two advantages to the creation of Bolshevism: the promotion of its centuries-old desire for world domination; and the crushing of its centuries-old rival, the Russian Orthodox institution.[72] Rome believed it had nothing to lose in establishing, via its Illuminati, the Bolshevik movement in Russia.

And now we must return to the history of South Africa. For the international Communist movement worked tirelessly for the conquest of South Africa. And now we can place this ceaseless assault in perspective, and many otherwise-incomprehensible deeds and events will now be more understandable.

Since before the beginning of the twentieth century, immensely-powerful international forces have sought to gain control over South Africa. We have now seen the origin and the background of these forces. Let us proceed to see precisely how they went about their work of conquering this country. These forces are directly responsible for the situation in South Africa today.

---

[70] *The Plot Against South Africa*, pgs.60,61.
[71] *The Vatican Billions*, pgs.202,203.
[72] *The Vatican Billions*, pgs.124,125.

CHAPTER THIRTEEN

THE CONSPIRATORS AGAINST SOUTH AFRICA

The British Empire, in the second half of the nineteenth century, was at the height of its power. But the sinister conspiratorial forces were intent on using the might of the Empire to bring about their own goal of a one-world government. The discovery of diamonds and gold within the boundaries of the two Boer republics - the richest deposits in the world - drew the attention of the shadowy figures working for world control. They determined to own this vast mineral wealth.

It was about this time that Cecil John Rhodes entered the South African situation, and with him sinister internationalist forces. He gained a virtual monopoly over the diamond fields in 1888, becoming immensely powerful within the Cape Colony, and Britain itself.

Rhodes was an extremely ruthless and ambitious man. At Oxford, his professor had been John Ruskin, a Socialist who taught that the rich elite should rule the masses, and that what mankind needed was a one-world government. He believed that the Oxford undergraduates were a privileged, ruling class who should extend the British Empire. Rhodes drank deeply of this doctrine.[73]

In a book called *The Anglo-American Establishment,* published in 1981, Carroll Quigley, a professor at the Jesuit-run Georgetown University in the USA, wrote that Rhodes, in his first will, left all his wealth to the Secretary of State for the Colonies and to the Attorney-General of Griqualand West, to be used to create a *secret society* patterned on the *Jesuits.* The reference to the Jesuits was made in a "Confession of Faith" which Rhodes wrote in 1875, and enclosed in his will two years later. And in a letter to the trustee of his third will, Rhodes told how to form this secret society, saying that the Constitution of the Jesuits should be obtained, and the words, "English Empire", inserted in the place of "Roman Catholic Religion".[74]

It must be borne in mind that Quigley was a professor in a Jesuit

---

[73] *The Other End of the Lifeboat,* by Otto Scott, pgs.8-11. Regnery Books, Chicago. 1985.
[74] *Understanding the New Age,* by Roy Livesey, pgs.121,122. New Wine Press, Chichester, England. 1989.

university. It certainly appears that he was deliberately promoting *another* view of conspiracy - *not* one concerning the Jesuits, but concerning Rhodes.[75] This becomes very likely when one considers that other writers about conspiracy used a reference Quigley made to a conspiracy (an "International Anglophile network") in another book, *Tragedy and Hope,* to go off in all kinds of directions *except* the direction of the Jesuits![76] It would appear that Quigley, in true Jesuitical style, wanted to draw the attention of researchers *away* from the Jesuits, and onto Rhodes; and in order to do this, he mentioned that Rhodes wanted to model his secret society on the Jesuits. But this does not mean that the information he gave about Rhodes was incorrect! He possibly banked on the fact that few, today, know anything about the Jesuits, and would ignore them in their zeal to look into Rhodes.

It is a fact that Rhodes was intimately involved with the (Jesuit-controlled) Illuminati. In the 1890's, he, Alfred Beit, Friedrich Eckstein, and the Rothschilds of London and Paris, formed Rand Mines, Ltd., because of the Johannesburg gold boom.[77] The Rothschild banking family was, and is, a major part of the Illuminati,[78] as seen in the previous chapter.

Rhodes, to promote his schemes, organised a conspiratorial network which included Lord Alfred Milner and a group of Oxford graduates assigned to South Africa, known as "Milner's Kindergarten".[79] Milner, as was pointed out in the previous chapter, paid over 21 million roubles towards financing the Russian revolution. He was at one time leader of the secret Round Table organisation, which was supported by the house of Rothschild. This again shows the close connection between British Imperialists, Communists, and the Jesuit/Illuminati forces.

A plan was formulated against the various nations of southern Africa: a plan that has been relentlessly pursued throughout the twentieth century, despite severe setbacks at times; a truly Communist plan. It was to force the various colonies, republics, and independent

---

[75] *Understanding the New Age,* pg.118.
[76] *Understanding the New Age,* pgs.115,116,119.
[77] *The Other End of the Lifeboat,* pg.7.
[78] *Understanding the New Age,* by Roy Livesey, pgs.180-183. New Wine Press. 1986.
[79] *The New American,* October 22, 1990.

black nations of southern Africa into a single state, in order to control southern Africa totally and exploit its vast wealth. This book will, in the following pages, reveal how these powerful forces have sought to achieve this - and how successful they have been. It has taken them over 100 years, but with the unbanning of the African National Congress and its master, the South African Communist Party, in 1990, the final stage towards the achievement of this goal began. South Africa started to totter the last few steps towards submerging itself into the New World Order envisioned by the conspirators; and fell into their waiting arms in April 1994.

The first step was to destroy the sovereign independence of all nations in southern Africa, and then secondly, to merge all these conquered peoples into a single union: first the white nations, then the black nations. Communism! The denial of any distinction between races, the removal of all barriers.

To accomplish this, the might of the British Empire had to be used, to conquer the black nations and the Boer republics. Let us see how this was done.

The Boers' South African Republic (the Transvaal) had a number of problems in the early 1870's. Its president, Thomas Burgers, was very unpopular; the republic was almost bankrupt; and there was trouble with the Bapedi tribe.

In Natal the Zulus, under their king, Cetshwayo, were a threat to the whites; and relations between the Zulus and the South African Republic were also very tense. Lord Caernarvon, the British Colonial Secretary, desiring a federation of the states in southern Africa, decided to annex the Transvaal, believing that the Orange Free State, the other Boer republic, would then join his federation scheme. On 12th April 1877, Sir Theophilus Shepstone, under orders from Caernarvon, annexed the Transvaal, with very little trouble, for Britain.

Relations did not improve between the British and the Zulus, and in 1879 the Zulu War began. The British invaded Zululand. At Isandhlwana, on the 22nd January 1879, where 384 whites and 491 Basuto allies were encamped, some 24 000 Zulus massacred all but 51 of the British garrison. The Zulus themselves lost over 3000 men in this battle.

At Rorke's Drift, on the Buffalo River, 170 British troops repulsed a Zulu army numbering 4000.

The war continued for months. In July, at Ulundi, the Zulus were finally decisively defeated. In August, Cetshwayo was captured and sent to Cape Town, and Zululand was divided into districts ruled by petty chiefs, who answered to the British.

Also in 1879, in the Transvaal, the British subdued the Bapedi. However, relations between the Boers and their British rulers went from bad to worse.

In addition, the Basuto rebelled in that year, and by 1880 East Griqualand was in rebellion as well, though there it was soon brought under control. Eventually, in 1884, Britain subdued the Basuto.

The restless Boers in the Transvaal finally rebelled against the British. Paul Kruger and two others were chosen to jointly govern the republic that was declared to be established in December 1880. The First Anglo-Boer War began on the 16th December. In August 1881, at the Convention of Pretoria, the independence of the Transvaal was recognised. However, it could not make treaties with other powers without Britain's consent, and the British Resident at Pretoria could veto laws which affected the blacks.

Kruger became president in 1883. The following year, the British surrendered the right to veto Transvaal legislation, and the Transvaal was permitted to make treaties with the Orange Free State and with black tribes to the north.

Rhodes had a clever plan to gain control over the gold-rich Transvaal. He planned to inspire an "Uitlander" rebellion against Kruger (the Uitlanders were British subjects who had gone to the Transvaal in search of wealth); then, a punitive expedition led by a man named Jameson was to capture Pretoria; and, by persuading the Cape High Commissioner that the Uitlanders' rights had been violated, forcing them to rebel against tyranny, he wanted to get the High Commissioner to supervise elections in the Transvaal republic, through which (since the Uitlanders greatly outnumbered the Boers) an

Uitlander would become president. And that president would then place the Transvaal in a federation with the British colonies of the Cape and Natal.[80]

To anyone familiar with recent South African history, all this sounds very familiar. It is almost exactly the same plan as has been used in the last few decades to bring about black Marxist rule over South Africa, as shall be seen: the black tribes were incited to rebel against the white government; force was exerted from outside South Africa's borders by means of a terrible terrorist war; the cry about "civil rights" and "tyranny" went up for decades, and the rebellion was therefore seen as justified; and finally, the cry for elections, supervised by the United Nations, through which a black Marxist puppet government of the internationalists was elected.

Jameson, however, failed in his campaign. He was captured by the Boers, and handed over to the British.[81] This was a setback for Rhodes. But the British, led by Alfred Milner, continued to deliberately *seek* war with the Boers. In 1899, British troops, urged on by Rhodes, were massed in large numbers on the border of the Boers' South African Republic (the Transvaal). President Kruger demanded their removal. This demand was ignored, and in that year the South African War (also known as the Boer War) began, between Britain and the Afrikaners.

The Boers fought very valiantly: 40 000 of them, at war against the greatest military power on earth; Afrikaner farmers against an enormous and disciplined army, which eventually numbered 400 000. Initially very successful, the brave Boers were finally defeated by the sheer weight of the British military might, as well as by the terrible "scorched earth" policy of the British, and the disease-ridden concentration camps they set up, in which 20,000 Afrikaner women and children died. Boer resistance was finally broken, and the two Boer republics surrendered in 1902. Britain had won, but at great cost. The honour of the British Empire was gone.[82] It was an ugly, unnecessary war; a deliberate war of conquest by Britain, for the purpose of gaining control over the immense wealth of South Africa,

---

[80] *The Other End of the Lifeboat*, pg.13.
[81] *The Other End of the Lifeboat*, pgs.13,14.
[82] *The Other End of the Lifeboat*, pgs.16-23.

and completing the first stage in its subjection to the New World Order envisioned by the conspirators, and controlled by Rome: the sovereignty of the various nations of South Africa was destroyed.

Now came the next phase in the plot: to *merge* all the nations of South Africa into one. Lord Milner, after Rhodes' death, was the main instrument of the conspiracy. He planned the merger in stages. First, the Afrikaner and British settlers had to be united, by merging the two former Boer republics of the Transvaal and the Orange Free State with the British colonies of the Cape and Natal. At this stage the black nations and the Coloureds were not considered. British and Boer - the two white races - had to be united first. Only after this was achieved, would the internationalists work for the incorporation of the various black races into a unitary South Africa.

The conspirators went to work. The *London Times* promoted the concept of union. "Closer Union Societies" were established in South Africa by Milner's men. The *Johannesburg Star* pushed for union, its editor being a Milner man, as did other papers. The Boers were made to believe that they would control the new government. They did not realise that the conspirators actually had their fingers in the new government that came into being, through two *Boer* leaders who in reality were part of the conspiracy, being pro-Empire men: Louis Botha and Jan Smuts.[83]

In 1910, the Union of South Africa was created, consisting of the provinces of the Cape, Natal, Transvaal, and Orange Free State. Louis Botha was the first prime minister, and Jan Smuts held three portfolios.

Stage One was complete. The Jesuit-controlled, Communist internationalist forces had succeeded in destroying the sovereignty of the Boer republics, and in creating the Union of South Africa. A country ruled, on the surface, by Afrikaners, but influenced, and manipulated to some extent, by the one-worlders. The year was 1910. South Africa was no longer the name of a geographical area alone, but was now the name of a country. And this is where the first part of this book must end. The forces which sought to gain control over it have been described. Now, in Part Two, we examine how those forces have used terror and murder to reduce South Africa from a leading country

---

[83] *The Other End of the Lifeboat*, pgs.30-33.

of the world to the Communist-controlled land it is today. And we shall see the role played by religious institutions and figures who, in the name of Christ, justified the atrocities committed by the terror organisations which operated in South Africa. They shall be exposed for what they really are: wolves in sheep's clothing, blind leaders of the blind, servants of Satan masquerading as servants of Christ. Behind their diabolical deeds is the evil one's desire to destroy the true Church of the living God, and the preaching of the Gospel of the Son of God. What we have witnessed, and what we are witnessing, is the outworking in this country of a great spiritual warfare in the heavens, a warfare that has been raging ever since the Lord Jesus Christ was on earth in the flesh. In this warfare, the gates of hell seek to prevail against the Church of Christ. The Lord has promised that they shall never succeed (Matt.16:18), but they never cease in their relentless assault. Satan seeks to bring the preaching of the Gospel, and thus the growth of the Church of Christ, to an end throughout the world. The fall of South Africa to the forces of international Communism in 1994, could lead to strong attempts to suppress the preaching of the Gospel of Christ, with, inevitably, the persecution of Christians.

And furthermore - a fact very few in the rest of the (officially) non-Communist, non-Romanist world are aware of - the fall of South Africa inevitably means the weakening of their own freedoms. Probably no place on earth was ruled by a government as anti-Communist, and even as anti-Romanist, as South Africa. And while other countries have enjoyed freedoms as great, or greater, than this one did, their *governments* are by no means as anti-Communist, as anti-Romanist, as South Africa's was. This is why they so readily turned on it and betrayed it - those who supposedly were its allies. The position of those living in the other countries of what is called the free world is far more precarious than they realise. They may at this time enjoy much freedom, but they are not ruled by their own governments: these are increasingly receiving their orders from the seven-hilled city on the Tiber. If such a bastion of anti-Communism and anti-Romanism as South Africa can topple, what of these other countries? Those who live in them may yet discover, to their cost, that the betrayal of South Africa by their own supposedly "freedom-loving" governments was a stepping-stone to their own enslavement.

PART TWO

CHAPTER FOURTEEN

THE VICTORY OF AFRIKANER NATIONALISM

The Union of South Africa, as seen in the previous chapter, was created in 1910. The plan of the conspirators was to unite the two European nations, British and Boer, by forming one country out of the two British colonies and the two Boer republics. This had now been achieved. An Afrikaner was prime minister, but he was a tool in the hands of the one-worlders. His cabinet minister, Jan Smuts, was even more so. The plotters had to work step by step, slowly, so as not to arouse the suspicion of the people.

Why did the Jesuit-controlled Illuminati forces want South Africa to be Communist? The reason is simple: a Communist state is easier to control, for their own ends, than a Capitalist state. Communist leaders, no matter how dictatorial, no matter how powerful, are merely puppets in their hands. A free, Capitalistic South Africa would never be ruled by them, but an enslaved, Communistic society would. Popery itself has always been an absolutist, dictatorial system; its Jesuits, in particular, are old masters at total bondage, total enslavement. And the Illuminati was organized along Jesuit lines from the very beginning. Communism is merely a pawn-system in their hands.

We have seen how the first step was to unite the two white races. Once this was achieved in 1910, the next step - a far more difficult one - was to merge the whites with the black nations in a single state: a classless, raceless society, a society of pawns, slaves of the masters.

Do the one-worlders really *care* about the black races? Are they really interested in their advancement? Are they truly concerned about equal rights, equal opportunities? South Africa became the target of a worldwide hate campaign, its racial laws attacked by the Reds and the liberal almost-Reds from the four quarters of the globe. But the internationalists do not care in the least about South Africa's blacks. All they care about is the advancement of their own cause, the step-by-step enslavement of the world. And here is the proof!

As early as 1912, Israel Cohen, a Communist writer, wrote a book called *A Racial Programme for the Twentieth Century*. In it he stated:

"We must recognise that the most effective weapon of our party is racial tension. By drumming it into the heads of the blacks that they have been oppressed for centuries we can mould them according to the programme of the Communist party....In our propaganda we must particularly make use of the notions of colonialism and imperialism....we must endeavour to inculcate a guilt complex among the whites with regard to the exploitation of the Negroes...."[84]

It cannot be denied that this plan has been eminently successful in South Africa. By exploiting the notions of "colonialism" and "imperialism", exaggerating their evils, ignoring their positive aspects, and literally harping on and on about "oppression" and "exploitation" (in Cohen's words, "drumming it into the heads of the blacks") until even those who did not believe it began to do so, the conspirators used the blacks as pawns to achieve their own purposes. It was not the blacks they were concerned about, it was their own plans and their own pockets. Apartheid was the issue they could exploit, to create racial tension (in Cohen's words, "the most effective weapon of our party".). The motive was not philanthropic, it was lust: lust for power and wealth.

The great tragedy is that millions of blacks throughout Africa have been led to believe that the Marxists sympathise with them, and are concerned for their well-being and advancement. But Cohen's words quoted above reveal the real motive of the conspirators. The truth is that both Marx and Engels *despised* blacks! Publicly, they pretended to be their friends; but privately, they equated them with animals and idiots. Marx declared that the blacks of Africa were "insignificant" and "irrelevant".[85] So much for the supposed concern that Communists have for the black races! They are nothing but pawns to advance the cause.

In order to make use of the blacks in South Africa, black organisations had to be either created or controlled, and used to agitate

---

[84] *The Plot Against South Africa*, pg.134.
[85] *The Plot Against South Africa*, pgs.134-135.

and stir.

The African National Congress (ANC), which was destined to play such a major role in the years to come, was founded in 1912. It was not involved in terrorism in its early years. It was founded for the purpose of uniting the black tribes and persuading the white authorities to abolish racial discrimination. But it was closely watched by the Communist International. We shall see presently what transpired in the 1920's, radically altering the ANC.

After World War One, Lord Milner placed Jan Smuts in the limelight. He became a world-famous statesman, and was greatly honoured.[86] He became *very* influential in planning the League of Nations. This was an attempt to create an eventual world government. It finally came to nothing, but the United Nations Organisation built on it. The Illuminati was hoping for much from Smuts. He was "their" man. But the Lord did not permit their plans to succeed so early in the century. The Afrikaners stood in their way, and thwarted their plans. Let us see how they did it.

At the end of World War One in 1918, the Afrikaner was a defeated person in every possible way, as a result of the Boer War and the struggle with Britain ever since then. There was much bitterness. A group of Afrikaners formed a secret organisation, called the "Broederbond" (Brotherhood), in 1918. Closely linked to the Dutch Reformed denomination and to the National Party of the day, its purpose was to put the Afrikaner in total control of every aspect of South African life. At first it was more of a cultural, semi-religious organisation. But not for long. It rapidly began to play an increasingly influential role in politics, a role that was to grow with the passing years.[87]

Thus two important "births", politically speaking, occurred in the first decade after the creation of the Union in 1910: the birth of the ANC in 1912, and the birth of the Broederbond in 1918.

---

[86] *The Other End of the Lifeboat*, pg.37.
[87] *The Super Afrikaners*, by Ivor Wilkins and Hans Strydom. Jonathan Ball Publishers, Johannesburg. 1980.

In line with Israel Cohen's policy of using the weapon of racial tension, the Communist International decided to gain total control of the African National Congress. At the Sixth Congress of the Communist International in Moscow in 1928, it was resolved that: "The Communist Party of SA should pay particular attention to the ANC. Our aim should be to transform the ANC into a fighting nationalist revolutionary organisation against the white bourgeoisie".[88] To accomplish this, Communists began to infiltrate the ANC leadership.[89]

In 1934 the chairman of the Afrikaner Broederbond, Professor J.C. van Rooy, said in a secret circular that the Broederbond must govern South Africa. Three years after World War Two ended, this came to pass. In the 1948 elections the National Party came to power. This party was controlled by the Broederbond. These Afrikaners had defeated the attempts of the one-worlders to gain total control of the country. Afrikaner nationalism had triumphed over Jesuit/Illuminati internationalism, causing the latter to suffer a major set-back; and this was by the will of God. For the Broederbond was fiercely anti-Communist, anti-internationalist, and anti-Romanist. Its membership was strictly controlled, and was open only to Afrikaans Protestant men. For centuries the Dutch Reformed institution had had a sound grasp of the terrible threat posed to Protestant freedom by the Roman Catholic institution. This we examined in Part One of this book. Its ministers regularly warned of "die Roomse gevaar" (the Romish danger). As was explained in Part One, there were many aspects of Dutch Reformed Protestantism that were far from being scriptural, and the vast majority of Afrikaners, for all their religion, were by no means truly regenerated Christians, though they almost all professed to be; but life under a Dutch Reformed/Broederbond-dominated National Party was far, far better, for both whites and blacks, than it would have been under a Papal-dominated government, or a Communist one.

---

[88] According to *Umsebenzi*, the SACP journal, Vol.2, No.1, 1986; as quoted in *The Aida Parker Newsletter*, Issue No.168, October/November 1993.
[89] *Gold in the Furnace: South Africa on Trial*, by George E. Smock, pg.75. Huntington House, Inc., Shreveport, Louisiana. 1987.

There was far more religious freedom, far more economic prosperity, far more political freedom. South Africa under a Protestant government (I do not say a Christian government, but a Protestant one) developed into one of the leading countries of the world, and *the* most advanced country of sub-Saharan Africa. Any comparison between the non-Romanist, non-Communist nations of the West and those which are Romanist or Communist will reveal that the latter trail far behind in every way. The Lord, in his mercy, permitted a National Party victory in 1948 so as to defeat the plans of the one-worlders. While the rest of the world moved towards the New World Order planned by the Jesuit/Illuminati forces, South Africa remained separate from it all for decades: free, immensely wealthy, safe, strong.

To cite one example of the anti-Romanist position of the Broederbond/National Party for decades: a strict immigration policy was set up, which ensured that Roman Catholic immigration to South Africa was controlled. In the early 1960's, for example, there was a considerable decline in immigrants from Portuguese territories, Italy, Greece, and the Mediterranean. This of course meant that Protestant immigration increased while Roman Catholic immigration decreased.[90]

Is it any wonder, then, that the Vatican for so long supported the Communist struggle against South Africa? It was seen, in Part One, that Rome had what it considered to be very good reasons for wanting to bring about a radical change of government in South Africa, and that one of these was the fact that this land was not a Roman Catholic land. This remained a reason for its actions against this country throughout the twentieth century. Here was a country that was not under Papal influence; that was, in fact, actively opposed to the Papacy. By any means, it had to be brought down. And it was prepared to employ the forces of Communism to do so.

The 1948 election was a victory for Afrikaner nationalists, and a major setback for Jesuit/Illuminati internationalists. But the latter did not give up. Through much violence, terror, and bloodshed over decades, through "church" support, and the infiltration of the National Party itself, the beginning of the last decade of the century saw the beginning of the end of a non-Communist South Africa.

---

[90] *The Super Afrikaners*, pgs.148-152.

CHAPTER FIFTEEN

APARTHEID

Apartheid! The very word itself became synonymous with South Africa in the past few decades. The international Communist movement, international media, liberals, leftist "churches", and many other groups turned South Africa into the outcast of the world by their constant reference to its apartheid policies. Deliberately ignoring the fact that apartheid in one form or another is practiced in many, many countries of the world; deliberately exaggerating its evils; deliberately overlooking the far more atrocious "human rights" abuses in various Communist lands, the worldwide conspiratorial forces launched the most vicious smear campaign in the history of the world. South Africa had to fall, and apartheid was the ideal excuse.

Let it be stated right here and now: there were certainly abuses under apartheid. Evils were committed, and justified, because of apartheid. All men are depraved by nature, ever since the fall of Adam, and no political system on earth has ever been, or will ever be, free of all evil. In every country on earth, under every type of government, wicked deeds have been committed by those in power. But let us examine the reasons why the South African government instituted its policy of "separate development", or apartheid.

South Africa is a complex, diverse country. Its racial and cultural mosaic is very intricate. One of the purposes for Part One of this book (in addition to showing the hand of the Lord in the events that fashioned this country) is to show how this very complex situation developed. South Africa is made up of people from Europe, Africa, Asia, as well as those of mixed race. There are at least thirteen distinguishable peoples in the country. There are two main white groups, the English and the Afrikaners. There are Asiatics, mainly Indians, and there are Coloureds. And there are nine major black nations, each one differing from the others in language, culture, traditions, and religion. These are further divided into over 750 smaller tribes. As for language, within the main black tongues, there are 23 subgroups, and a large number of dialects. Thus, in reality, there is *no* simple "black majority", as the world press has been so bent on declaring. The friction between some of these is very great, for example between the Zulus and the Xhosas, and violent clashes between them have occurred for centuries, and still do.

Such diversity posed a major problem to the National Party government when it came to power in 1948. It was also a fact that for the most part, the different peoples of South Africa *wanted* to preserve their heritages. Not just the whites, but many *blacks* as well, were in favour of a policy of separate development. It could be seen that this was the only logical and fair answer to this massive problem; the only workable solution. If ever there was going to be anything like a peaceful coexistence, a policy of separate development had to be implemented.

The internationalists hated it, of course, because it went against their plans for a unitary state, and that is why they fought so long and hard against it (and NOT because they really cared about the abuses of the policy).

No-one can deny that ultimately the policy was taken too far; that what came to be known as "petty apartheid" was unnecessary, cruel, stupid, and degrading; but that does not alter the fact that the basic idea - separate development - was the only workable solution.

The areas where, traditionally, particular black tribes lived, were called "homelands" or "bantustans". The plan was for each homeland to develop separately. In time, some of these were granted their independence. The world, of course, did not recognise them.

History reveals that the most workable solution for interracial peace and harmony is for each race to govern itself on its own land. Wherever one race has attempted to govern another, conflict has followed. And therefore this aspect of separate development - what can be called "grand apartheid" as opposed to "petty apartheid" - made sense. Just as, in Europe, the British had Britain, the Germans had Germany, and the French had France, so the ideal in southern Africa would be for the various races to have their own land and their own system of government.

But there was another problem, a far more complex one. Millions of blacks had migrated to the urban centres looking for employment. The government felt that they should be citizens of their own homelands, not citizens of South Africa. And so certain other apartheid laws came into being: the Mixed Marriages and Immorality Acts; the Population Registration Act; the Group Areas Act; and the Pass and Influx Laws. We shall take a brief look at each of these.

The Mixed Marriages and Immorality Acts forbade sexual intercourse or marriage between members of the different races. As every Christian knows, sexual intercourse outside of marriage is a grievous sin in the eyes of the Lord, whether between people of different races or people of the same race; but the Bible does not forbid *marriage* between two people of different races. The Old Testament mentality of the Dutch Reformed-dominated National Party members caused them to view marriages between people of different races as sinful, for they saw in the Old Testament that the Israelites were forbidden to marry those of other nations (e.g. Deut.7:1-4). What they failed to understand, however, was that the Lord had forbidden this because those other nations were heathen nations, and Israel worshipped the true and living God. The Lord forbids marriages between his people and those who do not worship him, not between members of different races. The Old Testament has a number of examples of men of God who married women of other nations. In the New Testament, the Church of Christ is made up of people from ALL nations (Rev.7:9,10), forming a new, "holy nation" (1 Pet.2:9); and in this "nation" there are no distinctions of race (Gal.3:27,28; Eph.2:11-22). Christians must marry Christians (1 Cor.7:39; 2 Cor.6:14). It is not their race that is important, but whether they both worship the true God or not.

The Population Registration Act classified everyone according to race. While necessary, this was not always done carefully, and often caused much suffering.

The Group Areas Act designated where each racial group in SA could, and could not, live. Although it is best for each race to govern itself on its own land (and this is why black homelands were created), there will always be people of other races within its borders, even if they have their own homelands, and are citizens of those (and within their own limits, those countries which encourage a certain amount of immigration often enrich themselves greatly); and, from a moral standpoint, these people should not be forcefully settled in specially designated areas alone, and prohibited from living amongst the rest of the population. Such a policy actually encourages racial hatred. The Group Areas Act resulted in the forced removal of blacks from areas designated for whites, and this caused great misery for many.

The Pass and Influx Laws required all in South Africa to have identity documents which specified their race group. Blacks could not enter white areas without them. Their purpose was to control the numbers of rural blacks moving to urban areas, which were very overcrowded. Again, the intention may have been good originally, an attempt to solve a massive problem, but there were abuses.

Apartheid, then, was an attempt to solve a huge and complex problem in South Africa. Many aspects of it were good and beneficial, and were accepted favourably by many in all race groups. Other aspects of it were cruel and derogatory, unnecessary and even plain stupid.

History confirms that the ideal solution to racial tension is for each race to govern itself. Sometimes, however, when the different races have been scrambled together, and not all parties are agreeable to partition, the ideal is not attainable without suffering and bloodshed. In such a case, the second-best solution is a federal one. If the whites in South Africa had never sought the cheaper black labour force that black migration provided, perhaps the ideal could have been attained, for then there would have been no sprawling black townships on the outskirts of white cities, with huge numbers of black people no longer looking to their traditional homelands, but to South Africa, as "home". But the reality must be faced. The ideal could be attained if all the races concerned agreed to implement it; but they did not do so. And so the only fair system would have been to have given equal privileges to *all* the inhabitants of South Africa, but in a federal system, with each nation governing a particular territory, but allowing people of other nations to live there. The government, tragically, when it finally dismantled apartheid, did not establish a federal system in its place, choosing rather to cave in to the ANC's demand for a "unitary state".

In addition the government, when it dismantled apartheid, went further: it released Marxist terrorists, it unbanned Marxist organisations. Granting the black inhabitants of SA equal status with whites did *not* mean that the Communist organisations had to be unbanned! - but that is what happened. It was not a South Africa in which all races would have equal status as citizens that the international conspirators wanted: they wanted a *Marxist* South Africa! It was not a South Africa in which all would be equal, but diversity would be acknowledged and respected, that they wanted: they wanted a *classless, raceless* South Africa! The tragedy was that, in addition to the good that was done when unnecessary and ugly racial laws were removed, a vast amount of evil was also done when diabolical terror organisations were unbanned and thus unleashed on the South African public, which lost no time in working for the complete and final collapse of the South African government, and the handing over of the country to the forces of international Communism, which in turn serve the interests of the one-worlders. This shall be seen in due course.

Apartheid was the excuse the plotters needed, and they exploited it to the full. But the upliftment of the blacks in South Africa was never the motive for their actions: the advancement of their own cause was the only motive they ever had. As the history of black Africa shows, Marxism has never brought peace, happiness, or prosperity to the black races. It has brought more misery than ever before. And this fact the black races of South Africa will learn to their cost, now that a Marxist dictatorship has risen from the ruins of once-prosperous South Africa.

CHAPTER SIXTEEN

THE ANC BANNED AND MANDELA IMPRISONED

The African National Congress was the black organisation the Communist Party decided to infiltrate and use to achieve its objectives in South Africa. As noted earlier, it was resolved in 1928 that the Communist Party of South Africa, working under orders from Moscow, would transform the ANC into a revolutionary organisation.

In the 1940's, men such as Nelson Mandela, Walter Sisulu, and Oliver Tambo joined the ANC; men whose names would become synonymous with the organisation in the years to come. At the ANC conference in 1949, these men staged a coup, culminating in Walter Sisulu becoming general secretary, and two Communists being elected to the National Executive Committee. From that date on, the ANC became far more radical.[91]

In 1950, the South African government passed the Suppression of Communism Act. This caused the ANC to become even more Communistic, as many Communists now joined it so as to continue operating; for the ANC was not perceived as a Communist front organisation by most. In 1955, the ANC adopted the "Freedom Charter" as its own constitution. This was a Communist document, advocating nationalisation of industry, etc.

In 1959 a split occurred. Some blacks were expelled from the ANC after a power struggle, and they formed another Communist organisation, the Pan Africanist Congress (PAC). This organisation was also destined to play a major role in the terrorist assault on South Africa.

And then came the Sharpeville event in 1960.

The Marxist terrorists of the ANC and PAC periodically staged confrontations with the South African security forces, for the purpose of painting them in the worst possible light. The Sharpeville event was precisely such a confrontation. But the truth is far different from what the world press chose to report.

---

[91] *Revolution or Reconciliation?* by Rachel Tingle, pgs.198,199. Christian Studies Centre, London. 1992.

This is what the world hears: in March 1960, some 10 000 blacks marched on a police station in Sharpeville. The police opened fire, and 69 blacks were killed, and 180 wounded. But let us delve a little deeper, and look at what led up to the events of that day, and what the media deliberately chose to ignore.

January 25, 1960: in Cato Manor not far from Durban, the police had made some arrests. Suddenly they were surrounded by a huge crowd of black people, who had been drinking, and who demanded the release of those arrested. The police were attacked, amidst cries of "Kill the cops!" Nine policemen were brutally massacred, literally hacked to pieces.

This terrible atrocity was *ignored* by most of the foreign press. But two months later, on March 21, the police at Sharpeville were faced with an angry crowd of many thousands. Cato Manor was fresh in their minds. Since the previous night, the crowds of blacks had been agitating around the police station. Repeatedly, the crowd charged the police barricades. The commanding officer ordered his men to load, but not to fire until ordered to. But the policemen were tired and tense. Some of them had been on duty for 24 hours.

Then the crowd surged forward, chanting "Cato Manor!" The gates were torn down, a police officer was thrown to the ground. The police opened fire. 69 were killed, and 180 wounded.

That was the confrontation the Communists wanted. It was not the last time they would deliberately sacrifice black lives to advance their "cause", as we shall see. They did not care how many black lives were lost, just as long as they finally achieved power. The international media howled with rage. The South African police were blasted as evil sadists, the whites in general as evil oppressors of the blacks. What was *not* widely reported was that Robert Sobukwe, the PAC founder, had *urged* the blacks to break the pass laws, and to demonstrate outside police stations.[92]

The Sharpeville event caused mob violence to erupt nationwide. Blacks killed blacks. The ANC called for a nationwide strike. The government declared a state of emergency, and then, in April, it

---

[92] *The Aida Parker Newsletter*, No.49, January 29, 1985.

banned the ANC and the PAC. They then went underground, and continued their terror campaigns.

In banning these organisations, the government dealt a severe blow to the plans of the conspirators. That ban remained in force until 1990, when a thoroughly-infiltrated National Party under F.W. de Klerk, bearing very little resemblance to the National Party of the past, lifted the ban. Violence and bloodshed increased dramatically from the very moment these organisations were unbanned. Their banning in 1960 was in the best interests of the security of South Africa; their unbanning in 1990, thirty years later, was a tragedy of immense proportions.

In 1961, South Africa became a republic. Also in that year, *Mkhonto we Sizwe* (meaning "Spear of the Nation"), the ANC's armed wing, was formed, and Nelson Mandela became its Commander. The ANC was under the control of the South African Communist Party, and the Soviet Union supplied it with arms, as part of its worldwide strategy to advance the Communist cause. An ANC official said of the Soviet Union, "We will cherish their friendship for many years to come"; and, "They are our allies of old time. We are not ashamed to have Communists in our ranks."[93]

In 1963, the ANC suffered another blow, as severe as its banning three years before. After a number of bomb attacks orchestrated by Mkhonto we Sizwe (usually known as "MK" for short), most of its leaders were arrested, including Walter Sisulu, Govan Mbeki, and Nelson Mandela. The police also recovered a number of documents. One of these gave minute details of the plans of MK's "Operation Mayibuye", which was a blueprint for seizing control by means of sabotage, revolution, terrorism, and guerrilla warfare.

As the years went by, Nelson Mandela was portrayed in the world press as a hero who had been unjustly imprisoned by the hated "apartheid regime" of South Africa. But the truth is that he and the others had planned the manufacture of 45 000 anti-personnel mines, 210 000 hand grenades, bombs, pipe bombs, syringe bombs, and bottle

---

[93] *Gold in the Furnace: South Africa on Trial*, pg. 76.

bombs! They had planned to overthrow the South African government. It was not for unjust reasons that Mandela was arrested and imprisoned; it was, in essence, for high treason![94]

These facts have been completely ignored by the international media, as have the following: Mandela had written a document entitled *How to be a Good Communist,* and had written of the coming of a "Communist world", of wiping out the enemies of Communism, etc. Another document, 94 pages long and written in his own handwriting, declared that "traitors and informers should be ruthlessly eliminated". He was, and remained, a committed Communist - but the world is hardly aware of it, thanks to the media cover-up of facts like these.

When arrested and tried, he at no time challenged the authenticity of these documents (so much for the oft-repeated cry that "he spent 27 years of his life unjustly imprisoned for his opposition to apartheid"); in fact, counsel for the defence stated that, "in the face of the overwhelming bulk of evidence", it would be "futile to refute any of the charges". The documents were so incriminating that the prosecution believed it could have obtained convictions on these alone. Mandela and the others, although they could have received the death sentence, were found guilty of armed insurrection and were sentenced, after an extremely fair hearing in open court, to life imprisonment. Even the liberal *Rand Daily Mail* said, in an editorial for June 17, 1964, "the sentences pronounced by Mr Justice de Wet yesterday at the conclusion of the Rivonia Trial were both wise and just....The sentences could not have been less severe than those imposed....The men found guilty had organised sabotage on a wide scale and had plotted armed revolution. As the judge pointed out, the crime of which they were found guilty was essentially high treason."[95]

The remaining ANC leaders continued operating as exiles, Oliver Tambo being the leader-in-exile; but the ANC's terror campaign was severely curtailed.[96]

---

[94] *Gold in the Furnace: South Africa on Trial,* pg.76; and *The Aida Parker Newsletter,* Issue No.168, October/November 1993.
[95] *The Aida Parker Newsletter,* Issue No.168, October/November 1993.
[96] *Gold in the Furnace: South Africa on Trial,* pgs.76,77;*Revolution or Reconciliation?* pg.200; and

Such is the truth about Nelson Mandela and the other leaders of the African National Congress: Communist terrorists who had planned armed insurrection and the violent overthrow of the South African government. And yet, 27 years later, these same revolutionaries were free men, legally entitled to build up the ANC within South Africa's borders (while it continued with the same murderous terror tactics that it had been using for decades), and overseeing the surrender of South Africa into their bloodstained hands. What took place, during those 27 years between 1963 and 1990, that led to their release and the betrayal of South Africa into the hands of its enemies? Please read on.

The Aida Parker Newsletter, Issue No.168, October/November 1993.

CHAPTER SEVENTEEN

THE VATICAN, THE WCC, AND "LIBERATION THEOLOGY"

After World War Two, the Vatican came to the conclusion that Communism was going to become the dominant world political system, and so it felt that it was necessary for the Roman Catholic institution to *align* itself with Communism in order to conquer the world. This has ever been Rome's policy: to test which way the political wind is blowing, and to act accordingly, striving to harness that wind for its own objectives.

When the pro-Nazi, anti-Communist pope, Pius XII, died in 1958, a pro-Communist pope, John XXIII, came to power. In addition, pro-Communist priests were proliferating. These "worker priests", as they were called, saw Communism as identical with "Christianity" (i.e. Romanism) on sociological and economic grounds. They claimed that the New Testament taught basic Communist principles. They believed that Christ and Lenin were both social revolutionaries, preaching the same "gospel".[97] They were the early proponents of aspects of the diabolical doctrine that was to become known as "liberation theology": essentially, Catholic-Communism.

John XXIII wasted no time in establishing ties with Socialists and Communists, including the Kremlin itself. Roman Catholics who supported the Communists were no longer condemned. He wrote two encyclicals, in 1961 and 1963, which were decidedly pro-Red. It was not long before the alliance between the Vatican and Moscow was well-established. The Papal institution had undergone a radical transformation.[98]

John is most famous for calling the Second Vatican Council, or Vatican II as it is known, in the early 1960's, its purpose supposedly being to update the Roman Catholic "Church". Vatican II really gave impetus to what later came to be called "liberation theology". When

---

[97] *The Vatican Moscow Washington Alliance*, by Avro Manhattan, pgs.78-83. Chick Publications, Chino, California. Second American Edition. 1986.
[98] *The Vatican Moscow Washington Alliance*, pgs.134-159.

John died his successor, Paul VI, was even more pro-Communist than he had been.[99] The merging of Roman Catholicism with Communism continued to steam ahead. Pro-Communist priests were sent, in particular, to Latin America and Africa, where they were to profoundly influence the Marxist revolutions on these continents. From the "Christ the Worker" image promoted by the worker-priests, "Christ the Liberator" was to emerge in Latin America: a Marxist "Christ", a guerrilla, a revolutionary, gun in hand, "liberating" the "oppressed" from Capitalism and the "oppressors". This blasphemous image of Christ was inspired by Vatican II.[100] And it was this concept that gave rise to liberation theology proper. In 1971 a priest named Gustavo Gutiérrez wrote *A Theology of Liberation,* and the movement had a name.[101]

Priests and nuns in Latin America joined Marxist guerrilla armies. Jesuits wrote Marxist-inspired works. They taught a Communist "Christ": making much of the fact that he had no property, his disciples were workers, etc. The masses, ignorant of the Scriptures, believed the distortion.

Liberation theology was born in Popery; and the Vatican was to play a huge role in supporting the Marxist revolutions in Africa, quietly at first, and then more and more noisily. Black people began to view the Roman Catholic institution as a powerful ally in their "struggle".[102] This was the case in South Africa, no less than in other African countries. The part Rome played in this land's revolution was immense, as the following pages will testify.

The World Council of Churches (WCC) also played a huge part in the revolutionary assault on South Africa. It is a radical, pro-Marxist, antichristian organisation serving the interests of Satan, a monstrous and deadly conglomeration of institutions masquerading as "churches" and justifying unspeakable horrors in the name of Christ.

---

[99] *The Vatican Moscow Washington Alliance,* pgs.161-170.
[100] *The Vatican Moscow Washington Alliance,* pgs.260-270.
[101] *Newsweek,* April 14, 1986.
[102] *The Vatican Moscow Washington Alliance,* pgs.300-314.

The WCC began in 1948 with 147 Protestant and Orthodox denominations. Today it numbers close to 300 denominations, representing some 400 million people.[103] It is an attempt to unite all "churches", a veritable Babel, an ecumenical monster playing right into the hands of the Vatican. The Roman Catholic institution is not presently a member but there is very close co-operation between the two, with at least a quarter of the WCC's staff being Roman Catholics.[104] It is heavily infiltrated by Communist agents, and has actively supported Communist revolutions worldwide.

Significantly, the National Church Council of the USA (NCC), which was the model for the WCC, was financed by contributions from, in particular, the Rockefeller and Carnegie foundations; and Rockefeller later financed the WCC's establishment in Geneva - just as he had the UN site in New York.[105] The WCC was thus financed by the Illuminati! And the Illuminati is controlled by the Jesuits. A further piece of evidence showing the Jesuit/Illuminati connections with the WCC is that John Foster Dulles, legal advisor to the Rockefeller family and later US Secretary of State, was appointed chairman of the Commission for International Relations of the WCC in Geneva, his task being to integrate and co-ordinate the WCC's work with the UN's work.[106] In fact, the WCC could be said to be the *spiritual* arm of the United Nations! As Jurgen Moltman, a leading theologian of the "Evangelical Church of Germany" and the WCC, said: "The churches should therefore make special efforts to get rid of national sovereignty and promote the development of the United Nations and a world government."[107]

What the reader must always bear in mind is that a church is not a true Christian church merely because it calls itself one. After the Protestant Reformation, Papal agents infiltrated Protestant churches

---

[103] *The Truth About the World Council of Churches*, by M.H. Reynolds. Fundamental Evangelistic Association, Los Osos, California (tract).
[104] *Watch!* July to September 1990, Vol.2, No.3. Christian Research Institute, Swansea, United Kingdom.
[105] *The Plot Against South Africa*, pg.174.
[106] *The Plot Against South Africa*, pg.175.
[107] *The Plot Against South Africa*, pg.173.

and over a period of many years did much to move them increasingly away from the Scriptures. In the nineteenth century the insidious effects of evolution, "higher criticism", liberalism, etc., began to be increasingly apparent within much of what went by the name of "Protestant". Churches and denominations began to preach a social message rather than the true Gospel. A great departure from biblical truths occurred, and this accelerated in the twentieth century. Most Protestant churches today bear little or no resemblance to true Christian churches. And most are members of the WCC, proclaiming a politicised, Socialist "gospel" instead of the true Gospel of Jesus Christ.

In 1966, some WCC officials organised a conference in Geneva, on the theme, "Christians in the Technical and Social Revolutions of our Time". Richard Shaull, an American theologian, gave a radical speech. He viewed Christ as a socio-political revolutionary, and advocated that the "Church" should get involved in the revolutionary process occurring in the Third World. He advocated a Marxist analysis of society: the revolutionary change of society.[108] Other speakers gave radical lectures as well. And its report stated that a significant number of "Christians" had assumed a revolutionary position. Influenced deeply by the Marxist concept of "institutional violence", the report stated: "It cannot be said that the only possible position for the Christian is one of absolute non-violence....Wherever small elites rule at the expense of the majority, political change.....should be actively promoted and supported....in cases where such political changes are needed .the use by Christians of revolutionary methods - by which is meant violent overthrow of existing political order - cannot be excluded *a priori*."[109]

The Lord Jesus Christ was never a socio-political revolutionary. He never once advocated the overthrow of the existing government, nor did he ever lead any insurrection, armed or otherwise. He preached about a *spiritual,* not a political kingdom: the kingdom of heaven (Matt.4:17). He emphatically condemned the use of the sword to advance his kingdom (Matt.26:52; Jn.18:36). The Scriptures teach that

---

[108] *Revolution or Reconciliation?* pgs.13-15.
[109] *Revolution or Reconciliation?* pgs.18,19.

the Church must obey the authorities, however dictatorial or tyrannical (Rom.13:1-7). Men, claiming to be Christians, who follow the teachings of Marx and advocate revolution, are in no way true Christians, disciples of the Son of the living God. They are simply religious terrorists, or otherwise men who hide behind a cloak of religion in order to perform revolutionary acts. The WCC report quoted above, in stating that political change can be legitimately brought about by "Christians" using violence, reveals the thoroughly antichristian, Marxist nature of that organisation. But worse was to come.

The "Christian Institute of South Africa", founded in 1963 by ecclesiastical leaders led by Beyers Naudé, became more radical after 1966 as Naudé was influenced by the WCC Church and Society Conference. It supported the Black Consciousness movement. In 1967 it joined the South African Council of Churches.[110] Beyers Naudé would play a very important role in the so-called "struggle". The Christian Institute was banned in 1977.

The 1968 General Assembly of the WCC came out in support of the idea of Third World revolutions. The "Church and Society Conference" of the WCC recommended a post-assembly programme to eliminate "racism" in general, and "*white* racism" in particular; and the proposal was adopted. Consequently, in 1969, the WCC-organised "Consultation on Racism" was held. A delegation of US Black Power radicals, and two *ANC* members, attended. One of them was Oliver Tambo, ANC leader-in-exile.

White-ruled Western societies were accused, in typical Marxist fashion, of exploitation and racism in order to accumulate wealth. Oliver Tambo demanded that WCC member-churches "throw their moral and material resources" behind the revolutionaries. And Channing Phillips, of the United Church of Christ, Washington DC, advocated "the power of violence". The Consultation urged the WCC to support revolutionaries in the Third World. And it recommended that the WCC serve as the co-ordinating centre for implementing strategies for the "struggle" against "racism" in southern Africa by the "churches".[111]

---

[110]*Revolution or Reconciliation?* pgs.75-77.
[111]*Revolution or Reconciliation?* pgs.20-25.

Here we see the way in which the international Communist movement succeeded in gaining the support of the so-called "churches" of the world. "Racism" was the issue that was exploited (and in South Africa, this was of course equated with apartheid); but it was merely the fuel to ignite the fire. Conflict had to be created between races, false abuses had to be manufactured and any real ones had to be exaggerated, in order to goad the blacks into rebellion and revolution, thinking they were fighting racism when in reality they were merely pawns, cannon-fodder for the advancement of international Communism, which in turn was promoting the Jesuit/Illuminati plan for world domination by the Papacy. The religious bodies that made up the WCC, many of them never having been scripturally-based and many others having moved away from any sound scriptural foundation they might once have had, were by this time so committed to a "gospel" of mere social action, that it is not surprising that they adopted the proposal to eliminate "white racism", as if that was what Christianity was all about. So far removed were the member-churches of the WCC from the true, biblical Gospel of Jesus Christ, that they could permit a terrorist like Oliver Tambo to address them, and then succumb to his demands!

The "churches" had been brought into the Marxist assault on southern Africa, under the guise of struggling against "racism". And their involvement would increase, year by year, in financial and other practical ways, as we shall see.

In August 1969, the WCC's General Committee, doing the bidding of its Communist overlords, called on churches to "move beyond charity, grants and traditional programming....to become agents for the radical reconstruction of society". And it proposed establishing a "Programme to Combat Racism" (PCR), involving all departments of the WCC. A Special Fund was set up, from which grants were made to organisations fighting "racism".[112]

"The radical reconstruction of society"! This was nothing less than classic Marxism, which seeks the destruction of Capitalism and the creation of a Communistic world, the destruction of freedom and the creation of a world of slaves, docile and obedient to the elite masters.

---

[112] *Revolution or Reconciliation?* pg.27.

And this, of course, is precisely the goal of the Papal system, the religion of Antichrist: a world in total obedience to the Roman pontiff.

Of the first grant made from the Special Fund in 1970, US $120 000 went to so-called "liberation movements" to be found primarily in southern Africa: the MPLA in Angola; its rivals UNITA and GRAE; FRELIMO in Mozambique; the Patriotic Front in Rhodesia; SWAPO in South West Africa; the ANC in South Africa; and also the PAIGC of Guinea and the Cape Verde Islands. This caused an uproar around the world, and in South Africa a number of member-churches of the South African Council of Churches (the South African division of the WCC) almost withdrew from the SACC; but finally, all retained membership.[113] The conspirators were following a definite plan, about which more shall be said later: one by one, South Africa's neighbouring or nearby countries fell to the so-called "liberation movements" (in reality, Marxist terrorist organisations, called "liberation movements" by the Marxists themselves, who sought to deceive the black masses into believing that they were interested in their political and social "liberation"). Mozambique, Angola, Rhodesia, South West Africa - each succumbed eventually to the terrorist onslaught, until South Africa was surrounded.

In practical terms, the support, by the WCC's Programme to Combat Racism, for these organisations meant that donations, contributed by the faithful of all kinds of so-called "churches", were being used to finance revolutionary violence in southern Africa - the killing of thousands upon thousands of people. And yet the member-churches of the SACC did not withdraw their membership, even when they knew what was going on! What a terrible blot upon these institutions, all claiming to be Christian churches and naming the name of Christ!

To their credit, the Salvation Army and the Presbyterian Church of Ireland formally withdrew from the WCC. In the Anglican institution, the outcry caused an emergency debate to be held by its General Synod; and yet, not only did it not withdraw from the WCC, but it actually ended up deciding for "*fuller* participation" in the WCC, and "*increased* contributions"![114]

---

[113]*Revolution or Reconciliation?* pgs.29,30.
[114]*Revolution or Reconciliation?* pgs.30-33.

That a body professing to be Christian could, in the light of the evidence, opt for fuller participation in the bloodstained WCC, and commit itself to giving even more money to it, is so horrific that there is no possible way, judging it by its behaviour alone, that it can be considered a Christian church. It is nothing less than a daughter of the Papal Whore (Rev.17:5), and like its evil Mother it has the blood of multitudes upon its hands. And blood is upon the other member-institutions of the WCC, which, both for doctrinal and practical reasons (an example being their support for terror groups), cannot by any stretch of the imagination be termed true Christian churches.

In the years following 1970, the grants increased, despite the outcries in, for example, the British press, and from many individuals - and despite the fact that these terrorist organisations were murdering missionaries and others. A world body naming the name of Christ, supporting the murderers of others naming the name of Christ! Such a body serves the devil.

In 1971, the Central Committee of the WCC declared that, in order to receive grants from the Special Fund, "The purpose of the [revolutionary] organisations must not be in conflict with the general purposes of the WCC and its units, and the grants are to be used for humanitarian activities." As the WCC was giving money to terrorist organisations, it was guilty of supporting those organisations, regardless of how the money was used! Besides, even if it could be proved that the revolutionaries did indeed use the grants for purposes other than the purchasing of arms, etc., the granting of this money simply enabled them to use *other* money for arms! But further, even though it stated that the money was to be used for "humanitarian activities", the WCC also declared that it would not control how the grants were used. In fact, the secretary general of the WCC admitted, in 1970, that it was impossible to guarantee that the money would not be used for arms.[115]

A significant statement in this declaration was that the purposes of the revolutionary groups "must not be in conflict with the general purposes of the WCC". As it continued to support the revolutionary groups, financially and in other ways, year after year after year, quite

---

[115] *Revolution or Reconciliation?* pgs.41,42.

obviously the purposes were identical. They serve the same earthly masters - the conspirators behind the scenes - and the same diabolical master, "the spirit that now worketh in the children of disobedience" (Eph.2:2): the devil.

Another thing the Central Committee stated in 1971 was that it did not pass judgement on the "victims of racism who are driven to violence". Once again it revealed, by this statement, that it was not of God. There is no justification for people to murder others, regardless of the circumstances. The spirit behind the WCC is not the Spirit of Christ.

Of course, the grants of the PCR to the terror groups helped to give publicity, and to *legitimise* them in the eyes of many. For the WCC has succeeded in convincing much of the world that it is a truly Christian organisation. If the WCC supported the "liberation movements", then surely they must be worthy of the support of the world!

"Contextual Theology" took root in South Africa in the early 1970's. It was spawned in the US, being originally promoted by a white Methodist minister, Basil Moore. But it was the book, *Black Theology and Black Power,* written by black US "theologian" James Cone and published in 1969, that in 1971 was a major inspiration in South Africa. The first book on Black Theology to be published in South Africa was *Essays on Black Theology.* South African Black Theology became the "theological" side of South Africa's Black Consciousness Movement - which was very similar to, and drew much inspiration from, the US' Black Power movement.[116]

South Africa was getting its own version of liberation theology, the false, revolutionary "gospel" of "liberation" from "oppression" by means of violence, that was to be preached with such vigour to the black masses in the years to come, stirring up hatred and causing the deaths of thousands of people. The glorious and ever-blessed name of Jesus Christ, the holy Son of the living God, was blasphemously used by cold-blooded revolutionaries in ecclesiastical attire to galvanise thousands of blacks into becoming expendable pawns to advance what they were told was the "Kingdom of God", but which was in reality to

---

[116] *Revolution or Reconciliation?* pgs.70-74.

advance the goals of those who wanted South Africa to fall to the international Communist movement.

CHAPTER EIGHTEEN

WHY SOUTH AFRICA WAS TARGETED

After the ANC was banned in 1960 and went underground, and after Nelson Mandela and others were arrested a few years later and sentenced to life imprisonment, its leadership, led by Oliver Tambo, operated from outside its borders, and conducted an ongoing terror campaign against South Africa. ANC headquarters were established in Zambia, bases were established in other southern African states, and offices were opened in London, New Delhi, and Moscow. As the years went by, in addition to the support it received from the World Council of Churches and various other "church" groups, it also received support from the United Nations, the Soviet Union, the Communist-bloc countries of Eastern Europe, Libya, and various Western governments as well.

Its armed wing, Mkhonto we Sizwe (MK), did not cease with the arrest of Mandela and the others. MK members were trained in Angola, Libya and elsewhere, and potential leaders were trained in the Soviet Union itself. After receiving specialised training, they infiltrated South Africa and carried out terrorist bomb attacks.

Infiltration was vital to the success of the revolution. In the early 1970's, the revolutionaries infiltrated black youth groups, trade unions, and white universities.[117] This infiltration was to pay off handsomely by 1976.

South Africa's great wealth made it a particularly important prize for the Communist forces to win. In the words of Soviet President Brezhnev:

"Our aim is to gain control of the two great treasure houses on which the West depends - the energy treasure of the Persian Gulf and the mineral treasure house of central and southern Africa."[118]

Indeed, South Africa is a treasure house of mineral wealth, the

---

[117] *The McAlvany Intelligence Advisor*, December 1986. Edited and published in Phoenix, Arizona, by Donald S. McAlvany.
[118] *South Africa--the Shocking Facts*, by Jed Smock. The Campus Ministry, Lexington, Kentucky. 1986. (pamphlet)

greatest anywhere on earth. The Soviet Union was the other great source of the world's mineral needs - and that was already closed to the West. If Moscow controlled South Africa, it would control up to 99% of the world's known platinum, 97% of its vanadium, 93% of its manganese, 84% of its chrome, and 68% of its gold.[119] With that kind of power in its hands, it could cripple the West's high-tech electronic society.

The Vatican desired South Africa for its immense wealth, and because it was not part of the world order which the Vatican was seeking to establish. The fall of South Africa would also mean the weakening of the United States of America - the ultimate target of Vatican global conquest. The Soviet global strategy in many ways paralleled the Vatican's, and for this reason was being manipulated by the Jesuit forces in its war against South Africa. Romanism desires world domination; so does Communism. Romanism desires the fall of the West; so does Communism. Romanism desires the wealth of the West; so does Communism. Romanism desires the elimination of biblical Christianity; so does Communism. These are the reasons behind the Vatican's support for Communism in South Africa and elsewhere.

The ultimate goal is the conquest of the United States of America, the most powerful of all Western countries. For many, many long years, the Vatican has been working for the downfall of the US. Due to the military strength of that land, it had to be severely weakened from within, by infiltration; and also by the destruction of its allies in the West - such as South Africa. It is a fairly well-known fact that the US has been heavily infiltrated by Communist agents, right up to the top levels of government.[120] But what is hardly known at all, is that agents of the Roman Catholic institution have *also* been infiltrating the US government for many, many years.[121]

---

[119] *South Africa--the Shocking Facts.*
[120] See, for example, *None Dare Call It Treason*, by John A. Stormer. Liberty Bell Press, Florissant, Missouri. 1964.
[121] See *The Vatican Moscow Washington Alliance*, pgs.350-356; *The Southern Cross* (published by the Southern African Roman Catholic hierarchy, Cape Town), December 28, 1986; February 12, 1989; August 2, 1992; and November 22, 1992; *Church and State*

This massive interference, by Roman Catholic and Communistic agents, in the top echelons of American government, will explain a fact that has perplexed so many in recent decades: that, despite the fact that the United States should have been doing all in its power to keep South Africa from falling to the forces of international Marxism, *it was doing the very opposite!* It was fighting against South Africa's government! It was an enemy to South Africa, not a friend - and it bears a huge amount of responsibility for the ruin of South Africa, as shall be seen in the following pages!

Yes, the US government during the past few decades was South Africa's enemy. Its goal was to destabilise the country and see to it that the ANC became the government![122] For many years, the CIA built up a network of opposition groups in South Africa, and infiltrated political, cultural, academic, religious and other groups.[123] And this was because the US government had been so heavily infiltrated by Vatican and Communist agents, working not only for the destruction of South Africa, but for that of the USA as well.

The picture, then, is this: the conspiracy is nothing less than world domination. The free Western nations stand in the way of that goal, and must be conquered. Leading them all is the United States. So its government was heavily infiltrated, in order to do two things: firstly, to work from the inside to move the United States in the direction of a Socialist, and ultimately Papal-controlled, society; and secondly, to use such influence as the infiltrators already possessed in the US government, media, etc., to actually *support* the revolutionary forces fighting to gain control over other free countries, such as South Africa.

(published by Americans United for Separation of Church and State, Silver Spring, Maryland), July/August 1989; April 1990; and January 1991; *Battle Cry* (published by Chick Publications, Chino, California), January/February 1990; *Milwaukee Journal*, December 8, 1990; *Col. North, Wm. Casey, and the Knights of Malta*, by Betty J. Mills, Republic Research, New Haven, Indiana; *Time*, February 24, 1992.
[122] *The McAlvany Intelligence Advisor*, October 1986.
[123] *The Plot Against South Africa*, pgs.199-202.

CHAPTER NINETEEN

THE CONFLICT ESCALATES, AND ANC/"CHURCH" CO-OPERATION INCREASES

The conspirators had decreed that the African National Congress, now totally under the control of the South African Communist Party, was to become the government of South Africa. To this end, the United Nations, in 1974, formally declared the ANC to be "the authentic representative of the overwhelming majority of the peoples of South Africa."[124] This was a blatant lie. Only a small percentage of any of the peoples of South Africa ever fully supported the ANC. Millions were *intimidated* into doing so, but that is a different matter. Even by June 1991, seventeen years later, the ANC, by its own admission, only had a membership of about 500 000:[125] a very tiny percentage in a country of over 35 million people! But the UN had decreed it, because the conspirators desired it: the ANC was "the authentic representative" of the majority. And because the UN had spoken, the world believed it. And because the world believed it, the world supported the ANC.

In South Africa itself, so-called "church" leaders were deeply involved, by the mid-1970's, in the revolutionary onslaught - even justifying *murder* by distorting the Scriptures, as the following testimony reveals.

A young black woman, Salamina Borephe, a former ANC member, testified before a study committee of the Republican Party in Washington that in 1975 she attended the Congress of South African Students (COSAS), which was, she was told, a branch of the ANC (the ANC being banned, of course, at that time). Priests praised Communism. Anglican priests told her and the others that local black councillors (seen as sellouts by the ANC) must *die*. In a meeting held in the Roman Catholic "church" building of Evanton and Sharpeville in September 1975, the priests referred to the Bible to explain why local councillors should be murdered. They also called for the killing

---

[124] *Gold in the Furnace: South Africa on Trial*, pg. 77.
[125] *Revolution or Reconciliation?* pg. 206.

of policemen. And they compared Nelson Mandela with Moses in the book of Exodus.[126]

Here were men, claiming to be ministers of the Gospel and servants of Christ, deceiving young and naïve blacks into believing a false "gospel" of deliverance from political oppression through murder. In classic liberation theology style, they turned to the biblical account of the exodus of the Israelites from Egypt (a favourite theme of liberation theologians), and depicted the blacks in South Africa as being in the position of Israel of old, needing a deliverer (Mandela) to free them from the tyranny of "pharaoh" (the white government). To thousands of restless young black people, ignorant of the Scriptures but religious and full of confidence in their priests, it made perfect sense. How could they know that the exodus from Egypt, that mighty deliverance wrought by the hand of God, typified the deliverance from the dominion of sin which is wrought by Christ in all his elect? Their priests did not tell them, because they did not believe it. To these wolves in sheep's clothing, the Bible was useful to advance the Marxist ideology among religious people by perverting its teachings to make it appear as if God supported the revolution of the "poor and oppressed" against the "rich oppressors". Roman Catholic and Anglican priests, and the religious leaders of many other institutions were deliberately teaching their followers the doctrines of Marx in a religious disguise - "the `gospel' according to Marx" - the so-called "theology of liberation"! Tragically, their lies were believed. Convinced that God was on their side, and that murder was justified when committed by the "oppressed" in South Africa, these young people were soon committing terrorist crimes with the full blessing of their priests and pastors.

In 1976 the Soweto riots occurred.

The African National Congress/South African Communist Party (ANC/SACP) infiltration paid off. Black *schoolchildren* were the pawns sacrificed by the revolutionaries to advance their own goals. As had occurred at Sharpeville in 1960, violent confrontation with the police was deliberately provoked. It began in Soweto, the sprawling black township on the outskirts of Johannesburg. The ANC persuaded

---

[126] *The Plot Against South Africa*, pg.180.

the most gullible section of the population - children - to go to war against the state and its security forces. The children were told, "Liberation before education!" In other words, they were urged to ignore their schooling until the country had been "liberated" from white rule. Even children under ten years old were armed and trained to kill![127] Massive student unrest occurred, involving thousands of protesting schoolchildren. Blacks killed blacks. The police acted forcefully. Riots erupted in other parts of the country. Over the months, 200 were killed, and 800 were arrested. Meanwhile, Communist propaganda filled the black townships. The South African Students' Organisation (SASO) urged children to be in the very *forefront* of the riots, so that the police would look like savages when children were killed. Thousands of black people were intimidated into joining the riots. Children, women, and the elderly were forced into the front lines, to face police bullets.[128]

The ANC and SACP recruited thousands of students for terrorist training outside South Africa.[129] Black schools were *forced* to close in the years that followed. And always the slogan was heard: "Revolution now, education later!"[130] That education never came for literally thousands of those children. Many of that "lost generation" became the battle-hardened gunmen who in the 1980's and early 1990's robbed banks and committed other crimes,[131] many of them in the service of the ANC, many others, no doubt, simply because they could find no employment, being uneducated. Such was the legacy of the 1976 riots.

By the late 1970's, the SACP/ANC revolutionaries had infiltrated a large number of South African organisations, such as AZASO (Azanian Students Organisation), AZAPO (Azanian People's Organisation ["Azania" being the name some revolutionaries wanted to call South Africa]), COSAS (Congress of South African Students),

---

[127] *The Aida Parker Newsletter*, Issue No.148, December 1991.
[128] *Gold in the Furnace: South Africa on Trial*, pgs.77-80.
[129] *The McAlvany Intelligence Advisor*, December 1986.
[130] *Gold in the Furnace: South Africa on Trial*, pg.80.
[131] *The Aida Parker Newsletter*, Issue No.148, December 1991.

MWASA (Media Workers Association of SA - thus increasing ANC influence in the media), SATAC (South African Teachers Action Committee), BPS (Black Priests Solidarity Group), etc.[132]

The "armed struggle" was intensified. Bombs placed in white areas became a popular ANC tactic. The targets were civilians, and the purpose was to instil fear in the white population.

In 1977, a book entitled *Farewell to Innocence*, written by Allan Boesak, was published. Boesak, a Coloured minister and radical revolutionary, had specialised in Black Theology during his studies in Holland. His book was influenced greatly by the teachings of James Cone. Using the biblical account of the Exodus and Lk.4:18,19, Boesak wrote: "The gospel of Jesus Christ *is* the gospel of liberation". God, he wrote, sides in South Africa with the blacks against the whites; and blacks could determine to use violence in the "struggle". His book became a vital text-book of Black Theology in South Africa. And Boesak himself became one of the most influential liberation theologians in the country. He officially and openly joined the ANC in 1991, but he was vocally and actively supportive of the armed revolution, and thus of the ANC, for many years before that, serving the interests of that organisation very well both in South Africa and abroad.

In June 1980, the World Council of Churches' Programme to Combat Racism (PCR) held a "Consultation on Racism" in Holland.[133] This conference involved 300 so-called "churches" from around the world, and resulted in the expansion of the PCR.

Oliver Tambo, ANC leader-in-exile, an Anglican who had once considered entering the Anglican ministry, addressed this conference. He made this very revealing statement:

"The church that the oppressed people of our country demand is one that openly, publicly and actively fights for the.... liberation of man, as part of the world forces engaged in the process of bringing into

---

[132] *The McAlvany Intelligence Advisor*, December 1986.
[133] *Signposts*, Vol.6, No.4, 1987. Signpost Publications and Research Centre, Arcadia, South Africa.

being a new world order...."[134]

Tambo admitted that there were "world forces" seeking to create a "new world order." He spoke of this long before it became popularised during the Bush Administration in the US from 1988 to 1992, revealing that it was planned by the conspirators long before. Almost certainly, not even he was aware of exactly who was at the very pinnacle of those "forces". He was a Communist, dedicated to the teachings of Marxism-Leninism. He almost certainly had absolutely no idea that behind international Communism, behind even the Illuminati and other new-world-order organisations, there stood a much older, much more experienced, much more powerful, much wealthier institution; at the forefront of which was the Jesuit Order, which for over 400 years had been tirelessly working for a new world order, governed by the Papacy. At least as far back as the time of the Jesuit Adam Weishaupt in 1776, the Jesuits were speaking of a new world order. This date, in Roman numerals, and the Latin words, "Novus Ordo Seclorum", are to be seen on the US one-dollar note.

Tambo, in these words, called upon the "Church" to involve itself in the revolution - little realising that there was a "Church" behind the very creation of the Communist forces he was serving: not a true Christian church, of course, but the Great Whore of Revelation 17, the Mother of Harlots and Abominations of the earth, mystical Babylon itself. He did not know it, and nor did the many others gathered at that conference. They listened to his words, and agreed with him: the "Church" must be actively involved in the revolution.

Tambo's words were also very ominous. For in his statement, "The church that the oppressed people of our country demand", we can see the Communist belief that religious institutions must serve Communism; that the Communist forces have the right to dictate to churches how they must function, and what they must do; and that if they do not obey, they must be eliminated. Communists view churches as tools of the revolution: instead of preaching salvation in Christ, they must preach "salvation" from "political oppression", from Capitalism, or they have no purpose and must be destroyed. There were many ecclesiastical leaders who, hearing Tambo's words, doubtless realised that their religious careers, perhaps their very lives, were at stake

---

[134] *Revolution or Reconciliation?* pg.34.

unless they towed the ANC's line. Thus, while there were those ecclesiastics who supported the ANC because they themselves were Marxists, there were many more who supported it because they feared for their futures if they did not. They saw the handwriting on the wall. Religious hirelings, not true shepherds, the true Gospel of Jesus Christ was foreign to them. Their positions were careers, not divine callings; knowing not the Lord, they tested the political wind and acted to save themselves.

Those true Christian ministers who refuse to preach another gospel, a false gospel, but stand fast in the truth and boldly proclaim it, will suffer persecution. For the true Church is not moulded according to the demands of worldly leaders, but is the Church of *Jesus Christ,* founded upon him, having him as its head, and obeying him alone.

Tambo went on to say, blasphemously:

"When those who worship Christ shall have….taken up arms against those who hold the majority in subjection by force of arms, then shall it truly be said of such worshippers also: blessed are the peacemakers, for they shall be called the sons of God."[135]

A blatant liberation theology statement by this life-long Marxist! He was saying, in effect, that the true worshippers of Christ are those who take up arms to overthrow oppressive governments - in South Africa, the "white minority government". This is utterly at variance with Romans 13:1-6, and 1 Peter 2:13,14, which teach Christians to be *subject* to the government, regardless of what type of government it is (Paul wrote these words while the Roman Caesar ruled), and that to resist it is to resist the ordinance of God, which is sinful. But Tambo, completely ignoring the plain teachings of the New Testament regarding obedience to authority, perverted the meaning of another Scripture in order to justify his antichristian statement. He quoted Matt.5:9: "Blessed are the peacemakers: for they shall be called the children of God." He said that "Christians" who fight against an oppressive government are the true peacemakers, the true children of God! As if, by violent revolution, a man could be a peacemaker! But this was simply typical liberation theology: taking a particular text out of context, and giving it a meaning it does not have, and one which

---

[135] *Revolution or Reconciliation?* pg.34.

contradicts the plain teaching of other texts. But the men who heard him speak were utterly destitute of the grace of God, and the true meaning of the Bible was foreign to them: they could readily accept Tambo's wicked interpretation of Christ's blessed words, because they knew not the Lord who had spoken them, and cared not a whit for "rightly dividing the word of truth" (2 Tim.2:15). Inasmuch as the Bible could be made to serve their political purposes, it was of use to them; beyond that, they had no use for it, and no understanding of it.

Tambo, at this conference, issued a number of demands: more support for the ANC; the severing of all links with the South African government; the withdrawal of all the member-churches' investment in South Africa; the "education" of all "Christians" worldwide to fight "racism"; etc. His words did not fall on deaf ears: the WCC was only too willing to carry out these demands. That very year, as a consequence of his speech, the WCC Central Committee called for *sanctions* against South Africa, and invited its member-churches to *support* the terrorist organisations, and to mobilise their members.[136] In the following years, sanctions caused great misery to millions of South Africa's blacks. And the mobilisation of the members of the various member-denominations of the SACC and WCC resulted in vast financial and other support for the terrorist armies of the ANC, SACP, and PAC, as we shall see.

It was also decided, as a result of Tambo's speech, that sympathetic SA "clergymen" should visit Nicaragua to learn how to make the revolution work. And many, particularly Roman Catholic priests, did precisely that.[137]

Nicaragua! This Latin American country fell to the Marxist Sandinistas after a bloody revolution - and the Sandinistas were led by Roman Catholic (particularly Jesuit) priests![138] *This* was the country which South Africa's revolutionary priests visited, in order to learn further skills in terrorism and subversion. "False apostles, deceitful

---

[136] *Revolution or Reconciliation?* pgs.34,35.
[137] *The Aida Parker Newsletter*, April 1988.
[138] *The Vatican Moscow Washington Alliance*, pgs.323-325. Also *The Aida Parker Newsletter*, Issue No.117, "The Priests Take on Pretoria: `Comrade Jesus' and the Revolution" (an *APN* Special Issue).

workers, transforming themselves as the apostles of Christ", but in reality ministers of Satan (2 Cor.11:13-15).

The revolutionary forces conducted a guerrilla campaign against South Africa from outside its borders, from neighbouring states, for many, many years. It was part of the overall strategy of weakening and isolating the country, but on its own it would never have been successful. There was absolutely no possibility of it being defeated solely by military means at this time (1980). The South African Defence Force was just too powerful. British General Sir Walter Walker, a former head of NATO forces, wrote in his book, *The Next Domino,* in 1980: "South Africa's conventional capability is so superior that its conventional military deterrent is more than equal both in a regional and continental conflict. In terms of conventional warfare it would be a tremendous undertaking even for a superpower such as the US or the USSR to invade South Africa." He also wrote, "I am….qualified to judge the quality of leadership in the higher echelons of their [SA's] Armed Forces and the Army in particular. I doubt if such strong men, high leadership and sheer professionalism can be matched by any other country in the world today."[139]

Every young white male, unless he had medical reasons exempting him, gave two years of his life to compulsory military service, defending the borders of the country, and a few weeks every year or so after that for a number of years. There was also, of course, a permanent force of thousands of disciplined black and white volunteers. Highly efficient, technologically advanced, the SADF was well able to protect South Africa's inhabitants.

But the Communist strategy for the conquest of South Africa was a five-part one. And a combination of all of these is what finally brought South Africa down.

Firstly, there was *external encirclement.* Gradually, one by one, the neighbouring states fell to the revolutionary forces, and became Marxist states. Not as large, or as powerful, as their giant southern neighbour, the Soviet strategy was to bring them down first, until SA was surrounded by hostile neighbours: Angola, Mozambique, Zimbabwe, Zambia. These states were armed by the USSR.

---

[139] Quoted in *The Plot Against South Africa*, pg.222.

Secondly, there was *economic warfare*. South Africa was to be isolated economically, through sanctions and disinvestment. The WCC adopted a policy of disinvestment against SA in 1972. In 1979 Desmond Tutu, SA's radical black Anglican bishop and general secretary of the SACC at the time, called for foreign countries to cease coal imports from SA. In 1980, after Oliver Tambo's speech to the WCC, calls for sanctions by the WCC and the SACC increased. We shall see how, by 1986, these calls bore much fruit.

Thirdly, there was the policy of thoroughly demoralising the white people of South Africa. They were isolated from the rest of the world, and made to feel that they were the worst people on earth. This was done in order to drive them to the point of surrender, instilling in them the attitude that the only thing to do was to negotiate the best peace possible with the ANC. This "warfare" was promoted by the liberal media, the universities, and the left-leaning "churches" and religious organisations.

Fourthly, there was of course *internal revolution*. The Soviet Union, working through the SA Communist Party, which in turn controlled and worked through the ANC and its military wing, MK, conducted an internal terror campaign of murder, sabotage, arson, in white residential areas, in urban centres, on farms, and in the black townships. As the SACP and ANC were banned, they operated through a variety of front organisations.

Fifthly, *negotiations* resulting in piecemeal surrender, step by step, were to be used.[140]

Such was the strategy. And it was to prove successful. The decade of the 1970's had witnessed the escalation of the conflict. The decade of the 1980's was, however, to be the decisive decade: the internal revolution became more violent, international pressure was tremendously intensified, and by 1990 the South African government had capitulated, releasing Nelson Mandela and unbanning the SACP, the ANC, and other organisations. This tremendous victory for the revolutionary forces was the beginning of the end of South Africa as a free, non-Communist country. The early 1990's were filled with one great victory after another for the revolutionaries, as the old South Africa died a slow and agonising death.

---

[140] *Signposts*, Vol.6, No.3, 1987.

CHAPTER TWENTY

THE EARLY 1980's: ROMAN CATHOLIC SUPPORT FOR THE ANC

The conspirators operate on many fronts. Two of the organisations that have played a very large role behind the scenes in manipulating the US government are the Trilateral Commission and the Council on Foreign Relations (CFR), sometimes referred to as America's "invisible government".

The CFR is an Illuminati front organisation. It was conceived at a meeting of English and US Round Table groups in Paris in 1919; and it was formed in 1921 by such men as J.P. Morgan, John D. Rockefeller, Paul Warburg, and Jacob Schiff (representing Rothschild). These men represented the international bankers of the day, and their goal was a New World Order.[141] Colonel Edward House, the American most responsible for the CFR's creation, stated that his objective was "Socialism as dreamed of by Karl Marx". Today CFR members include bankers, politicians, lawyers, etc. It works "to maintain and gradually increase the authority of the UN".[142]

The Trilateral Commission was conceived by Zbigniew Brzezinski, the head of the Russian Studies Department at Columbia University. With the assistance of David Rockefeller, it was launched in 1973. The plan was to *merge* economics, defence, and politics.[143] Its members are almost equally drawn from North America, Europe and Japan. And its stated purpose? To "abolish the narrow dictates of national interest" and "to build a new world order".[144]

The Trilateral Commission and the CFR, not surprisingly as they are part of the network of organisations working for the world government desired by the Papacy (though many within these organisations are quite unaware of this fact), supported the ANC and

---

[141] *Understanding the New Age*, pgs.165-8. 1986 edition.
[142] *The Aida Parker Newsletter*, Issue No.142, March/April 1991.
[143] *Understanding the New Age*, pgs.171-3.
[144] *The Aida Parker Newsletter*, Issue No.142, March/April 1991.

wanted to see it become the government of South Africa.

Professor Samuel Huntington, a US academic, was a top ideologue to the Trilateral Commission and the CFR. And ever since 1981, he was a key policy consultant to SA's National Party government! Its Department of Foreign Affairs, in particular, was deeply under his influence. This powerful department, led by Foreign Affairs Minister Pik Botha, became virtually an agent for the One World scheme of the CFR[145] - and thus of the forces behind the CFR. Changes were beginning to occur by the early 1980's. "Reform" was in the air, which would eventually prove to be capitulation. And it was being guided by the Department of Foreign Affairs, receiving its orders from the US.

But nine more years were to pass before the schemes of the CFR were to come to full fruition under President F.W. de Klerk. In 1981 the groundwork was just being laid.

The CFR's influence in SA was constantly expanding. Many South African mining magnates, academics, industrialists, politicians, and religious leaders were receiving guidance from it.[146] South African super-industrialist Harry Oppenheimer was one of those with very close ties to the CFR/Trilateral Commission combine, as well as to another organisation, the Bilderbergers.

The Bilderbergers derived their name from the venue of their first conference, held in 1954: the Hotel de Bilderberg in a small town in Holland. Powerful men, international financiers and politicians from Europe and the USA (including, again, David Rockefeller), came together to promote a common European market, a "United States of Europe".[147] They viewed European union as a further step towards world government.

The House of Rothschild banking establishment, and the Rockefellers, control the Bilderbergers. Influential South Africans have, from time to time, attended meetings and worked for SA's

---

[145] *The Aida Parker Newsletter,* Issue Nos.158, October 1992, and 160, January/February 1993.
[146] *The Aida Parker Newsletter,* Issue No.142, March/April 1991.
[147] *Understanding the New Age,* pgs.159-162; also *New Age Bulletin,* Number Twelve, August 1989. Published by Roy and Rae Livesey, Kidderminster, Worcs., UK.

destruction. The Bilderbergers work for Communist goals, the destruction of national borders.[148]

Oppenheimer controlled one of the largest business/banking/media empires in the world, including most of South Africa's diamond mines, over 60% of its stock market, most of its newspapers (which consequently were very liberal and pro-ANC), and 600 corporations. He was one of the chief patrons of the SA Institute for International Affairs, which is the South African counterpart of the US' CFR,[149] with tentacles reaching into all areas of South African life, especially the Foreign Affairs Department.[150]

Thus we find that, by 1981, the noose was beginning to tighten. Powerful men, in powerful organisations, were inexorably turning South Africa away from its conservative, anti-Communist foundations, weakening its resistance, softening it up, preparing it for its absorption into the one-world system planned by the Jesuit/Illuminati forces.

The Institute for Contextual Theology (ICT) was established in 1981. Closely allied with the South African Council of Churches and also the South African Catholic Bishops Conference (SACBC), and funded by foreign religious groups such as the Catholic Fund for Overseas Development (CAFOD), Christian Aid, and Trocare (the Irish Roman Catholic aid agency), this radical organisation promoted liberation theology in South Africa.

Its first general secretary was Frank Chikane - who later became SACC general secretary. A later general secretary of the ICT was Roman Catholic priest, Smangaliso Mkhatshwa, who had been general secretary of the SACBC.[151] Thus it can be seen how these various religious organisations overlapped, all furthering the Marxist revolution, all working for the same ultimate goal. For Rome, of course, the plan was to use the revolutionaries as the muscle to usher in eventual Roman Catholic control over South Africa; and it was prepared to work hand in hand with the liberal Protestant

---

[148] *The Aida Parker Newsletter*, Issue No.165, July 1993.
[149] *The McAlvany Intelligence Advisor*, March 1989.
[150] *The McAlvany Intelligence Advisor*, Winter 1990. Special Report.
[151] *Revolution or Reconciliation?* pgs.80-83.

denominations in order to bring this about. Romanism despises Protestantism, and seeks to absorb into its fold all the so-called "separated brethren" (merely the modern term for heretics, which is what Rome considers all Protestants to be). But while she is working, through the Ecumenical Movement, for the destruction of Protestantism, she is simultaneously working *with* various Protestant bodies, notably the WCC and its local branches around the world, in the political arena. She will use any means at her disposal to achieve her goals. In a country like South Africa, where the majority of the population adhere to some Protestant denomination or other, she *must* work hand in hand with them, while at the same time steering them in the direction of eventual "union" with (in reality, absorption by) her.

The ICT - ecumenical, radical - promoted a combination of American Black Theology and Latin American Liberation Theology. When it was established, it declared that it would seek to set up "Basic Christian Communities" (BCC's). These began in Latin America, where they consisted of groups of the poor who were taught, by their Romish priests, how to apply liberation theology. These Roman Catholic Basic Communities were also known there as the "alternative Church". Extremely effective, they politicised the masses.[152] They were the equivalent of the classic Marxist cells which worked so well in bringing about the downfall of Czarist Russia. They consisted of about ten or twelve families in any average-sized village, who were led and indoctrinated by priests (particularly Jesuits) and other Romish religious workers. The purpose of the teaching was to develop a political approach to economic and social problems by means of civil disruption and even violence.[153]

The ICT sought to establish identical BCC's in South Africa. It worked closely with a Roman Catholic organisation, the Lumko Institute, which produced much material on these "Small Christian Communities" (SCC's), as they were also called.[154] From 1981 to 1989, the groundwork was being laid. We shall later see how they began to be implemented in 1989.

---

[152] *Revolution or Reconciliation?* pgs.84-89.
[153] *The Vatican Moscow Washington Alliance*, pgs. 322,323.
[154] *Revolution or Reconciliation?* pgs.90-92.

Liberation theology in South Africa was up and running. *Inter Nos,* the monthly publication of the South African Catholic Bishops Conference, in its October and December issues of 1982, called on the "Church" to identify with the "oppressed" in South Africa by supporting trade unions. It suggested that churches could help by preaching a "gospel" of "social justice", inviting trade union leaders to address church congregations, providing trade unions with venues for meetings, financing unions, etc.[155]

Trade unions have always been very important to revolutionaries. They also became extremely useful to the Papacy. After a Papal visit to Communist Poland in 1979, a revolutionary trade union movement called "Solidarity" was born, the child of the Vatican.[156] This Catholic-Communist organisation was used greatly by Rome in the 1980's, until eventually it came to power, Catholic-Communism sweeping away atheistic Communism.

In South Africa, black trade unions became front organisations for the banned ANC and SACP. When the Roman Catholic bishops called on the "Church" to support the trade unions, they knew exactly what they were doing: enlisting the support of the so-called "churches" for these front organisations of the Marxists. And of course, calls such as this, followed by the opening of "church" buildings for trade union meetings, etc., were very instrumental in convincing black revolutionaries that the "Church" was their ally. For it must be remembered that the objective, as far as Rome was concerned, was power: power over the masses, the expansion of Roman Catholic power in South Africa.

Also in the October issue of *Inter Nos,* Capitalism, Communism, and "Christianity" were discussed, Marxism and "Christianity" were compared, and common ground was discovered (that is, common ground between Marxism and liberation theology, or Catholic-Communism, which of course there is, as liberation theology perverts the Bible so as to make it appear to the ignorant to be advocating Marxism).

And in the December issue, a priest named Joe MacMahon

---

[155] *Signposts,* No.1, 1983.
[156] *The Vatican Moscow Washington Alliance,* pg.54.

acknowledged that Marxist concepts had been infiltrated into "Christian" (i.e. Roman Catholic and liberal Protestant) thinking. He recommended that Black Theology should take on the ideas of the founder of the Italian Communist Party, Gramsci. The political allegiance of the Roman bishops in South Africa was plain. The SACBC sided unashamedly with Communism.

The depth of support by the Roman Catholic hierarchy for the ANC terrorists was evident in many ways. Roman Catholic archbishop, Denis Hurley, thoroughly pro-ANC, was one of the foremost advocates of liberation theology in South Africa. He was a vigorous defender of the revolutionary forces which were committing such terrible atrocities throughout southern Africa. While the ANC was waging a terror campaign against SA, SWAPO (the South West African People's Organisation) was doing the same thing against South West Africa (now Namibia). In January 1983 Hurley, head of the SA Catholic Bishops Conference, gave a lecture in Johannesburg on Namibia. Even *Roman Catholics themselves* later accused him of throwing a smokescreen around SWAPO![157]

The ANC was at this time involved in terrible acts of sabotage, etc., throughout South Africa. A number of bomb blasts occurred around the country. On May 20,1983, for example, the ANC planted a car bomb in Pretoria, South Africa's capital, which killed nineteen people and injured 239. And yet, *in that very year,* Denis Hurley, who played a leading role in the campaign against South Africa in West Germany, said in that country that the ANC was the natural expression of the African wish for liberation.[158] He told a press conference in Bonn that "a majority of SA Blacks" were "happy about the acts of sabotage conducted by the ANC".[159]

Such a statement was patently untrue: the vast majority of blacks did *not* support the ANC's terror campaign. But what did this high official of the Roman Catholic institution care about truth? For many,

---

[157] *U.C.A. News,* 10/86. United Christian Action Press Release, South Africa.
[158] *U.C.A. News,* 10/86.
[159] *The Rand Daily Mail,* February 23, 1983; quoted in *The Aida Parker Newsletter,* April 1988.

many centuries, Rome has justified acts of terror and murder to advance its own cause; it was merely doing, in South Africa, what it had always done.

The United Democratic Front (UDF) had come into being. This movement was nothing less than the internal wing of the ANC, which was still banned. The headquarters of the UDF had the same address, in Johannesburg, as the SACC! Two of its patrons were Desmond Tutu (Anglican) and Allan Boesak (World Alliance of Reformed Churches). Another was Romish priest, Smangaliso Mkhatshwa. Denis Hurley also had strong links with the UDF. He was also involved in the establishment of the End Conscription Campaign (ECC)[160] in 1983. The ECC, pro-Communist, pro-ANC, worked in collaboration with the War Resistance League in New York, a Communist front organisation backed by Moscow.[161] Every young white male, as noted previously, had to undergo compulsory military service in South Africa. The ECC sought to bring this to an end, so as to weaken the South African Defence Force. It thus served the interests of the revolutionaries admirably. Both the South African Council of Churches and the SA Catholic Bishops Conference signed a declaration of support for its call to end conscription.[162] Anything that would weaken South Africa and strengthen the so-called "liberation struggle" was supported by these wolves in sheep's clothing, masquerading as servants of God.

The Education Section of the SA Catholic Bishops Conference published, in 1983, a study course for school children. In it, black homeland leaders were depicted as government puppets, aiding the government in its oppression of the masses. It condemned black policemen, black soldiers, black councillors, and Coloured and Indian parliamentary representatives as "collaborators" and traitors. It was illustrated with pictures of black children raising their fists and saying, "We won't work for the whites any more! Europeans get out! We won't pay any more taxes! Schools are useless! The chiefs are oppressing us! Give us land!" And this highly significant one: "We'll

---

[160] *The Aida Parker Newsletter*, April 1988.
[161] *The McAlvany Intelligence Advisor*, April 1987.
[162] *Signposts*, Vol.6, No.4, 1987.

never allow the Christians to rule us!"[163]

In publishing this study course, the Papal representatives in South Africa gave justification to the restless youth in the townships, already stirred up by Communist agents, to commit acts of violence and murder! What kind of abominable institution is this, that would actually publish and distribute such a document among *school children?* It claims to be the only true Church, but its works identify it, beyond any shadow of doubt, as the Great Whore of biblical prophecy. In the years that followed, many, many black policemen, soldiers, and councillors were brutally massacred by mobs of young blacks who had labelled them "collaborators" with the "apartheid regime", and thus traitors in the eyes of the revolutionaries. From whom did many of them learn such ideas? From the bishops of the Romish system. Who taught them to hate whites, to despise education (causing them to burn down schools across the country), etc.? The bishops of Rome. Who taught them, even, to despise the very word "Christian", unless it referred to the type of "Christian" who praised Marx, took up arms against the government, and justified terrorism in the name of Christ? Again, the bishops of Rome. They filled the minds of impressionable children and teenagers with hatred. Coming to them as religious holy men, they fanned the flames of revolution. Those flames were to engulf literally thousands of blacks throughout the 1980's and into the 1990's.

Rome has not changed. She remains what she has ever been, a bloodthirsty religio-political system that will stop at nothing to achieve her purposes. Even the poisoning of the minds of children, turning them into killers.

---

[163]*U.C.A. News*, 11/86, quoted in *The Plot Against South Africa*, pgs.181-183.

CHAPTER TWENTY-ONE

1983: THE SACC THOROUGHLY EXPOSED

In 1983 the South African government published a potential bombshell against the South African Council of Churches: the Eloff Commission of Inquiry into the SACC.[164] Unfortunately it was not disseminated widely enough, and therefore its contents were not generally known.

The Report of this judicial Inquiry discovered that the SACC was a highly politicised organisation working closely with the ANC, militant black consciousness groups, and trade unions, in order to radically transform South African society (pgs.161-179, 224-236). A huge section of its income was used to support political groups, trade unions, etc. (pgs.324-345). Its annual conference in 1974 passed a resolution, the "Hammanskraal Resolution", which showed its sympathy with the violent deeds of the Marxist terrorists, and justified their terrorism on "theological" grounds (pgs.188-191).

The Report showed the links, going back many years, between the SACC and the ANC. For example, it cited Anglican bishop, Desmond Tutu, who had had discussions with Oliver Tambo and other ANC leaders, as saying that Tambo had "Christian convictions" (pg.172). Tutu also stated that he believed force might become inevitable, and he justified this. He called guerrillas "our brothers and sisters" (pg.175).

Peter Storey, a Methodist minister and past president of the SACC, said that the SACC declared its deep understanding of those who had resorted to guerrilla warfare (pg.174). He stated that the SACC's motive for providing funds for the legal defence of so-called "political crimes" (terrorist crimes) was partly to show solidarity with, and understanding of, the actions of those who used violence (pg.177).

This man's statements show the real nature of the SACC! An umbrella organisation for a large number of institutions claiming to be churches of Christ, with "deep understanding" for Marxist guerrillas! - so deep that it readily provided funds out of its coffers for the legal

---

[164]*Report of the Commission of Inquiry into South African Council of Churches,* printed by the Government Printer, Pretoria, 1983. C.F. Eloff, Chairman of the Commission.

defence of guerrillas who had committed atrocious crimes! Men who had bombed, stabbed, shot, or burnt people to death!

The Scriptures declare that murderers "shall have their part in the lake which burneth with fire and brimstone" (Rev.21:8). In Gal.5:19-21, such "works of the flesh" as hatred, wrath, strife, and murders are listed; and it says that "they which do such things shall not inherit the kingdom of God." Throughout the Old and the New Testaments, murder is shown to be a terrible sin before God, a transgression of his eternal law; and yet the SACC, claiming to represent "God's people", used its funds to defend people guilty of murder and other sins - and justified doing so! This diabolical organisation is *not* a Christian body. It is not serving Christ as it claims, but the devil.

The Eloff Commission found that the man behind Desmond Tutu was a white man named Wolfram Kistner, who was closely tied with the German "churches" which supplied over half the SACC's funds (pg.90ff.). He was director of the SACC's main branch, the Division for Justice and Reconciliation. Kistner did not believe that churches should concern themselves only with man's spiritual needs, but believed in a political and economic "gospel". And he said that his views coincided with those of Durban's Roman Catholic archbishop, Denis Hurley. He believed in civil disobedience; in resisting the state (contrary to the plain teaching of Scripture: Rom.13:1-7). He compared South Africa with Nazi Germany (a favourite trick of liberation theologians, quickly believed by the gullible and those ignorant of history, but utterly absurd). He acknowledged that sections of liberation theology come from Marxist works, such as the concept of "structural violence" - violence which supposedly has its roots in the structures of a society. This typically Marxist concept is contrary to the Word of God, which teaches plainly that violence springs from the depravity of man's heart, his sinful nature (e.g. Gen.6:5,11-13). When institutions claiming to be churches ignore or deny the biblical teaching of sin and human depravity, and instead blame "society's structures" (in South Africa's case, apartheid) for wicked deeds, they are not churches of Christ. Sin is made out to be "structural", not individual. This is Marxism, but not Christianity.

Kistner encouraged "church" contact with trade unions. He

favoured strikes and boycotts by blacks and Coloureds. The Eloff Commission came to the conclusion that the SACC's support for trade unions was not because it desired to help the blacks, but because the unions could be used in the "liberation struggle". This conclusion was absolutely correct.

Kistner also motivated the SACC to initiate a propaganda campaign to emphasize the *negative* aspects of black homelands, migrant labour, resettlement, etc., in SA and elsewhere. He also called for "Christians" to prepare for underground activities of "non-violent" opposition. Such activities would of course be illegal, and they would also *not* be non-violent.

The Eloff Commission also discovered a most significant fact, which the SACC itself always sought to hide: it *did not* enjoy the support of a large number of blacks, or black ministers! A number of black denominations were *not* members of it! (pgs.133-135). Furthermore, it acted apart from its member-churches, rather than with them: the Report stated that it had become a self-sustaining bureaucracy not responsible to its member-churches, and supported mainly by overseas donors (pgs.135-140).

While it is true that it was not responsible to them, this does not mean that the Anglican, Methodist, and other institutions did not concur with it in its support of terrorist organisations. The evidence reveals clearly that they did.

It certainly received more funds from foreign sources than from South African ones. And how were these funds used? In 1984, the SACC spent only R54 000 (1.2%) of its total income of over R5.4 million on "spiritual matters". But it spent R2 million on secular grants! Its secret Asingeni Discretionary Fund spent over R1 million that year. This fund was used for the assistance of "victims of apartheid", trade unions involved in labour disputes, black consciousness groups, etc.[165] In other words, for furthering the cause of the revolution! There can be no doubt about the true nature of this organisation. It is a dangerous, antichristian body, a true daughter of its parent, the World Council of Churches.

---

[165] *The Sunday Times* (Johannesburg), June 30, 1985.

The 1984 Unit 11 Core Group meeting of the WCC stated that the "PCR [its Programme to Combat Racism, examined earlier] could help the churches to understand theologically that the commitment to peace and justice may well involve conflict and violence".[166] It is not surprising that churches needed help in understanding this theologically: for such a doctrine can certainly not be found anywhere in the Bible! In typical liberation theology fashion, the South African state was portrayed as being at war with the "oppressed"; and "peace and justice" would only be ushered in when the government was overthrown and a "government of the people" (a Communist government) was installed. Conflict and violence, then, was portrayed as necessary and just in order to remove "tyranny".

Also in 1984 (as it had done in 1980), the Central Committee of the WCC called for more "contextualisation" of theology. Various WCC projects promoted "contextual theologies": the Racism in Theology project; the Theological Education Fund; etc.[167]

The continual calls for disinvestment, made by the SACC, the SACBC, etc., were not being ignored. In September 1984, the chairman of Chase Manhattan Bank, Willard Butcher, announced that the bank was cutting its ties with South Africa. The SA Rand suffered as a result. David Rockefeller was formerly chairman of this bank.[168] The conspirators were moving to isolate South Africa and force it into their One World Order schemes.

---

[166] *Revolution or Reconciliation?* pg.51.
[167] *Revolution or Reconciliation?* pgs.51,52.
[168] *The Aida Parker Newsletter,* Issue No.124, December 1988.

CHAPTER TWENTY-TWO

1985: MASSIVE INTENSIFICATION OF "CHURCH" INVOLVEMENT IN THE REVOLUTION

In 1985, Gavin Rilly, then chairman of Oppenheimer's Anglo American Corporation, initiated talks with the ANC in Zambia. Some saw this as an attempt, by big business in SA, to negotiate the best deal possible with the ANC before it came to power, having accepted that it eventually would be the government of SA. But the truth is that international financiers *wanted* the ANC to come to power in SA! They were financing international Communism. They saw it as a means to even greater control over nations. And they, in turn, were serving the interests of the Jesuit/Illuminati forces working for world control.

After Relly's talks with the ANC, that organisation went from strength to strength, economically.

The involvement of the "churches" in the ANC/SACP's revolution was massively intensified in 1985. And yet this was the year in which the ANC issued the call to make South Africa "ungovernable". So-called "liberated zones" were created in the black townships. The Soviet flag flew in some places.[169] And this was also the year in which the hideous "necklace" murder method came into being, openly advocated by the ANC. Those within the black townships whom the revolutionaries accused of being collaborators with the government, black moderates, black anti-Communists, etc., were caught by mobs of screaming, chanting "comrades"; tyres were placed around their necks; these were filled with petrol, and then ignited. The poor victims died an agonising, slow death, while all around them the crowds laughed, kicking them, pelting them with stones, stabbing them with sharpened objects. The ANC's spokesman, Tim Ngubane, said at California State University on October 10, 1985, "We want to make the death of a

---

[169] *The McAlvany Intelligence Advisor*, December 1986.

collaborator so grotesque that people will never even think of it".[170] Hundreds died by means of this gruesome murder method, and yet the so-called "churches" intensified their support for the ANC as never before. For blacks in the townships, the Papal Dark Ages, and the days of the Papal Inquisition, when multitudes were put to death by various hideous means because the Papacy decreed it, had returned. The "necklace" was not condemned by the priests of Rome, because the ANC was serving its purposes. Nor was it condemned by the cringing, cowardly clerics of the various Protestant institutions that were (and are) nothing less than the harlot daughters of the Mother Whore of Rome. The government of SA was constantly and loudly condemned as the most brutal the world had seen since Nazi Germany, but the burning to death of hundreds of blacks by the power-hungry, murderous ANC "comrades" drew hardly a murmur of protest.

1985, too, saw the beginnings of so-called "People's Courts", illegal back-yard "courts", with *children* meting out the penalties, such as up to 500 lashes for not supporting the ANC. Many died under such torture. And yet religious groups actually supported these "courts"! A Roman Catholic nun actually *presided* over one![171]

Oh, let none think that Rome has changed! Let none assume that the nightmare days of the Inquisition have passed forever! Wherever it has the opportunity, Rome persecutes, and tortures, and kills. And many of the Protestant institutions ape the Mother Harlot in all this.

Black town councillors were targeted, and labelled as collaborators with the "apartheid regime". As one example, T.B. Kinikini, a town councillor in KwaNobuhle, was ordered to resign. A successful businessman, a man who had greatly assisted his fellow-blacks, his house was stoned when he refused, and one of his businesses was burned down; and in March 1985, he and his two sons were brutally killed. The bodies of him and one of his sons were set alight. His other son's body was not found.[172]

All this was known by the religious groups; and yet their

---

[170] *The Aida Parker Newsletter*, Issue No.169, December 1993.
[171] *The Aida Parker Newsletter*, Issue No.148, December 1991.
[172] *Gold in the Furnace: South Africa on Trial*, pgs.85,86.

involvement in the revolution *intensified* in 1985.

In June 1985, the ANC's National Consultative Conference was held in Kabwe, Zambia. According to the official ANC report, it was recommended that: "We should aim to create ANC units within the established churches and independent churches and other religious bodies";[173] and, "By raising the political consciousness of this community [the religious community], influencing them to accept the politics of the Movement [the ANC]....all should strive to convert them into centres of resistance and struggle."[174] In other words, the ANC, knowing full well the religious nature of the vast majority of SA's inhabitants, knew that, if ever it was to be successful, it had to have even greater support from the churchgoing masses than before. As we shall see, it was successful: not only did it increase its influence within the established, liberal denominations, but also within various other religious bodies, including even the supposedly "evangelical".

It was also recommended at the conference that "the Movement should encourage trends within the churches and religious organisations that come closer to the struggling people. We should find ways of supporting the call by the churches for the downfall of the fascist regime". So, the ANC purposed to do all it could to make the churches even more radical, more revolutionary. As for finding ways to support the churches' call for the downfall of the government, it simply followed its old methods, as we can now see with hindsight. Both the ANC and the religious bodies were working for the same end. Religion served revolution, and revolution served religion.

The report also declared: "We should seek ways of intensifying church involvement in the End Conscription Campaign." The ANC well knew that the SADF was far, far more powerful than its own military wing, MK. South Africans, at this time, knew they were at war, their country was threatened by international Communism, and they gladly supported military conscription. If the churches could become more intensely opposed to conscription, the country's military might would eventually be greatly weakened. The churches were the key, in such a deeply religious country.

---

[173] *The Aida Parker Newsletter*, April 1988.
[174] *Revolution or Reconciliation?* pgs.138-140.

The report also made this chilling declaration: "We should organise Mkhonto we Sizwe [the ANC's armed wing] even among the churches". In other words, this terrorist army was to become a part of the religious bodies of SA! Churches were to be taught to accept MK as SA's legitimate army, fighting a legitimate battle.

And which countries were to be looked to for guidance in this mobilisation of the churchgoing masses? "To enrich our work on the Christian front, we should send delegates to study the Nicaraguan and Polish Christian roles in their struggles".[175] How very revealing! Both were Roman Catholic countries. The Vatican supported the Catholic-Communist terrorists in Nicaragua, and the Catholic-Communist radical trade unionists in Poland.[176] The ANC, in sending delegates to learn from the so-called "Christians" (Romanists) in these countries, was learning the techniques and strategies of trained Roman Catholic revolutionaries, and applying these to the South African conflict.

To promote these goals within the churches, a new ANC department was established: the "Department of Religious Affairs"! And it was run by activist Anglican priest, Fumanekile Gqiba, who called for the "crushing" of "the wicked".[177] By "the wicked", of course, this religious hypocrite meant the SA government.

The emblem of the ANC's Department of Religious Affairs was interesting. It consisted of a boat carrying a cross. Superimposed on the cross were the crescent moon and star of Islam. Apart from the Islamic symbols, this emblem was *very similar* to the emblems of the WCC and SACC![178] This left no doubt as to what type of "Christianity" the ANC favoured, or to the very close alliance between it and the WCC/SACC.

Desmond Tutu, certainly one of the most powerful and influential ecclesiastical figures in the revolutionary assault on SA (the other "top players" being Denis Hurley, Allan Boesak, Beyers Naudé, and Frank Chikane), in 1985 attended the funerals of blacks killed in clashes with

---

[175] *The Aida Parker Newsletter*, April 1988.
[176] *The Vatican Moscow Washington Alliance*, pgs.53-57, 316-326, etc.
[177] *Revolution or Reconciliation?* pg.142.
[178] *Signposts*, Vol.7, No.1, 1988.

the police, and addressed the crowds at some of these, even though their coffins were draped with the colours of the ANC. His wife attended the funeral of those killed in South Africa's raid on the ANC base in Gaborone, Botswana. Members of the SACC were present as well, alongside members of the ANC Executive.[179] Both Tutu and the SACC were sending a very clear message to the terrorists: we are with you all the way in the armed revolution.

Something of the heretical theology of Desmond Tutu can be gleaned from the following: he went on record as saying that Jesus may have been an illegitimate son, and that the Holy Spirit is not limited to the Christian Church - that even Mahatma Gandhi was possessed by the Holy Spirit![180] Yet this man, holding to such heresies, was ordained as a bishop, and later an archbishop, in the Anglican institution!

The campaign to end compulsory military conscription intensified. The SA Catholic Bishops Conference called for the ending of it, in 1985. Its statement said that Roman Catholics must "promote peace" by working for an end to conscription by whatever ways lay open to them.[181] Its leaflet, *The Call to End Conscription,* was widely distributed in Roman Catholic "churches".[182] How could an end to conscription, when SA was at war, promote peace? The SACBC, in the true spirit of liberation theology (Catholic-Communism), blamed the government and its security forces for the violence and bloodshed: those who, in Marxist fashion, are labelled the "oppressors". The plan was simple, but highly effective: the revolutionaries caused unrest; the army and police came in to restore law and order, as is their duty (Rom.13:3,4); and then the liberal media, the leftist "churches", etc., screamed that the apartheid government was a dictatorship, bent on

---

[179] *The Natal Witness* (Pietermaritzburg, South Africa), June 24, 1985.
[180] As quoted from *The Cape Times,* October 24, 1980, and from a speech in St Alban's Cathedral, Pretoria, November 23, 1978, in *Gospel Defence League,* May 1986. Published by the Gospel Defence League, Cape Town.
[181] *The Southern Cross,* July 7, 1985.
[182] *Signposts,* Vol.4, No.4, 1985.

oppressing and murdering innocent people. And the gullible and the naïve, ever ready to believe whatever their papers and religious leaders told them, were persuaded that the way to promote peace was to put an end to conscription, for this (they were led to believe) provided the evil, cruel, murderous state with the manpower to carry out its tyrannical oppression.

Beyers Naudé, SACC general secretary in 1985, told the conference of the SACC that unrest in the country had developed to such an extent, that it could be called the beginnings of a civil war.[183] Of course, the liberation theologians never once laid the blame for the unrest at the feet of the revolutionary organisations, the SACC, or the SACBC, but always at the feet of the "apartheid regime", as they loved to call the government.

As the unrest in the black townships escalated in 1985, the national conference of the SACC sent a telex to the State President, *demanding* the immediate withdrawal of the army and riot police from the townships.[184] The vast majority of blacks in the townships were only too pleased that the army and riot police were there, for their presence brought a measure of peace and security. But the Communist revolutionaries were unable to strike fear into township residents, and thus intimidate them into supporting the revolution, as much as they would have liked, as long as the army and riot police were there. Hence the SACC demand for their withdrawal. It was all so cleverly orchestrated. Of course, they blamed the army and police for the violence, not the revolutionaries.

The Vatican, for its part, did not merely use the bishops and priests within South Africa to support the Marxist forces, but mustered its forces in other parts of the world as well. A notable example was a Brazilian cardinal by the name of Arns: one of the world's most powerful Papists, he was the head of the largest, and one of the most radical, archdioceses in the world, and a member of the United Nations Committee for Humanitarian Issues.[185] In 1985 Arns was refused

---

[183] *The Natal Mercury* (Durban, South Africa), June 26, 1985.
[184] *The Natal Mercury*, June 28, 1985.
[185] *The Sunday Tribune* (Durban, South Africa), June

permission to come to South Africa, after the government learned that he was coming to participate in the End Conscription Campaign. Although he denied all knowledge of the Campaign, it was discovered that in fact he *had* been invited to participate, and was scheduled to speak! When the government asked him for a written statement that he would not participate, he refused to give one. The government nevertheless accepted his earlier verbal assurance, but the cardinal retracted. Then his visa was withdrawn. The fact that he had lied about his intentions meant nothing to the radical, Red-supporting "clergy" in South Africa: the government's action was criticised by the SACC, the Methodist denomination of SA, and the End Conscription Campaign, among others.[186]

The Irish Republican Army has always been a servant of the Papacy in Ireland.[187] In its attempts to bring British control of Northern Ireland to an end, it has used the same kinds of terror tactics as the ANC used in South Africa. This radical terrorist organisation's political wing is called Sinn Fein. At its Party Congress in 1985, Sinn Fein president, Gerry Adams, said: "We do not hypocritically call upon the ANC to renounce violence. We stand shoulder to shoulder with them in their right to develop their struggle by whatever means are forced upon them. To the ANC we extend our unconditional solidarity. To our black brothers and sisters in the struggle we send this simple message of support: Fight on!"[188] These words reveal, firstly, that there is an international terrorist network, made up of various terrorist organisations around the world, supposedly widely divergent and fighting for different goals, but in reality interlocking and even at times overlapping, and working for the same ultimate ends; secondly, that the ANC's war was the Vatican's war: for the IRA is under the Vatican's control. IRA support for the ANC was yet another link in the

---

30, 1985.
[186] *The Natal Mercury* and *The Natal Witness*, June 27, 1985.
[187] See *Catholic Terror in Ireland*, by Avro Manhattan. Chick Publications, Chino, California. 1988.
[188] *Victims Against Terrorism Update*, August 1988. Published by Victims Against Terrorism, Lyndhurst, South Africa. Also *The Aida Parker Newsletter*, No.122, October 1988.

chain of international Roman Catholic support for the Marxist ANC.

Action From Ireland, an Irish Roman Catholic organisation allegedly concerned about "justice" in the Third World, but in reality serving the Vatican in promoting Communism, became involved in the South African situation. Irish store workers, saying they opposed apartheid in South Africa, went on strike in July 1985 (no doubt encouraged to do so by their priests), refusing to handle South African goods. Action From Ireland helped the strikers contact Desmond Tutu, and he invited them to South Africa.[189]

In the United States, the Romish bishops called for an end to South Africa's apartheid policy in August 1985. The head of the US bishops endorsed the demands of the SA bishops: the release of all "political prisoners" (terrorists), an end to police occupation of black townships, etc.[190] The worldwide anti-apartheid movement was growing, and Rome was very deeply involved.

In South Africa itself in 1985, at a meeting held in Cape Town and arranged by the Roman Catholic Justice and Peace Commission, it was agreed that the Roman Catholic institution should work more closely with trade unions, as well as with organisations "fighting for justice", such as the United Democratic Front. "Church" buildings and their facilities would in future be open for these groups to use.[191] Rome well knew that the UDF was the internal wing of the ANC. Allan Boesak was not its only patron: another was Romish priest, Smangaliso Mkhatshwa, secretary of the SACBC. He was banned from 1976 to 1983.[192]

Knowing the power of the printed page, the SA Catholic Bishops Conference started publishing a newspaper in 1985: the *New Nation*. A radical political paper, it supported the United Democratic Front (UDF). The paper was financed by the Roman Catholic institution in Germany. Its editor was Zwelakhe Sisulu, son of former ANC secretary Walter Sisulu. His mother was a national president of the UDF. The UDF was a powerful means of intimidation in the black townships. Children and teachers were threatened. Black policemen

---

[189] *The Southern Cross*, July 7, 1985.
[190] *The Southern Cross*, August 25, 1985.
[191] *The Southern Cross*, August 18, 1985.
[192] *Signposts*, Vol.4, No.3, 1985.

were ostracised from their families and friends.[193] And yet the SACBC supported this organisation. Even the paper's name - *New Nation* - clearly revealed the intention of the Papal emissaries: they sought to erect a new nation on the rubble of the old South Africa, a nation radically different from the one that went before, a Catholic-Communist nation.

On October 26, 1985, 22 women were arrested outside the police station in Moroka after demonstrating with slogans. Four of them were nuns! They called for the army's withdrawal from the black townships.[194]

On July 20, 1985, there was a massive funeral, at Cradock, for four black civic leaders, who had been murdered. The mourners sang "liberation" songs, and gave black power salutes. There was a huge red flag, with the hammer-and-sickle emblem on it, waving in the breeze: the flag of the Soviet Union. There were flags of the outlawed ANC. There was a banner which read, "SA Communist Party". And priests and other clerics were present, walking in the very shadow of the hammer-and-sickle! It was not Marx and Christ who walked hand in hand that day, but Marx and the false "Christ" of liberation theology, the radical, bloodthirsty "Christ" invented in the wicked imaginations of men. Tragically, this was the "Christ" who had been preached to the masses. They did not know the difference between the true and the false.

When Beyers Naudé and Allan Boesak, two of the leading revolutionaries in clerical dress, arrived, they were carried shoulder-high by the crowds, which showed how popular they were among the revolutionaries. Both men spoke at the funeral, condemning the state of emergency the government had imposed in order to restore law and order, and calling for the release of "political prisoners" (terrorists).[195] These men, who called themselves "men of God" and whom the deceived masses *believed* to be "men of God", preached anti-

---

[193] *Signposts*, Vol.5, No.3, 1986. Also *U.C.A. News*, 10/86.
[194] *The Southern Cross*, November 17, 1985.
[195] *The Sunday Times* and *The Sunday Tribune*, July 21, 1985.

government sermons, and said nothing about the pro-Communist position of the "mourners". In the name of Christ, they spoke of political revolution, not spiritual redemption. They knew nothing of the Gospel of Christ; they knew only the "gospel" of Marx.

In August, Allan Boesak planned a march on Pollsmoor prison, where Nelson Mandela was incarcerated, to demand his release. He was arrested before the illegal march began, but the marchers went ahead anyway, on August 28. The crowd of about 4000 was led by Protestant ministers, Romish priests, and nuns. Fourteen "clergymen" and two nuns were arrested.[196]

The calls for the release of Nelson Mandela were increasing. He was turned into the symbol of heroic resistance to apartheid by the international media, revolutionary organisations, and religious institutions sympathetic to the "struggle". Around the world he was labelled a hero, a patriot, a true leader, unjustly imprisoned by the white authorities of racist South Africa. The real truth about the reasons for his imprisonment was never told. And the world believed the media reports. If ever the South African government could be pressurised into releasing Mandela, this would be a massive victory for the Communist forces, for it would boost the morale of the revolutionaries. It would be a strong signal that the SA government was capitulating, and that total victory was not far away. Very few in South Africa could have realised, in 1985, that his release was only five years away.

The international and local media, of course, played an extremely important role in the SA revolution. Scenes were *deliberately* "staged" for the cameras. German reporters, for example, threw sweets into rubbish bins and photographed black children rummaging in the bins for them, and then published the photos with captions about starving black children living on the whites' refuse. Camera crews *deliberately incited* racial unrest, in order to film it. Some TV crews had prior knowledge of future "unrest incidents", and set themselves up to film these. In September 1985, Soweto children were *paid* by a TV crew to burn their school books in front of the cameras. Also in September, demonstrators at the University of Cape Town *waited* for the foreign

---

[196] *The Natal Mercury*, August 29, 1985.

media to arrive before going on the rampage.[197]

The plain truth of the matter is that the notion of an "independent press" is a fallacy. It is *controlled*. This was admitted as long ago as 1914 by John Swinton, former chief editor of the *New York Times,* in a speech given at the annual dinner of American Associated Press. He said, "There can be no question of an independent press. Not one of you dares to utter his honest opinion. We are the instruments and vassals of the rich men behind the scenes. We are puppets. These men pull the strings and we dance...."[198]

Who controls the international media? About a century ago a book was written entitled *America or Rome, Christ or the Pope?* by John L. Brandt. He wrote that, already in his day, many who collected the news items and wrote the dispatches for Associated Press were Roman Catholics or Roman Catholic sympathisers. They suppressed or published items as it suited their purposes. In London and Chicago, Associated Press was controlled by Irish Romanists and others. Already in those days it was made public that thousands of Jesuits were purchasing newspapers, etc., under their own names but for the Vatican. Romish archbishop Vaughan said: "Our media....has its hand on the Associated Press, the largest dailies of Boston, New York, Chicago, Philadelphia, San Francisco, Los Angeles, and many other cities are under its spell, and so secret, subtle and clandestine is the work that many are unaware of it."[199]

The vast influence which the Vatican wields over the mass media is a documented fact. D.J. Beswick, in *The Broadcasting Controversy, the Pope and Catholic Action,* wrote: "A study of the sources I have mentioned, and various others, indicates that throughout the western world the flow of information in the mass media, and particularly the programming of radio and television, is fundamentally a Catholic Action phenomenon."[200] Albert Close, in *Jesuit Plots from*

---

[197] *The Plot Against South Africa,* pgs.110-114.
[198] *The Plot Against South Africa,* pg.110.
[199] *The Protestant Challenge,* Vol.XXII, No.4, July/August 1992. The Canadian Protestant League, Burlington, Ontario.
[200] *The Broadcasting Controversy, the Pope and Catholic Action,* by D.J. Beswick, pg.5. Published in Wellington, New Zealand, 1976.

Elizabethan to Modern Times, wrote: "There can be no shadow of doubt that the Jesuits and the Anglo-Romanist party in Britain have gained great influence over the Cable Services, Press Agencies, B.B.C., and chief newspapers of Great Britain"; "In the course of nearly a hundred years, Rome has saturated the whole British Press with hundreds of these Roman Catholic Reporters and sub-Editors."[201] The Vatican makes use of the Jesuit/Illuminati forces to powerfully influence the media. In SA, billionaire industrialist Harry Oppenheimer's Anglo-American Corporation controlled most of the newspapers, and these were pro-ANC for years.

Years before SA fell to the ANC, Joachim Chissano, then deputy to President Samora Machel of Marxist Mozambique, said that the ANC would not, by itself, beat the SA security forces. But then he added, "But that doesn't matter. We know that the whites in southern Africa are so influenced by their media that they will give up their position of power."[202] He was right. The Vatican/Illuminati/Communist conspirators were (and are) masters at disinformation and media-manipulation.

It was in 1985 that the famous "Kairos Document" was published.[203]

It was copyrighted by the Institute for Contextual Theology, that radical religious organisation. The document was signed by over 150 religious leaders and theologians from 22 denominations in South Africa, many of whom had been involved with ICT, and advocated Black Theology.[204] Some were senior UDF officials.[205]

It called the terrorists who were committing terrible acts of violence "Christians" (pg.2). In attacking what it called "State

---

[201] *Jesuit Plots from Elizabethan to Modern Times,* by Albert Close, pgs.169,170. The Protestant Truth Society, London.
[202] *The Plot Against South Africa,* pg.115.
[203] *The Kairos Document,* Skotaville Publishers, Braamfontein, South Africa. All references to this document are from the Second Revised Edition, 1987. However, according to the Preface, editing was kept to a minimum.
[204] *Revolution or Reconciliation?* pg.97.
[205] *Signposts,* Vol.5, No.1, 1986.

Theology", "the theological justification of the status quo", it rejected the true meaning of Rom.13:1-7, claiming that this text is *not* "an absolute and universal principle that is equally valid for all times and in all circumstances", but was written to Christians who felt they were "exonerated from obeying any State at all". It declared that *oppressive* governments need not be obeyed (pgs.3-5); in fact, that "once it is established beyond doubt that a particular ruler is a tyrant or that a particular regime is tyrannical, it forfeits the moral right to govern and the people acquire the right to resist" (pg.22). This completely ignores the fact that Jesus, who lived under a tyrannical regime, never once taught his followers to resist a tyrant just because he is a tyrant. The document employed Acts 5:29 to justify the revolution against the South African state (pg.6), entirely ignoring the fact that this text refers to what Christians must do only when they are forbidden to perform their Christian duties, and *not* to violent rebellion against the state merely because it is tyrannical (or perceived to be)!

It dealt favourably with Communism, stating that the SA state, in order to have a concrete symbol of evil, "has invented, or rather taken over, the myth of communism". It said that "millions of Christians in South Africa (not to mention the rest of the world)" were regarded as atheists by the state - implying that millions of Christians were Communists (pg.7). This was a blatant lie, of course, as no true Christian is a Communist.

Using the book of Exodus (as liberation theologians love to do), it called for an intensification of "the struggle" to remove "injustice and oppression" (pg.12). The Church, it declared, had to consult with the political groups that represented the grievances of the people (i.e. the ANC, UDF, etc.). It condemned what it called "the structural, institutional and unrepentant violence of the State and especially the oppressive and naked violence of the police and the army", but it refused to call what the *revolutionaries* were doing "violence", declaring instead that "throwing stones, burning cars and buildings and *sometimes killing collaborators*" was part of the "struggle for liberation", which the state and the media had "*chosen to call* violence"! (italics added).The violence of the "oppressed" was simply the "desperate attempts" of the people to defend themselves (pg.13). It said: "Christians....must quite simply participate in the struggle for liberation and for a just society" (pg.28). This included civil disobedience: "The campaigns of the people, from consumer boycotts to stayaways, need to be supported and encouraged by the Church" (pg.28); "the Church will have to be involved at times in *civil disobedience*" (pg.30).

Clearly, the conspirators felt confident that liberation theology had penetrated so deeply into South Africa's religious denominations that it was now possible to publish such a document and get away with it. These denominations had sunk so low that this vile document was accepted as being a Christian statement! It plainly justified violence, as long as it was the violence of the "oppressed", not the "oppressor"; it encouraged the murder of black moderates by calling them "collaborators" with the state; etc. Here was a document, issued by men whom the deceived masses believed to be ministers of Christ, openly and blatantly *justifying* the atrocities of the ANC, SACP and PAC. It was saying, in effect: "Your revolution is just! God himself is on your side! Fight and kill, if necessary, to overthrow the white government! Christians *must* participate in the revolution! You are not a good Christian unless you do!"

Despite the fact that a Roman Catholic priest, Patrick Hartin, wrote in the Romanist weekly, *The Southern Cross,* that the Kairos Document was a plea for condoning violence on the part of the "oppressed" in the name of Christianity, and that this was wrong,[206] the editorial of that issue stated that the Bible recognises the legitimacy of violence to defend violated rights when all else fails. It in no way condemned the veiled Marxism of the document. It made the state out to be the aggressor, and the revolutionaries to be simply poor, suffering souls with a legitimate cause.

Although SA's Roman Catholic bishops said that they were not in complete agreement with every point raised in the Kairos Document, they welcomed what they called its "call and challenge".[207]

The Kairos Document played a major part in legitimising the armed revolution in the eyes of many who professed to be "Christians". It was a horrifying testimony to the true nature of what so often passes for "Christianity" in the world today, for it was hailed by

---

[206] *The Southern Cross,* November 3, 1985.
[207] *The Southern Cross,* December 1, 1985.

religious leaders around the world. The thick cloud of spiritual darkness that engulfed Europe in the Dark Ages is, in our days, rolling across the entire world. And with spiritual darkness comes persecution, horrifying atrocities sanctioned by the "Church".

CHAPTER TWENTY-THREE

1985: "EVANGELICALS" JOIN THE RADICALS; THE CALL FOR SANCTIONS

In an ANC publication read out to the Supreme Court in Pietermaritzburg on October 29, 1985, it was stated that many Christians in South Africa were engaged in mobilising the masses, and that they formed a part of the military and political fighting forces of the ANC.[208]

These were not *true* Christians, of course. They were not men and women who had been regenerated by the Holy Spirit, made new creatures in Christ, saved by grace through faith. But the fact was that large numbers of people, belonging to various religious denominations, were active Marxist guerrillas. Some of them, of course, were simply using a cloak of religion to give their wicked deeds legitimacy. Others were so deceived by the political "gospel" being preached around the world by radical Communist clergymen, that they believed they were serving Christ by working for the destruction of the South African state by violence. The only "Christianity" they knew was the false version, which was no Christianity at all.

Oliver Tambo had told the World Council of Churches in 1980 that the present epoch demanded "Christians" such as the Roman Catholic priest, Torres, who joined guerrilla forces in Colombia in the 1960's;[209] and many who called themselves "Christians" in South Africa heeded his call and joined the ANC and other Marxist organisations. But for almost 2000 years, there have been multitudes who called themselves "Christians" who were not, but were in spiritual darkness, slaves of sin and Satan; and the 1980's were no exception.

One of the concerns of the revolutionaries was how to involve those who called themselves "Evangelicals" in the "struggle": those

---

[208] *The Natal Mercury*, October 30, 1985.
[209] As reported in the ANC magazine, *Sechaba*, November 1980. See *The Natal Mercury*, October 30, 1985.

who professed that the Gospel was spiritual, not political, and that the Church was a spiritual organism, not a political organisation. All true Christians are evangelical, of course; but as with the name, "Christian", itself, those who call themselves "Evangelicals" include many who are as lost as those within the liberal institutions.

A major step in wooing *these* "Evangelicals" was taken in 1985 by the Pietermaritzburg-based, professedly "evangelical" organisation, Africa Enterprise (AE). Christians, sound in the faith, were not deceived by AE's evangelical facade, for they could see that the "gospel" preached was not the Gospel of Christ: it was shot through with Arminianism, so-called "entertainment evangelism", Romanism, Ecumenism, and liberation theology. But multitudes *were* deceived by its evangelical-sounding terminology, its emphasis on missions, etc.

In September 1985, AE organised what was called the National Initiative for Reconciliation (NIR), which was held in Pietermaritzburg for three days. In its policies, the NIR showed itself to be identical with the SACC! Speakers included Roman Catholic archbishop, Denis Hurley, and Anglican bishop, Desmond Tutu - two of the country's (and indeed the world's) leading revolutionary priests. The "initiatives" decided upon at the NIR were virtually identical with those presented to the State President by a religious delegation a month before, and with those of the UDF/ANC: "initiatives" such as an end to the state of emergency, the removal of the security forces from the townships, the release of all "political prisoners", etc.[210]

Things were becoming increasingly confusing for the average, churchgoing (though unregenerate) South African. The lines between the liberal, politically-motivated "churches" and religious institutions, and those professing to be evangelical, were becoming increasingly blurred. The average churchgoer was unable to discern the terrible truth: that in fact, *there was no difference*. Liberals and supposed "Evangelicals", appearing to be at opposite poles, were actually working for the same goals. Deception abounded. Like sheep, the country's religious citizens (and 75% of South Africa's inhabitants professed to be "Christians") were being herded in the direction the conspirators wanted them to go. Not knowing the Lord Jesus Christ, never having been regenerated, they were unable to discern between

---

[210] *Signposts*, Vol.4, No.5, 1985.

false Christian and true Christian, false Church and true Church, false Christ and true Christ. Jesus said, "Not every one that saith unto me, Lord, Lord, shall enter into the kingdom of heaven; but he that doeth the will of my Father which is in heaven" (Matt.7:21). To multitudes of professing "Christians" he will say, on the great day of judgement, "I never knew you: depart from me, ye that work iniquity" (vs.23). They name the name of Christ, but do not depart from iniquity (2 Tim.2:19): they are "Christians" in name only.

Roman Catholics, liberal Protestants, supposedly "Evangelical" Protestants: all were actively working for the downfall of the South African government, and for the transformation of South Africa into a Communist state.

The violence of the revolutionaries was being increasingly justified within ecclesiastical circles. Beyers Naudé, SACC general secretary, told the Anglican institution's synod in England in November 1985 that he believed churches needed to reconsider their traditional stand on violence, in the light of events in South Africa. For this he was given a standing ovation! He told a press conference later that SA churches had stated that they were generally against violence, but that such a statement had virtually lost all meaning for those in SA struggling for "liberation".[211] These were thinly-veiled words in support of violence.

Then, in December 1985, ecclesiastical leaders from South Africa openly met with members of the ANC and PAC in Harare, Zimbabwe. The ecclesiastical wolves included Romish archbishop, George Daniel, Anglican archbishop, Philip Russell, and leaders of the Methodist and Presbyterian institutions, as well as of the WCC. They met to "exchange ideas" on how to overcome apartheid.[212] Would the Lord Jesus Christ have sat down to exchange ideas with avowed enemies of the Gospel? Would he have discussed with them how to overthrow a government? Yet here were men, professing to be his servants, doing precisely that! Satan has his church, too, and men such as these are a part of it.

---

[211] *The Natal Mercury*, November 23, 1985.
[212] *The Daily News* (Durban, South Africa), December 6, 1985.

Also in Harare, Zimbabwe, in late 1985, the WCC and the SACC organised the Harare Consultation on the issue of South Africa, involving radical "church" leaders, and ANC and PAC representatives. It used the Kairos Document as a basis. It issued the "Harare Declaration", calling on all countries to apply sanctions against South Africa. The world heeded their call: the very next year massive sanctions were applied. It also called on all churches to support the "liberation movements", and on all churches worldwide to keep the 16th of June 1986 as a "World Day of Prayer to End Unjust Rule in South Africa".[213] What did the WCC or SACC care that economic sanctions would deprive millions of blacks of their jobs, increasing the suffering? In fact, that is precisely what the radicals desired: the more unemployment and starvation, the more restlessness; the more restlessness, the more pliable the masses would be in the hands of the radicals.

Clearly, by December 1985, the international conspiracy against SA was scenting victory. On December 22, the Roman Antichrist himself, John Paul II, spoke out against "racism" in SA, and *praised* the anti-apartheid demonstrations, saying the "Church" viewed such actions with "approval and support".[214] In saying this, the most powerful religious figure on earth gave his support to the Marxist killers filling the country with terror.

---

[213] *Revolution or Reconciliation?* pgs.118-121.
[214] *The Southern Cross*, January 12, 1986.

CHAPTER TWENTY-FOUR

1986: FURTHER INTENSIFICATION OF ECCLESIASTICAL EVIL

In the wake of the meetings between religious leaders and the ANC in late 1985, Romish archbishop Denis Hurley said on 26 January 1986 that the bishops of SA had adopted a "change of attitude", and that in future, they would talk more directly to the ANC and other so-called "liberation movements".[215] This of course gave the impression that prior to this there had been little contact between the revolutionaries and the Romish representatives; but in the light of the evidence this was a false impression. In reality, this statement simply served to give the ANC and the other organisations further legitimacy.

In April, a delegation of the SA Catholic Bishops Conference, headed by Hurley, travelled to Lusaka, Zambia, to meet with the ANC. They discussed ways in which each group could help end apartheid, and agreed that the violence in SA was caused by apartheid.[216] How utterly absurd! The violence in SA was the direct result of the ANC's armed revolution! But in typical Communistic fashion, the existing order of things was blamed, not the revolutionaries.

The meeting agreed that the Roman Catholic institution had to "mobilise its white adherents" to act against apartheid, and that it was important for military conscription to be brought to an end. Important to whom? To the ANC and the SA Communist Party, of course. The ANC also said that it was stepping up the armed struggle; and it refused to condemn the use of bombs and "necklace" murders. But the bishops, far from condemning this stance, simply declared that, while they did not agree with the ANC's use of violence (impossible to believe in the light of Rome's history), they "understood the reasons" why it had resorted to violence, and that, as it was playing an important role against apartheid, it was therefore important to keep in contact with it.[217]

---

[215] *The Southern Cross*, February 9, 1986.
[216] *Signposts*, Vol.5, No.4, 1986.
[217] *Signposts*, Vol.5, No.4, 1986; and *The Southern Cross*, May 4, 1986.

Hurley said that the ANC seemed optimistic that a spirit of liberation had been aroused in SA, that could not be quenched. The ANC and the bishops agreed that the present government could not be an agent for change, but was the main obstacle.[218]

Three influential "church" delegations had now openly met with the ANC: the delegation of Roman Catholic, Anglican, Methodist, Presbyterian, and WCC leaders in late 1985; the WCC/SACC conference, also in late 1985; and now the SACBC delegation. Active religious support for the terrorist organisations was now blatant. No wonder the ANC seemed optimistic! A "spirit of liberation" (revolution) had indeed been aroused in SA - and Romanists, Anglicans, Methodists, Presbyterians, and others were the ones who had aroused it! And one must not fail to note how the bishops brushed over the ANC's use of horrifying violence. Ignoring the terrible atrocities committed in the name of "liberation", they were *not* merely keeping in contact with the ANC (though that would have been bad enough), but they were actively and enthusiastically working *with* it. Much evidence has already been given; but much more will follow.

Roman Catholicism has never been against violence, if it will serve its purposes. Centuries of Papal history prove that.

On January 26, 1986, a Roman Catholic "Mass for Peace" was celebrated in the black township of Mamelodi, near Pretoria. Two petrol bombs (used by the revolutionaries in the townships) were held aloft by a black priest, and later taken up with the bread and wine during the offertory procession. Romish bishop, Mansyet Biyase, said the mass was to strengthen the people's fight for liberation.[219]

In the previous chapter, it was seen that the WCC/SACC/ANC/PAC Harare Declaration had declared that 16 June 1986 was to be a "World Day of Prayer to End Unjust Rule in South Africa". This of course was Soweto Day, which was held every year by the revolutionaries to commemorate the police action taken against the rioters back in 1976, who were viewed as heroes by the ANC. On June 15, 1986, in the Roman Catholic weekly, *The Southern Cross,* the Roman Catholic Justice and Reconciliation Commission issued a full-

---

[218] *The Southern Cross,* May 4, 1986.
[219] *Signposts,* Vol.5, No.2, 1986.

page, blood-red poster for Soweto Day, picturing a black man carrying a dead black boy, and the words, "World Day of Prayer to End Unjust Rule". It *also* had these words: "A man can have no greater love, than to lay down his life for his friends" - the words of Jesus in John 15:13! This was liberation theology, blatant and vile. When Jesus said to his disciples, "Greater love hath no man than this, that a man lay down his life for his friends", his very next sentence was, "Ye are my friends, if ye do whatsoever I command you" (Jn.15:14). Jesus laid down his life for his friends. The friend of Christ is the one who does what he has commanded. No terrorist is obeying the commands of the Lord! It is also true, by comparing Jn.15:13 with the preceding verse, that the greatest proof of the love between Christians is when one Christian lays down his life for another. "Hereby perceive we the love of God, because he laid down his life for us: and we ought to lay down our lives for the brethren" (1 Jn.3:16). But those who died in the Soweto riots of 1976 did not in any way whatsoever fulfil this Scripture. They were not Christians laying down their lives for their fellow-Christians in the cause of the Gospel, but rioters disobeying the government, in direct violation of Romans 13:1-6. But Rome, knowing the ignorance of the masses regarding the Word of God, took Jn.15:13 out of context, and distorted its meaning to give (supposed) scriptural justification to the revolutionaries in their unlawful deeds.

As widespread violence continued to rock South Africa, a state of emergency was declared. The government knew very well that Roman Catholic priests were deeply involved in the internal revolution. In fact, when the SA Catholic Bishops Conference sent a delegation to meet State President P.W. Botha on 17 November 1986, he told them that the SACBC's radical newspaper, *The New Nation,* was dangerous. He told the SACBC to "get their house in order".[220] And as part of the state of emergency, a number of priests were detained, and some were even deported.[221] They were found to be dangerous to the wellbeing of society. They were working for the violent overthrow of the government. One notable example was Popish priest and SACBC

---

[220] *The Natal Witness,* November 18, 1986.
[221] *The Southern Cross,* July 13, 1986.

general secretary, Smangaliso Mkhatshwa, who was arrested in May for illegally possessing arms and ammunition.[222] Again the question must be asked: can such men be the servants of God? It is impossible. Not only their vile doctrines, but their ungodly lives, show them to be the servants of Antichrist, not Christ.

The editorial of the Romanist weekly, *The Southern Cross,* 10 August 1986, declared that the Roman Catholic institution worked for peace. However, it went on to say: "To take up arms to secure rights....can only be legitimate when all peaceful negotiations have failed. It can be called for only by those who are recognised as leaders. The system that is sought to be overthrown must be truly tyrannical. It is the last resort after peaceful means have failed."

This astoundingly revealing statement was perfectly in keeping with the Vatican document, *The Instruction on Christian Freedom and Liberation,* paragraph 79: "A last resort: These principles must be especially applied in the extreme case where there is recourse to armed struggle, which the Church's magisterium admits as a last resort to put an end to an obvious and prolonged tyranny".

The Papal hierarchy in SA had not actually come out and *officially* declared that the masses should take up arms to overthrow the state. But it had most certainly declared the SA government to be tyrannical. And it had most certainly declared Mandela, Tambo, etc., to be the legitimate leaders. And it very openly supported the ANC. So it mattered little that it had not *officially* declared that there was no alternative but the armed struggle: to the multitudes of the blinded faithful in the townships, it was as good as said. Speaking at the Durban Technikon, to a different type of audience, Denis Hurley would only go so far as to say that a community had the right to overthrow a tyrant, and that therefore the "Church" had to involve itself in politics, and guide the people, and exhaust all non-violent means;[223] but the message being received at grassroots level, in the sprawling townships among the radical young "comrades" was far stronger: all non-violent means have been exhausted; the "Church" is fully behind the armed struggle.

---

[222] *The Plot Against South Africa,* pg.181.
[223] *The Sunday Tribune,* August 17, 1986.

Consider, for example, the following. A Popish priest, Stanley Sabelo Ntwasa, said that even though many regard it as folly to throw stones and petrol bombs at armoured personnel carriers, for those involved it was a sign of the fulfilment of what all people of goodwill hoped for! He said he was impressed by the youths' willingness to pay with their lives that others might live.[224] When priests at grassroots level were making statements such as these, the message being received by the revolutionaries was loud and clear: the armed struggle had received the blessing of the "Church".

The SA Catholic Bishops Conference received huge funds from a French Catholic-Communist organisation, CCFD (Catholic Committee Against Hunger and For Development). Between 1981 and 1986, the CCFD gave over R3.5 million to the SACBC's *New Nation* newspaper, the SACBC itself, the campaign against conscription, etc. In 1986 alone, the CCFD allocated R399 550 for the *New Nation*. It also provided funds for the study of liberation theology and black theology.[225]

Meanwhile, in the United States, the Vatican was mobilising its vast machinery against South Africa. The United States Catholic Conference's administrative board requested Roman Catholic dioceses and other "church" entities to remove their funds from companies doing business in South Africa, if the SA government did not begin to dismantle apartheid and negotiate with "black leaders" (i.e. the ANC) by May 15, 1987.[226] In accordance with this, the Jesuits' Georgetown University, the oldest Roman Catholic university in the USA, voted on September 19 to divest the university of its holdings in companies doing business in South Africa. The resolution called for selling stock in corporations such as IBM, Mobil, and General Motors, if these did not leave SA within 90 days of their Annual General Meetings.[227] Significantly, IBM and GM decided to pull out of SA in October - a month later!

Baltimore Diocese, USA, declared that it would begin divesting its

---

[224] *Signposts*, Vol.5, No.5, 1986.
[225] *Signposts*, Vol.7, No.3, 1988.
[226] *The Southern Cross*, October 5, 1986.
[227] *The Southern Cross*, October 19, 1986.

holdings in companies doing business in SA unless they ceased business by December 31. The companies were IBM, GM, Mobil, Burroughs, Chevron, and Texaco.[228]

What must be understood here is that the Roman Catholic institution in the United States is immensely wealthy. It has invested millions of dollars with literally hundreds of corporations, trusts, banks and industrial giants (including IBM and General Motors[229]), making it one of the most influential factors in the economic activities of the US.[230] This is why, when the Vatican said, "Jump," these companies jumped. They ceased doing business in South Africa. "The merchants of the earth" were under her power, and they obeyed when she spoke (see Rev.18:3). She used her phenomenal economic muscle, in the United States and around the world, to pressurise the South African government into surrendering to the ANC.

Universities across America erupted in anti-SA demonstrations. Students insisted that their universities divest from American companies doing business in SA. Funds were raised for the ANC by student bodies. SA was labelled the "most wicked, racist, Fascist, immoral country in the world". There were protests, rallies, sit-ins, marches, arrests, on campus after campus across the US. None of this was sporadic: it was very carefully orchestrated. The *faculty members* of many US universities had themselves been involved in the protests in the US in the 1960's. They were leftists, and many of them were outright Marxists, who were now teaching their anti-Americanism and pro-Sovietism to their students. So they supported the anti-SA demonstrations.[231] And both student bodies and supportive faculty members were receiving orders from "higher authorities": it was all part of the increased worldwide assault on South Africa in 1986 by the conspirators. Students, fresh out of high school, naïve and gullible, were merely pawns in a deadly global game. Probably not one in a thousand could have instantly found South Africa on the map, let alone have had any sound grasp of its complex society. They were fed the propaganda the conspirators wanted them to have, and they swallowed

---

[228] *The Southern Cross*, October 19, 1986.
[229] *The Vatican Billions*, pgs.160,161.
[230] *The Vatican Billions*, pg.155.
[231] *Gold in the Furnace: South Africa on Trial*, pgs.11-15.

it.

When the US Congress passed the "Comprehensive Anti-Apartheid Act" (CAAA) in 1986, sanctions against South Africa began to take terrible effect. Almost every country in the world applied them. This resulted in vast unemployment among blacks, and untold deprivation and suffering. But this was precisely what the South African Communist Party/African National Congress alliance wanted: for the suffering and misery produced a revolutionary climate, a breakdown in law and order, and the beginnings of a potential civil war. South Africa's blacks were *expendable* in the "struggle"; all that mattered to the SACP/ANC alliance was power.

We have examined, in some detail, the activities of the Roman Catholic institution in 1986, both within South Africa and internationally, in destabilising and isolating the country to bring it to its knees. But what of the World Council of Churches? What part did *it* play in promoting the revolution, in that year?

Under the auspices of the World Council of Churches' Programme to Combat Racism (PCR), a Youth Conference was held in Harare, Zimbabwe, in July 1986. Present at the conference were members of the ANC, PAC, and SWAPO (South West African Peoples' Organisation. SWAPO had not yet come to power in South West Africa. Note that these conferences were usually held in one of SA's neighbouring Marxist-Socialist countries, like Zimbabwe or Zambia. The ANC and other revolutionary groups were based in these countries during the years that they were banned in SA). It must be borne in mind that the WCC is looked upon, by most of the world, as a Christian organisation, so that this conference was viewed as a Christian conference. And yet the participants reaffirmed the legitimacy of the armed struggle, vowing to destroy the South African system! The WCC "Message to the Youth of the World" ended this way: "We, therefore, uphold the faith of Christ crucified, and share in the redemptive purposes of God in Jesus Christ. `Now, when these things begin to take place, look up and raise your heads, because your liberation is drawing near.' We uphold the liberation of God in our acts of liberation."[232] This was classic liberation theology: evangelical-sounding terminology coupled with the distortion of Scripture to justify violence and revolution. The text of Scripture that was employed was Luke 21:28. The King James Version reads: "And when these things begin to come to pass, then look up, and lift up your heads: for your redemption draweth nigh." Read in context, these words, spoken by the Lord Jesus Christ, have absolutely nothing to do with political "liberation"! And yet, as used in this WCC document, it was made to appear as if it had to do with the revolutionary "liberation" of people from political "oppression". And the statement, "We uphold the liberation of God in our acts of liberation," gave the impression that the armed struggle was sanctioned by God; that the bombings, and burnings, and shootings, were pleasing to him.

Such was the "Christianity" of the WCC. This world body is a satanic Babel, not a Christian institution. The pious-sounding phrases that it utters from time to time are nothing but a religious mask. Behind that mask lurks a diabolical organisation, which has provided terrorist groups with millions of dollars to enable them to carry out their atrocious deeds.

Desmond Tutu, of course, ever in the vanguard of the ecclesiastical Reds, continued to utter his "religious revolutionary" speeches. In January 1986 he said that the situation in South Africa was such that violence (on the government's part) could justifiably be met with violence (by the ANC). He said that although he did not subscribe to the ANC's methods, he agreed with its principles.[233] This was nothing less than giving ecclesiastical support to the ANC's terror campaign, his feeble personal disclaimer notwithstanding.

And what of the Kairos Document? In 1986 the Kairos National Office was mobilising *religious youth groups* to implement the document. Marxists have always known that young people can be very easily manipulated to serve their purposes. The SACC youth, the Student Union for Christian Action, Young Christian Students, The

---

[232] *Ecumenical Press Service*, WCC, issue 21, July 16-31, 1986, quoted in *Gospel Defence League*, May 1987.
[233] *The Natal Witness*, January 28, 1986.

Catholic Students' Association, Anglican Youth, Catholic Youth, InterChurch Youth - all were deeply involved in implementing and promoting the Kairos Document. It was to be spread in schools, universities, church youth clubs, etc., throughout South Africa. Furthermore, training in *civil disobedience* was to be given.[234] Of course, some of the young people in these youth organisations were radical activists themselves, agents serving their ecclesiastical and political masters. And they steered the gullible and the naïve in the direction that they wanted them to go.

Religious services were also radically altered to further the "struggle". A book of Kairos liturgies for the Easter festival was published in 1986. In this book it was suggested that sermons on "Good Friday" should emphasize that "Jesus was killed because....he sided with the poor and oppressed and opposed their oppressors"; and that the aim of the sermon on "Easter Sunday" should be "to see the uprisings of the people....as the resurrection of Christ in South Africa today". Another suggested sermon stated that "our Easter experience" is "the struggle for liberation in South Africa today".[235]

Once again, what we have here is classic liberation theology: the perversion of the Gospel to make Jesus appear to have been a revolutionary, a guerrilla fighter, leading a popular uprising against the authorities. In truth, he was, and is, the Son of God, who died on the cross for the sins of his elect, and rose from the dead for their justification (Rom.4:25). But in South African liberation theology, he was a "freedom fighter" who was caught and executed, just as many terrorists had been in South Africa; and he was "resurrected" in South Africa as the people rose up against the authorities

The blasphemous "theology" of the Kairos Document was of course unacceptable to Evangelicals. The Institute for Contextual Theology, therefore, in 1985 established a project known as "Concerned Evangelicals"; and in 1986 this published *Evangelical Witness in South Africa*. This was ICT's attempt to win over Evangelicals to its position. It was liberation theology - but in "evangelical" dress. It was a "confession" of white support for apartheid, and it also called on blacks to repent of something: to repent

---

[234] *Revolution or Reconciliation?* pgs.111,112.
[235] *Revolution or Reconciliation?* pgs.113,114.

of not being more deeply involved in the "struggle"!²³⁶ Thus, according to this book, those blacks who had not fought against apartheid (moderate, non-Communist blacks) had sinned as much as the whites who supported it. It was signed by 132 members of the Baptist denomination, the International Assemblies of God, the Apostolic Faith Mission, and other bodies. The authors, however, were not named. It called for a full-scale confrontation with the South African government, saying that the "Law of Satan" and "Order of Hell" must be resisted. It criticised the evangelical doctrine of saving souls, and waiting for the Lord to return. It claimed that Christ was a revolutionary. It attacked the doctrine of obedience to authority found in Romans 13, saying that "racist missionaries" developed the "tradition" of obedience to authority, to maintain Western imperialism.[237]

Once again it must be said: such is the spiritual darkness today, that those who profess to be "Evangelicals" are for the most part as lost, as spiritually dead in trespasses and sins, as spiritually blind, as any theological liberal. And, as with the "National Initiative for Reconciliation" organised by the Africa Enterprise organisation, which was examined earlier, many professing Evangelicals simply swallowed the blend of theological liberalism and theological conservatism that was becoming increasingly popular. They were too ignorant of the Scriptures to know that what they were swallowing was poison. Claiming to be "filled with the Holy Spirit", claiming to be Bible-believers, they showed, by their lack of any spiritual discernment, that they were not following the Holy Spirit, but seducing spirits; not the doctrines of Holy Scripture, but doctrines of devils. Spiritual blindness is not only found within Roman Catholicism and openly liberal Protestantism. Sometimes, those with Bibles in their hands and scriptural terminology on their lips are just as blind. The Holy Spirit must open the eyes, and open the ears, or none can see or hear.

The African Communist, No.104, 1986, stated that because the majority of the working-class in South Africa claimed to be Christians, "revolutionaries should then look for ways, and means, of involving

---

[236] *Revolution or Reconciliation?* pgs.114-117.
[237] *Gospel Defence League,* October 1986.

the Church in the national liberation struggle".[238] That very year, 1986, was a good year for the ANC/SACP in this regard. "Church" involvement in the revolution intensified as never before.

And yet ANC-inspired violence was more horrifying than ever. The "necklace" murders continued. The ANC's Radio Freedom declared on May 4 that the "necklace" murders and other forms of killing were legitimate, thus spurring the young "comrades" in the townships to further acts of barbarity. A few examples will suffice. In April, in Lebowa, ANC "comrades" grabbed an 80-year-old blind black woman, beat her with wire cables, put a tyre around her neck, poured petrol on her, and set her alight. 32 other black people, mainly elderly women, were burnt to death the same day. One man, after being set alight, was still alive after the tyre was burnt out. His son was forced by the "comrades" to kill him with a knife. Sometimes, the killers *ate* the flesh of their "necklaced" victims.[239]

In September Alfred Nzo, the ANC's secretary general, told the London *Sunday Times* that collaborators "had to be eliminated". When asked if this included necklacing, he nodded emphatically and said, "If the people decide to use necklacing, we support it."[240]

From August 1985 to mid-May 1986, over 400 blacks were killed by the "comrades".[241] And in the townships, the governing bodies were being overthrown and so-called "people's power" was taking over. The radicals organised street, block and area committees to govern the towns. These kept a list of all people in the blocks, and if a "counter-revolutionary" (i.e. a non-Marxist) lived in a particular block, his house was located, and his every move watched.[242] "People's courts" were established, "people's education" was taught in many black schools, and the Soviets were praised.[243] A reign of terror was spreading through the townships. Where were the voices of protest from the Roman Catholic institution, the South African Council of

---

[238] *Revolution or Reconciliation?* pgs.135,136.
[239] *Gold in the Furnace: South Africa on Trial,* pgs.71-74.
[240] *The Aida Parker Newsletter,* Issue No.169, December 1993.
[241] *Gold in the Furnace: South Africa on Trial,* pg.89.
[242] *Signposts,* Vol.5, No.3, 1986.
[243] *The McAlvany Intelligence Advisor,* December 1986.

Churches, the Anglican and Methodist institutions, always quick to condemn the security forces? They were ominously silent.

CHAPTER TWENTY-FIVE

1987: "THE ARMED STRUGGLE IS A THEOLOGICAL DUTY!"

In early May 1987, a week-long conference on South Africa and South West Africa, organised by the World Council of Churches' Programme to Combat Racism, was held in Lusaka, Zambia, to review the implementation of the Harare Declaration. It was opened by the Zambian president, Kenneth Kaunda. Kaunda was a Socialist dictator himself. When he opened the conference, he urged American and European churches to influence their governments to exert more international pressure on South Africa.[244] Leaders of the ANC, PAC and SWAPO attended as delegates, not merely observers, and addressed the conference.[245] And on May 10, executive members of the South African Council of Churches met ANC and PAC officials.

The conference called on the central committee of the World Council of Churches to recognise "that an armed struggle against an unjust regime was a moral and theological right and duty", according to the Anglican archbishop of Central Africa, Khotso Makhulu.[246] Such a wicked, unscriptural statement could confidently be made because the ignorance of the Bible was so great among Protestants that they could not see it for the lie that it was. When Paul preached to the Bereans, they "searched the scriptures daily, whether those things were so"(Acts 17:11). He who does not preach what the Word of God declares, preaches error, a false message. But few, today, of the multitudes who profess to be Christians (and while multitudes profess to be, only a tiny minority are true Christians) ever search the Scriptures: despite the fact that the Bible is far more readily available to people than at any other period in the history of the world, there are very, very few who know what it proclaims. And the religious leaders know it, and take advantage of their ignorance.

In Romans 13, when Paul wrote, "Let every soul be subject unto the higher powers", and, "Whosoever therefore resisteth the power,

---

[244] *The Natal Witness*, May 5, 1987.
[245] *Revolution or Reconciliation?* pgs.121,122.
[246] *The Citizen* (Johannesburg), May 11, 1987.

resisteth the ordinance of God: and they that resist shall receive to themselves damnation" (vss.1,2), he was writing at a time when Caesar ruled with an iron fist. The early Christians were not living under an elected government, answerable to the people, but under an absolute dictatorship. And yet the Lord, through Paul, instructed them to be subject. Today, however, we have so-called "servants of Christ" preaching the *very opposite* of what Paul and the other apostles preached, declaring that it is a moral and theological right and duty to take up arms against an unjust regime! No men of God these, but servants of Satan.

The "Lusaka Statement" of May 1987, which was agreed to by the SACC, WCC and ANC, contained the following:[247]

"….the South African regime and its colonial domination of Namibia is illegitimate". South West Africa/Namibia was under the government of South Africa; but SWAPO was waging a guerrilla war to gain control of it.

"We again commit ourselves .to work….for the removal of the present rulers who persistently usurp the stewardship of God's authority". Where in the New Testament are Christians exhorted, or even permitted, to remove the rulers by violence?

"We affirm the unquestionable right of the people of Namibia and South Africa to secure justice and peace through the liberation movements. While remaining committed to peaceful change we recognise that the nature of the South African regime….compels the movements to the use of force along with other means to end oppression". Here was a statement in open support of the terrorist tactics of the ANC, PAC and SWAPO.

"….SWAPO, the sole and authentic representative of the people of Namibia". Just as the ANC had been falsely declared to be the sole and authentic representative of the people of South Africa, so the Lusaka Statement now falsely declared SWAPO to be the sole and authentic representative of Namibia's people. Just over two years later, SWAPO came to power in Namibia, by massive intimidation and with the assistance of the United Nations, "church" groups, etc.

The Lusaka Statement also declared that churches should support

---

[247]*Revolution or Reconciliation?* pgs.125-126.

sanctions against South Africa, and that they must *repent* of not having supported revolution.[248]

In a later "Action Plan", the WCC was called upon to encourage its member-churches to support the "liberation movements" as the *legitimate representatives* of the people. The SACC's AGM voted to adopt the Lusaka Statement in July, and the Anglican denomination did so in November.[249]

The SACC's Justice and Reconciliation department distributed the book, *Violence and Nonviolence in South Africa,* by Walter Wink, to its member-churches in 1987. This book advocated violence if non-violent means appeared to have failed. Clearly, the SACC was enthusiastically supporting the violent revolution against South Africa.[250]

The Lusaka Statement was issued in May 1987. *In that very month,* on May 20, a car bomb blast occurred in Johannesburg, South Africa. This was the tenth bomb blast in Johannesburg that year, and the twenty-fifth in the country. It occurred on the fourth anniversary of the blast in Pretoria, in 1983, which killed nineteen people and injured 239, and for which the ANC had claimed responsibility.[251] *This* was the kind of action which the WCC, SACC, and other religious groups had given their support to. The administrative board of the SA Catholic Bishops Conference, it is true, condemned the bomb blast, saying it was opposed to the use of violence by either security or "liberation forces";[252] but this condemnation had a terribly hollow ring to it, in the light of all the solid evidence of SACBC/ANC collaboration. Having said that it condemned the violence, it continued to actively and enthusiastically support the perpetrators of the violence. Actions so often speak so much louder than words.

Despite the terrible carnage being wrought by the ANC and the other terrorist organisations, "church" support for them continued, and

---

[248] *Gospel Defence League*, September 1987.
[249] *Revolution or Reconciliation?* pgs.126,127.
[250] *Revolution or Reconciliation?* pgs.129,130.
[251] *The Citizen*, May 21, 1987.
[252] *The Southern Cross*, June 7, 1987.

intensified. The Methodist denomination of South Africa, for example, in 1987 reaffirmed its call to *lift the ban* on "liberation movements". Its Cape Synod adopted the motion calling for the lifting of the ban for the following reasons:

these movements were South African movements that had consistently worked for the liberation of all South Africans;

the armed struggle had only been adopted after 50 years of non-violence had failed to achieve results;

and no future for South Africa could be considered in isolation from these movements![253]

If one was not told that a *religious denomination,* professing to be Christian, had given the above reasons for unbanning murderous, Marxist organisations, one would probably have assumed that they were given by a Marxist organisation itself. Few could possibly have guessed that they were reasons given by a Protestant denomination! But they were. The Methodist institution viewed the people of SA as being in need of "liberation" by Marxist murderers who, it felt, were unjustly banned, and furthermore that they were essential to the future of the country. The leadership positions in this and other denominations in SA were filled with unregenerate wolves in sheep's clothing who, in the name of God and the Lord Jesus Christ, were preaching another "gospel" - one far, far different from the Gospel of the grace of God. And what was true in SA was true throughout the world.

Allan Boesak was hard at work in 1987, as always. This leading South African liberation theologian said on June 21, at the German Kirchentag in Frankfurt, "The New Jerusalem is not a future world somewhere else. No, the New Jerusalem comes from heaven into *this* reality....this City [of God] does not need to wait for `eternity.' This New Jerusalem will arise from the ashes of all that which today is called `Pretoria.'" And he identified Pretoria, SA's capital, with the "Babylon" of the book of Revelation.[254] This man, in his book, *Comfort and Protest,* called the SA government "the beast from the sea", empowered by Satan, which was to be "slain by the sword", and

---

[253] *The Citizen,* June 8, 1987.
[254] *Gospel Defence League,* August 1987.

that those who "slew" it would be doing God's bidding!²⁵⁵

Thus, in liberation theology, whenever an "unjust regime" (i.e. a non-Communist government) is overthrown, and a Communist government is installed, there the "New Jerusalem" has been established. The book of Revelation says: "And I John saw the holy city, new Jerusalem, coming down from God out of heaven, prepared as a bride adorned for her husband" (Rev.21:2). In this beautiful chapter of God's Word, the New Jerusalem symbolises the true Church, the "wife" of Christ (Rev.21:9-11, compared with Eph.5:22-33). In the political "gospel" of liberation theology, this lovely truth is cast aside, and the New Jerusalem is declared to be a Communist dictatorship.

Identifying Pretoria with "Babylon" in Rev.17 and 18 is utterly preposterous. As if "Babylon the Great, the Mother of Harlots and Abominations of the earth" (Rev.17:5), only came into existence when Pretoria became the capital of South Africa! That mystical "Babylon", that Great Whore (Rev.17:1,2), is none other than the Roman Catholic institution, as has been recognised by Christians throughout the centuries: the description given in Scripture perfectly fits the Roman Catholic system, and that alone. Everything - its wicked deeds, its predominant colours, its blasphemies, its political intrigues, its immense wealth, its paganism, its persecuting spirit - is perfectly described.

But by identifying Pretoria with "Babylon", Boesak created further "justification" for the armed revolution - for Rev.17 and 18 reveal that "Babylon" will be violently destroyed, and that this violent destruction is the judgement of God upon it. This also explains why he called the SA government "the beast from the sea"; for Rev.13 describes the "slaying with the sword" of this "beast". From the final book in the Bible, then, as is done from so many other biblical books, texts are found which so-called "theologians" pervert so as to make it appear as if the Bible supports armed revolution. And who, among the multitudes of unlearned black people in the sprawling townships, would argue with the learned Allan Boesak? Very few indeed.

Desmond Tutu also continued doing as much as he could to

---

²⁵⁵*Gospel Defence League*, September 1987.

support the terrorist organisations. He said that, if he was a young man, he would reject Tutu because there was nothing to show for his advocacy of non-violence. He said that the time might come when the "Church" would have to decide which was the lesser evil - apartheid or violence. And he added that a time can come when it is justifiable to overthrow an unjust system by force.[256] Although he did not, by these statements, advocate revolution directly, they were none-too-subtle hints that perhaps the time for non-violence was now past, or soon would be.

And what of the Roman Catholic institution in 1987? Its deep involvement in revolution was admitted by SWAPO, when that organisation denied responsibility for a bomb blast on September 20 that destroyed a Roman Catholic "church" building in northern Namibia: "The Church is fighting for the same cause that SWAPO is fighting for - peace, justice and freedom in Namibia."[257]

A Roman Catholic nun, Bernard Ncube, who was closely linked to the UDF and had been detained several times, was the president of the Transvaal branch of FEDSAW (the Federation of South African Women), a UDF affiliate with strong Communist ties, in 1987.[258] As for the notorious Institute for Contextual Theology, the steering committee included three Romish priests: Lebamang Sebidi, chairman; Smangaliso Mkhatshwa, general secretary of the SACBC; and Albert Nolan, a foremost liberation theology author; as well as nun Bernard Ncube. There were, in fact, more Roman Catholics on the steering committee than any others.[259]

During 1986 and 1987, the SA Catholic Bishops Conference received R11.3 million from the European Community.[260] The EC was of course predominantly Roman Catholic.

The pope of Rome, John Paul II, planned to visit various southern African countries in September 1988, and many South African Roman Catholics were hoping that he would visit South Africa as well. But Romanist bishop, Wilfred Napier, president of the SACBC, made it

---

[256] *The Natal Witness*, January 14, 1987.
[257] *The Southern Cross*, October 18, 1987.
[258] *Signposts*, Vol.7, No.3, 1988.
[259] *Signposts*, Vol.6, No.6, 1987.
[260] *Signposts*, Vol.7, No.3, 1988.

clear in 1987 that the pope would not come. According to him, if the pope visited SA in September 1988, this would be seen as legitimizing the white government, which did not govern for the common good. He said that "the people" were saying that it would be almost unthinkable that the South African Police, who were the "instruments of repression", should be entrusted with the security of the pope.[261]

South Africa, of course, could well do without the presence of the Roman Antichrist. It was no loss, in fact it was a great blessing, that he did not pay a "pastoral visit" to this suffering land. But Napier's statements revealed, with stark clarity, that the Vatican fully supported the Marxist terrorists who were causing such suffering and bloodshed in SA. Not that evidence was lacking before, of course!

No-one should underestimate the effect the pope's decision not to visit SA had upon the duped masses. Revered throughout Africa, even by non-Romanists, as a great "holy man" and representative of Christ, and adored by Romanists as the "Holy Father", the vicar of Christ, his refusal sent a powerful message to the masses in the black townships: the pope supported the armed struggle! He had set himself against the SA government! It was illegitimate! It had no right to govern! And therefore it had to be overthrown! This was the will of God, for had not "Christ's vicar" made it clear?

There was much irony in the fact that, as it turned out, the Roman pontiff, due to bad weather, was forced to make a landing in South Africa anyway, on his way to the little country of Lesotho, and the "instruments of repression", the South African Police, were entrusted with his security after all, as they escorted him by car to the Lesotho border!

By October 1987, some 400 people had been "necklaced", and 200 more burned to death in other ways, according to the head of intelligence of the security branch of the SA Police.[262] The question must be asked: *who was oppressing whom?* The real oppression came, not from the security forces, but from the ANC/SACP revolutionaries, who were filling the lives of innocent black people with terror. These

---

[261] *The Southern Cross*, November 22, 1987.
[262] *Victims Against Terrorism Update*, Vol.1, No.6, November 1987.

Communists spoke of liberation, of peace and justice. But to "liberate", they placed tyres around people's necks and filled them with petrol and set them alight; to promote "peace", they waged a dreadful terrorist war; to establish "justice", they committed atrocities so terrible they almost defy belief.

They did not, in truth, seek any of these things. They sought only power, total power, absolute power. And it mattered nothing to them how many black lives were lost in order to achieve it.

The people of Nicaragua could have told the blacks of South Africa all about Marxist-style "liberation", "peace" and "justice". There, the Marxist Sandinistas had waged a terrible guerrilla war and ultimately had come to power. The Sandinistas were supported by the *Jesuits* and other Roman Catholic priestly orders, and the Sandinista government had Jesuits serving in it. Liberation theology had been devastatingly effective in Nicaragua. In 1987 Oliver Tambo, head of the ANC, was embraced by Nicaraguan President Daniel Ortega, and received the Order of Carlos Fonseca - the highest award of the Sandinista government - for his "fight against apartheid".[263] Yet another indication of Roman Catholic support for the ANC.

According to the testimonies of former ANC terrorists, blacks were often recruited against their wills, and taken to Zambia, Angola, Mozambique, etc., for training. Sometimes the training was done in the USSR itself. The ANC camps in these countries were horrifying places, the recruits living in appalling conditions. The ANC *leadership,* however, lived very well. The indoctrination in the camps was blatantly Marxist.[264] ANC training was also conducted in Libya, Lebanon, South Yemen, and Eastern Europe.[265]

As for the PAC, its recruits were trained in Uganda, Syria, Lebanon, and China. It also often sent its recruits to Libya for training. The Libyans, however, were not interested in the black "cause", but rather in the establishment of an Arabic, Muslim empire throughout Africa. To this end, pressure was exerted on the black recruits to

---

[263] *Victims Against Terrorism* Update, Vol.1, No.5, September 1987.
[264] *Victims Against Terrorism* Update, Vol.1, No.3, February 1987.
[265] *Signposts*, Vol.9, No.4, 1990.

convert to Islam. Those who did so, were treated far better than the others. Communism was also taught to the recruits.

Various other terrorist organisations trained their recruits in Libya as well, including the IRA (Roman Catholic) and the PLO (Muslim). As far back as the early 1970's, meetings took place between the ANC and IRA in Libya, the USSR, Eastern Europe, Lebanon, and South Yemen.[266] PAC leaders had discussions with the IRA in Britain, and the two stated that they were ready to work *together* in SA. The PLO, as well, was quite prepared to work in SA with the PAC.[267] This reveals that, in the twilight world of international terrorism, Communism and Islam merge with Roman Catholicism. Seemingly-diverse groups, with apparently little or nothing in common, support one another, standing shoulder to shoulder in the international "struggle". For truly, the battle *is* international. Behind it all is the centuries-old Vatican conspiracy, under the direction of the Jesuit/Illuminati forces, to enchain the world to the feet of the pope. The network centres in Rome, even though many of those involved do not know it. Christians have the prophetic Word, and the available evidence verifies it. While Communism, or Islam for that matter, can be used to further its ambitions, the Vatican will readily make use of the forces of either one. Communism and Islam have ambitions of their own, of course, and are also prepared to use anyone to further *their* goals. It was thus mutually beneficial for the Roman Catholic IRA and the Marxist ANC or PAC to work together, for the ANC and the Muslim PLO to work together, etc. Victory for one was seen as a further step towards victory for the others. A setback for one was a setback for all. The common thread, uniting them all, was the destruction of the existing order, and the creation of the new.

---

[266] *Signposts,* Vol.9, No.4, 1990.
[267] *Victims Against Terrorism Update,* Vol.1, No.3, February 1987.

CHAPTER TWENTY-SIX

1988: WHEN "STANDING FOR THE TRUTH" MEANT SUPPORTING TERROR

The deep involvement of various "churches" in the armed revolution against South Africa was admitted by Mrs Winnie Mandela, wife of the ANC's Nelson Mandela. A fiery, radical revolutionary and heroine of the young "comrades" in the townships, she said in an address to a graduation ceremony at the Federal Theological Seminary in Pietermaritzburg in March 1988: "We say to [SA State President] Botha: You touch the churches, you have unleashed the wrath of the nation. We shall stand by our churches, enough is enough."[268]

But the fact that Roman Catholic, Anglican, Methodist, and other religious institutions were deeply involved in the revolution on the side of the ANC was not enough: the ANC wanted the involvement of those "churches" not yet engaged in the revolution! On the ANC's "Radio Freedom" broadcast on March 1, 1988, it was stated: "the democratic movement [the ANC] must be given a voice in all the churches - its directives must be relayed from inside the churches. From today, all the church services must be services that further the democratic call. The church must be for liberation. Its services must be for the struggle of the people against the apartheid regime."[269] Thus the ANC presumed to have the power and the right to dictate how the churches should act, and what they should teach. In typical Communist fashion, churches were expected to serve the Communist cause; they were viewed merely as tools of the Communist system. As long as they obeyed orders, they would be tolerated, even protected; but what if they did not? *True* Christian churches would never agree to such demands: what would the future hold for such churches, and thus for true Christians, in an ANC-ruled South Africa? Oh, those so-called "churches" in membership with the Communist-supporting SACC readily agreed to propagate the ANC's message, having become nothing more than puppets dancing to the ANC's tune; and they knew that as long as they continued to tow the line in an ANC-governed

---

[268] *The Natal Witness Echo*, March 31, 1988.
[269] *Revolution or Reconciliation?* pg.145.

South Africa, all would be well for them. But what would happen to those true churches of Christ which in the past refused to preach the ANC's "gospel", and would in the future continue to refuse to do so? We shall see, as we proceed, that restrictions, and even persecution, of the true Christian Church in South Africa may not be too far away.

By 1988, all SACC member-churches were being pressurised to endorse the Lusaka Statement, the WCC/ANC document based on the Kairos Document and drawn up in 1987. In fact, the Statement itself had declared that its proposals should be made *compulsory* and churches "monitored" to be certain that they were implementing them![270] Religious freedom was plainly not part of the ANC's vision.

We shall continue to trace the unholy alliance between the ANC and the wicked institutions claiming to be "churches" in South Africa. The New Testament clearly defines what a church of Christ is; and neither the Roman Catholic, Anglican, Methodist, nor any of the other institutions which supported the ANC qualified. But how were the blinded masses to know this? They had not heard the true Gospel, only a false one. The only Scriptures they really knew were those their priests and ministers distorted to support the political "gospel". The only "churches" they were aware of were those which were merely religious branches of the ANC/SACP. These are days of gross spiritual darkness around the world, and the Lord's true servants are few and far between. The testimony to the true Gospel is a small and feeble one today. The world looks at the innumerable "churches" and believes that Christianity is flourishing as never before; but the humble Christian, who loves his Lord and studies his Word, knows the difference between the giant denominational monstrosities filled with unregenerate, ungodly men, and those despised but godly few who have gone forth to Christ "without the camp" (Heb.13:13), assembling in small local churches or even (in these dark days) too far from any other believers to meet with any, full of love for the Lord and his holy Word, striving to be separate from the world and desiring to live holy lives to the glory of God.

At the January 1988 quarterly meetings of Methodist "churches"

---

[270] *Gospel Defence League*, June 1988.

around South Africa, a study document called *Should We Become a Peace Church?* was distributed. Although the document was eventually scrapped, its proposals revealed the depths to which the hierarchy of this denomination had sunk. The proposals were that Methodists should not participate in military service in any form; that Methodists who supported the resolution must participate in "non-violent action" (e.g. strikes, stayaways, funeral demonstrations, and non-collaboration with government agencies - actions which almost always led to terrible violence); and all this in order to bring about social change.[271]

In a word, the Methodist institution would be committed to civil disobedience! - something the Scriptures expressly forbid, but much to the advantage of the radical ANC/SACP alliance. In fact, the document openly stated that the proposals were designed to put Methodists "on the side of the oppressed" in their "struggle" (usual liberation theology terminology). The Methodist institution, most certainly, was one of those Winnie Mandela had in mind when she warned the State President not to touch "our churches". But it was by no means the only one.

The "Church and Society Department" of the United Congregational denomination of South Africa (UCCSA) made the following proposals to the UCCSA Executive Committee in 1988: ....the Church cannot deny the liberation movement the right to take up arms"; "this is an ethically superior choice to passive acceptance of injustice"; and, "the UCCSA accepts the Lusaka Statement".[272]

The *Romish* religious leaders continued to be in the very forefront of the "struggle", as always. The SA government knew it, and from time to time took action. In April, it closed down the radical Roman Catholic newspaper, *The New Nation*.[273] Famous SA liberation theologian, Romish priest Albert Nolan, declared that there would be an *increase* in direct "church" involvement in opposing racially biased laws and policies. He said that Roman Catholic bishops might go to

---

[271] *Signposts*, Vol.7, No.2, 1988.
[272] *Gospel Defence League*, June 1988.
[273] *The Southern Cross*, April 17, 1988.

jail as the confrontation over "apartheid" developed.[274]

On April 8, the leaders of the 500 priests and monks of the Missionary Oblates of Mary Immaculate sent a letter to the State President, P.W. Botha, in which they declared their support for the SACBC. They also "decried" the "occupation of Namibia to the detriment of the aspirations of the Namibian people and the unnecessary prolongation of a war situation in that country". They "decried" the "elements of destabilisation in the Southern African countries, in particular where the SADF is present (e.g. Angola)". They also noted the presence of the military in black residential areas of SA.[275] In this way they sought to discredit the SADF. They failed to point out, of course, that the military was usually very welcome in the townships, because ordinary men and women were then able to go about their daily tasks in peace and safety; or that the SADF was involved in a full-scale war of defence against Communist expansionism from SA's frontline states.

On the occasion of Nelson Mandela's 70th birthday (spent in prison), South Africa's Roman Catholic bishops sent him a message, saying that they were praying for him that eventually they and he would "celebrate in freedom the bond of our common dignity as children of the same Father, and sisters and brothers in the one Lord Jesus Christ".[276] Not quite two years later, he was free.

In December, a ceremony to mark the unveiling of the tombstones of four blacks killed two years before was attended by ANC activist and avowed Marxist Harry Gwala and UDF president Archie Gumede. Gwala said: "We will never retreat. We will continue the struggle", and referred to the dead as "comrades". And yet Roman Catholic archbishop, Denis Hurley, celebrated mass, and pronounced a blessing over the tombstones, sprinkling them with "holy water"![277] A clear example of RC/ANC collaboration! The signal sent to the revolutionaries was: these men were Christians; they served Christ as they fought against the state.

---

[274] *The Southern Cross*, August 14, 1988.
[275] *The Southern Cross*, April 24, 1988.
[276] *The Southern Cross*, August 7, 1988.
[277] *The Natal Witness*, December 12, 1988.

Just how deeply the Roman Catholic institution was involved in the revolution, just how sinister that involvement was, and just how terrifying it was for young blacks who tried to escape the clutches of the religious and political revolutionaries, is apparent from the following:[278] Godfrey Sitole, a 21-year-old black man from Atteridgeville, became involved, while at school, with the "Student Christian Movement" (SCM), a front for COSAS, the Congress of South African Students, a radical ANC-supporting organisation. The SCM claimed to instruct students in religion; but it had a far more sinister purpose. Membership was *compulsory*. The meetings were held at a Roman Catholic "church". At the meetings the members were taught about detention laws, and what to do if stopped by a policeman. The Popish priest explained the meaning of Socialism, and why one should resist oppressive laws. Godfrey said that the priest was well aware of the evil things they were doing, but he helped them. He told them what slogans to put on T-shirts, and gave them the money for printing. The "comrades" were aware that, if the police were after them, they could go to the Roman Catholic "church" or to the priest's home. The priest told them that the police had no right to search a "church" building. He told them to practice two-day fasts, because they might have to hide in the bush for two days at a time.

After two or three meetings, the priest introduced them to a COSAS official. They *had* to join. They were told that COSAS would deal with bad teachers. Later, when Godfrey wanted to resign, they accused him of working with the system. He said that he knew it was dangerous not to attend the meetings in the "church". He was caught by the "comrades", who tried to burn him to death, but the police arrived just in time.

Godfrey escaped an agonising death, but not all were so fortunate. His testimony reveals the diabolical collaboration that took place between Roman Catholic priests and the Marxist guerrillas, especially in the simmering black townships. Lurking beneath their white collars and black robes were Red ideologists who would stop at nothing, not even murder, to accomplish their goals. And many in the townships came to live in fear of these men who blasphemously claimed to be the representatives of Christ.

---

[278]*Victims Against Terrorism Update*, July 1988.

In liberation theology, such festivals as Easter provide ideal opportunities for promoting this false gospel. On "Good Friday" in 1988, Romish archbishop Denis Hurley and other religious leaders presided at a dawn service which was held to "link" the suffering theme of "Good Friday" with South Africans working for "justice and freedom".[279] Eighteen radical organisations, as well as the *New Nation* newspaper, had been banned by the government. Paddy Kearney, director of Diakonia, an ecumenical agency, said that the silencing by the government of these organisations and the *New Nation* was a silencing of God! He thus equated the revolution with the will of God, and thereby deceived many ignorant souls. Hurley, leading the prayers, prayed that God would look upon those who suffered under banning and restrictions, and (by implication) he compared them with Christ, whom the leaders of his day had tried to silence. What a blasphemous perversion of the truth! The Bible says of the Lord Christ, "For Christ also hath once suffered for sins, the just for the unjust" (1 Pet.3:18). He who was perfectly just, perfectly holy, harmless, and undefiled (Heb.7:26), suffered for the sins of his people; but those who had been banned in South Africa were unjust, unholy, harmful terrorists, defiled by sin! Those who sought to silence Christ were servants of the devil who hated the holy Son of God; but the South African government, in banning these radical organisations, was seeking to maintain law and order as these organisations sought to overthrow the state by violence. This was a typical example of liberation theology's false doctrine.

During the service, which was held in the Central Methodist building in Durban, nineteen people, representing the silenced organisations, stood at the front of the "church" wearing gags. Afterwards they, with religious leaders, priests, nuns, and seminarians, led hundreds of people up the main street of Durban to St. Paul's Anglican building. They carried large crosses and walked in silence. Later the gags were symbolically removed. In this way the Marxist religious leaders showed their blatant support for the revolution, giving religious legitimacy to it.

On May 1, 1988, for the fifth consecutive year, "churches" in

---

[279] *The Southern Cross,* April 24, 1988.

Durban and Pietermaritzburg celebrated "Worker Sunday", with special services, etc. To help focus on the role of workers, they were invited to attend services in their work clothes, and to bring symbols of their work. The theme was taken, as it was each year, from a statement on "Workers' Rights", drawn up by Durban "churches" in 1983.[280] This was blatant Communism in religious dress. "Workers of the World Unite!" was the great rallying cry of classic Communism, and these "churches" were promoting the Communist concept of using the "workers" to overthrow the government. They were sowing discontent among the middle and lower classes, ripening them for revolution. Also in May, the strongest "church" delegation to ever attend a major labour union gathering took part in the special conference of COSATU (the Congress of South African Trade Unions), the giant trade union umbrella organisation affiliated with the ANC/SACP. The conference was called to consider how to respond to the government's tougher line on unions. The SACC and the SACBC were invited. Rob Lambeth, a member of the SACBC delegation and secretary of the "Church and Work Commission", said that the "Church" was seen to be the natural ally of the worker movement in SA. As regards the Roman Catholic institution and its relations with unions, he said that it had "always stood in solidarity with workers", and that there was a "positive relationship" between it and the unions.[281] Here was yet further proof, by way of admission, of the active participation of Popery and other religious institutions in the "worker movement", which served the Catholic-Communist cause. The Papal institution began to woo the "proletariat" soon after World War Two, when the "worker-priest" movement began. These worker-priests joined trade unions, etc., in various European countries, working in factories and living in the workers' hostels. They preached a Communistic "gospel". Under the Roman pope, John XXIII, in the 1960's, the image of "Christ the Worker" became extremely popular, with Christ being depicted as one of the "proletariat", a working-class man, a carpenter. This image was enthusiastically received by Romanists who were manual labourers. And in Latin America, it was a small step from "Christ the Worker", holding the tools of a trade in his hands, to

---

[280] *The Natal Witness*, April 29, 1988.
[281] *The Natal Witness Echo*, May 26, 1988.

"Christ the Liberator", toting a gun: the "Christ" of liberation theology.[282]

It was, likewise, a small step in South Africa.

Yet another significant meeting took place in May. About 200 religious leaders held an emergency meeting to consider new, "non-violent" ways to "resist apartheid". It was sponsored by the SACC. The Roman Catholic institution, which was not a member of the SACC, and a number of independent African "churches", also took part.

Some of the suggestions included civil disobedience in areas such as tax payments and military service. It ended with a "service of witness and solidarity" at the main Roman Catholic building in Soweto.[283] And Anglican archbishop, Desmond Tutu, preached. In his sermon, Tutu said: "We....have determined that we shall obey God and not man".[284] He was referring to the words of the apostles in Acts 5:29; but Tutu was a liberation theologian, and he distorted the true meaning of the Scriptures as all liberation theologians do. The New Testament emphatically teaches that Christians are to obey the authorities, as has often been shown in this book. But if a government forbids Christians to do what the Word of God commands, *then* the government must be disobeyed in order to obey God. *That* is what Acts 5:29 is about, as any reading of the verse in its context will show. Tutu, however, used this verse to try to justify disobedience to the government's *lawful* authority. This was a sinful perversion of the Scriptures.

In a statement read on behalf of the convocation by Frank Chikane, the general secretary of the SACC, the religious leaders declared that as "Christians", they had to regard the "suffering and oppression of people of God, as a violation of the Body of Christ". "We have no choice but to oppose the present regime....We now commit ourselves .to end unjust rule in our country". The convocation distinguished between the legitimate authority which conformed to the Gospel, and

---

[282] *The Vatican Moscow Washington Alliance,* pgs.260-270.
[283] *The Natal Witness,* May 31, 1988.
[284] *The Citizen,* June 1, 1988.

the illegitimate kind which did not.[285] But where in all the New Testament are we told that an authority is only legitimate when it conforms to the Gospel? The Roman Empire did not conform to the Gospel, and yet it was while that empire held sway that Paul told Christians to obey and submit to the secular authority! The "ending of unjust rule" is *not* the task of the true Church of Christ. But when these religious leaders spoke of the "people of God" and "Body of Christ", they had in mind the adherents of their religious institutions, not those whom the *Scriptures* call the members of Christ's body, the Church of the living God.

One other significant event took place in May. The "Standing for the Truth" defiance campaign was launched at a convocation of "churches" in Johannesburg. The purpose of the campaign was for "churches" to move from merely condemning apartheid, to "non-violent" action to *end* apartheid (and by "ending apartheid", of course, they meant an end to the white government).

The SA Catholic Bishops Conference issued a statement in August, saying that the SACBC had agreed to participate in the campaign, and reaffirming its membership and support for it.[286]

To say that its purpose was to use "non-violent" action meant absolutely nothing. Its deliberate purpose was to provoke the police by breaking the law, and many died on both sides.

Internationally, the "church" campaign against South Africa continued to intensify in 1988. The World Council of Churches declared that it would give R360 000 to SWAPO from its fund to combat racism. The PAC would receive R110 000, and the ANC R250 000.[287] SWAPO may have received more than the others at this time because the WCC scented victory for SWAPO in Namibia in the very near future. The international Communist strategy was first to encircle South Africa, and then to carry out the final assault on South Africa itself. Namibia had to fall first.

At the Lambeth Conference in 1988, the world's Anglican bishops

---

[285] *The Citizen*, June 1, 1988.
[286] *The Southern Cross*, September 10, 1988.
[287] *The Citizen*, October 5, 1988.

called on their churches to exert pressure on their governments to pressurise the SA government into "ending apartheid". The bishops supported sanctions, aid to anti-apartheid groups and to the frontline states (SA's neighbours), and the unbanning of the ANC. The Conference declared that it "understood" those who, "after exhausting all other ways, chose the way of armed struggle as the only way to justice".[288] Yet another justification, by a religious institution, of the murderous tactics of the ANC, PAC and SWAPO. Yet another example of the depths to which this denomination, like all other major denominations, had sunk.

Roman Catholic and Protestant groups in France issued a joint statement after the murder of an ANC official in that country on March 29, demanding that the French government combat apartheid "with economic and diplomatic pressures". The statement was signed by the president of the French bishops' Commission for Justice and Peace; the president of the Catholic Committee Against Hunger and For Development; and a representative of the Protestant Federation of France.[289]

The United States Catholic Conference publicly expressed support for a US bill proposing comprehensive sanctions against SA, on 19 May 1988.[290] And on October 25, representatives of several religious bodies, including the US Catholic Conference, met in New York to lay plans to escalate pressures for change in South Africa.[291] Also in October, the South African Crisis Co-ordinating Committee was launched in the US, at the request of SA liberation theologians. Its purpose was to "organize a co-ordinated and sustained ecumenical response to the crisis in SA". It was run by US "church" leaders.[292]

The pope of Rome was kept constantly informed about events in South Africa; and he made his position plain. When a joint delegation from the SACBC and the SACC visited him in May 1988 to discuss the South African situation, he told Anglican archbishop Tutu, Methodist president Khoza Mgogo and others that apartheid was "unacceptable". He urged the religious leaders to use "only peaceful

---

[288] *The Natal Witness,* August 8, 1988.
[289] *The Southern Cross,* April 24, 1988.
[290] *The Southern Cross,* June 5, 1988.
[291] *The Southern Cross,* November 20, 1988.
[292] *Signposts,* Vol.8, No.4, 1989.

means" in fighting apartheid.[293] On the surface, his statements appeared mild enough; but that which was unacceptable to the Roman pontiff was being vigorously assaulted by the agents of that pontiff around the world. For the purpose of the global Roman Catholic hierarchy is to make all political structures "acceptable" to the pope, i.e. to subjugate them all to his dominion. And his call for only peaceful means to be used was a hollow one indeed, in the light of the past and contemporary history of Romanism around the world. It was what he was *expected* to say, and he said it; but what is intended for public consumption is not always intended for the servants of the pope to obey.

On July 18, the pope expressed his *admiration* for Nelson Mandela, saying that he had a great respect for the human story of the man.[294] Yet another bit of evidence as to the Vatican's support of the ANC's revolution against South Africa; yet another powerful signal sent to the restless "comrades" in the townships.

At the end of the previous chapter, it was seen that there was a strong connection between the ANC and the Roman Catholic IRA, the terrorist organisation working in Northern Ireland and England. In January 1988, Ronnie Kasrils, the ANC's military intelligence chief, met with Patrick McFlegharty of the Provisional IRA in Cork, Ireland, and a joint working party was established to explore areas where mutual assistance might be possible. The source of arms for both terrorist groups was the same: Moscow, via Libya.[295] So the collaboration between the two was strengthened; and, as the Vatican was behind the IRA,[296] we once again see how the hand of Rome was involved in the South African revolution, using its Irish "baby" to assist in the advancement of the ANC's war.

---

[293] *The Natal Witness*, May 28, 1988; and *The Southern Cross*, June 12, 1988.
[294] *The Natal Witness*, July 19, 1988.
[295] *The Aida Parker Newsletter*, No.122, October 1988; and *Signposts*, Vol.9, No.4, 1990.
[296] *Catholic Terror in Ireland*, by Avro Manhattan.

CHAPTER TWENTY-SEVEN

1989: THE "PASTORAL PLAN", PROTEST MARCHES, AND "PROGRESSIVE CHRISTIANS"

South Africans could never have suspected, as 1988 passed into history and 1989 dawned, that this year would mark the beginning of the end of the South Africa they had always known, and the onset of the violent "labour pains" which would culminate in the bloody birth of the "New South Africa": the South Africa which the Vatican and Moscow and Washington and London desired. A "Democratic People's Republic". A Communist state.

The new "child" had been conceived many, many years before, and had been developing slowly, almost secretly, unseen by the world at large, in the womb of the Jesuit/Illuminati forces. The death of the old South Africa, and the birth of the new, had been carefully orchestrated.

There was external encirclement. One by one, the countries to the north of South Africa had experienced bloody revolutions, and one by one they had succumbed. Now South Africa was encircled by Marxist states, hostile to their giant southern neighbour, favourable to the ANC/SACP alliance, and armed by the Soviet Union. This external encirclement was deliberate. It was calculated. South Africa was surrounded.

There was also economic isolation. This, too, was deliberate. Massive global sanctions had been applied against South Africa, greatly increasing the level of unemployment and consequently the misery of millions, making them willing cannon-fodder in the hands of the revolutionaries.

In addition to being externally surrounded by hostile states and isolated economically, there was the terrible internal revolution: gruesome murders, sabotage, arson, bombings, "necklacings", etc., had become so frequent and commonplace that South Africans could hardly remember a time when these things had not been a part of daily life.

All of this led, of course, to the demoralisation of the public. White South Africans were constantly being told that they were the worst people on earth, a nation of racists, of Nazis, of slave-owners. The whole world hated them. The media, the liberal religious institutions, the universities, all had done an excellent job of demoralising the population. South Africans were weary, very weary; and more and more began to simply give up. Increasingly, they began to feel that the only solution was to negotiate "the best peace possible" with the ANC. And this, too, was deliberate. Morale was at an all-time low. The time was right for "negotiations" and piecemeal surrender.

First, however, a new man was needed at the helm. State President P.W. Botha had begun the process of dismantling apartheid. Shops, hospitals, restaurants, hotels, beaches, parks, etc., were integrated. Coloureds and Indians were given their own houses in Parliament. The "Mixed Marriages" Act, job discrimination, influx laws, were all scrapped. But he refused to unban the ANC and SA Communist Party, or to negotiate with them. A new man was needed; and in F.W. de Klerk, the international conspirators found their man.

The National Party (NP) had ruled South Africa since 1948. But for over a decade, it had been infiltrated by men working for the New World Order desired by the Vatican, international Communism, and the powerful "shadow governments" which hold the real reins of power in the United States, Britain, and elsewhere. Various powerful men in the NP government were New World Order disciples, working *from within* the NP to deliver South Africa into the New World Order, in exchange, no doubt, for promises of prominent positions in the future order of things. It was almost impossible for the Afrikaners to realise this, the NP having been for so many years the bastion of Afrikaner nationalism. But as we shall see, the evidence is overwhelming.

Those within the National Party who wanted - actually *wanted* - to deliver the country into the hands of the ANC/SACP, in accordance with the conspirators' plans, knew that P.W. Botha had to be removed. In 1989, the NP rejected his leadership, and F.W. de Klerk became NP leader and State President of South Africa.

It was not long before he began to give clear indications of the direction in which he was taking the country, as shall be seen.

On June 26, de Klerk visited the *Vatican,* and met with Roman Catholic Cardinal Agostino Casaroli, the Vatican's Secretary of

State.[297] One very big question arises: *Why?* South Africa was not a Roman Catholic country. De Klerk was not a Roman Catholic. Ah, but he was a one-worlder, and the movement towards a united world, ruled by a world government, is orchestrated by the Vatican, as it has been for centuries. Whether or not de Klerk was aware of this is impossible to say. Within the one-world conspiracy, there are many different degrees of knowledge. The threads are numerous and intricate, and doubtless there are only a very few men who are fully aware of all the threads that make up the web. Even within the Jesuit Order itself, many are deliberately kept in the dark about much. There are men, both within and without the priesthood, who frequently tread the corridors of the Vatican, who are only aware of that corner of the global tapestry which they have been assigned to work on. All roads lead to Rome, as Scripture testifies and as history verifies; but not all the roads are discerned by all who are involved, nor how they interlock and overlap. But Scripture says of the Great Whore, mystical Babylon, the Papal system with its headquarters in the city on seven hills, that "the kings of the earth have committed fornication" with her (Rev.17:2). They know her power, and they seek her favour. For many centuries it has been so. And thus does her power over the nations of the earth increase.

On May 14, 1989, after ten years of preparation, a major step forward in the Roman Catholic institution's grassroots subversive activity in South Africa was taken. Its "Pastoral Plan" was launched, the purpose of which was (ostensibly) to invite South Africa's Roman Catholics to become a "community serving humanity"; to improve the quality of "Christianity" within the "Church".[298] But the real purpose of this Plan was far more sinister.

It involved the creation of "Small Christian Communities": neighbourhood communities, meeting weekly in people's homes, and forming a huge network, with the potential to undermine the very foundations of society. The concept came from Latin America, where liberation theology had been so astoundingly successful. The "Catholic Basic Communities", as they were called there, numbered over 53 000

---

[297] *The Natal Witness*, June 27, 1989.
[298] *The Southern Cross*, May 14, 1989.

in Brazil alone by 1982. They were the equivalent of the classic Marxist cell groups which were extremely successful in pre-Soviet Russia, and they were usually led by priests, most often Jesuits. The indoctrination was "meant to develop a political approach to economic and social problems via active disruption or even violent militancy. The `communidades de base' are, therefore, powerful revolutionary tools in the hands of a militant Catholic Church preparing them for use during the forthcoming commotion."[299]

Now these base communities were being established all across South Africa, to mobilise Roman Catholics against the state. In late 1989 the present author was told, by members of the security forces monitoring the radical religious groups in South Africa, that they were well aware of what the "Pastoral Plan" was really all about. Unfortunately, just a few short months later in early 1990, the ANC and other revolutionary organisations were unbanned, and subversive activity against the state was allowed (*by* the state!) to proceed almost unhindered. The National Party under F.W. de Klerk was willingly surrendering, step by step, to the ANC. The enemy could no longer be treated as the enemy by the security forces.

The radical "Commission of Church and Work" of the SA Catholic Bishops Conference made some highly significant statements in its bulletin, *Church and Work*. It said that the Roman Catholic institution in South Africa was, in 1989, placed on a path towards becoming a "social movement" with the potential to "move beyond protest to various forms of non-violent resistance to oppression and exploitation". It declared that the "Church" sought to "re-organise itself" so as to galvanise the people in its parishes, to *transform* the economy and the state.[300] This of course would be by means of the implementation of the Pastoral Plan and the creation of base communities. These statements were Socialistic ones, plain and simple. As for the resistance being "non-violent", they well knew that this was simply not true. When laws are broken by those who deliberately rebel against them, seeking and even provoking confrontation with the

---

[299] *The Vatican Moscow Washington Alliance*, pgs.322,323.
[300] *Church and Work*, Vol.1, No.2, pgs.7,8. Bulletin of the Commission of Church and Work of the SACBC, Congella, South Africa.

security forces, there is violence.

The bulletin stated that the Roman Catholic hierarchy sought to "empower" the trade unions, "to give expression to the aspirations of the poor and marginalised majority in society. When the majority are mobilized in the new social movements which are supported by the church, and when these are sufficiently strong to create a *mass opposition movement* the potential for a *counter-power to the state* exists" (italics added). The South African state was seen as the great enemy, striving for the slavery of the masses, not their emancipation.[301] These were undisguised Marxist statements. "Workers of the World Unite!" was the cry of classic Communism, and trade unions have always played a major role in Communist revolutions. Clearly, according to this bulletin, the Romanist hierarchy sought to build up a sufficiently powerful grassroots movement to bring down the South African government. And this is further borne out by the following statement from the bulletin:

"The Catholic just war theory argues that violence can be justified [against the state] if the immediate shorter term suffering is outweighed by the longer term good which is achieved. In other words, in South Africa, the liberation movements' achievement of democracy, social equality, dignity and an end to institutionalised racism would outweigh the numerous deaths on the road to freedom".[302] The reader is exhorted to read the above quotation again, and to let it sink in. It is saying that the barbaric, murderous tactics of the ANC, SACP, and PAC, which resulted in terrible bloodshed and suffering in South Africa, could be *justified* if these terrorist groups ultimately achieved "democracy, social equality, dignity and an end to institutionalised racism"!

Although the article did not openly advocate this, saying that it had problems, it also did not condemn it outright either. Far from condemning it, it declared that this was the Roman Catholic "just war" theory; and that the violence in South Africa *could* be justifiable.

Here were men, claiming to be members and leaders of the religious institution which calls itself the only true Church on earth, strongly suggesting that the use of horrific violence by the Marxist

---

[301] *Church and Work*, pg.8.
[302] *Church and Work*, pgs.8,9.

guerrilla movements in South Africa, resulting in the deaths of large numbers of people, was justifiable in order to achieve "longer term good"! And there are people who think that Rome has changed; that it is not what it once was; that it has reformed, and is now a respectable, holy, pure Christian church. It is the same monstrous, murderous institution that it always was. Where is even the *resemblance* to a church of Christ, as set forth in the pages of the New Testament? There is none. It bears none of the marks of a true Christian church. The Lord Jesus Christ, the great Head of the true Church, is not present within its walls. He is not there. It is the synagogue of Satan, the Harlot and Mother of Harlots. The Holy Spirit does not dwell within the hearts of its priests and bishops and popes, nor within the hearts of its common followers, but the spirit of Antichrist is certainly present there.

The bulletin also admitted that Roman Catholic priests allowed student groups and workers the use of "church" buildings and were often present at meetings, and that they "challenged the actions of the police and the army".[303] It would not be amiss to say that the ANC/SACP alliance could *never* have succeeded in its goals without the overt and covert support of the Roman Catholic system in South Africa, or that of the various other religious institutions which so actively supported it.

The Papal system's direct, blatant support for the ANC's bloody revolution was manifest on August 4, 1989. Some days before, on July 23, two young Roman Catholics were killed when a limpet mine they were thought to have been planting near the magistrate's court in Athlone exploded. Their burial occurred on August 4, concelebrated by a bishop and no less than seven priests, and attended by approximately 3500 people. Desmond Tutu and Allan Boesak were also present. The priest who preached at the requiem, Peter-John Pearson, said that the two young people had both been "devout Catholics who were committed to the struggle because of their faith. Their Christian ideals led them to become active members of young congresses working for a democratic, free South Africa."[304]

---

[303] *Church and Work*, pg.11.
[304] *The Southern Cross*, August 20, 1989.

These two devout Papists were inspired by their devilish Romish doctrines ("Christian ideals", according to the priest!) to commit a terrorist act; and when they were killed, they were treated as martyrs! According to the police, a banner in the colours of the ANC hung from the "church" steeple, and other banners, some displaying the hammer-and-sickle emblem of the Communist Party, decked the walls. The police were shouted at when they tried to seize the flags of these illegal organisations. At the cemetery, when police removed two ANC flags from the coffins, a brick and stone were thrown at them. Rome was openly flaunting its vile relationship with the SACP/ANC alliance. Despite all the cosmetic surgery done to the Harlot's face in the past few decades, it was still the same bloodstained Harlot that it had ever been. It had entered into a love affair with the SACP/ANC, in order to promote its own sinister objectives; and it did not care in the least what barbaric methods the SACP/ANC used, as long as its own long-term goals were achieved thereby.

In Britain in 1989, the Roman Catholic institution continued its anti-South Africa campaign. It strongly supported the Southern Africa Coalition, an organisation consisting of "churches" in Britain which joined up with trade unions and other groups to urge the imposition of greater sanctions against SA. Several major Roman Catholic societies supported it, and two archbishops were among its patrons.[305] The Romish bishops of England and Wales also called on individual Romanists to end such things as investment in SA.[306] Again we see the international nature of the Vatican's assault on this country.

The month of September 1989 saw a number of protest marches, led by religious leaders, throughout South Africa. On September 13, thousands of people marched in Cape Town. The Roman Catholic participants were led by a bishop and two priests. Dominican and Holy Family nuns, members of the Cape Town Roman Catholic Justice and Peace Commission, and pupils of a Romish college also took part.[307] On the 15th, marches were held in Johannesburg, Pretoria, and Port

---

[305] *The Southern Cross*, October 1, 1989.
[306] *The Southern Cross*, December 17, 1989.
[307] *The Southern Cross*, September 24, 1989.

Elizabeth. Various religious leaders led the Johannesburg march on police headquarters: Romanist, Methodist, Anglican, and leaders of the SACC. Winnie Mandela held the ANC flag, alongside the SA Communist Party flag.[308] The Johannesburg marchers handed the police a memorandum against "police brutality". The crowd numbered about 30 000. Romish archbishop Hurley was one of the marchers, along with bishops, priests and nuns. The master of ceremonies at a prayer service which preceded the march, and which was held in the Anglican cathedral, was radical Romish priest, Smangaliso Mkhatshwa. Jay Naidoo, general secretary of the giant trade union organisation, COSATU, spoke during the service, and said: "We salute the church that today stands with the oppressed in our country."[309]

"Police brutality", of course, had become a favourite phrase of the revolutionary forces in South Africa. Although the truth is that the South African Police did a great deal of good in the black townships, they had been depicted in the worst possible light by the End Conscription Campaign, the SACC, the SACBC, and other groups. These did all they could to denigrate the police - a typical Marxist tactic. Despite the fact that the majority of residents *wanted* the police to stay in the townships, these groups continued to demand that the SAP and SADF leave. The purpose, of course, was to make it impossible for the police to carry out their duties; to be hated by all sections of the society. This would greatly benefit the radicals, because a helpless, despised police force is a powerless one.[310]

On the 21st, over 7000 people, led by various religious leaders, marched through Pietermaritzburg, after a service that was held in the Anglican cathedral. This author personally witnessed and photographed this march. The flags of the banned ANC and SA Communist Party flew openly.[311] It was a sight the author will never forget: to see the international emblem of Communism displayed freely in the country once known around the world as probably the most anti-Communist on earth, to hear the chanting mob, to see the clenched-fist salute, and the confusion on the faces of the spectators.

---

[308] *The Citizen*, September 16, 1989.
[309] *The Southern Cross*, October 1, 1989.
[310] *The Aida Parker Newsletter*, Issue No.131, September 1989.
[311] *The Natal Witness*, September 22, 1989.

Most South Africans were still blissfully unaware of what was occurring. Surely the country of their birth, once so safe and prosperous, could not possibly be on the brink of a Communist takeover? But then (they wondered) why were those Communist flags displayed so openly? Why were the police not clamping down? Why were the streets being taken over by chanting, shouting mobs with hate in their eyes? South Africans were confused, and many were scared. They could hardly believe their eyes. For so long they had fought to prevent a Communist takeover; had sacrificed so much in its defence; had lost so many of their sons on the borders of the country, where they had bravely fought the Communist guerrilla armies seeking to overrun their beloved land. And now the enemy they had fought for so long seemed to be right in their midst, taking over their city centres, flying their terrible flags without interference. And most confusing of all, the enemy was led by *religious* leaders, who held prayer services and prayed for the success of the Communist revolution! South Africans, the vast majority of them, did not understand. The wool had been pulled over their eyes. They had no idea what was in store for them.

The most prominent "minister" at the Pietermaritzburg march was Methodist bishop Mgogo. But also present, marching arm in arm with the others, not far from the ANC and Communist Party flags, was supposed "Evangelical", Michael Cassidy, leader of Africa Enterprise (AE).[312] This organisation was discussed in an earlier chapter. Considered to be an evangelical Christian organisation by many people within and without South Africa, it was in reality ecumenical, charismatic, and very sympathetic to liberation theology. In April, in fact, Michael Cassidy travelled with other AE men to Zambia, where he presented a copy of his new book to President Kenneth Kaunda, a man who had for many years supported the ANC's war against South Africa. Kaunda was actually asked (and agreed) to be patron of an upcoming AE mission to Zambia! In addition, while in Zambia, the AE delegation met with the ANC for "discussion".[313] It was far from being a Christian organisation.

The South African Police had actually received orders *not* to take

---

[312] *The Natal Witness*, September 22, 1989.
[313] *The Natal Witness*, April 26, 1989.

action against those flying the ANC and SACP flags.[314] The National Party government was "softening up" the population, accustoming them to the changes, preparing them for the greater shocks still to come. It was, one step at a time, caving in to the demands of the global conspirators.

On the 22nd, religious leaders led a march through the Durban city centre. The marchers numbered over 20 000. It began with a prayer service at Denis Hurley's cathedral. He led the service, but was joined by various other religious leaders, including Jewish and Muslim representatives. The march ended at the city hall, where many religious leaders, and leaders of the "Mass Democratic Movement" (an ANC-aligned movement), spoke against apartheid - under an ANC banner! The banner of the Communist Party was also visible, as were others. Hurley, as well as Anglican archbishop Nuttall, threatened to withdraw if the Communist flags were not removed. And so they were.[315] This of course was to give the impression that these religious leaders did not support Communism, and doubtless large numbers were convinced. But this one action in reality meant absolutely nothing, considering the very many *other* actions and statements by Hurley and others in *support* of the ANC/SACP alliance.

On September 22, the World Council of Churches announced its annual grants from the Special Fund of its "Program to Combat Racism" (PCR), which was examined earlier in this book. SWAPO (the South West African Peoples' Organisation, a Marxist terror group) received R462 000, the ANC R280 000, and the PAC R187 600.[316] Once again, SWAPO received the largest amount at this time because victory was imminent. With the fall of South West Africa and the birth of Namibia, South Africa's external encirclement would be complete, and from then on all the energies of the World Council of Churches could be directed against South Africa alone.

Did the WCC care that SWAPO was a terrorist, Marxist organisation, that had committed terrible, brutal atrocities for many

---

[314] *The Aida Parker Newsletter*, Issue No.131, September 1989.
[315] *The Southern Cross*, October 8, 1989.
[316] *Gospel Defence League*, October 1989.

years? Not at all. In fact, *before* the grants were announced, some of those who had been imprisoned by SWAPO in its camps showed the scars which they had received while being tortured. And yet the grants were still given! A SWAPO-sympathising religious "minister" *admitted* that the Council of Churches in Namibia (CCN) had *known* about the tortures since *1976*. And yet they kept quiet, and continued to support SWAPO![317]

Some of the released prisoners of SWAPO had been enticed to SWAPO camps in Angola and Zambia by promises of scholarships, made by SWAPO and by the Council of Churches in Namibia. When released, they were so aware of the collaboration between SWAPO and the CCN in the revolution that they refused to be sent to camps controlled by the CCN! How tragic that these men now associated Christianity with the brutal tortures they had received, because men claiming to be ministers, presiding over institutions professing to be churches, had actively and enthusiastically supported SWAPO's bloody terror campaign. In the name of Christ, they had justified SWAPO's atrocities. The *false* "gospel" was now so widespread throughout southern Africa, that multitudes were unaware of any other. To huge numbers of people, "Christianity" meant the demonic doctrine of "liberation theology": Jesus was a social revolutionary, a guerrilla fighter, "sin" was found only within the structures of the present society and the "oppressors", not within every human heart, and "salvation" occurred when the present order collapsed, and a so-called "People's Democracy" rose from its ashes. The dreadful plight of these benighted souls can be compared, in some measure, to that of the Europeans during the Papal Dark Ages, when "Christianity" simply meant Papal oppression to vast multitudes. As long as one obeyed orders, one was safe; if not, awful tortures and a hideous death awaited one.

The CCN had always acted as SWAPO's internal wing. It really originated in 1967, with the Christian Institute, founded by the Anglican denomination and espousing liberation theology. In 1973, the Christian Centre took over its work. Members included Lutherans and Roman Catholics. Although Lutheranism was the largest denomination in South West Africa, the Roman Catholic institution was large too,

---

[317] *Gospel Defence League*, October 1989.

and both were very active in supporting SWAPO. In 1978 it was disbanded and the CCN was founded. Methodists and United Congregationalists were now members as well. By 1985, there were sixteen known SWAPO members employed by the CCN.[318]

In June 1981, the CCN received a "Report on Namibia" from the South African Catholic Bishops Conference, written partly by Denis Hurley. This report called SWAPO "first and foremost a national liberation movement" that was Marxist only because the USSR and other Marxist countries assisted it! The report gave six instances of alleged South African security force brutalities, but did not interview any victim of SWAPO atrocities.

SWAPO could never have won the revolutionary war against South West Africa/Namibia by military means alone. The South African Defence Force was just too powerful, and SWAPO was just too hopelessly inept. But unfortunately for the peoples of South West Africa, the SA government had caved in to international pressure, and had decided to relinquish its administration of South West Africa. When the elections were held, SWAPO won. But it did so by cheating, coercion, blackmail and intimidation. It had the support of the trade unions, the Council of Churches in Namibia, and Anglican, Romanist, and Lutheran institutions. People were intimidated into voting for it. Many SWAPO supporters registered as voters more than once. And false Lutheran baptismal certificates for children much younger than the voting age of eighteen were in wide circulation![319]

Oh, what a perversion of true, biblical Christianity! How great will be the judgement of God upon such men!

SWAPO received vast financial support from the WCC, the Organisation of African Unity, North America, Western Europe, and the Eastern bloc. And of course, the United Nations was in favour of a SWAPO victory, and did all it could to make certain that SWAPO won. The elections were under UN supervision, but in no way was the UN neutral! Years before, after all, it had declared SWAPO to be "the

---

[318] *The Aida Parker Newsletter*, Spring 1989, Issue No.129, "SWA/Namibia: Quo Vadis?" (An *APN* Special Issue).
[319] *The Aida Parker Newsletter*, Spring 1989, Issue No. 129.

sole and authentic voice" of the Namibian people.[320]

SWA/Namibia's "independence" in 1990 served as a chilling warning of what South Africa could expect when the time came for its first supposedly "free and fair" multiracial elections. It was a graphic reminder of how those who cannot come to power through fair means can do so through foul, by using radical "churches", the UN, and the barrel of a gun.

On September 23, 1989, the southern Transvaal region of "Young Christian Students" (YCS), a Roman Catholic group, held a public rally in the Central Methodist Church Hall in Johannesburg, on the theme, "Unban the truth - unban Jesus". It was part of the ecumenical "Standing for the Truth" campaign launched by religious leaders in May 1988.[321]

"Unban the truth - unban Jesus"! The ANC, the SACP, the PAC, and many other radical organisations were banned. This slogan, then, equated Jesus with these organisations; it was stating that their Communist ideology was the truth, and that this "truth" was the same as that of the One who is "the way, the truth, and the life" (Jn.14:6), and that, in banning these groups, the government had banned Jesus! It was, in a nutshell, calling the Lord Jesus Christ a Communist guerrilla fighter. This is the very essence of liberation theology: that the Gospel of Jesus Christ and the Communist ideology of Karl Marx are one and the same. Jesus, in liberation theology, is declared to be on the side of the "poor and oppressed" (the Communist guerrillas and their dupes), and against the "oppressors" (the state and its security forces). The "Kingdom of God" will be ushered in when a Marxist paradise (!) is created. That is the "gospel" of liberation theology, but it is *not* the true Gospel of Jesus Christ, the Son of God.

The chaplain of YCS, priest Chris Langeveld, said that the "Church" had to become part of the defiance campaign to exert pressure for "peace" and to create a situation forcing the government into negotiations. And Methodist bishop Peter Storey saluted the YCS for "calling the youth of the Church back to the commitment of Jesus

---

[320] *The Aida Parker Newsletter*, Spring 1989, Issue No. 129.
[321] *The Southern Cross*, October 8, 1989.

Christ".[322] The New Testament expressly forbids this type of defiance of the secular authorities. As revolutionaries the world over know, the only type of pressure that will force governments into negotiations is widespread violence and anarchy. The YCS chaplain, as a servant of his "Church", knew that Rome was committed to supporting precisely this type of pressure. As for Methodist Storey's comment, urging young people to defy the government had absolutely nothing to do with "the commitment of Jesus Christ". But these ecclesiastical leaders walked in spiritual darkness, as blind leaders of the blind (Matt.15:14). The name of Christ was on their lips, but the Spirit of Christ was not in their hearts.

Would true Christians, who rejected liberation theology and spoke out against the blatant perversion of the Gospel by Romanist, Anglican, Methodist, and other religious leaders, be persecuted under an ANC government? Would these very religious leaders call for such persecution? Let it be understood, incredible as it may seem to some, that brutal persecution of those opposed to liberation theology in South Africa began years ago, and that a document published in 1989 by liberation theology advocates, entitled *The Road to Damascus,* was a direct attack upon the true Gospel and true Christians, and led to increased persecution of those opposed to the hideous and satanic message of liberation theology! We must now turn to an examination of these things, for their significance cannot be underestimated.

The ANC favoured *a* "gospel". It was of course not the true Gospel of the grace of God, but the false "gospel" of liberation theology. In January 1989 John Lamola, of the ANC's Religion Department, declared that it was the Church's "central religious duty" and "evangelical obligation to see to the overthrow of the apartheid regime". He justified the use of violence to accomplish this.[323] And Andrew Mlangeni, a leading ANC figure and a Roman Catholic, said in late 1989 that "clergy" influenced the formation of ANC policies, and that the "Church" would play an important role in a "post-apartheid South Africa" (in other words, in a Communist South

---

[322] *The Southern Cross*, October 8, 1989.
[323] *Revolution or Reconciliation?* pgs.146,147.

Africa).³²⁴ By the "Church", he meant those religious institutions which were pro-ANC, and no others, as will become clear.

The advocates of liberation theology call themselves "progressive" or "prophetic Christians". Those who do not agree with them are labelled "Right-Wing Christian Groups" (RWCG's). Broadly, this term is used to describe *all kinds* of religious groups which reject liberation theology and believe that it is not the Christian's duty to work for the overthrow of the government.³²⁵ All false religious institutions claiming to be Christian hold to *some* true doctrine, and many false groups believe (rightly) that it is wrong to oppose the state, or to support revolution; and all such groups are lumped together under the term, "Right-Wing Christian Groups", by the so-called "progressive Christians", even though differing widely on many other doctrines. Obviously included under this term, then, would be *true* Christian churches, and true believers, even though they would have nothing in common with other "right-wing" groups targeted by the "progressives".

The Institute for Contextual Theology was at the forefront of this assault. In 1985 the ICT decided to *study* the groups which criticised liberation theology and the Kairos Document; and in 1988 the ICT's AGM had as its theme a study of "right-wing religion" in South Africa. It worked with the University of Cape Town's Religious Studies Department in studying this subject. This led to a conference in Harare in August 1989, on "right-wing religion". The papers from this conference contained attacks on such scriptural doctrines as the deity of Christ, his virgin birth, atonement, resurrection, second coming, as well as on the doctrine of salvation.³²⁶ This is because the Christ of God is not the Christ of liberation theology: *that* "Christ" is a revolutionary, a guerrilla fighter; and the doctrine of salvation as set forth in Holy Scripture is not the doctrine of liberation theology: *that* doctrine is one of "salvation" from political "oppression" by violent revolution.

Then in July 1989, the ICT document, *The Road to Damascus: Kairos and Conversion,* was published in South Africa, and also in

---

[324] *The Southern Cross,* January 28, 1990.
[325] *Revolution or Reconciliation?* pgs.150-152.
[326] *Revolution or Reconciliation?* pgs.152-154.

Britain by the Catholic Institute for International Relations and Christian Aid.[327] Thus it was an ecumenical project in which Rome played a major part. It was signed by over 500 liberation theologians from South Africa and Namibia, including such "leading lights" as Desmond Tutu, Allan Boesak, Beyers Naudé, Frank Chikane, and Smangaliso Mkhatshwa, as well as liberation theologians from five other Third World countries (pgs.23-33). It particularly attacked what it termed "the religious right, right-wing Christianity, conservative Christianity"; in summary, "anti-communist evangelicals" (according to the Preamble). It stated categorically: "we denounce all forms of right-wing Christianity as heretical" (pg.13). It distorted the true meaning of Romans 13 (pg.14). It declared that "right-wing Christianity .distorts even the authority of the Bible by treating it as a book from heaven that must be obeyed without understanding or critical comprehension. In some countries, this is called fundamentalism" (pg.14). The only true Christians were said to be those who advocated liberation theology; and those who did not were said to be *persecutors* of the Church! Such "Right-Wing Christians" were accused of idolatry, heresy, apostasy, hypocrisy, and blasphemy! (pgs.10-18).

What a diabolically clever assault on the true Gospel! The very ones who were the *real* persecutors, apostates, idolaters, heretics, hypocrites, blasphemers, and servants of Satan, shifted the charges to others! In this way they deluded multitudes of blacks into believing that *their* version of "Christianity" was the true one, especially since *The Road to Damascus* was widely distributed in English, Afrikaans, Zulu and Sotho.

For centuries, the Roman Catholic institution, claiming to be the "one true Church", persecuted those who refused to acknowledge her, calling *them* persecutors, apostates, idolaters, heretics, hypocrites, blasphemers, Satan-worshippers; today, this evil institution is doing the same thing; but now she is aided by her abominable "Protestant" daughters (Rev.17:5). The Ecumenical Movement has resulted in "Protestant" institutions having the same persecuting spirit that animated the Roman Harlot for centuries.

---

[327] *The Road to Damascus: Kairos and Conversion*, Skotaville Publishers, Braamfontein. © ICT, 1989.

The Road to Damascus followed the typical liberation theology line. It turned the Lord Jesus into a political liberator, seeking the "liberation" of those who are "oppressed, discriminated against or marginalized….the victims of racism, sexism, political repression" (pg.8, including footnote 5). It made him into a prophet of a "new world order" (pg.8). It completely distorted the truth about him. It also distorted the account of the conversion of Saul of Tarsus, stating that, as he had been converted from being a persecutor of Christians, so today those who "persecute" the radical terrorist-supporting "Christians" must be converted (pgs.19,20). The truth, however, was that the religious radicals were *not* true Christians, but people who supported those who bombed innocent people, burned people to death, tortured them, etc. The true Christians whom Saul was persecuting were being persecuted simply for their faith, for worshipping the Lord and serving him, *not* for participating in riots and revolutions!

The document stated that Christians *must* work for justice and (political) liberation - that this is their mission; and that those not involved in such a work worship a false God (pg.10). It brushed over Communism as being merely a convenient scapegoat for the state, declaring that the "progressive Christians" (i.e. the religious radicals) were branded as "Communists" for the same reason (pg.12). "A further characteristic of right-wing Christianity," it stated, "is that it is fanatically *anti-Communist"* (pg.15).

Inevitably, such a radical document led to *persecution* of "right-wing believers" by the pro-Marxist "Church". And although the term, "right-wing believers", is very broad and includes many non-Christian groups, it *also* includes all *true* believers in Christ, who have been regenerated by his Word and Spirit, have called upon his name in repentance and saving faith, and have been washed from their sins in his blood.

Pastors in the black townships were put under pressure to teach liberation theology. The revolutionaries used to force black "right-wing believers" to open their wicked, illegal "People's Courts" with prayer and Bible readings. "Right-wing believers" were threatened with necklacing if they did not participate in killings. Their children were forced to be in the front of attacks, and if they were not seen to be participating enthusiastically, they were labelled as "informers" and "sell-outs".[328]

All indications are, then, that under an ANC government, the radical "Church" (Rome and its "Protestant" daughters - those within the SACC and other radical groups) will *continue* to war against all who oppose it. In Nicaragua, when the Marxist Sandinistas came to power, the pro-Marxist "Church" spearheaded the attack on "right-wing Christians". Ominously, Roman Catholic priest Smangaliso Mkhatshwa said in 1990 that ICT representatives had visited Nicaragua to learn from it, and that even after the "people's government" was in power in South Africa, they must *continue to sustain* theological support for this government.[329]

For while true Christians, believing that it is the Lord who "removeth kings, and setteth up kings" (Dan.2:21), will submit themselves in all lawful matters to a Marxist government, in accordance with Rom.13:1-7, they will *never* obey any government decree forbidding them to preach the true Gospel, or to worship the Lord as his Word decrees, or to live as his Word commands. In this they will obey Acts 5:29. And *for* this, they may indeed face persecution. The Lord's will be done.

Certain events of immense significance which occurred in 1989 must be mentioned In this year the world witnessed what was portrayed enthusiastically by the international media as the "collapse of Communism" in the Soviet Union and Eastern Europe. It is outside the purposes of this book to examine these events in detail. Suffice it to say, here, that there is a vast body of evidence to show that Communism in the old USSR and Eastern Europe did *not* collapse in 1989: that it was a deliberate Communist smokescreen, designed to fool the West into disarming, and into financially supporting the now supposedly "former" Communist regimes; and it worked. Just some of the evidence that this "fall" was stage-managed is the following: it was planned *years before* it actually happened;[330] the same people remained in power behind the scenes; after 1989, in almost every one

---

[328] *Revolution or Reconciliation?* pgs.157-159.
[329] *Revolution or Reconciliation?* pgs.159-165.
[330] *New Lies for Old,* by Anatoly Golitsyn. Dodd, Mead and Company, Inc., New York. 1984.

of the Eastern European countries, Communists resumed open control, having been re-elected (in what were no doubt rigged elections, as was to occur in South Africa in 1994) under the new names of "Social Democrats", etc.; and around the world after 1989, Communism continued to expand, Communist guerrilla forces continued to receive funds and support from Moscow, and South Africa fell to the Communist forces in 1994.

CHAPTER TWENTY-EIGHT

1990: UNLEASHING THE BEAR

February 2, 1990, was the date on which President F.W. de Klerk officially and publicly initiated the process of surrendering South Africa into the hands of its enemies.

On that day, after years, indeed decades, of pressure from the international community, the United Nations, the Vatican, the World Council of Churches, the South African Council of Churches, trade unions, the South African Communist Party, the African National Congress, and a vast array of other groups, de Klerk announced that the SACP, ANC, PAC, and other revolutionary organisations were unbanned, and that Nelson Mandela would be released. The international conspirators had won a resounding victory, and South Africa was on the slippery slide to total disaster.

The National Party government had been capitulating for a long time prior to this date, of course. But on February 2, this capitulation was made official, and the revolutionary forces that South Africa's sons had sacrificed so much to keep at bay were unleashed on the Republic, legally, with a stroke of the pen. The enemy was now free to operate within South Africa's borders, and during the next few years would drench this lovely land in the blood of thousands upon thousands of people.

As Nelson Mandela, living symbol of the ANC, walked out of prison a free man on February 11, being ecstatically hailed around the world as the saviour of South Africa, and as the jubilant hordes of ANC, SACP and PAC "exiles" began to prepare to flood back into the country, ordinary law-abiding citizens of all races shuddered. This was the much-vaunted "New South Africa", and it did not take long for South Africans to find out exactly what it would be like.

The ANC lost no time in taking advantage of the new opportunities that were presented to it. It had *no intention* of forsaking its armed revolution: it could now conduct it with far more ease, and success, than ever before. Nelson Mandela, after his release, actually called for the "armed struggle" to be *intensified*.[331] ANC insurgents continued to secretly establish hideouts and caches of weapons in South Africa.[332]

The ANC had a definite strategy to seize power. The armed revolution was a prominent part of that strategy. In addition, it planned to use mass mobilisation: strikes, mass defiance, rent boycotts, rallies, etc. All of these would serve to mobilise the masses, and would of course lead to violence (which the ANC desired). From February 21 to March 6, 84 people were killed, and 129 injured.

The ANC also planned to destroy the independent black national states and homelands. In early 1990, these erupted in ANC-inspired violence. The only two not touched by the violence were the Transkei and KaNgwane - because both were pro-ANC.

Another important part of the ANC's strategy was the use of underground structures: trained agents sought to infiltrate and control political organisations, unions, the media, etc. This of course is standard Marxist policy. And internationally, the ANC continued to insist that sanctions against SA be maintained.[333]

The ANC, in a document dated January 8, 1990, praised the religious leaders' "Standing for the Truth" campaign, saluting prominent religious figures who had sided with the ANC.[334] And it also stated: "There is also a continuing responsibility on the part of the religious community to deepen their engagement in the struggle to end apartheid....In the period ahead of us, greater rather than less involvement will be expected of the religious community."[335] And indeed, as soon as the terrorist organisations were unbanned and Mandela was released, the pro-Red "churches" lost no time in fulfilling the ANC's wish. In April, 40 South African religious leaders met with ANC officials to discuss the return of "exiles". The head of the ANC's Religious Affairs Department, Anglican priest John Lamola, said that the discussion would be about the churches' response to the exiles' "plight". The religious delegates included representatives from the

---

[331] *Signposts*, Vol.9, No.2, 1990.
[332] *The Citizen*, July 23, 1990.
[333] *Signposts*, Vol.9, No.2, 1990.
[334] *Signposts*, Vol.9, No.2, 1990.
[335] *Revolution or Reconciliation*, pgs.145,146.

SACC, the SACBC, and the Muslim, Hindu and Jewish communities.[336]

Lamola declared that the role of the religious community in SA was "an affirmation of the morality of the liberation struggle, particularly as led by the ANC."[337] In other words, he was saying that the "churches", by their open support of the ANC and other terrorist groups, had declared the revolution to be right and good and proper! And in this he was correct: that is precisely what they had done. Lamola, after all, had stated in January 1989 that it was the Church's "central religious duty" and "evangelical obligation to see to the overthrow of the apartheid regime"; and he had justified the use of violence.[338] In November 1991, he was to become personal assistant to Frank Chikane, general secretary of the SACC.[339]

The ANC declared, in April, that it would work to transform religious communities "into solid centres of resistance and struggle".[340] The pro-Marxist "churches" had been such centres for many years already; but they would be still further "Communized" in the years ahead.

In May, the National Party and the ANC held talks and reached agreement on certain matters. Mandela said that they were now *closer* to each other. Further talks were planned. President de Klerk called the talks "an important breakthrough".[341] The South African Catholic Bishops Conference issued a statement calling the meeting between the two "one of the most welcome events in recent South African history".[342] Indeed, from the perspective of the SACBC, it was most welcome, for it indicated that the NP was losing ground, and rapidly, to the ANC.

The first few months of 1990 saw incredible changes taking place in South Africa, and none of them for the better. Not just Nelson Mandela, but many other terrorists in prison were released, and were

---

[336] *The Citizen*, April 23, 1990.
[337] *Revolution or Reconciliation?* pgs.147,148.
[338] *Revolution or Reconciliation?* pgs.146,147.
[339] *Revolution or Reconciliation?* pg.148.
[340] *Revolution or Reconciliation?* pg.148.
[341] *The Citizen*, May 5, 1990.
[342] *The Southern Cross*, May 27, 1990.

permitted to publicly proclaim their ideology; the Communist leaders continued to call for an intensified "armed struggle"; the government and the ANC began to negotiate, with the government constantly giving in to the ANC's demands; there was talk of uniting the ANC's armed wing, Mkhonto we Sizwe (MK), with the SA Defence Force; etc. And inevitably, the violence and killings escalated. In the townships, black political leaders were murdered, the people were intimidated, and at least nineteen people were brutally "necklaced", as the now legalized ANC and other terrorist organisations unleashed a tidal wave of terror.[343]

After the release of "political prisoners" (i.e. terrorists) in 1989 and especially after the release of Mandela in February 1990, there was an upsurge in *witchcraft cases and witch-burnings,* according to the Human Sciences Research Council. Many of the youths who burned to death those accused of witchcraft flew the ANC and SACP flags.[344] In other words, they reverted to their traditional beliefs as they began to scent victory politically, showing just how thin was the veneer of "Christianity" they assumed. The SACC and SACBC spoke of the "Christians" who supported the revolution, but in truth these people were unregenerate, deceived souls, many of them equally comfortable with their ancient tribal beliefs as with the so-called "Christianity" (which was no Christianity at all) of the SACC and of Popery.

Nelson Mandela began to travel the world, drumming up support for the ANC, and being praised by the world media as a moderate, wise, reasonable, dignified man who had suffered unjustly at the hands of the "oppressive white government" of South Africa, by being imprisoned for 27 years. Little or nothing was said about the *reasons* for his imprisonment, or his definite Communist links. He was hailed everywhere as the future president of South Africa.

The Vatican's Jesuit/Illuminati forces, operating through a maze of organizations in SA and around the world, had worked long and hard for Mandela's release, knowing what a massive boost this would give to the revolutionary forces. On June 15, Mandela had a private

---

[343] *Signposts,* Vol.9, No.3, 1990.
[344] *Roca Report,* No.43, July 1992. Published by Roca, Menlo Park, South Africa.

audience with the pope of Rome, John Paul II, in the Vatican. Welcoming Mandela, the one whom God's Word identifies as the Antichrist said, "Thanks be to God that we can meet." Later he said to Mandela, "God bless your initiatives." The two men were photographed holding hands. Mandela asked John Paul to take a clear position in support of sanctions against South Africa. According to Mandela, the pontiff did *not* ask the ANC to renounce violence. He told the press that the pope "apparently understands the situation better than some of you do. He has made no such request."[345]

The Vatican was clearly jubilant. Its years of work were paying off: the fall of the Republic of South Africa was now not too far away. The pope did not ask the ANC to renounce violence, because it knew that violence was the only way for it to achieve victory, and because the Papacy has always supported violence if its goals are furthered thereby. The ANC was doing the Vatican's bidding in South Africa, and the pope was perfectly willing to "bless" its initiatives, knowing full well that these included the use of horrifying violence.

Millions of Roman Catholics worldwide saw that their pope, the head of their "Church" and the man they considered to be the Vicar of Christ upon earth, had joyfully welcomed Mandela as a friend and hero. These millions, ignorant of the sinister forces at work behind the scenes, assumed that Nelson Mandela was a good, moderate man, a man who favoured the Roman Catholic "Church", the best man to rule South Africa.

Also in June, Mandela visited the United States, where so much of the ANC's support had come from over the years. Guests at exclusive dinners paid up to $50 000 to dine with him, and the funds went to the Mandela Freedom Fund.[346] He was enthusiastically welcomed by American religious leaders - Roman Catholic, Protestant, Orthodox, Jewish and Muslim. They praised him highly, gave him huge sums of money, and declared their support for continued sanctions.[347] Spiritually blind ministers of Satan, they rejoiced at the release of a convicted Communist terrorist, and eagerly anticipated the long-

---

[345] *The Citizen,* June 16, 1990; and *The Southern Cross,* July 1, 1990.
[346] *The Citizen,* June 18, 1990.
[347] *The Southern Cross,* July 8, 1990.

awaited ANC victory in South Africa.

Speaking at a Harlem, New York "church" service, Mandela said that the ANC was an organisation brought up in the atmosphere of religion. "The religious influence in the ANC has been strong right from the beginning; our first president, Dr Dube, was a well-known religious leader," he said. Then, regarding the role of the US "churches" in South Africa's revolution, he said: "You are our comrades in arms, you are our brothers and sisters...."[348]

Again it must be pointed out that the ANC could never have met with the success it did without the active support of religious institutions, and that religious Communism is the most dangerous type of all. Many ignorant people are fooled into believing that the ANC is not, therefore, hostile to Christianity. But there is biblical Christianity, and there is the perverted, wicked "Christianity" of the Papacy, the World Council of Churches, etc., which is "Christian" *in name only*, and it is *this* that the ANC favours, and nothing else!

Consider the following. In July 1990, the South African Communist Party declared that it "regretted" supporting Soviet intervention in Hungary, Czechoslovakia and Afghanistan; had ceased to support *all* Soviet foreign policy decisions; and that it was in favour of religious freedom in a secular state! It declared, "Believers are welcome to join our party," and, "We Communists feel we are closer to the moral content of Christianity, Muslim, Hindu and Jewish teaching than many an apartheid *dominee* (minister)".[349] This was a typical Communist smokescreen. Various Communist states guaranteed religious freedom on paper in the past - even as they persecuted Christians. Yes, "believers" were welcome to join - but to do so, they would have to comply with Communist Party doctrine and methodology, and thus the only ones who would join would be those who were pro-Red themselves, not true Christians. That Communism is close to the "moral content" of the *false* "Christianity" of Romanism, the World Council of Churches, etc., cannot be doubted; but it is far removed from *true, biblical* Christianity.

As for saying that it regretted supporting Soviet expansionism, and that it was no longer supporting every Soviet foreign policy decision,

---

[348] *The Citizen*, June 22, 1990.
[349] *The Sunday Times*, July 22, 1990.

this too was a deliberate smokescreen. In light of the cleverly-orchestrated "changes" in the USSR and Eastern Europe in 1989, designed by the Communist conspirators to lull the West into a false sense of security, the SACP made these statements, making it appear as if it, too, was changing, and as if there were serious divisions within the international Communist movement, so that Communism in South Africa or elsewhere was no great threat any more. It was all a lie.

In July, President de Klerk hosted a "Church Conference" in Pretoria. He had asked churches to contribute guidelines to the process of negotiations and the content of a new constitution for the country. Over 200 delegates from over 100 denominations were present. The SACC boycotted the conference, but agreed to a later one, to be held in November, on condition that SACC general secretary, Frank Chikane, was co-chairman. The July conference was considered an "exploratory exercise" to give the "less experienced churches the opportunity of discussing socio-political matters".[350]

These "less experienced churches" were those which had either not previously been involved in liberation theology and revolutionary activism, or if they had, their involvement had been very minor. Thus, the ANC/SACC had succeeded in involving even more "churches" in the "struggle" than ever before, and under the *leadership* of the SACC!

Accordingly as planned, the "National Conference of Churches" was held in Rustenburg from the 5th to the 9th of November. It was controlled from beginning to end by the SACC. Frank Chikane, who was also a United Democratic Front vice-president, was co-chairman of the conference. Barney Pityana, director of the World Council of Churches' Programme to Combat Racism, was conference co-ordinator. Of the 26 foreign observers, 22 came from ecumenical organisations such as the WCC and others. Of the thirteen main speakers, nine had close ties with the SACC. Beyers Naudé, prominent SA liberation theologian, was a key speaker. A specially-invited guest was the president of AZAPO, the radical "Azanian People's Organisation". "Azania" was the name certain radical groups gave to South Africa.

---

[350] *Gospel Defence League*, August 1990.

The conference promoted a Socialistic redistribution of land and wealth, accepted the principle of "one man, one vote", and a "transfer of economic power".

The "Rustenburg Declaration", which issued from the conference, was in favour of liberation theology. It defined sin as "structural", not personal, in accordance with liberation theology doctrine, which of course was in line with Marxism. Colonialism and apartheid were the great sins.

It also *lied* about the groups represented at the conference! Obviously it wanted to convey the impression that it was the only authentic voice of the South African churches. It said that there were 330 representatives of 80 denominations and 40 organisations participating in the conference, and it claimed to represent 95% of all South African churches. Later, however, after being challenged, it said that there were 230 representatives of 107 denominations and organisations. Yet once again it was lying: there were 40 denominations and 48 organisations represented![351]

We see, therefore, that in accordance with the ANC's express wishes, as set forth in its January 8 document, the radical "churches" were indeed "deepening their engagement" in the so-called "struggle". They were doing all in their power to ensure victory for the ANC in South Africa.

In November, the World Council of Churches announced the year's grants from its "Special Fund of the Programme to Combat Racism": US $549 000. Of this, $235 000 went to the ANC and PAC.[352] WCC financial support for these terrorist groups was continuing.

It is very revealing to examine the income of the South African Council of Churches. The plain truth is that *most* of the people within the member-churches of the SACC *did not support the SACC!* This was evident from the extremely small proportion of the SACC's budget which came from the annual affiliation fees of the member-

---

[351] *Signposts*, Vol.10, No.1, 1991; and *Frontline Fellowship News*, 1990/6 Special Edition. Published by Frontline Fellowship, Newlands, South Africa.
[352] *Gospel Defence League*, November/December 1990.

denominations. From 1975 to 1981, only 0.3% of the SACC's average yearly income came from its members; in each of the years 1987-1990, members' fees were only 0.2% of the total income; in 1990, 21 of the 37 member-institutions had outstanding fees![353] Quite plainly, the majority of the members of the various denominations that were in membership with the SACC did not approve of what the SACC was doing, or of what the leaders of their denominations were doing, in supporting it! And yet the SACC loved to portray itself as the authentic voice of the vast majority of "Christians" in South Africa. This was a lie, and the SACC knew it was a lie, but it continued propagating it anyway.

Where, then, did most of the SACC's money come from? The answer: foreign donors. From 1987 to 1990, 96.6% came from such donations and grants, mainly from European and North American religious organisations.[354]

Most of the SACC's money was given over to its "Justice and Society" department. This was used for (among other things) supporting political activists who fled South Africa to escape arrest, or to join the ANC or PAC; providing legal aid to those accused of terrorist and other offences; and aid to the families of "exiles", most of the beneficiaries being ANC or PAC members.[355] Hardly what one could call using money for the Lord's work! But the SACC was not doing the Lord's work. It was "Christian" in name only, and it was doing the work of the devil.

In September 1990, the South African Defence Force, despite massive military build-ups in SA's frontline states,[356] announced drastic cuts. These included the disbandment of an electronic workshop and a signal unit; the closure of an air force base by the end of 1991; the disbandment of three squadrons, and of a light aircraft flying school; etc.[357] The government of F.W. de Klerk was surrendering to the forces of Communism, and a major part of that

---

[353] *Revolution or Reconciliation?* pgs.167-169.
[354] *Revolution or Reconciliation?* pgs.169-171.
[355] *Revolution or Reconciliation?* pgs.172-180.
[356] *The McAlvany Intelligence Advisor*, Winter 1990. Special Report.
[357] *The Citizen*, September 28, 1990.

surrender included the severe weakening of the Defence Force. These announcements were just the beginning. Step by step, South Africa's once-mighty security forces were being destroyed. Step by step, the National Party government pursued its policy of handing over power to the ANC/SACP alliance.

CHAPTER TWENTY-NINE

1991: "REAPING A WHIRLWIND THE CHURCHES HELPED TO SOW"

In February 1991, John Kane-Berman, the executive director of the South African Institute of Race Relations, a multiracial, anti-apartheid body, stated that the "Christian" leadership in South Africa "has helped to legitimise violence as an instrument of liberation", and that "black people in the townships are reaping a whirlwind of violence that the churches have helped to sow."[358]

Immediately, screams of outrage were heard from the radical religious leaders. Frank Chikane said, "we are disgusted by the vicious and unwarranted attack on the churches by Mr John Kane-Berman," and, "we have always believed and still believe the apartheid system is the primary cause of violence in our country." How apartheid could still be responsible, when apartheid as a political system was now dead in South Africa (apart from the fact that as yet blacks had not participated in a general election), Mr Chikane conveniently failed to say. He indignantly referred to Mr Kane-Berman's statements as a "vicious *and unwarranted* attack on the [ANC-supporting, pro-Marxist] churches"; yet not only is there the simply overwhelming evidence that the statements were true, but the ANC Youth League *admitted* it, in its response, as reported in *The Citizen* of February 6, 1991. It declared that "the Church advocated the use of organised violence employed by a disciplined liberation movement to advance the cause of liberation."[359] What Frank Chikane denied, the ANC Youth League itself confirmed! The ANC well knew, and had frequently acknowledged, the immense help given to it by the radical "churches"; but a prominent leader of those very "churches", who was perfectly aware of the truthfulness of the charges, tried to deny it.

Meanwhile, in the black townships, the "whirlwind of violence that the churches helped to sow" continued to rage, and daily life for multiplied thousands of black people was one of despair and sheer terror.

---

[358] *Revolution or Reconciliation?* pg.4.
[359] *Revolution or Reconciliation?* pgs.5,6.

In January 1991, Oliver Tambo, speaking at a huge rally in Durban, said that the ANC would *intensify* its campaign of "mass action". The decision to do so had been made in December 1990, by its National Consultative Conference. It had decided to use mass action, demonstrations, etc., to take mass action into the white areas, to build "self-defence units", and to formulate a national "peace committee" which would include "churches", COSATU, and youth. It also planned to discredit the government internationally.[360]

The South African Institute of Race Relations, in its publication, *Spotlight,* stated that the immediate aims of the ANC's mass mobilisation campaign included forcing the government to abdicate; forcing it to give in to the establishment of an interim government, and to agree to the ANC's demand for a constituent assembly which would prepare a new constitution; generating increased support for and membership of the ANC; forcing homeland governments and black councils to collapse; etc. In addition, it had other aims, not publicly acknowledged. These included destroying the power of Chief Buthelezi, the ANC's rival amongst the Zulu people; creating a climate of fear and instability, and the perception that only the ANC could limit this; and discrediting the security forces.[361]

We shall see, in the following pages, just how it pursued these objectives, and just how successful it was in achieving some of them.

At the Durban rally, Tambo was presented with a spear and shield by fiery ANC veteran Harry Gwala, who said, "We are not begging for freedom, we will take it by force if we have to."[362] The armed revolution was certainly not over! And yet "church" support for this terrorist organisation continued unabated. A message from Roman Catholic archbishop, Denis Hurley, was even read to the crowd before the meeting began.

The Roman Catholic institution was deeply involved in assisting returning ANC "exiles". Priest Emmanuel Lafont was a key organiser

---

[360] *The Aida Parker Newsletter,* Issue No.143, May/June 1991.
[361] *The Citizen,* April 19, 1991.
[362] *The Natal Mercury,* January 14, 1991.

of their reception and registration, together with nun Shelagh Mary Waspe of the Johannesburg Roman Catholic Justice and Peace Commission. And the Catholic Renewal Centre in Kensington South was the *main venue* for their reception and registration.[363]

The United Nations, too, was involved: the government actually agreed to allow the UN to help repatriate "exiles".[364] Both the UN and the ANC welcomed this decision, and not surprisingly: the UN had always been fully on the ANC's side, and had helped a number of other Marxist terrorist groups, most recently SWAPO in South West Africa. For many, many years, the South African government had been very anti-UN, but now this had changed: little by little, the UN started to involve itself in South Africa's affairs, with the approval of the National Party government. This was because the National Party was no longer the National Party of the past. It was now controlled by men who were in favour of the "New World Order" desired by the Vatican, the Illuminati, the UN, and international Communism. These men fervently wanted to see South Africa take its place in the New World Order, as did the conspirators internationally, who had laboured so long and hard for precisely that.

Consider the following. In Cape Town in March 1991, the United States ambassador to South Africa, William Swing, told an engineering conference that a "new world order" was sweeping aside the old, and that South Africa was part of the revolution. He said some called it "freedom fever", others called it a "democracy surge". "Bipolarity as well as ideological confrontation are giving way increasingly to pragmatism, consensus politics and some rather unorthodox alliances". He said this was largely due to the "failures of Communism". The "collapse" of Communism in Europe, he declared, meant that one-party governments in Third World countries were now looking to other systems and were now receptive to multi-party democracy, and would consequently be examining "South Africa's transition to democracy". And he stated that "an increased emergence of multilateralism" would include "an enhanced role for the United Nations", best illustrated by the recent UN action in the Gulf War.[365]

---

[363] *The Southern Cross*, March 17, 1991.
[364] *The Natal Mercury*, March 23, 1991.
[365] *The Sunday Tribune*, March 24, 1991.

How diabolically clever the conspirators had been! By fooling the world into believing that the changes in Eastern Europe meant that Communism was dead, that those countries were now "free" and "democratic", and that the "New World Order" was something wonderful, an order in which all countries of the world would be united in peace, living as one big, happy global family, they had succeeded in concealing the fact that the New World Order was *precisely* what international Communism had always been working for! Communism was not dead in Eastern Europe or anywhere else, and the peoples of those countries were not truly "free". The tactics had simply changed: by making it appear to the world as if Communism was dead, and all the old Communists had suddenly been converted into freedom-loving democrats - whereas in reality, behind the scenes, the same men, the same powerful forces, were in control as before - the world had been deceived. A major step towards global enslavement had been taken, hidden behind such terms as "freedom", "democracy", and the "death of Communism". And the United Nations was to play a major role in the future.

And deep in the shadows, behind the United Nations, behind international Communism, behind the liberal, closet-Socialist rulers of the US, behind the pro-Marxist World Council of Churches, behind the leftist world media, were the Jesuit/Illuminati forces working for the subjugation of the whole world to the Vatican.

Seen in this context, South Africa's "transition to democracy", spoken of by William Swing and heard often on the lips of the ANC/SACP leadership, world leaders, etc., meant its fall to the ANC/SACP alliance, and thus its absorption into the New World Order.

Knowing the deep aversion most South Africans had to Communism, the ANC, in its efforts to win the support of the population, never mentioned the fact that it was controlled by the South African Communist Party. Both the ANC and its affiliated trade union movement were very reluctant to identify just how many Communist Party members were involved in their leadership positions - or who they were. But the fact was that Communist Party members held *top positions* in the ANC and the unions; and the Communist

Party was *deeply involved* in all aspects of the ANC's negotiations with the government.[366] This was because, as has been shown in this book, the ANC years ago came under the control of the SACP, which in turn was controlled from Moscow. Yet millions of South Africans remained ignorant of this fact. Yes, they saw that it was allied to the SACP, but had no idea that it was *controlled by* the SACP. The ANC readily admitted its alliance with the SACP. At its national conference in Durban in 1991, it confirmed and vigorously defended this alliance. Very significantly, it added that, "within the churches", this alliance was not seen as a problem![367] As far as the Roman Catholic and SACC-affiliated "churches" were concerned, this was very true.

From time to time, ANC leaders gave the game away. Chris Hani, leader of MK, the ANC's armed wing, when speaking in the US in 1991 where he was a guest of the Communist Party USA, said that the ANC retained "a very close relationship with the USSR", and that the Soviets continued to train ANC cadres at their military academies. He said, "We have enough guerrillas to resume the armed struggle although I hope this does not happen. We have accepted the mistakes and shortcomings of Socialism in other countries. We are studying their mistakes to ensure that *when we rule South Africa as a Communist government* we do not make the same mistakes" (italics added).[368]

This statement revealed that the ANC was a Communist organisation. It also revealed that Communism in the territory of the old USSR was certainly not dead. Moscow continued to support the Communist ANC. In various Communist countries, the powers that be had simply reformed themselves in order to be even more effective, while giving the world the impression that Communism had collapsed.

The *religious* influence on the South African Communist Party was actually admitted by Jeremy Cronin, a member of the SACP's central committee. Addressing a meeting of the Johannesburg Roman Catholic Justice and Peace Commission on the subject of "The Communist Party and Religion", on April 23, 1991, he said that some of the most

---

[366] *The Sunday Times,* April 28 and May 5, 1991.
[367] *The Citizen,* July 5, 1991.
[368] *The Aida Parker Newsletter,* Issue No.143, May/June 1991.

dedicated members of the SACP were "committed Christians", and that "Communism shares with Christianity a belief in the all-important value of the human person". He himself had attended a Roman Catholic school.[369]

Communism has absolutely *no* respect for the "value of the human person", as the multiplied millions of victims of Communism would testify, if they could. But then, nor has Romanism, as its own multiplied millions of victims would testify, if *they* could. Nor has the Communist-supporting World Council of Churches or its various national affiliates. Such "Christians" as were members of these institutions could easily join the Communist Party, because they were strangers to the saving grace of God, not true Christians at all. Rome, of course, had objectives of its own in supporting the Communist Party. It was the muscle which the Vatican was using to bring about the collapse of South Africa, and thereby to promote its own objectives in the country.

Since the unbanning of the ANC and other groups in 1990, the violence had increased dramatically, especially between the ANC and Inkatha, the predominantly Zulu organisation based in Natal. The majority of the Zulus were politically conservative, anti-Communist, and absolutely opposed to the ANC. The ANC deceptively shifted the blame for the violence to Inkatha and the security forces, whereas in fact it had been initiated by the ANC. Nelson Mandela, speaking on May 16, 1991, warned the government that if it failed to stop the violence, it could spread to white areas. He said, "When they ["our people"] realise that the government is working with the black organisations that are killing our people, they will arm themselves and go to the white areas, and kill innocent people there."[370] Even though he added that the ANC, PAC, and AZAPO did not support this, it was nevertheless a thinly-veiled *suggestion* to black militants. The ANC/SACP tactic was, first, to initiate the violence; and then secondly, to blame it on Inkatha when its members retaliated, or on the government when the security forces clamped down to restore law and order! The media, of course, took the ANC's version of events at face

---

[369] *The Southern Cross*, May 12, 1991.
[370] *The Citizen*, May 17, 1991.

value.

On June 16, Mandela said that the ANC would not compromise over its demands for a constituent assembly and an interim government, and warned of more mass action if these demands were not met.[371] According to the Communist strategy, the first stage of its planned takeover of the country involved removing power from the hands of the government, and establishing an interim government dominated by the ANC. Chris Hani, the ANC's military chief, said on the same day that the ANC would negotiate for "democracy", not special co-existence with the National Party government. "The aim of negotiations," he said, "is to take power from the government and to transfer power from the minority to the majority."[372] In other words, the ANC was involved in the negotiations, not in order to compromise, to give as well as take, but solely for the purpose of bulldozing its way to power. It was not negotiating, it was demanding - and the government was giving in to every demand.

Hani also said that the ANC was the only organisation representing all of South Africa's people - which, although patently untrue, was nevertheless perfectly in keeping with the United Nations' declaration in 1974 that the ANC was the "authentic representative of the overwhelming majority of the peoples of South Africa". According to the ANC itself, by June 1991 it only had about 500 000 members![373] That was far below the membership figures of Chief Buthelezi's Inkatha Freedom Party, the largest political party in South Africa. But the ANC was the puppet of far greater powers, and regardless of popular support, they were going to see to it that their puppet came to power, either by negotiations or by violence. It was in June, in fact, that the ANC confirmed for the first time that its leadership had ordered a "back-up" plan of armed revolution, if its negotiations with the government failed. This included establishing arms caches in South Africa, to create a national uprising.[374]

The unbanning of the ANC just over a year earlier had not in any way made that organisation give up the armed revolution. It had

---

[371] *The Citizen*, June 17, 1991.
[372] *The Citizen*, June 17, 1991.
[373] *Revolution or Reconciliation?* pg.206.
[374] *The Citizen*, June 24, 1991.

simply made it far easier for it to conduct such a revolution, for it could now do so from within South Africa's borders! The country was teetering on the brink of an ANC-inspired bloodbath.

The World Council of Churches' Programme to Combat Racism (PCR) continued to financially support the ANC and PAC. From 1970 to 1991, it gave a total of US $726 500 to the PAC, and $1 351 500 to the ANC! These grants were, for the most part, funded by appeals to member-churches, governments, etc. The principal British donor was the Methodist institution.[375]

The world's Anglican leaders said in April 1991 that sanctions against SA had been successful in bringing about change, and should only be lifted after consultation with black leaders (by whom they meant the ANC). They said that they were "deeply distressed" at the government's failure to protect black people - but conveniently overlooked the fact that whenever the security forces were sent in to do so, the ANC and other radical groups demanded their withdrawal. They also gave "thanks to God" for the release, over a year earlier, of Nelson Mandela, and also for the radical Rustenburg Conference, examined in the previous chapter.[376] The worldwide Anglican institution was plainly and publicly on the side of the terrorists.

The South African Council of Churches and the South African Catholic Bishops Conference acted as channels for large sums of money from the European Community to radical organisations in South Africa. The EC had been using the SACC and SACBC for this purpose since 1985. By June 1991, a total of approximately R420 million, or 87.5 million pounds sterling, had been allocated. The EC had stated that these funds were to be used for "welfare and humanitarian" purposes; but as it declined to monitor how they were spent, this meant absolutely nothing. The evidence points to the funds being used for *political* purposes.[377] The EC was heavily Roman Catholic, so once again we see evidence of the Vatican's full-fledged support for the South African revolution.

The evidence continued to mount up. For example, on June 16,

---

[375] *Revolution or Reconciliation?* pgs.36,37.
[376] *The Citizen*, April 15, 1991.
[377] *Revolution or Reconciliation?* pgs.181-191.

1991, to commemorate "Soweto Day" as the day had become known among the radicals, the Regina Mundi Roman Catholic "church" in Soweto was filled with 1500 members of the PAC, AZAPO, and the Workers Organisation for Socialist Action (WOSA).[378]

Also in June, Roman Catholic cardinal Roger Etchegaray, Vatican envoy and president of the Pontifical Council of Justice and Peace, visited South Africa on a "fact-finding mission". A Vatican statement said that his visit was meant to "confirm the constant concern of the Apostolic See in view of a peaceful socio-political evolution of South Africa". He met President de Klerk and Pik Botha, the Minister of Foreign Affairs, on June 20. He also met members of the Inkatha Freedom Party, ANC, PAC, AZAPO, and the South African Council of Churches.[379] A high-ranking Vatican official meeting with leaders of all the political organisations was very ominous. The Vatican was certainly keeping a watchful eye on developments in South Africa.

On July 10, Romish archbishop Denis Hurley said that sanctions against SA should be lifted. The SA Roman Catholic bishops had supported sanctions since 1986, and Hurley said that these sanctions had "certainly made a difference" to the country. But he wanted the new government to have a better economy when it came to power, and he thought that a realistic assessment was that "majority rule" would be achieved in two years - the sooner the better.[380] And after meeting in full session in August, the Romish bishops of southern Africa said in a statement that the time for sanctions was past.[381]

After causing untold suffering to millions by supporting economic sanctions, Hurley and the other Papal leaders now called for their lifting so that an ANC government (for that is what Hurley meant by "majority rule" - even though the ANC did not truly represent the majority) could inherit a better economy! Black suffering meant nothing to these men, if it forwarded the revolution. Only when the ANC appeared to be on the brink of victory did they call for the lifting of sanctions.

As it turned out, an ANC victory was not officially achieved in two

---

[378] *The Citizen*, June 17, 1991.
[379] *The Southern Cross*, June 30, 1991.
[380] *The Southern Cross*, July 28, 1991.
[381] *The Southern Cross*, September 1, 1991.

years. But Hurley was not too far off in his prognostication, for by mid-1993 the ANC was virtually running the country, even though it did not officially come to power until April 1994.

Romish bishop Wilfred Napier, president of the SACBC, made a number of highly significant statements in an interview published on July 28, 1991.[382] Concerning a papal visit to South Africa - something long desired by many Roman Catholics - he said that the ANC had been consulted about this some years before, but had been against it because they felt that the government would use such a visit to its own advantage. However, they were told that the pope's speeches would reflect the wishes of the local bishops; and when they heard that, "the ANC were quite at ease", although, Napier added, they might still have some reservations. His words revealed the extremely close relationship between the Romish bishops and the ANC. Not only was the latter consulted about a possible papal visit, but once it knew that the papal speeches would reflect the wishes of the bishops in South Africa, it was "quite at ease", knowing that the bishops were fully on its side, and that therefore the pope would be as well!

Napier said that the pope could be a catalyst for change; and he cited the case of Chile, where within a year of the pope's visit General Pinochet had been ousted. In this he was absolutely correct: such is the Roman pontiff's power over the millions of Roman Catholics, that the world's politicians compete for his favour; and woe betide any political leader who dares to cross him! Modern history contains examples of radical social changes following in the wake of a papal visit to a country.

Napier also said that, when a "majority government" came to power, priests might be needed in some areas to fulfil functions of *government,* because of the low standard of education [among blacks], and that some priests might be given permission to work in politics, for a time. Certainly in the 1980's the Communist government of Nicaragua had a number of Roman Catholic priests in various government positions.[383] And indeed, when the ANC came to power in

---

[382] *The Southern Cross,* July 28, 1991.
[383] *The Vatican Moscow Washington Alliance,* pgs. 323-325.

April 1994, there *were* priests in the government.

Napier went on to say that the "Renew" programme in the Roman Catholic institution was one of breaking the parishes down into smaller units, "Christian communities", which some bishops saw as a better method for implementing the "Pastoral Plan". Although some people, he said, viewed these communities as Communist, they were not. The purpose of the "Pastoral Plan" was examined in an earlier chapter of this book. It was *most certainly* a Marxist concept, and had been very effective in Brazil. Naturally this bishop of Rome would want to allay the fears of many, even within the Roman Catholic community, by denying that it was Communist, but the evidence proved otherwise.

The liberal media has always supported the Marxist cause, and been very sympathetic to the Roman Catholic institution. This is because, as was seen in an earlier chapter, much of the mass media industry is either under the control of, or heavily influenced by, the "Church" of Rome, especially in the United States, but also elsewhere. In South Africa, most of its English press and some of its Afrikaans press was controlled by Harry Oppenheimer's Anglo American Corporation; and those papers supported the revolution.[384] On August 25, 1991, the contribution of the Roman Catholic institution to the media industry in South Africa was the subject of a meeting of the "St. Matthews Guild". Christopher Bennett, a Roman Catholic and a radio personality, addressed the meeting. He said that Roman Catholic influence on the South African media was visible and invisible. Visible influences included religious broadcasts. The invisible influences included radio and TV presenters who were Roman Catholics. He said that the invisible influence of Roman Catholicism on the media was a powerful and growing force, and he believed this process would continue.[385] Certainly, this powerful influence could be detected in the support given, in the liberal media, to the ANC and the other Communist forces conducting the armed revolution. Even the state-controlled SA Broadcasting Corporation became increasingly pro-ANC.

---

[384] *The McAlvany Intelligence Advisor*, December 1986.
[385] *The Southern Cross*, September 8, 1991.

1991 was the most murderous year in South Africa's history. In August, the police reported that *28 000* people had died in criminal violence in the previous fifteen months! A few thousand members of the Inkatha Freedom Party, the ANC's powerful rival and its number one target, were killed. Murders of policemen escalated drastically in that year. To a very large extent, the murderers were encouraged by the strong efforts to undermine the South African Police that had been made by the SACC and the SACBC, aided by leftist lawyers, the leftist press, etc.[386]

Under pressure from the ANC, the National Party government in 1991 *released 57 000 convicted felons* - followed by thousands more some time later.[387] This incredible capitulation, condemned by all the attorneys-general of South Africa as well as by many lawyers and criminologists, sent shock-waves throughout the country, and without question contributed to the horrifying violence of that year and the following ones. Literally before their very eyes, South Africans were witnessing their country sink into a state of lawlessness and near-anarchy, as their government, in order to please the ANC, ceased to carry out the primary function of any government, which is the maintenance of law and order. The country, already engulfed in barbaric violence, its law-abiding citizens forced to besiege themselves in their own homes while Marxist terrorists were permitted to roam free, now had to contend with tens of thousands of additional criminals suddenly unleashed onto the streets.

And meanwhile, despite the "negotiations", and despite denials by the ANC, intelligence reports revealed that it was building a conventional armed force outside South Africa, assisted by the USSR, Tanzania, Botswana, Uganda, Lesotho, Libya and the Palestine Liberation Organisation.[388] The ANC's military might was growing, and South Africa's security forces were shrinking.

---

[386] *The Aida Parker Newsletter*, Issue No. 148, December 1991.
[387] *The Aida Parker Newsletter*, Issue No.148, December 1991.
[388] *The Aida Parker Newsletter*, Issue No.148, December 1991.

CHAPTER THIRTY

1992: US PRESSURE, NP RETREAT, ANC ADVANCE

By early 1992, the "Congress for a Democratic South Africa" (CODESA) was well in place, and was rapidly usurping Parliament as the primary decision-making authority in South Africa. It was an unelected body, consisting of members of various parties but completely dominated by the National Party government and the ANC, and it was working to transform SA into a "democratic" (i.e. Marxist) country. The NP had undergone such a radical change that it was unrecognisable as the NP of the past. Although there were frequent apparent clashes between it and the ANC on various details, the simple reality was that the NP, pressurised by the Bush Administration in the US, the US State Department and various Western countries[389] (who in turn were receiving orders from the Jesuit/Illuminati conspirators), was in the process of handing over power to the ANC/SACP alliance. Parliament itself was reduced to virtually rubber-stamping the agreements reached at CODESA. In fact, a member of the ANC's National Executive Committee said that the government was "only relevant insofar as it will give legal effect to decisions taken by CODESA."[390] Unofficially, the ANC was already beginning to govern the country to a large extent. The international conspirators were winning. South Africa was in the late stages of the first phase of a classic Marxist-Leninist revolution: Phase One was to establish a coalition government between Communists and non-Communists; and Phase Two was to establish a "People's Democracy" (a Communist state), after all non-Communists had been purged out of the government. The same pattern had been followed in Russia, China, Cuba, Nicaragua, and Rhodesia.[391]

South Africa in early 1992 was a country in the grip of an economic depression; it was experiencing absolutely horrifying

---

[389] *The McAlvany Intelligence Advisor*, February/March 1992.
[390] *Roca Report*, No.38, February 1992.
[391] *The McAlvany Intelligence Advisor*, February/March 1992.

violence; and its people were confused, demoralised, and frightened. Then came the referendum.

In March 1992, the National Party government held a referendum, ostensibly to give whites the opportunity to vote either "Yes" or "No" to the NP's reforms. An overwhelming majority of whites voted Yes, giving the NP the justification it sought to continue surrendering control of the country into the hands of the ANC/SACP alliance.

But now for the ugly truth.

Before the referendum, President de Klerk sent letters to 70 foreign governments to obtain their support for a "Yes" vote. They responded in his favour, threatening South Africa with a return to sanctions, international isolation, etc., if whites voted No.[392] This was deliberate interference in South Africa's affairs, a successful attempt to frighten whites into voting Yes. The entire referendum, in fact, was deliberately and shamelessly *manipulated,* by the NP government using vast funds, as well as by the media, big business, and external pressure. The leftist media, controlled by the Oppenheimer empire and for so long pro-Marxist, and powerfully influenced by the Roman Catholic institution, went all out for a Yes vote, using fear tactics, threatening what would (supposedly) happen to South Africa if whites voted No, comparing a No vote to a return to the Dark Ages, to the millions of lives lost in Nazi Germany, etc., and not giving those parties opposed to a Yes vote a fair hearing. Big business supplied at least R50 million to the campaign to ensure a Yes vote. Thousands of white workers were threatened that they would lose their jobs, that they would even be fired, if they voted No.[393] The entire campaign was a cleverly-manipulated plot to bulldoze the whites into going along with NP "reforms". What most did not realise, however, was that, by voting Yes, they did not, in fact, give their assent to reforms (which most sensible whites had long ago realised were necessary anyway), but they had unwittingly ensured that an interim government would soon be in power, dominated by the ANC, which would eventually lead to a full-

---

[392] *Roca Report,* No.39, March 1992.
[393] *The Aida Parker Newsletter,* Issue No.152, April 1992.

fledged ANC government.[394] They had voted, not for good and useful reforms, but for the continued surrender of South Africa into the hands of its enemies. They had been lied to, threatened, and generally bludgeoned into voting Yes.

Meanwhile, the ANC continued to rapidly prepare military structures to seize power by violence and bloodshed if the "negotiations" (negotiated surrender) ever failed. It repeatedly affirmed that it would only hand over control of its armed wing, Mkhonto we Sizwe (MK), to an *interim government* which would *merge* all existing armies: the SADF, MK, and those of the independent homelands of Transkei, Venda, Bophuthatswana, and Ciskei.[395] Until then, it had absolutely no intention of disbanding this private (and illegal) army. It was, in fact, strengthening and increasing it. Large supplies of Russian arms were being smuggled into South Africa by MK, and stashed in secret arms dumps. MK had an estimated 10 000 highly-trained guerrillas in the frontline states. They were trained in Cuba, Libya, China, Russia, and by the PLO. MK was establishing "Self-Defence Units" in the townships, called "Township Defence Forces" (TDF's), for the purpose of controlling the residents by intimidation. The world was being told that Communism was dead, that the Commonwealth of Independent States (the old Soviet Union) was not Communist, but this was simply not true: with its *re-organised* KGB, it was *still* supplying the Marxist ANC guerrillas with military equipment![396]

The British *Intelligence Digest* declared: "Increasingly, South Africans are coming to realise that they are facing a classic Marxist/Leninist revolution, organised by dedicated South African communists trained in the former Eastern bloc and by Western communists. Surprising to many will be the information received by *ID* sources in South Africa that the revolution is still being directed by communist cadres in Eastern Europe, and the former Soviet Union."[397]

---

[394] *Roca Report*, No.40, April 1992.
[395] *Roca Report*, No.39, March 1992.
[396] *The McAlvany Intelligence Advisor*, February/March 1992.
[397] *The Aida Parker Newsletter*, Issue No.156, Aug

ANC financial backing continued to come from the internationalists. In early 1992 it was reported that the American Rockefeller Foundation and the ANC were going to jointly launch a $5 billion "SA Trust for Equity and Development".[398]

In April 1992, a number of ANC members were directly implicated in armed actions. Some even wore police uniforms, deliberately posing as policemen as they carried out armed attacks! ANC arms caches were also discovered. And yet the government, bending over backwards in order to keep the negotiations on track, simply claimed that the ANC could not control its members, and merely took action against the individuals concerned, and not the ANC itself.[399] The truth was, of course, that those individuals were acting on orders from the ANC! - but the government *wanted* the population to believe that the ANC as an organisation was against the armed actions of some of its members. For the National Party was a thoroughly-infiltrated, pro-New World Order party, being dictated to by the US State Department, which wanted to see the ANC come to power, and which had massively financed terrorist organisations in South Africa for many years.[400]

The United States was forcing South Africa, as well as Brazil and Argentina, to shut down their huge arms industries, ostensibly to "promote world disarmament". The real reason, however, was so that the *US military* would then be able to enforce its will anywhere in the world, without resistance. As stated by US Army Chief of Staff General Gordon Sullivan, his re-organisation of the US defence structure "supports the role of the US as the pre-eminent power of our age".[401] As the US became increasingly Socialist, as its policies increasingly harmonised with those of Russia, and as it increasingly came under the influence, and in some areas control, of the Vatican, its military began to advance the cause of the New World Order internationally, which was, in essence, to advance the interests of the

---

1992.
[398] *Roca Report*, No.38, February 1992.
[399] *Roca Report*, No.41, May 1992.
[400] *The McAlvany Intelligence Advisor*, February/March 1992.
[401] *The Aida Parker Newsletter*, Issue No.152, April 1992.

Vatican. The armed forces of the United States were becoming the pope's armed forces.

In obedience to the orders it received from Washington, the National Party government began to literally drain the life out of the once-mighty South African Defence Force; this at a crucial time in the country's history, when the ANC was rapidly increasing the size and strength of its own private army. General Magnus Malan, South Africa's Minister of Defence, was replaced in July 1991, under pressure from the ANC and Washington, by Roelf Meyer, a liberal with almost no military experience. According to Colonel J. Breytenbach, one of South Africa's most highly-decorated officers, Roelf Meyer "destroyed the life of the defence force by draining its already near-comatose body of its discipline, in perhaps the most idiotic shambles ever inflicted on a modern army Meyer .has achieved in six months or less what SA's enemies could not achieve in nearly 80 years of often very violent and desperate conflict."[402] When Meyer was appointed, *Africa Confidential* reported that he "was moved in as Minister of Defence to oversee the decline of the SADF as a political factor." And the *Aida Parker Newsletter* stated, "He was there to dismantle, on the instructions of Washington and the State Department, Africa's finest fighting force and perhaps the fifth best military machine in the world."[403]

Meanwhile, there were some very strange goings-on in Botswana, one of South Africa's neighbouring countries. A large US air force base was under construction in the desert in Botswana in 1992. According to the *McAlvany Intelligence Advisor,* a "well-placed source" in the National Party said that the US had threatened the South African government in early 1990 that South Africa could be attacked from this base; but that, after President de Klerk unbanned the ANC and SACP, construction on the base ceased. However, in January 1992, over 300 members of the US 325th Infantry Brigade conducted desert-warfare exercises there.[404] It was clearly not closed down! In

---

[402] *The McAlvany Intelligence Advisor*, February/March 1992.
[403] *The Aida Parker Newsletter,* Issue No.160, January/February 1993.
[404] *The McAlvany Intelligence Advisor,* February/March 1992.

addition, The US Peace Corps, which always has many CIA agents, had over 200 people stationed in Botswana in 1992 - the largest presence per capita anywhere in the world.[405]

This R1 billion base, being built only 250 miles from Pretoria, was codenamed "Operation Eagle". The US Information Service in Johannesburg denied that there was any US involvement in military construction in Botswana. The truth, however, was that the US had indeed commissioned it, and was funding it. According to Howard Phillips, head of the US Conservative Caucus, "There are those who believe that it is in preparation for the possibility that a UN peacekeeping force might be needed a year or two down the road, to keep recalcitrant White and Black anti-Communists from resisting the authority of a newly installed Marxist regime in SA, brought to power under the auspices of the ANC."[406]

For many long years, the United States and the United Nations had given massive assistance to the Communist ANC. Now the NP government was surrendering power to the ANC through negotiations. But there were millions of South Africans, both black and white, who were fiercely anti-Communist, and who were beginning to resist this piecemeal, creeping surrender of the country into Communist hands: Zulus belonging to the Inkatha Freedom Party, Afrikaners and other whites belonging to the Conservative Party, Xhosas in the Ciskei, and others. The conspirators were well aware that these conservative, anti-Communist groups posed a major threat to their plans to install the ANC as the government. And it was beginning to look more and more as if the mysterious US air force base in Botswana might indeed be for the purpose of forcefully ensuring an ANC victory if necessary, and then for ensuring that the ANC would *maintain* its control over South Africa once it came to power.

Certainly, the US military was becoming increasingly involved in serving United Nations interests around the world, including Africa. In late 1992, US President George Bush sent 28 000 troops into Somalia, saying that this military operation was to make it possible for food to

---

[405] *The Aida Parker Newsletter*, Issue No.154, June 1992.
[406] *The Aida Parker Newsletter*, Issue No.154, June 1992.

reach the starving, and that troops were there on "God's work". Yet thousands of people had been starving there since 1990. It was only in late 1992 that the US became involved. And what about the many other parts of the world which were in as great a plight as Somalia? Why was the US not interested in helping the people living in those places? We can be certain of this: the US did not get involved in Somalia for humanitarian reasons. It did so for motives far more selfish. And for South Africa, the implications were very sinister indeed. With the US presence in Somalia, the US air base in Botswana, and the fortress-like US embassy erected in Pretoria itself, the signs all pointed to plans for increased US military intervention in Africa, and particularly South Africa. As the *London Times* editor, Simon Jenkins, wrote: "Three-quarters of the globe is now at risk of attack from America or its UN proxies."[407]

Again it must be stated: the United States military was being deployed, around the world, to achieve the objectives of the One-World conspirators. The New World Order desired by the Vatican, international Communism, and the closet Socialists in Washington, was coming into being mainly through "negotiations", accords, pacts, etc. But wherever resistance to the New World Order (World Government) was encountered, the US military was being deployed to force the resisters into line.

In 1992 the ANC also began to openly court the Islamic states. Mandela visited Saudi Arabia, the United Arab Emirates, and Iran. These had all supported the ANC. In July, he was awarded an honorary doctorate at Teheran University. He said: "The people of Africa will make Iran's Islamic revolution a model for their revolutionary moves." He also met the Ayatollah Khameini, and laid a wreath at the tomb of the Ayatollah Khomeini.[408] The bloody revolution that swept Khomeini to power - a model for Africa! Chilling words indeed.

---

[407] *The Aida Parker Newsletter*, Issue No.160, January/February 1993.
[408] British *Intelligence Digest*, 29.7.92, as reported in *The Aida Parker Newsletter*, Issue No.156, August 1992.

SA had only a very tiny Muslim population - not even half a million. But for many long years Muslim states and terrorist organisations had done much for the ANC, and increasingly the close ties between the two were evident. When in early 1992 Mandela met Muslim terrorist leader, Yasser Arafat, at the PLO headquarters in Tunisia, he said, "We regard the PLO as one of the most progressive movements in the world and we are going to continue that friendship."[409]

President de Klerk actually admitted, when he received the "International Man of the Year Award" on April 30, 1992, that the international community *demanded* that South Africa think exclusively and become *one nation*.[410] This was an admission that the conspirators, the Jesuit/Illuminati forces pulling the strings behind the scenes in the UN, Moscow, and Washington, were exerting tremendous pressure on South Africa to follow the Communist path and become a "unitary state".

What was once unthinkable was now happening: relations between the National Party and *Russia* improved in 1992, with diplomatic ties being established. And according to Western intelligence sources, the first four Russian diplomats to be accredited to Pretoria were top KGB officials.[411] The Communist KGB was not dead: it had simply been renamed, as part of the giant smokescreen the Soviets had succeeded in erecting. In June, President de Klerk visited Russia; invited President Boris Yeltsin to visit South Africa (an invitation he accepted); and promised to give Russia R100 million in revolving credit, to facilitate trade. When he landed in Moscow, a Russian military band played "Die Stem van Suid Afrika" (The Call of South Africa), the national anthem; and above the Kremlin, the SA flag flew. De Klerk, strolling in Moscow's Red Square, said that both Communism (in Russia) and apartheid (in South Africa) were now gone. And he urged Russian entrepreneurs to make use of South Africa as a gateway to southern Africa. Both countries undertook to

---

[409] *Roca Report*, No.38, February 1992.
[410] *Roca Report*, No.41, May 1992.
[411] *The McAlvany Intelligence Advisor*, February/March 1992.

encourage contact and exchanges at all levels.[412]

These were indeed strange times! South Africa and Russia were once at opposite poles: the former one of the most anti-Communist countries on earth, staunchly conservative, and the latter the world's leading Communist country, engaged in supporting a decades-long war against South Africa. What had happened? It was not Russia that had changed: its leaders still remained dedicated Communists, but they had succeeded in convincing the world that they had become anti-Communists, and that Communism was now dead. It was *South Africa* that had changed: its ruling party had shifted from the right to the left, so slowly and subtly that it had hardly been noticed until it was too late. And now, with Russia pretending to be anti-Communist, it was possible for President de Klerk to actually visit Moscow, the world headquarters of the international Communist terror network; promise credit to Russia; hear the national anthem played by South Africa's decades-long adversaries; see the flag flying from the building where terrible plots against South Africa had been hatched, and were still being hatched; declare that both Communism and apartheid were dead - false and true respectively; and permit KGB officials to take up residence in Pretoria.

---

[412] *The Citizen*, June 2, 1992.

CHAPTER THIRTY-ONE

1992: "PRAY FOR THE DOWNFALL OF THE SINISTER GOVERNMENT!"

Religious involvement in the ongoing revolution intensified during 1992.

On May 4, a six-day train boycott was called by the South African Council of Churches, in conjunction with the ANC and SACP. And Romish "liberation" priest, Smangaliso Mkhatshwa, had previously led a week-long sit-in at the offices of Spoornet, the rail transport company.[413] Anything to cause disruptions, anything to stir up discontent.

On May 8, the SA Catholic Bishops Conference joined its voice to those calling for an *international monitoring force,* to monitor the violence.[414] If SA allowed international monitors to enter the country, the radicals knew, these would work for an ANC victory. That was why they were calling for them.

In May, the SACC called on "Christians" to "pray unceasingly" for the "downfall of the sinister government". This call was made on the eve of a "National Week of Prayer and Healing". It called the government "illegitimate" and "immoral". Then it proclaimed "People's Power" in this statement: "Justice demands that the voice of the people be heard. Any attempt to silence that voice is to face the wrath of God as much as it is to face the anger of an already frustrated people".[415] This was a thinly-disguised call for further violence against the state, and gave supposedly divine justification to the revolutionaries in their efforts. As liberation theology always does, it claimed that God was on the side of the "oppressed", which of course meant that he was on the side of the Marxists; for that is what these radical clergymen had in mind. To declare the government to be illegitimate was utterly unscriptural, according to such passages as Rom.13:1-7 and others. Paul did not call the government of the Roman Empire illegitimate, even though it was very cruel and dictatorial. It

---

[413] *Roca Report,* No.41, May 1992.
[414] *The Southern Cross,* May 24, 1992.
[415] *The Citizen,* May 29, 1992.

was ordained by God, for that time and place, just as the South African government was ordained by God.

On May 23, a delegation of ecclesiastical leaders, led by Frank Chikane of the SACC, met with President de Klerk and handed him a memorandum on the violence. Roman Catholic "brother", Jude Pieterse, secretary general of the SACBC, said that "church" leaders felt strongly that security forces were involved in perpetuating violence. He also said that violence came to the Transvaal when Inkatha was launched as a party.[416] Typical of the radical clergy, he shifted blame for the violence from the ANC to the security forces and Inkatha. Marxists have used this tactic for decades, and it is very effective. Pieterse also declared that the Roman Catholic institution, along with other bodies, was developing an "education for democracy programme" to be carried out among grassroots communities before elections for a "democratic government". Naturally (although he did not say so), huge numbers of black voters would be "educated" to vote for the ANC. This programme was in fact developed, and was very successful in rallying people to the ANC's side. Wherever priestcraft reigns worldwide, the people look to their priests as God's holy representatives, to be trusted blindly.

Also in May, six religious leaders took part in the second plenary session of CODESA (known as CODESA II). Three opened the session, and three closed it. They were representatives of the Dutch Reformed, Anglican and Roman Catholic institutions, and of the Jewish, Hindu and Muslim religions.[417] Such a religious Babel had never before taken part in the political process in this way.

In June 1992, a report released by the London-based Christian Studies Centre caused a stir. It stated that sections of the SA "Church", aided by overseas funds, had "sympathised with the liberation movements - especially the African National Congress - to such an extent that they have simply turned a blind eye to the methods such organisations have been prepared to employ to gain power, or have developed a theology which actually justifies violence." This statement was absolutely true, as this book amply demonstrates. The Marxist-

---

[416] *The Southern Cross*, June 7, 1992.
[417] *The Citizen*, May 12, 1992.

supporting "clergy", however, reacted in shocked indignation. The presiding bishop of the Methodist denomination of South Africa, Stanley Mogoba, rejected the report's claim, saying that the statements were "not only devoid of truth, but do the cause of the Christian Gospel an injustice and immense harm."[418] To say that the report's statements were devoid of truth was to *make* a statement that was devoid of truth! - and the blasphemous heresies of *liberation theology* were responsible for doing the cause of the *true* Gospel of Christ harm, for multitudes believed that the Gospel was the message of liberation theology, and not the Gospel of the saving grace of God as revealed in the Bible.

Meanwhile, the hideous violence racking South Africa continued. From May 15 to 30, the township of Sharpeville erupted. An ANC family was killed on May 15. Then Winnie Mandela came to the township and told the ANC people to form "street committees", and that soon it would be time to fight. Shortly after this, an Inkatha man was burnt to death by necklacing. ANC "comrades" went from house to house, insisting that all young men had to join them. People were shot, necklaced, etc. One man's burnt body was placed on top of a chimney, as a warning to all not to oppose the ANC. Even children attacked the police and Inkatha members, saying, "If we find you in the township after 6.00 p.m., we'll kill you."[419]

On May 31, Mandela said in a speech that whites could become targets of angry blacks in spreading violence. And he added, "You are going to see mass action on a scale you have never seen before."[420] By saying this, he was implicitly *encouraging* blacks to attack whites.

He had promised large-scale mass action; and it happened. In June the ANC, declaring that it would render South Africa ungovernable, launched a "mass action" campaign to topple the government, involving marches, sit-ins, strikes, etc.[421] It was called "Operation Exit". On June 2, a massive hospital strike was launched, affecting

---

[418] *The Natal Witness,* June 22, 1992.
[419] *The Aida Parker Newsletter,* Issue No.154, June 1992.
[420] *Roca Report,* No.42, June 1992.
[421] *Natal Witness Echo,* June 18, 1992.

many hospitals. Workers were intimidated and even killed.[422] The National Education, Health and Allied Workers Union (NEHAWU), which was ANC-aligned, planned to continue the strike until the country was brought to a standstill.[423]

According to SA's law and order minister, between February 2, 1990 and May 25, 1992, over 3000 attacks against policemen had been initiated by the ANC; and several hundred ANC members had been arrested for possession of unlicensed firearms. Harry Gwala, ANC leader in Pietermaritzburg, actually *admitted* that the ANC was killing Inkatha leaders.[424] During the first half of 1992, 1181 people were killed in 4489 incidents of political violence, 109 policemen were killed, and 23 people were necklaced.[425] And yet the government did nothing, and the religious leaders continued to heartily support this murderous organisation.

The black people were being told that the ANC had their interests at heart; that all would have an equal share of the wealth under an ANC government; etc. But as always with Communists, while they claim that all men are equal, some are manifestly more equal than others. By 1992 the ANC/SACP leaders were living in the lap of luxury. It had not taken them long to settle in to the extravagant lifestyles they so readily condemned their enemies for!

Nelson Mandela, himself, lived in the wealthy Johannesburg suburb of Houghton. While he was in prison, his wife Winnie had a house built for them in Soweto, at a cost of R750 000: a house with fifteen rooms. Oliver Tambo lived in Sandhurst - the most expensive suburb in the country. *His* mansion cost R3 million, and the entire ground floor was laid out in marble! Thabo Mbeki lived for months at the Carlton Court, at a cost of R500 a night. Chris Hani sent his daughter to a private school, at a cost of R10 000 a year. Children of other revolutionary leaders went to extremely expensive private schools as well.[426] Not for these men the sacrifices they called upon their duped followers to make! While millions upon millions of blacks

---

[422] *Roca Report*, No.42, June 1992.
[423] *Roca Report*, No.43, July 1992.
[424] *Roca Report*, No.42, June 1992.
[425] *Roca Report*, No.43, July 1992.
[426] *The Aida Parker Newsletter*, Issue No.157, September 1992.

had lost their jobs as a result of ANC-inspired sanctions, and were living in shacks and utter squalor, their "leaders" were wallowing in comfort and ease. While the education of millions upon millions of black children was being constantly disrupted by ANC-inspired campaigns, resulting in a generation of black youth lacking even the basics of education, their "leaders" made certain that *their* children did not suffer.

And what of two of South Africa's leading liberation theologians, Allan Boesak and Frank Chikane? Boesak, admittedly, was now the Western Cape leader of the ANC rather than a "minister" (not that he ever was a true minister of the Gospel). He now lived in Cape Town's wealthy Upper Constantia area, in a house costing approximately R595 000. As for Chikane, the secretary general of the SACC, he lived in a R750 000, eight-bedroomed double-storey mansion, built *for* him by the SACC, in Diepkloof township. The house was paid for by "churches" in Norway, Switzerland, and Canada.[427]

Proof positive, if more were needed, that the *real* purpose of the Marxist revolution was not to improve the living conditions of the masses, but to massively enrich the revolutionary leaders. The masses were merely the cannon fodder the leaders used to achieve power and wealth for themselves.

By mid-1992, the ANC's real support in South Africa was at an all-time low. At Evaton in June, Mandela was actually *jeered* by angry young blacks, who told him that *he* would be necklaced if he did not do as they demanded! Attendance at ANC rallies had dropped dramatically. The only reason strikes and stayaways were successful was because of massive and brutal intimidation. The ANC was not (despite its claims) the largest political organisation in the country.[428] It desperately needed a boost to its plan for large-scale mass action. In the words of the *Guardian Weekly*, July 3, 1992, "Mass mobilisation (on the scale needed by the ANC) requires an enormously powerful sense of outrage, and it's not entirely clear that such sentiment exists in

---

[427] *The Aida Parker Newsletter*, Issue No.157, September 1992.
[428] *The Aida Parker Newsletter*, Issue No.155, July 1992.

today's South Africa." It went on: "Clearly, an 'apartheid' atrocity was needed to reawaken dormant passions and the ANC was presented with one on June 17".[429] This was the terrible massacre at Boipatong, and it was just the boost that the ANC needed.

On June 17, 1992, at Boipatong township, over 45 black people were brutally killed in a single massacre. The ANC screamed that blacks were being killed just because they were blacks. It blamed Inkatha and the security forces. Justice R.J. Goldstone, however, of the Goldstone Commission, found no evidence of police or government involvement in the massacre; and according to Chief Buthelezi, at least ten of the victims were actually Inkatha members - yet they were buried as ANC supporters![430]

Certain facts started to come to light. On June *13*, four days before the massacre, ANC "comrades" had moved through Boipatong, looking for Inkatha members and sympathisers, and even for Zulus who were not involved with Inkatha at all. A woman was the first victim - she was necklaced. Then others were killed. But the press were silent about these killings of Inkatha supporters, as were religious leaders - who four days later would be so vocal when ANC supporters were killed!

In April, 32 Zulu Inkatha supporters, mainly women and children, were attacked while they slept, and hacked to death, in Crossroads and Zonkisizwe squatter camps, by ANC supporters. And yet the media was almost completely silent, as were the religious leaders!

It is perfectly evident that the Boipatong massacre was to the advantage of the ANC; and it got as much political mileage out of it as possible, supported by its media and ecclesiastical allies. In the words of the *Roca Report:* "It is almost as though the ANC's propaganda machine had been primed, just waiting for an incident of this nature to again grab world headlines and world sympathy and to give the worldwide anti-apartheid movement the cause it needed to reactivate itself. Certainly the air waves echoed with allegations of government, police and Inkatha involvement almost before that tragic night

---

[429] *Roca Report,* No.43, July 1992.
[430] *Roca Report,* No.43, July 1992.

ended."[431]

In the words of a Zulu hostel dweller in Boipatong: "If the ANC takes power in South Africa, this country will be in ruins. Blood, not water, will flow from the taps."[432]

The radical "church" leaders lost no time in rallying to the side of the ANC after the Boipatong massacre. At a memorial service for the victims, an angry religious "minister", Ernest Sotsu, called on people to form defence units and "go to war"; and the other ecclesiastical leaders present - representatives of the Methodist, Presbyterian, and other denominations - did not object to his call.[433] In July, the SACC demanded that President de Klerk agree to an international monitoring group, commit himself to negotiating *multi-party* control of the security forces, and bring the Boipatong killers to book. It said that if these demands were not met by July 15, the "churches" would take a number of steps to pressure the government.[434] The ANC itself, using the Boipatong massacre to its advantage, called for the security forces, *and* the SA government, to be placed under the control of an international force: either the UN, the EC, the OAU, or the Commonwealth. The government gave in, partially, to this demand, by declaring after Boipatong that the international community did have a role to play in SA. Foreigners were called in to assist with the enquiries into the violence.[435] SA was surrendering its national sovereignty to the New World Order, one step at a time. The ANC was certainly profiting immensely from the Boipatong massacre!

After the massacre, a "Broad Forum" was formed, consisting of the ANC, PAC, COSATU, NACTU, and AZAPO. It was formed in order to *seize control* of the huge black townships in the Vaal triangle. It immediately imposed a (so-called) "enforced protection" programme: preventing residents from leaving the townships or going to work, unless able to provide "acceptable" reasons. Even then, marshals had to accompany them. The Forum claimed that these measures were for the protection of the people. An AZAPO leader said, "I think it is

---

[431] *Roca Report*, No.43, July 1992.
[432] *Roca Report*, No.43, July 1992.
[433] *The Citizen*, June 26, 1992.
[434] *The Natal Witness*, July 11, 1992.
[435] *Roca Report*, No.43, July 1992.

necessary that they [the township residents] are encouraged to follow and abide by what their fellow residents have decided." Any resident wishing to go out the township had to report to his "street committee leader" or branch leader. Residents, however, were in fear of the marshals, and their control over their lives. The young "comrades" had instituted a reign of terror. Cars were searched at roadblocks set up by the youths. And to prevent police work, residents were forced, in the dead of night, to dig two-metre-deep trenches across almost half the streets in Boipatong, and to patrol the streets.[436] In this way the radicals controlled the township, turning them into lawless areas where even the police found it almost impossible to go.

In his report given at the National Conference of the SACC, held in July 1992, the general secretary, Frank Chikane, laid the blame for the present crisis in SA, the breakdown of negotiations, and the violence, at the door of the "illegitimate" government, the military, and the police. Most delegates at the conference agreed to continue to *confront* the government, and to *mediate* between it and the ANC, although some wanted confrontation only. In the resolutions of the conference, the government was condemned.[437]

The ANC's violent campaign, meanwhile, was intensified in July; and yet the SACC had no words of condemnation for it. "We are going to identify and march towards the homes of police who killed our people during riots," Peter Mokaba, the ANC Youth League president, said on July 11. "We are going to harass their families so that they know that they are staying with killers. We are going to return to the 1985 period with the establishment of street and block committees."[438] The PAC, meanwhile, came up with a new slogan: "Kill a cop a day". These were the people the SACBC, the SACC, and other religious institutions were wholeheartedly supporting! Occasionally, some of the leaders of these institutions realised, perhaps, that their support for the revolutionaries, and particularly for the ANC, was too overt. For example, on 6 July 1992 Khoza Mgojo, president of the SACC, said in

---

[436] *The Sunday Times*, July 5, 1992; and *Roca Report*, No.44, August 1992.
[437] *Challenge*, No.9, September 1992. Contextual Publications, Johannesburg.
[438] *Roca Report*, No.43, July 1992.

his opening speech to its national conference, "We shall need to examine why we are perceived as the ANC at prayer."[439] The answer was certainly not difficult to find!

"Church" support for the ANC's campaign of mass action was blatant. An example was the occupation of the offices of the Transvaal Provincial Administration in Pretoria by five ANC members in July. They were led by Romish priest and ANC member, Smangaliso Mkhatshwa.[440]

The ANC/SACP/COSATU alliance pulled out of the CODESA talks because Inkatha, its hated rival, was making too much progress there, and also because it gave the ANC an excuse for its mass action.[441] On July 28, a delegation of "church" leaders, led by Roman Catholic archbishop, Wilfred Napier, met President de Klerk to attempt to re-start the negotiations, which had stalled. They also met Mandela, who welcomed their intervention.[442] In this way the ANC was made to look innocent, as if it was not its fault that the talks had stalled.

There are two ways, according to the Word of God, to identify a false teacher, a man claiming to be a servant of Christ but in reality serving the devil: by his doctrine, and by his conduct. Their support for Communist killers was proof positive that the radical "clergymen" were not servants of Christ; but in addition, their doctrines left no room for doubt either. For example, on 8 July 1992 Desmond Tutu, calling for SA to be made a secular state, in which Christians would not enjoy any special status, made the following statements: "God is clearly not a Christian. His concern is for all his children." "That God does not belong only to Christians must be abundantly obvious except to those who ignore the truth." "God accepts as pleasing to him those who live by the best lights available to them."[443] He was also reported, in *The Natal Witness*, as saying, in addition to his statement that God does not belong only to Christians: "That Christians do not have a

---

[439] *Signposts*, Vol.11, No.4, 1992.
[440] *The Natal Witness*, July 21, 1992.
[441] *The Aida Parker Newsletter*, Issue No.156, August 1992.
[442] *The Southern Cross*, August 9, 1992.
[443] *The Southern Cross*, July 19, 1992.

monopoly on God is an almost trite observation."[444] The present author wrote to the *Witness* in response to Tutu's antichristian statements, and his letter was published on October 23. This is what it said:

"The syncretistic statement by Desmond Tutu (in your article, "Church's Call Opposed", September 26) that `God does not belong only to Christians' deserves strong comment from Bible-believing Christians. The Bible proclaims, in no uncertain terms, the absolute uniqueness of Jesus Christ: that he is the only way to God the Father; that his is the only name under heaven given among men whereby men and women must be saved (Jn.14:6; Acts 4:12). This is denied by those who seek to convince men that other religions are `equally valid ways to God'; but to do so is to deny the plain teaching of the New Testament. Let it be made clear that all Bible-believing Christians reject with disgust the false `gospel' of Tutu and other syncretists who, professing to speak as `ministers' of Christ, preach a different `gospel' entirely."

Of course God is not a Christian! Tutu's statement was not only unscriptural, it was ridiculous. A Christian is a follower of Christ, the Son of God. But only Christians are the children of God (Jn.1:12,13; Rom.8:14-17). As for Tutu's statement that God accepts as pleasing to him those who live by the best lights available to them, this, too, was blatantly unscriptural: it was advocating salvation by works, whereas salvation is by grace through faith. The Lord Jesus Christ made it perfectly clear that he alone is the way to God the Father (Jn.14:6). These were just the latest utterances by Desmond Tutu revealing his spiritual blindness and unregenerate heart.

Progressive United Nations intervention in South Africa's affairs was accepted by the SA government in 1992. First there was a UN Security Council debate on SA, agreed to by the government. Mandela strongly attacked the government at this debate, accusing it of "state terrorism", and called for a special representative to be sent to SA. Consequently, Cyrus Vance was appointed as UN Special Envoy to South Africa.[445] Vance was an American Insider, a One-Worlder: a

---

[444] *The Natal Witness*, September 26, 1992.
[445] *Roca Report*, No.44, August 1992.

liberal Democrat, a past chairman of the Rockefeller Foundation. He had played an important part in the downfall of the Shah of Iran (which resulted in the coming to power of the Ayatollah Khomeini), and of the white government of Rhodesia (which resulted in the coming to power of Marxist Robert Mugabe). He was *very* pro-ANC.[446] Next, the ANC requested a group of international monitors to be sent to SA. As the *Sunday Times* reported, "The new world order has come to these shores."[447] Indeed it had. Internationalist pressure from the Vatican, Moscow, Washington, etc., and infiltration of the National Party government, had brought about this astounding series of events. South Africa was coming under New World Order control.

After Vance's arrival, a ten-member UN team arrived to monitor the ANC's week of mass action in August, as Mandela had requested. Team leader, Hisham Omayad of Ghana, revealed the UN's pro-ANC position when he told illegal ANC marchers in Krugersdorp on August 5, "The UN is very proud of you. We are with you all the way. We wish you all the best."[448] The UN was not hiding it: it was 100% behind the ANC, and would do everything in its power to ensure its victory! Many years before, it had declared the ANC to be the authentic representative of South Africa's peoples; and it had not changed its mind, despite the years of ANC-orchestrated terrorism and bloodshed.

The UN secretary-general recommended that 30 UN observers be stationed in SA. The government agreed. Increasingly, the UN was becoming ominously involved in SA's affairs.

---

[446] *The Aida Parker Newsletter*, Issue No.156, August 1992.
[447] *The Sunday Times*, July 19, 1992; as reported in *Roca Report*, No.44, August 1992.
[448] *Roca Report*, No.44, August 1992.

CHAPTER THIRTY-TWO

1992: THE "DECLARATION ON RELIGIOUS RIGHTS AND RESPONSIBILITIES"

For Christians, the most ominous event of 1992 was the publication, on July 4, of the *Draft Declaration on the Rights and Responsibilities of Religious People;* and its finalised version, the *Declaration on Religious Rights and Responsibilities,* in November the same year. This was, for Christians, the most dangerous document ever published in South Africa.

It all started in December 1990. A conference to produce guidelines for future relations between the state and religious groups met in Johannesburg. It was called the "National Interfaith Conference on Religion-State Relations"; and it was held at the initiative of the SA chapter of the World Conference on Religion and Peace (an organisation working to bring all religions together), and of Albie Sachs of the ANC's National Executive Committee, a man who was also a Communist Party member. One of the conference's goals was to produce a "Charter on Religious Freedom", based on the United Nations' "Declaration on the Elimination of All Forms of Intolerance and of Discrimination based on Religion or Belief". The Charter was drawn up over a period of time, and published on July 4, 1992 as the *Draft Declaration on the Rights and Responsibilities of Religious People.*[449]

Roman Catholic priest, Bonaventure Hinwood, was the official representative at the national level of the SA Catholic Bishops Conference on the WCRP body that drew up the document. When it was published, the SACBC accepted it in principle.[450]

That it was drawn up by an ecumenical, syncretistic body, in conjunction with the Marxist ANC/SACP, was ominous enough; but what it actually *declared* left no room for doubt that this draft document posed a terrible threat to the true Church of Christ in South Africa. It was designed to destroy the propagation of biblical Christianity in the country.

---

[449] *Signposts,* Vol.11, No.4, 1992.
[450] *The Southern Cross,* August 30, 1992.

The conference in December 1990 was addressed by a Muslim; by Albie Sachs of the ANC; by liberation theologian Frank Chikane; and by Denise Ackerman, a senior lecturer in theology at the University of the Western Cape, who proclaimed religious feminism. And the responses were by three so-called "Christian" theologians, three Muslims, three Jewish leaders, and three Hindus. A book of these lectures was published, entitled *Believers in the Future*. While the Muslims and Hindus quoted from *their* sacred books frequently, the so-called "Christians" did not quote once from the Bible in their lectures! Instead, they spoke of "Godself" (a New Age term), "God, our Father and Mother" (a feminist, New Age, anti-biblical, blasphemous way of addressing God), and "Ultimate Reality".[451] "Blind guides" indeed (Matt.23:16)!

The opening words of this Draft Declaration were, "We, representatives of many faiths in South Africa".[452] No true Christian could have, or would have, been involved in any such ecumenical, interfaith conference, for the Scriptures forbid it. The Lord Jesus Christ is absolutely unique: he is the only way to the Father (Jn.14:6), his is the only name under heaven whereby men must be saved (Acts 4:12), and there can be no fellowship, no communion, no concord, no agreement between believer and unbeliever (2 Cor.6:14-18).

In its opening paragraph, the Draft Declaration stated, "We, representatives of many faiths in South Africa....believe that our religions....must .play a role in the creation of a just social order." But this is *not* the task of the Christian Church! Nowhere in the New Testament is it stated that this is the Church's role. This statement reflected typical Marxist liberation theology: the idea that men must establish "the Kingdom of God" (a Communist state) on earth; that sin is "structural" (in society), rather than personal; that salvation is salvation from "oppression", rather than from one's own sins.

The first paragraph also declared: "We....are convinced that it is

---

[451] *Signposts*, Vol.11, No.4, 1992.
[452] *Draft Declaration on the Rights and Responsibilities of Religious People*. WCRP-SA (World Conference on Religion and Peace, South Africa), Pretoria West.

essential for us to promote understanding, respect and tolerance in matters of religion or belief, and reject any use of religion or belief that violates justice and human dignity." It is true that Christians must tolerate other religions in society. No Christian, or Christian church, is ever to do violence to those who reject the Lord Jesus Christ and his Gospel (Lk.9:52-56). But this document was advocating that Christians must treat other religions as equally valid ways to God! It implied that Christians must not condemn other religions as false! This no true Christian could ever agree to. Nor can any true Christian ever respect a false religion. Tolerance is one thing; but no Christian can respect a devilish religion. And all religions, other than the true faith of Christ, are devilish, according to God's Word. As for violating "justice and human dignity", this was extremely vague. Would preaching the Gospel be construed as "unjust"?

Another statement: "We....acknowledge the courageous role played by many religious people in upholding the values of justice, peace and human dignity in the midst of repression and division." Liberation theology, plain and simple! The drafters, of course, had in mind the SA government and its apartheid policy when they employed the words, "repression and division"; and the "courageous leaders" they had in mind were no doubt such men as Desmond Tutu, Denis Hurley, Beyers Naudé, Frank Chikane, Allan Boesak, and other pro-Red, radical "clergymen". But these men did not uphold justice, peace and human dignity! They upheld civil disobedience, violence, and misery! They were "grievous wolves" (Acts 20:29), whose very sermons stirred up men to hatred and bloodshed.

"We, therefore," the Draft Declaration went on, arrogantly, as if its authors were the spokesmen for all religious people, including true Christians, "join together as people of different faiths to promote reconciliation and reconstruction, and call upon the state to commit its resources to this task." Firstly, Christians cannot and will not "join together" with non-Christians in inter-faith ventures (2 Cor.6:14-18; Eph.5:11). Secondly, it is not the Church's task to "promote reconciliation and reconstruction" in society. Christians beseech men to be reconciled to *God,* by faith in his Son Jesus Christ (2 Cor.5:18-21): *that* is the work of reconciliation Christians are engaged in. The people of this world will always be at war; at enmity. Only when one is at peace with God, can one be at peace with one's fellow-man. But liberation theologians are not concerned with men being reconciled to God, for they themselves are strangers to God; they are not themselves reconciled to him.

Paragraph 1.1 stated, "People shall be free to have a religion or belief of their choice, save that the religion of children shall be determined by their parents, and no-one shall be coerced into accepting or practising any other belief." Certainly, none can be compelled, by force, to become Christians. It is the work of the Holy Spirit alone. True Christians, however, proclaim Christ to *all - including* children. For they are commanded to (Mk.16:15). And this can (and does at times) cause enmity between parent and child (Matt.10:34-37), should the child embrace the Gospel.

Para.1.2 stated, "Everyone has a duty to practise and encourage tolerance and respect towards people of other beliefs." Could it be construed as "intolerant" to tell a man that he is a lost sinner, bound for hell unless he repents? Could it be construed as "intolerant" to tell a man that Christ is the only way to the Father? Conceivably, it could; and that would pose a great threat to all true Christians.

Para.1.3: "Everyone has the duty to refrain from causing harm to other persons because of religious convictions and practices." True; but with the modern pseudo-science of psychology being virtually deified in society today, supposed "*mental* harm" could be something Christians are charged with causing in the future, when they tell men and women that they are sinners, lost and without hope unless Christ sets them free.

Para.1.4 was extremely dangerous: "While people are free to hold personal religious convictions, the *public expression* of religion shall not violate the common good of society or the rights of others" (italics added). The Christian's faith is not merely a private matter (Rom.10:9)! The wording of this sentence in the Draft Declaration was sufficiently vague to be broadly interpreted. Exactly what would violate the common good of society or the rights of others? It did not say. If such a sentence ever became law in South Africa, it could be used to forbid public preaching, tract distribution, etc. Ever since the very beginning of the Christian Church, there have been those in positions of authority who have sought to prevent the preaching of the Gospel to the multitudes (e.g. Acts 4:1-4,15-20); this Draft Declaration was an attempt to do the same in South Africa.

Para.1.5 declared: "Religions and their members should devote their energy and talents to the service of their fellow South Africans." Since when was that the Church's task? Nowhere in the New Testament does it say so! It is the Church's task to preach the Gospel to all men. But again, according to the doctrine of liberation theology, its task is to serve the "oppressed".

Para.1.6 stated that religions are "the conscience of society". This is not true: various religions (Popery, Islam, etc.) have promoted violence, and are still doing so, and have committed wicked acts throughout their history.

Para.2.1 contained perhaps the most dangerous statement of all in the Draft Declaration: "A religion shall be entitled to recognition by the state on the recommendation of the interfaith advisory body." Whether the state recognises biblical Christianity or not, is irrelevant to Christians. Obviously, it is a great blessing if a particular state grants religious liberty; but they are to serve God regardless of whether it does so or not! The WCRP and ANC planned to establish an advisory body to recommend which religions could be legally recognised in South Africa. What kind of a body did they have in mind? Para.3.1 made it clear: "To facilitate the implementation of this declaration and to act as a formal link between religions and the state, an independent interfaith advisory body should be established." A syncretistic body, in other words; and, given the nature of religious activism in South Africa, one can be certain that if ever such a body came into being, its members would be drawn primarily from the South African Council of Churches and the South African Catholic Bishops Conference! No doubt there would be some members from the Hindu, Muslim, and Jewish religions as well. This body, according to the desire of those who drew up this Draft Declaration, would dictate which religions would be entitled to state recognition, and therefore existence! And if a particular religion, or church, was not recognised, it would be illegal and persecuted!

Now, quite obviously, a true Christian church would never be recognised by such an interfaith body. Just as the Jewish religious leaders in the first century did not recognise the religion of Christ, but persecuted his followers (Acts 4:1-3; 5:27,28,40), so an "interfaith advisory body" would do the same in South Africa. It would be nothing less than an *inquisition* in this country. And we can be sure that in time to come, the Roman Catholic institution would come to dominate such a body. At the present time, because of the religious mosaic of South Africa, it has to tolerate the "multifaith" movement; but believing itself to be the only true religion, it would always seek to dominate and eventually totally control any such body.

"Members of this body shall enjoy good standing within their own religions, and be committed to the interfaith movement", para.3.2 stated. Who, then, would be appointed to such a body? Only ecumenicals/syncretists. And who would appoint the body? "The body shall be appointed by the Human Rights Commission in consultation with the major religions of South Africa" (para.3.3). The Human Rights Commission, however, was heavily-biased in favour of the ANC. It deliberately hid the truth about ANC atrocities! The appointees, then, should such a body come into being as the drafters would like, would not only be syncretistic, but also pro-Marxist. It would then be an ANC-controlled religious body.

True biblical Christianity is not, of course, one of the "major religions" of SA: true believers are a minority in SA, as they are anywhere in the world. By "major religions", the Declaration meant the denominations represented by the SACC, as well as Popery, and probably the Islamic, Hindu, and Jewish religions as well.

Returning to para.2, it was stated (Para.2.3): "The state shall guarantee to each religion the free exercise of spiritual authority among its members and jurisdiction in religious matters, *provided* this does not infringe on the provisions of the Bill of Rights and this declaration" (italics added). Very ominous indeed; the word "provided" was most important here. This group had declared itself to have the right to dictate what all religions in SA would be allowed to do.

Moving on to the fourth paragraph, 4.1 stated, "Religions shall at all times remain self-critical, and eliminate discrimination and intolerance based on gender, race, language or social status within their own communities." Again let it be said, that it is not the place of the state, nor of any "advisory body", dictate to a church how it should function. This typically Marxist statement was in line with the "non-sexist, non-racial, classless society" the Marxists aimed for. Communism seeks to remove the differences that do exist between sexes, races, and classes. No Christian, of course, is to act in a superior, sinful manner to anyone else. And in the Church, all are one in Christ Jesus: God is no respecter of persons regarding the salvation of people from different races, social classes, or from either sex; and when it comes to church membership there are to be no distinctions either (Gal.3:28). Nevertheless, the Lord has decreed that only men are to teach, speak, and be in authority in the local church (1 Tim.2:11-14; 1 Cor.14:34,35; 1 Tim.3:1-13; Titus 1:5,6). Many denominations now readily ordain women, but this is utterly antibiblical. Militant, ungodly feminism has infiltrated even the professing "Church" in our day. This is a satanic movement, a rebellion against the God-ordained roles of men and women. And the drafters of the Draft Declaration desired to make it a *crime* to obey the Bible on this matter! Should such a statement as was contained in this Declaration ever become law, churches seeking to obey the Scriptures by refusing to ordain women would be guilty of the modern "crime" of "discrimination based on gender". In this way the Communist forces would aim to control all aspects of the life and government of churches.

Para.4.2 stated: "Religions shall also oppose every form of exploitation and oppression in society at large." Of course Christians will never be in favour of evil exploitation, etc. But again it must be emphatically stated that it is not a Christian church's task to fight such things. As individuals, Christians can be involved in political and social matters, if they so desire; but it is not the task of a Christian church to be involved in such things. Furthermore, what the drafters meant by this was doubtless that Christians should become involved in marches, demonstrations, civil disobedience, sit-ins, etc., and other ungodly practices.

Paragraph 5 dealt with the matter of religious education. Para.5.1

stated: "The objective of all religious education shall be to engender an understanding, appreciation and tolerance of all religious traditions and to promote the national goals of a democratic, nonracial and nonsexist South African society." Firstly, one must note the dogmatic, arrogant wording: "The objective....*shall be* " Secondly, let the wording itself be analysed. Christians want to know something about other religions - so that they can be in a position to evangelise the adherents of them, and for no other reason. All religions are demonic in origin, and the devil himself is worshipped through them all. But by "understanding", the drafters meant that Christians must accept these false religions as valid! As for "tolerance", Christians practice this. They do not harm those of other religions. But regarding "appreciation" for other religions, that is impossible for the Christian. These false religions are damning millions of people. The devil is behind them all. Christ is absolutely unique, and no true Christian has any appreciation for false religions.

Nor is it the Church's task to promote the goals of a Communist South Africa, which is really what the wording of this point meant.

Para.5.2: "Children shall enjoy the right to education in religion or belief in accordance with the wishes of their parents or guardians...." Of course, if the points in this Declaration ever became law, this permission would only be given to those who belong to a religion recognised by the interfaith body!

In para.6.4, it was declared: "State schools shall not be used as platforms for proselytisation." In other words, no evangelism would be permitted at schools. Conceivably, a child who spoke to another child about Christ and the Gospel, could be violating such a law (if it ever became law)!

Paragraph 13 opened with a statement that sounded fine in itself: "Religions and individuals shall be free to promote and propagate their beliefs" (13.1). It was, however, "clarified" by 13.2: "This should be done with respect for the beliefs of others, without malice, slander or the denigration of any person or religion, avoiding the dissemination of malicious falsehoods and promotion of racial hatred." To denigrate means to blacken or defame. If a Christian calls a religion false, or exposes its evils, this could be construed as "slander", "denigration", "disseminating malicious falsehoods", etc., under such a law. Preaching from such a text as Acts 2:22,23 could conceivably be seen as "promotion of racial hatred" against the Jewish people; preaching from such a text as 2. Thess.2:3,4, and applying it to the Papacy as Christians throughout the centuries have done, could conceivably be seen as "lack of respect for the beliefs of others", "slander", "denigration of a person or religion", etc. Naming false ministers could be viewed as "defamation". Calling someone a child of the devil and an enemy of all righteousness, as Paul did in Acts 13:8-10, could be viewed as "malice" and "slander". A clever lawyer could interpret this paragraph in such ways! In the United States, similar cases are brought before the courts from time to time; and if ever such a paragraph as this became law in South Africa, Christians in this country could face great persecution.

Para.13.4 declared the following: "The promotion and propagation of any religious beliefs should not be directed at children under the age of eighteen, except with the permission of their parents." This was a statement of unadulterated Marxism. In the Soviet Union for decades, it was illegal for anyone to preach to children under the age of eighteen; the result, of course, being that by that age, they were well-indoctrinated in the teachings of Karl Marx, and usually wanted to know nothing about religious matters anyway. The long-term result of such a law in South Africa would be to direct the attention of the next generation away from religious matters, and particularly away from Christianity. Such a law would be one that no true Christian could obey, for the preaching of the Gospel to all men, women, and children is a law that must be obeyed above any law of man (Acts 5:28,29).

Para.14.1 declared: "Religions and individuals shall be free to publish and distribute literature and use other media to disseminate information about their doctrine, worship and pastoral affairs, provided that they do not denigrate or misrepresent the beliefs of others." This would naturally mean that any book, tape, or tract exposing a false religion would be illegal.

Finally, at the very end of the Draft Declaration, was the following "Commitment": "We believe that the principles contained in this declaration could contribute greatly to the authentic practice of religion, interfaith cooperation and social justice, and we therefore undertake to promote them among our fellow believers in this country and throughout the world."

The *authentic* practice of religion? In other words, biblical Christianity would be considered *non*-authentic. The drafters made it quite clear that this document was designed to contribute to the satanic interfaith movement, and to satanic liberation theology (religious Communism).

There can be no doubt that this document was aimed primarily at the suppression of biblical Christianity in South Africa. Satan is only interested in destroying biblical Christianity: all other religions are under his control anyway.

The drafters planned to finalise the document in November 1992, and requested that any suggestions for amendments or additions be submitted before September 30.

Accordingly, on November 22-24, 1992, about 120 members of many "Christian" denominations, and major religions, met in Pretoria and finalised the document. The SACBC was represented, and a number of Romish priests were present.[453] The finalised version was called the *Declaration on Religious Rights and Responsibilities*. It was hoped that this Declaration would be appended to a future Bill of Rights, in order to help with the *interpretation* of the clause on religious freedom!

The conference that met to finalise it was a religious Babel - an interfaith gathering that was an abomination to the Lord (2 Cor.6:14-18). Prayers were led by a Muslim, a Hindu, and a Bahai. Satan is the god that the members of these religions worship! A shaman also led in prayer: a man claiming to be a priest who is able to contact ancestral spirits and the spirits of living and inanimate things. A white man, he represented the *sangomas* (witchdoctors) at this conference! And yet men claiming to be Christian leaders were present - and said nothing. Clearly they were not true Christians, but blind leaders of the blind. No true Christian could have participated in such wickedness.

---

[453] *The Southern Cross*, December 13, 1992.

This witchdoctor called on the delegates to hum like bees, in imitation of the Australian aborigines, who do so in their religious rites. Then he called upon "the Great Spirit, the first movement", in his prayer. He asked "the milky way, our stellar family within the galaxy....the sun and the moon, the heavenly bodies....the powers of the four directions - the east and the west, the north and the south....the elements of sky and earth, of fire and water", to be present as they prayed. He went further, and called upon "the spirit of all the two-legged peoples", "the spirit of all four-legged creatures", "the winged creatures", and "all creeping things - all lowly beetles and worms and snakes", to be present as they prayed. He went further still, and invoked "the rock people, the living earth, and the dust, and the space between the dust .the tiniest atom and the emptiness at the heart of the atom", to be present as they prayed.[454]

This man invoked *demons* in his prayer! In calling upon the milky way, the sun, moon, and heavenly bodies, he was worshipping and praying to "the host of heaven", which the Lord forbids (Deut.17:3; 2 Kings 17:16; Acts 7:42,43). In calling upon the "spirit" of two-legged, four-legged, winged, and creeping creatures, he "changed the glory of the uncorruptible God into an image made like to corruptible man ['two-legged peoples'], and to birds ['the winged creatures'], and fourfooted beasts ['four-legged creatures'], and creeping things ['all lowly beetles and worms and snakes']" (Rom.1:23). He "worshipped and served the creature rather than the Creator" (Rom.1:25, margin); and so did every delegate present at that conference. In doing so, they worshipped devils: for demonic spirits are behind all false worship (1 Cor.10:19,20; Deut.32:17).

This finalised *Declaration on Religious Rights and Responsibilities* was not identical to the Draft Declaration. It was shorter; and a number of points in the Draft Declaration were dropped. No doubt this caused many to assume that the danger had to a large extent passed. Two things, however, need to be said here. Firstly, although a number of the more dangerous statements in the Draft Declaration did not find their way into the finalised version, the latter was still extremely dangerous (as shall be seen). Secondly (and this is

---

[454] *Signposts*, Vol.12, No.1, 1993.

why the Draft Declaration was analysed in such detail above), even though the final version was not identical with the draft, the *draft* was what they wanted! They obviously felt that they would have to tone down the finalised version for the time being; but we can be certain that the plan was to bide their time, and to push for the other points at a later stage. The final version was doubtless just the beginning. Desiring to eliminate biblical Christianity from South Africa, they doubtless planned to try again, and to keep trying until they were successful.

Let us examine the final version of this dangerous document.[455]

It began by declaring: "We who subscribe to this declaration… .acknowledge the courageous role played by many members of religious communities in upholding human dignity, justice and peace in the face of repression and division." This was obviously a reference to the pro-Red religious leaders who supported the revolution in South Africa. By "repression" they meant *government* actions, and by "human dignity, justice and peace", they meant the so-called "people's struggle": the Marxist revolution against the South African government.

To "uphold human dignity, justice and peace", these religious leaders supported the terrorist organisations in their vicious, bloody revolution. To "uphold human dignity, justice and peace" these wolves in sheep's clothing said little or nothing in condemnation of the barbaric necklace murder method. Woe unto such vile hypocrites! The Almighty God, who sees and knows all, has not forgotten. Woe unto them! The great day of judgement will indeed be a day of unspeakable terror to these wicked ones.

"We who subscribe to this declaration….are convinced that our religious communities can play a role in redressing past injustices and the construction of a just society". In the first place, this is not the Church's task, as has been said before; and in the second place, it will never happen! According to liberation theologians, sin is "structural": it is in society. If it is in individuals at all, then it is in the "oppressors" rather than the "oppressed." None of this, of course, is in any way

---

[455] *Declaration on Religious Rights and Responsibilities.* World Conference on Religion and Peace, South African Chapter, Krugersdorp.

scriptural.

"We who subscribe to this declaration....therefore .call upon religious communities to promote spiritual and moral values, reconciliation and reconstruction, in accordance with their own teachings." Nothing was said in this finalised document about an "interfaith advisory body", dictating which religions would be allowed to exist, and which would not. This naturally made this final version look much better than the draft version. But it must be remembered that it *was* the desire of those who drew up the draft version to see such a body established. That was their intention! For the time being, they postponed it; but it is highly unlikely that they scrapped it altogether. It could still be set up, in the future.

As for the statement, "in accordance with their own teachings", this would refer only to those religions permitted to exist by the state, on the advice of any future advisory body. And it must also be remembered that guarantees on paper mean little or nothing to Communists.

Point 1.1: "All persons shall be free to have and give expression to a system of values or religious beliefs and practices of their choice, and no-one shall be coerced into accepting or changing his/her religious affiliation." While sounding very good, much depends on what is meant by the word, "coerced". That was sufficiently ambiguous to be broadly interpreted! A smart lawyer could argue that dogmatic, persuasive statements are "coercion".

Point 1.2: "Everyone should respect and practise tolerance towards other people whatever their religious beliefs, provided that the expression of religion shall not violate the legal rights of others." Again, very ambiguous. Would it be a violation of one's rights to tell someone that his religion is wrong, or satanic?

Point 3.1: "Religious communities should, in accordance with their particular teachings, educate their communities in spiritual and moral values and promote these in society." All true Christian ministers educate their flocks in spiritual and moral values anyway, in accordance with the Word of God; they do not need any organisation to *tell* them to. And the question arises: could it be that the "values" they will be expected to teach will be those they are *told* to teach?

Point 3.3: "Religious communities should....direct their land resources to the benefit of the landless." This was straightforward Communism. The plain fact is that some will always have more land than others. The Bible does not say otherwise.

Point 3.4: "Religious communities should....remain self-critical at all times and strive to eliminate discrimination based on gender, race, language or social status in their own structures and among their members." This would constitute blatant interference in the affairs of the local church, if it became law. This conference arrogantly presumed to dictate to churches how they should act. According to the New Testament, in the local church there should not be discrimination based on race (Gal.2:11-14; Gal.3:28), or social status (Jas.2:1-13; Gal.3:28); and nor should women be treated any differently from men when it comes to church membership, fellowship at the Lord's table, etc. (Gal.3:28). The New Testament *does* teach, however (as seen earlier in this chapter), that women are not to teach, speak, nor to be in authority over men, in the local church (1 Tim.2:11-15; 1 Cor.14:34,35). As these are divine commandments, Christians will always seek to obey them, regardless of whether or not this is construed as "discrimination based on gender" - which is, in fact, what militant feminists consider it to be. It is the Lord's will for the government of his churches, and Christians are not to alter his commandments. There are very definite scriptural reasons for these commandments, as well.

One wonders how the government, or some advisory body, would plan to enforce the prohibition in this Declaration, should it ever become law!

Point 6 began by stating that religions have the right to propagate their teachings. But 6.1 stated: "The propagation of religious teachings should be done with respect for people of other religious communities, without denigrating them or violating their legal rights." This was a very dangerous statement! Christians, knowing that Christ alone is the way to the Father, and that all religions other than the true religion of Christ are false and devilish, will always tell this to the blinded adherents of these religions. Just as Paul "persuaded and turned away much people, saying that they be no gods, which are made with hands" (Acts 19:26), so Christians say the same today. Just as he preached that men "should turn from these vanities [false gods] unto the living God" (Acts 14:15), so Christians preach today. Paul boldly called the false gods "vanities"; but in South Africa, if these wicked plotters have their way, Christians will be forbidden by law to speak thus of the false gods of Romanism, Islam, Hinduism, Buddhism, etc. It would be a law that Christians would not be able to obey (Acts 5:29); but such a law would make persecution of Christians inevitable.

Finally, mention should be made of Point 7, which stated that religious communities shall have access to the public media. Point 7.2, however, declared: "To ensure such reasonable access and to avoid misunderstandings and intolerance, the broad religious spectrum of society should be represented on all boards responsible for religious media." This clause, if it became law, would close the door to the preaching of the true Gospel via radio or television! For the "narrow way" proclaimed by true Christians would be construed as intolerant by those who tread the "broad way" that leads to destruction (Matt.7:13,14). The "broad religious spectrum" that would be represented on all boards would indeed be the "broad way" of which Jesus spoke.

The document ended with an "Affirmation". It said that the signatories to the declaration were "convinced that there is an urgent need for all religious communities and the state to accept and implement the principles in this declaration", and recognised "that these principles will function within the framework of a Bill of Rights". Note the word, "will" - not "should" or "might"! Should this diabolical document ever become law in South Africa, true Christianity would be outlawed.

And who were the sponsors of this document? "The WCRP-SA gratefully acknowledges financial support for this project from: Anglo American and De Beers Chairman's Fund, Evangelisches Missionswerk (Germany), Niwano Peace Foundation (Japan), and the South African Catholic Bishops' Conference." We ought not to be surprised. The internationalists, in conjunction with Popery and other religious groups, financed the whole thing. The document was perfectly in keeping with their plan for South Africa.

CHAPTER THIRTY-THREE

1992: PROVIDING MARTYRS FOR THE CAUSE

In September 1992 the ANC/SACP alliance deliberately planned and staged a confrontation with the security forces of the tiny homeland of the Ciskei, which resulted in the deaths of twenty-nine people.

Ciskei was ruled by Brigadier Oupa Gqozo, a man staunchly anti-ANC. It had been granted its independence from South Africa years before, but the Communist forces refused to recognise it. The ANC/SACP alliance insisted that all the independent homelands had to be reincorporated into South Africa. The bloody confrontation that occurred in September had been deliberately planned by the ANC/SACP, for the following reasons: to gain international sympathy; to overthrow Gqozo; and to force the South African government to assume direct control over all the homelands, so that, when the ANC came to power in South Africa, *it* would control them. Ciskei was chosen as the first target because it was the weakest non-ANC homeland.

The march was organised by Chris Hani, general secretary of the South African Communist Party. He said, "The battle lines are drawn. Tomorrow we are going to Bisho [the capital of Ciskei] to remove Oupa Gqozo." He called Gqozo "de Klerk's puppet" and "kitchen boy". His speeches were deliberately inflammatory. He also called Chief Buthelezi of KwaZulu "that madman".[456]

Since August, huge quantities of weapons had been smuggled into Ciskei by the ANC/SACP, for the mass action.

On September 7, 40 000 ANC supporters marched to the Bisho stadium. Ronnie Kasrils, senior ANC/SACP member and MK intelligence chief, deliberately defying the court order (as he himself admitted later), led several hundred people through a gap in the fence. The Ciskeian troops shot twenty-nine people dead. And the world screamed with rage, siding with the ANC/SACP and condemning Gqozo. The entire event was a brilliant propaganda victory for the Communist forces. They cared nothing about the fact that they had

---

[456] *Roca Report,* No 45, September 1992.

purposely sacrificed twenty-nine of their own people for the cause. Kasrils said, "We had confrontation in mind." Indeed, maps were discovered detailing the plans to break through the gap.[457] But the international media, and governments worldwide, were not interested in the truth. They saw what they wanted to see, and that was all. As far as they were concerned, "innocent", "peaceful" ANC marchers had been gunned down by merciless, barbaric Ciskeian troops.

ANC Western Cape secretary, Tony Yengeni, said on September 10, "Gqozo must die." According to an SA Army chief, MK intended assassinating Gqozo. The ANC, of course, denied this.[458]

Predictably, the South African Catholic Bishops Conference sided with the ANC. It issued a statement expressing its "dismay" at the "senseless killing....of innocent people at Bisho", and extended sympathies to the victims and their families.[459] Those killed were not innocent: they had broken the law, they posed a massive security threat, and the Ciskeian troops had acted as troops in similar circumstances almost anywhere in the world would have done.

Just as predictably, the other radical, Marxist-supporting religious institutions took the side of the ANC/SACP as well. On September 17, some 80 members of the Institute for Contextual Theology protested at the South African Broadcasting Corporation (SABC), claiming that the SABC had not reported the ANC's march on Bisho correctly. Priest John Lamola of the SACC said: "We are not going to allow the SABC to continue to hoodwink our people." The petition delivered to the SABC condemned it for "portraying peaceful protest as Communist-inspired and demonic".[460] That was precisely what it was!

The WCC demonstrated its support for the ANC and SACP by sending its secretary-general, Emilio Castro, to address those at the funeral of the victims. He did so alongside the ANC's Walter Sisulu, the SACP's Chris Hani, and the Transkei's Bantu Holomisa.[461]

The pope of Rome himself, John Paul II, commented on the Bisho

---

[457] *Roca Report*, No.45, September 1992.
[458] *Roca Report*, No.45, September 1992.
[459] *The Southern Cross*, September 20, 1992.
[460] *The Citizen*, September 18, 1992.
[461] *The Sunday Tribune*, September 20, 1992.

tragedy. A Vatican message was forwarded on September 16, which stated that the pope "commends the dead to our heavenly Father's eternal love and invokes the divine gifts of strength and comfort on the injured and on affected families".[462] He certainly left no doubt as to who he sided with!

The Bisho tragedy gave an excuse to various foreign pro-Red ecclesiastical leaders to interfere increasingly in the South African situation, allegedly to help "stop the violence". A five-man delegation arrived on September 22 at the start of an ecumenical monitoring programme to "monitor violence", attempt to get negotiations going again, and prepare the masses for elections. It was headed by the representative of the Anglican institution at the United Nations, Sir Paul Reeves, and was invited to SA by the SACBC and SACC. Accompanying him were Christine Davis, Quaker president of the Council of Churches in Britain and Ireland; Melvin Talbert, a Methodist bishop and WCC member; Jorgen Estrup, a member of the Lutheran denomination of Denmark and a parliamentarian; and Boniface Tshosa Setlalekgose, Roman Catholic bishop of Botswana. Reeves said that the group "would do what Christians and the church have always done, which is to stand beside those who are victims of violence. It is of the essence and nature of the Christian faith that we share with God his search and hope for justice."[463] Such utter drivel was astounding. Since when has it been the divinely-given mission of the Church to stand beside those who provoke the state by sinful actions? One will search in vain in the New Testament for such a commission from the Lord Christ. And to speak of God as *searching and hoping* for justice! - as if the Almighty, the sovereign Lord of all creation, is stumbling around in confusion and uncertainty, searching and hoping for something so elusive to him that he needs mortal men to "share" in his search with him! Though "knight" is spelt with a *k*, it would be better to spell it without that letter when referring to Reeves, for his words reveal spiritual darkness indeed.

The ecumenical monitoring programme was a joint effort by the World Council of Churches and the National Ecumenical Forum, and was Vatican-approved. The plan was for groups of international

---

[462] *The Southern Cross*, September 27, 1992.
[463] *The Citizen*, September 23, 1992.

"church" leaders to visit SA for four to six weeks at any given time, to "monitor the situation."[464] In essence, this meant that they would assist the ANC/SACP alliance to achieve its goal of taking power.

So blatant was the radical "church" support for the ANC and its allies, that it was only after several religious leaders had received death threats, and Chief Buthelezi had sharply criticised "clergymen" for identifying with the ANC at its funeral marches, that several religious leaders - two leading Anglicans and the former head of the Congregational denomination - attended and participated in an Inkatha Freedom Party funeral! Those being buried had been victims of ANC violence.[465] It was quite obvious, however, that such actions were nothing more than token gestures. The sympathies of the liberal denominations lay with the ANC, not the IFP.

In the wake of the so-called "Ecumenical Eminent Persons Group" headed by Reeves, interfaith religious "observers" began arriving in South Africa in October, as arranged by the WCC and Roman Catholic, Dutch Reformed, and Pentecostal "churches" in South Africa.[466]

In October Sheena Duncan, senior vice-president of the SACC, said that ministers should use Sunday services to educate their congregations about democracy and prepare them for elections. She added that the Church's independence gave it an important role in helping prepare people for elections.[467] In a letter published in the *Natal Witness* newspaper on November 25, the present author wrote the following in response to her statements: "Given the well-known and well-documented support by the SACC for the ANC/SACP/Cosatu alliance, the ministers of the SACC's member-churches would doubtless be expected to educate their congregations in accordance with the wishes (a better word would be demands) of the so-called liberation movements (in reality, terrorist organisations)....the truth is that the member churches of the SACC are not independent: they are dancing to the tune of the Marxist

---

[464] *The Citizen*, September 23, 1992.
[465] *The Southern Cross*, October 25, 1992.
[466] *The Southern Cross*, October 25, 1992.
[467] *The Natal Witness*, October 24, 1992.

revolutionaries....The World Council of Churches, to which the SACC belongs, has provided huge financial assistance to these groups over many years, even though it is aware of the atrocities being committed by them. Bible-believing Christians do not take their orders from this ecclesiastical monstrosity, which is nothing less than the religious arm of the Marxist revolution in SA."

Nelson Mandela, committed Communist, gave an interview in 1992 in which he spoke of his own attitude towards religion. Although he said he was "not particularly religious or spiritual", he also declared, "I am not an atheist. Definitely not."[468] But he added that he did not usually regard this (to him) deeply personal matter as open for comment in the media. Indeed, for Communism to succeed in Africa, it *had to* be a form of *religious* Communism; and liberation theology was the ideal answer to this Communist dilemma. Mandela had obviously drunk quite deeply of this merger of Communism with religion. He spoke with affection of an Anglican prison chaplain named Hughes, whom he met while in prison, of André Schafer of the NG Kerk in Afrika (Dutch Reformed), and of Theo Kotze, Methodist chaplain. He said that he had enjoyed the ecumenical approach of the chaplains, who did not ask which church or religion people belonged to. And he said, "I never missed a service and often read the Scripture lessons." No doubt such statements were designed to reassure religious people that he was a religious man; and they probably did. But true Christians would not be fooled by such words. They know that attending services, and reading the Scriptures, do not prove one is a Christian.

He also enjoyed the visits of a Muslim Imam, with whom he often spoke at length. He was clearly impressed with Islam.

When at Pollsmoor Prison, it was a source of disappointment to him that only the Methodist chaplain was allowed to visit him, because he was a member of the Methodist denomination (and said during the interview that he still was). He became friends with his chaplain, Dudley Moore, and regularly received the Methodist sacrament of communion. It tells us much about this denomination claiming to be Christian, that it could have a convicted Communist guerrilla on its membership rolls, and that it could permit him to receive the

---

[468] *Challenge*, No.10, October/November 1992.

ordinance! Mandela said of the communion service: "The sacrament gave me a sense of inner quiet and calm. I used to come away from these services feeling a new person."[469] A new person he might have felt, but a "new creature" in Christ he was not (2 Cor.5:17).

On December 14, addressing the "Free Ethiopian Church of Southern Africa", Mandela praised the contribution of what he called "the broad Ecumenical Movement in South Africa and internationally" for its "unparalleled" struggle against the "heresy of apartheid". He named, in particular, Tutu, Chikane, and Naudé. He then outlined what the "Church" should be doing in SA (according to the revolutionaries). He said it "has no option but to join other agents of change and transformation".[470] Note the words, *no option*. This was an indication that the only type of "church" the ANC recognised was one that aided and abetted the revolution. It was clearly in favour of those religious groups that formed part of the "broad Ecumenical Movement" and fought apartheid, but of no others. In this light we must interpret another sentence of his on that occasion: "In the ANC we guarantee both the freedom of religion and the independence of the church." As far as the ANC was concerned, freedom of religion should only be extended to those religious institutions that joined the revolutionaries in their so-called "struggle".

The South African government in 1992 capitulated more and more to the ANC. On September 26, President de Klerk and Nelson Mandela signed a "Record of Understanding". The government agreed to release so-called "political prisoners" (another term for terrorists), fence in hostels (which contained mainly Inkatha Freedom Party supporters), and ban traditional weapons (used by Zulus). In other words, this agreement was an anti-IFP agreement. The ANC - the *real* cause of the violence - was left untouched!

The ANC, for its part, merely agreed to examine its programme of mass action. It did - and *recommitted* itself to it.

The two men also agreed to an interim government for South Africa![471] This was a major capitulation by the government. It was

---

[469] *Challenge*, No.10, October/November 1992.
[470] *Challenge*, No.12, February 1993.
[471] *Roca Report*, No.46, October 1992.

precisely what the ANC had been working to achieve. Essentially it meant that the government would surrender power.

Among the prisoners the government released, were Robert McBride, an MK commander who bombed a bar, killing three and injuring sixty-nine; two other MK officers who killed ten people, including four very young children, and injured twenty; and (as a concession to the militant white right-wing, so as to make it appear as if the government acted fairly) Barend Strydom, who killed black people in cold blood.[472] These unrepentant killers were released back into an already terrified society. An absolute mockery of justice, and another victory of immense proportions for the Communist forces.

By late 1992, the beautiful province of Natal, the traditional home of the great Zulu nation, was in a civil war, with ANC and IFP supporters killing one another. The government moved extra police and troops into the province. Professional hit squads were in operation. Guns were everywhere. ANC men were carrying out attacks dressed in police uniforms, and using the pro-ANC homeland of Transkei as a springboard from which the attacks were launched. By late 1992 a hundred people a month were being killed in Natal. The ANC had declared war on the Zulu-based, non-Communist IFP, and its leaders and supporters were being massacred. And yet, when one ANC member - Reggie Hadebe, deputy to ANC Natal leader Harry Gwala - was killed, the NP government offered a R25 000 reward for information leading to the arrest and conviction of the killers.[473] Clearly, the government was favouring the ANC - delivering the country piecemeal into its hands, in fact. Throughout the year, the government sidelined the IFP and its leader, Chief Mangosuthu Buthelezi, and capitulated on virtually every point to the ANC.

Afrikaners found it hard to believe that their National Party, under the presidency of FW de Klerk, was actually doing all in its power to see to it that the ANC came to power in South Africa eventually. But this was indeed the case. While calling the ANC its enemy, the government actually moved to *prevent the ANC/SACP from being discredited!* In 1992, a document was published by the South African Communist Party, entitled *State of the Nation: the Road to Victory*, the

---

[472] *Roca Report*, No.46, October 1992.
[473] *Roca Report*, No.47, November 1992.

Path to Power. The following astounding statement was made in this document: "Mr de Klerk gave express orders to the military and police not to discredit the movement, despite having ample information to do so". This he did as far back as 1990. The conservative, anti-Communist *Aida Parker Newsletter* (APN) confirmed it. In the November/December 1992 issue, it was revealed that in 1990, *APN* had begun work on an exposé of ANC torture camps in various African countries. In December 1990, *APN* was asked, by a cabinet minister in Pretoria, to drop this exposé, saying, "It is feared that such disclosures would affect negotiations"! *APN* did not drop it; and after it was published, close personal friends of Aida Parker were approached "by agents of a certain intelligence service", requesting them to spy on *APN!*[474]

The government of FW de Klerk was deliberately attempting to suppress any information that would discredit the Communist ANC! Incredible....but true. The National Party had come under the control of the shadowy international forces that desired an ANC puppet government in Pretoria for the purpose of controlling South Africa's immense riches.

The government's appointment of the Goldstone Commission, an otherwise most mysterious business, made sense in the light of this. Throughout 1992 the pro-ANC stance of the Commission became increasingly obvious. It seemed bent on destroying the credibility of the SA security forces. Goldstone gave certain findings to the ANC *for inspection,* even before submitting them to President de Klerk, who appointed him in the first place! Then, he organised a raid on the premises of the top-secret Directorate of Covert Collection, a Military Intelligence operation. The raiding team knew exactly where to find the documents they wanted. These documents were important in the disclosures of MI investigations into links between MK, the ANC's armed wing, and the Irish Republican Army. The leftist media had blasted these investigations as "dirty tricks", even though national security was at stake.[475]

---

[474] *The Aida Parker Newsletter,* Issue No.159, November/December 1992.
[475] *The Aida Parker Newsletter,* Issue No.159, November/December 1992.

This also once again reveals the connections between the ANC and the Roman Catholic IRA.

Further stunning evidence of the government's deliberate, step-by-step surrender of power to the ANC/SACP alliance, was to be found in a secret SACP policy paper issued in November 1992, entitled *Between the People's Offensive and Regime Crisis: Prospects for a Democratic Victory and Advance to Socialism.* This document was leaked to the SA government, which deliberately did nothing about it. It was also leaked to *The Aida Parker Newsletter,* which *did* do something. It published the document. It clearly revealed the government's capitulation, every step of the way, to the revolutionaries.

In it, it was stated that "the regime's" (i.e. NP government's) camp was divided; that consensus had developed between the government and the "liberation movement"; that the government had consistently given in, but never the "liberation movement"; that no agreement was possible on regional powers (i.e. that a federal system was out, and SA had to be a unitary state); that there was a "dominant position within the ruling bloc" that had sided, in essence, with the SA Communist Party; that opposition to "convergence" with the revolutionaries on the part of the government had weakened considerably, thanks to the efforts of the "most advanced" section of the NP (i.e. the liberal section); that "the partial neutralisation of the armed forces through interim government control will be achieved soon"; that the government's National Intelligence Service (NIS) had deliberately worked *against* the white Conservative Party and the Zulu-based Inkatha, and against elements within the military; that NIS had been involved, in a positive manner, with the pro-ANC *Vrye Weekblad* newspaper, and with certain leftist journalists; that the "dominant position" within the NP deliberately leaked the documents which precipitated what was called "Inkathagate" (revelations of government funding of Inkatha); that "thorough-going redistribution and affirmative action" was very much SACP policy; etc.[476]

This document, in a nutshell, revealed that a thoroughly infiltrated, thoroughly New World Order National Party was deliberately,

---

[476] *The Aida Parker Newsletter,* Issue No.162, April 1993.

definitely, inexorably handing over power to the Communist forces, in accordance with the wishes of the Jesuit/Illuminati forces internationally. It was not accidental, it was calculated. The greatest enemy conservative, anti-Communist, freedom-loving South Africans had, was their own government. The evidence had been accumulating for years, and by the end of 1992 it was simply overwhelming. Mind-boggling and overwhelming.

In December 1992, President de Klerk dropped another bombshell. Twenty-three senior army officers were either retired or suspended on his direct orders, as well as paid informers who had infiltrated deep into the ANC. The reason given for this was that there was evidence of criminal actions. Government officials, however, said that it was really done in order to remove elements in the security forces who opposed an interim government, and the absorption of the ANC's armed wing, MK, into the South African Defence Force. One source in Military Intelligence said that this axing was having a "terrible effect on the soldiers' morale. They cannot believe what they are seeing." Former chief of Military Intelligence, General Tienie Groenewald, said: "I have never before seen a government destroy its own power base as this one is doing." The ANC praised the purge, saying that it opened the way for joint ANC/government control of the Defence Force. The world, in general, applauded de Klerk's move.[477] It was yet another major capitulation to the ANC and its international backers.

And meanwhile, the ANC continued to illegally send recruits abroad for military training, by the thousands. Some were *children*.[478]

The International Freedom Foundation appointed the Douglas Commission in 1992 to investigate atrocities in ANC prison camps. In making its findings known, the Commission described what it called "a litany of unbridled and sustained horror". The brutality was appalling. Tortures and murders regularly took place. Top ANC officials were implicated in these: Hani, Slovo, Tambo, Kasrils, Nzo, etc. Douglas recommended punishment for the guilty. But the ANC, predictably, rejected the findings. And yet the report came on top of two others - one by Amnesty International, and the other an internal *ANC*

---

[477] *Roca Report*, No.49, January 1993.
[478] *Roca report*, No.48, December 1992.

investigation - both of which found evidence of abuses![479] The devastating information in these reports should have been international news, and should have put paid to the ANC's ambitions of ever ruling South Africa. But the government continued negotiating.

It was about this time that the Pan Africanist Congress (PAC) began to move increasingly into the limelight, due to the terrorist attacks of its armed wing, the Azanian Peoples Liberation Army (APLA). Not as popular as the ANC, it was nevertheless also supported by overseas funds, and was just as murderous. APLA declared war on whites. On November 29, 1992, it killed four and injured twenty in a single attack in Kingwilliamstown. In a December 3 attack in Queenstown, a limpet mine was used. APLA had never before used a limpet mine, and this fact was an indication of MK collusion with APLA. Although the ANC and PAC were supposedly two separate organisations, it began to appear as if the ANC could be assisting what many perceived (incorrectly) to be an organisation even more radical than the ANC - to make the ANC look good! The PAC was *as* radical as the ANC, but not more so. Certainly, however, when the ANC condemned the PAC attacks, it made itself appear to be less radical, more moderate.[480]

Step by step, the South African government was retreating from the firm stance it once had taken on UN intervention in South Africa's affairs. On September 10, 1992, foreign affairs minister Pik Botha urged the UN secretary general to send a special envoy to SA, saying: "We do not envisage an observer role only but help and involvement."[481] The ANC's strategy all along had been to cause such a massive, countrywide escalation of violence, while simultaneously seeing to it that the security forces were rendered almost impotent by the government itself, that the population at large, and the government, would say, "We need the United Nations." Once the UN entered SA, the ANC was assured of victory; for the UN had for many long years given it full support. Now it was happening: the government was caving in, surrendering the country into the hands of the world body, and thus of the Jesuit/Illuminati internationalists.

---

[479] *Roca Report*, No.49, January 1993.
[480] *Roca Report*, No.48, December 1992.
[481] *Roca Report*, No.45, September 1992.

CHAPTER THIRTY-FOUR

1993: ECCLESIASTICAL EULOGIES FOR A COMMUNIST THEY EQUATED WITH CHRIST

The African National Congress understood that it was essential to have as much support as possible from religious groups, not only to give it legitimacy in the eyes of the world and of South Africans themselves, but also because South Africa was (and is) such a religious country that the ANC could not hope to be successful without "church" support, and lots of it. It has been shown, in this book, to what extent various so-called "churches" and "church" organisations supported the revolutionaries through the years. It has also been shown that, while of course the liberal denominations and the Roman Catholic institution fully supported the ANC, that organisation desired to see those calling themselves *Evangelicals* doing so too. An organisation called "Concerned Evangelicals" attempted to win Evangelicals to the "revolutionary cause", by promoting liberation theology and the revolution in an evangelical dress - but so subtly that many Evangelicals would fall for it.

In the December/January 1993 issue of *Challenge,* a magazine of liberation theology published by "Contextual Publications" (the name reveals much!), Moss Ntlha of "Concerned Evangelicals" wrote about the anti-Communist, anti-ANC leaders of the independent homelands of Ciskei and Bophuthatswana, and of the self-governing territory of KwaZulu, all of whom claimed to be Protestant Evangelicals. The article called them tyrants and killers; called the police handling of the ANC's march on Bisho, Ciskei, in September 1992, "the tragic massacre of nearly 30 peaceful marchers"; hid certain historical facts; said nothing of the ANC's ruthless history; and called on Evangelicals to "re-position" their witness - "against oppression and tyranny" (but not a word about the oppression and tyranny of the so-called "liberators"!), "against state sponsored murder" (but not a word about ANC-sponsored murder!), etc.[482]

This was a deliberate *whitewashing* of the ANC/SACP alliance,

---

[482]*Challenge*, No.11, December/January 1993.

and a falsification of the true facts. It was an attempt to push Evangelicals, too, into the "struggle".

The liberal, leftist "churches", meanwhile, continued to give their wholehearted support to the ANC and its bloody revolution. On January 29, 1993, for example, Nelson Mandela addressed delegates at the Anglican Consultative Council conference in Cape Town, after meeting with the Anglican Archbishop of Canterbury, George Carey, the head of the world's Anglicans. Mandela praised the role of the "Church" in supporting what he called the "struggle for democracy" (the revolution). Carey, for his part, said that the Anglican institution was "passionately committed to justice and equality and shares the ANC's dream of a non-racial society in South Africa."[483] In a letter published in the *Natal Witness* on February 15, 1993, written in response to the statements of Mandela and Carey, the present author wrote:

"Let it be stated very clearly: there is the Church of Jesus Christ, consisting of all whom the Lord has called to himself through Christ; and there is a false `church', using the same terminology, but preaching falsehood, supporting revolutionary organisations, and blasphemously equating `salvation' with freedom from `political oppression'. The latter `church' supports the ANC's `struggle for democracy' - in reality a revolutionary war to gain power. The true Church does not support such wickedness, never has, and never will. George Carey, of the Anglican denomination, spoke piously of his denomination sharing `the ANC's dream of a non-racial society in South Africa'. The only thing the ANC dreams of is power by any means. The interests of `the people' (to use one of its favourite terms) have never been paramount. An organisation with such a track record of murder and torture certainly does not have the welfare of `the people' at heart. And `churches' that support it are not churches of Christ."

Since returning to South Africa, ANC exiles had received money from the National Coordinating Committee for Refugees (NCCR). And who were the members of this organisation? They were the South

---

[483] *The Natal Witness*, January 30, 1993.

African Council of Churches, the South African Catholic Bishops Conference, the World Conference on Religion and Peace, as well as the ANC, PAC, and AZAPO! Yet another piece of damning evidence of "church" support for the terrorist organisations. Money was sent to the NCCR by the United Nations; but these payments stopped when the organisation was dissolved on April 1, following the discovery of massive fraud![484] A telling insight into the false "Christianity" of these religious institutions!

Despite its unbanning three years before, despite all the concessions to it since then, the ANC by 1993 was still deeply involved in a terrorist war against the people of South Africa. This was proved once again when, in the midst of the government's negotiations with it, ANC members were arrested on February 1 with a huge shipment of arms they were smuggling into Natal, including RPG rockets and launchers capable of destroying armoured vehicles. The ANC fully supported the smuggling of arms into Natal. The government, once again, did nothing but protest - and the negotiations continued, the issue pushed aside.[485]

Communist Party control of the ANC was as strong as ever. In a letter written by SACP deputy general secretary, Charles Nqakula, which was leaked to the *Aida Parker Newsletter,* it was revealed that, of the 50 people on the ANC's National Executive Committee (its highest decision-making body), 33 were SACP members. Communists headed all the most sensitive administrative structures of the ANC. Many denied that they were Communists, but what did this matter? Their denials meant absolutely nothing.[486]

On January 29, 1993, Nelson Mandela denied that there was any ideological connection between the ANC and the SACP, and he said that the alliance would very likely be terminated once the ANC became a political party.[487] This was nonsense, of course. In April, the ANC's foreign affairs director, Thabo Mbeki, said that the organisation was considering redressing the "gross maldistribution of

---

[484] *Roca Report*, No.57, September 1993.
[485] *Roca Report*, No.50, February 1993.
[486] *The Aida Parker Newsletter,* Issue No.162, April 1993.
[487] *The Natal Witness,* January 30, 1993.

wealth" through independent law courts under a future government. "The ANC reserves nationalisation and the redistribution of resources as matters of possibility," he said. A spokesman for a major banking group said that it would be possible for the courts to ascertain an individual's net worth and appropriate his assets.[488] Such a policy was in perfect keeping with Communism, despite Mandela's denials of any ideological connection between the ANC and SACP! And of course, the overwhelming historical evidence contradicted his claim as well.

On March 2, six black children of members of the Inkatha Freedom Party were gunned down in a car ambush near Pietermaritzburg. ANC men were charged with the gruesome murders. On March 13, two white teenagers and the mother of one of them were killed near Johannesburg by gunmen who fired on their car. The gunmen originally intended to fire on a school bus carrying white children. APLA, the PAC's armed wing, claimed responsibility, but one of the two men charged with the murder was an ANC member until the end of 1992, and the other was an ANC supporter. Both were trained by MK, the ANC's armed wing. On March 20, a motorist was forced to stop and was told, "We are going to kill all the old white people and white children. This will be a year of terror." He was almost burnt to death in his car, but escaped just in time. A number of other whites were killed in the Johannesburg area, the Eastern Cape, and the Orange Free State. Clearly, the ANC and PAC were doing their best to provoke a race war. A year of terror 1993 was to prove to be indeed, as shall be seen.

Despite MK and APLA being the armed wings of two different organisations, the ANC and the PAC respectively, the evidence pointed to very close co-operation between the two. Meetings were held between them, supposedly "dissident" MK members joined APLA, and both guerrilla armies were supported by Transkei's military leader, Bantu Holomisa.[489] And three independent MK sources told the *Weekly Mail*, 3.12.93, that MK members played key roles in some of APLA's attacks in 1992. After the attacks, MK and

---

[488] *The Aida Parker Newsletter*, Issue No.163, May 1993.
[489] *Roca Report*, No.52, April 1993.

ANC members were sent out of the country for training, sometimes with APLA members. An East Rand MK commander said that there was "a crossover in the ranks on the ground", with APLA usually claiming responsibility for attacks. "The ANC needs to keep a clean image, but it also had to keep links with the PAC, especially the militant youth," he said.[490]

The ANC was employing a twin strategy. On the one hand, it was talking peace and negotiating with other organisations. Mandela admitted that ANC members were as involved in violence as anyone else, and Chris Hani said that he rejected calls for war and the ambushing of white women and children, and called for a "people's peace corps". On the other hand, ANC violence was actually *increasing!*[491] This twin strategy was to be employed throughout the months to come.

Meanwhile, the Jesuit/Illuminati/internationalist forces continued to dictate the terms of surrender to the de Klerk government. In early 1993, according to the US ambassador to the Vatican, Thomas Melady, United States and Vatican officials discussed South Africa's bid for diplomatic recognition.[492] Clearly its bid for such recognition depended much on what Rome and Washington decided.

"Well-placed sources in Washington" revealed in 1993 that the US State Department instructed de Klerk *not* to declare a state of emergency in South Africa, or call out the security forces for full-scale action, regardless of how many died at the hands of the ANC/SACP.[493] It mattered nothing to Washington how many died in South Africa, as long as the ANC, in which the US had invested hundreds of millions of dollars, eventually governed the country. For then the conspiratorial rulers of the US would (through their ANC puppet) be in control of SA's immense mineral wealth. And behind these men stood the Vatican.

Mandela called for the formation of a "peace corps", its commander to be appointed by the United Nations. The United States

---

[490] *Roca Report,* No.60, December 1993.
[491] *Roca Report,* No.52, April 1993.
[492] *The Southern Cross,* April 4, 1993.
[493] *The Aida Parker Newsletter,* Issue No.163, May 1993.

was increasingly, in 1993, serving the interests of the United Nations. US Secretary of State Warren Christopher, addressing a select audience in Chicago on March 22, emphasized that the US would have to marshal the West's collective strength to deal with ethnic conflicts. He said that the US had to develop the international means to *contain and prevent* such conflicts before they erupted![494] What he was asserting, in effect, was that the US was to become increasingly involved in the affairs of other nations, serving the interests of the UN. He said that UN peacekeeping capabilities had to be strengthened to permit prompt, preventive action. NATO, the OAU, and other organisations had to be adapted to support the UN in this. Increasingly, the distinction between the US and the UN was blurring.

Christopher's words received confirmation from two others. James L. Woods, the US' Deputy Secretary of Defence for African Affairs, said that the US, Russia, NATO and the OAU were among the states and institutions involved, or to be involved, in the *American quest to end or stifle* global, regional, and ethnic strife and violence! He said that "peace enforcement" involved military operations to restore peace, even though the parties might not consent to intervention and might still be fighting. And Anthony Lake, US National Security Advisor, stated that the US needed to help build the capacity of the OAU to engage early and effectively as peacekeepers. He added: "This implies an activist approach in nations that are disasters in the making."[495]

What the words of these men meant was that it was planned that the United States would increasingly play the role of the world's policeman; that it would lead and support others, such as the OAU, NATO, etc., who would also have such a role to play; that it, and these others, would increasingly serve the interests of the United Nations; and that (unknown, probably, to these men) the US would be serving the interests of the Vatican as the Vatican's muscle - its army - to accomplish its goals of world conquest.

---

[494] *The Aida Parker Newsletter*, Issue No.164, June 1993.
[495] *The Aida Parker Newsletter*, Issue No.164, June 1993
[495] *The Aida Parker Newsletter*, Issue No.164, June 1993.
[495] *The Aida Parker Newsletter*, Issue June 1993.

For South Africa, these plans were ominous; for conceivably, then, the US armed forces could eventually intervene militarily in South Africa. They would do so, of course, in support of the ANC, *not* of the moderate, anti-Communist, pro-Western forces in the country.

An event occurred on April 9, 1993, that was to plunge South Africa into probably its greatest crisis up to that time: the general secretary of the South African Communist Party, Chris Hani, was murdered by a white man.

The man was a Polish immigrant. He fatally shot Hani outside the latter's home. And the country literally exploded in ANC-orchestrated violence. The very next day, three whites in the Cape Town area were burnt to death, and others were killed elsewhere. Police stations were attacked around the country. On April 14, the ANC's day of protest and "mourning" for Hani's murder, there was more violence. Marches and rallies countrywide were very violent. In Cape Town's city centre, terrible destruction of property occurred, and one person was killed. In Port Elizabeth and Pietermaritzburg, in Durban and Johannesburg, there was widespread destruction of property. 50 000 people attacked a police station in Soweto. The police killed four and injured 250, and the ANC called it "unprovoked police brutality"![496] This was sheer nonsense, a blatant lie. The duty of the police was to maintain law and order, making use of such force as was necessary to accomplish this (Rom.13:3,4). They had a duty to clamp down hard. Regrettably, they did not clamp down hard enough. As always, the government used strong language, but did almost nothing.

The ANC/SACP/COSATU alliance announced, on April 16, that it was initiating a six-week campaign of what it called "rolling mass action" to force the government to meet its demands for an election date to be set by the end of May, and for the immediate installation of a "Transitional Executive Council" (TEC), which would give the alliance joint control over the security forces. South Africa was forced to the very brink of civil war.[497] Indeed, it was not too long before the government had capitulated on both points. The installation of a TEC would mean that the government would no longer be governing - as

---

[496] *Roca Report*, No.52, April 1993.
[497] *Roca Report*, No.52, April 1993.

the ANC well knew.

At least fifteen people died in violence connected with Hani's funeral, held on April 19. Outside the stadium where the funeral was held, a near-riot ensued. A nearby railway station was gutted, homes were damaged, and shops looted.

The police signed a pact with the ANC, that they would not intervene at the cemetery unless requested to do so by ANC marshals! This stupid action, this blatant capitulation to ANC demands, led *directly* to the destruction of a row of houses nearby. Two white men were hiding in one of those houses, and they were burnt to death. The police simply refused to intervene, despite receiving many phone calls begging them to do so.[498] The ANC was giving the orders, and the government and the police force were meekly obeying. Innocent men and women died, but not even their tragic and unnecessary deaths moved the government to take action against the Communist monsters.

Murder is murder, regardless of who the victim is, and the murder of Chris Hani, despite the fact that he was a top-ranking Communist with the blood of many on his hands, was still a sinful act. But let us now delve a little deeper behind the scenes, and pose the question: *why* was Chris Hani killed? Was his murder merely planned by a racist member of the Conservative Party, and carried out by a Polish immigrant with a hatred for Communism, or could it be that the *Communist forces themselves* had a hand in it?

Some very interesting points were made by the Returned Exiles Coordinating Committee (RECOC), in a pamphlet this organisation issued entitled *Hani: Let's Cool the Hysteria!* When there was a resurgence of neo-Nazi organisations worldwide in 1970, the Soviet KGB *infiltrated* them. Such agents are called "sleepers". Thus, within various right-wing groups, there are Communist agents, pretending to be right-wingers and anti-Communists. What was not well-known was that a bitter struggle for leadership had broken out in the ANC/SACP just before Hani's murder - and Hani had been at the centre of it.[499] Could it be that he was actually deliberately sacrificed by the ANC/SACP?

---

[498] *Roca Report*, No.53, May 1993.
[499] *Hani: Let's Cool the Hysteria!* Returned Exiles Coordinating Committee pamphlet, issued in 1993.

One thing is certain: only the ANC/SACP stood to gain anything from his murder. Firstly, it united the ANC again. Secondly, the ANC exploited it against the right-wing. Thirdly, it gave that organisation the "justification" to launch a mass action campaign countrywide. It was almost as if the ANC/SACP had been waiting for this murder to occur!

Some things were very mysterious indeed, and very suspicious: the murderer had aimlessly driven around in the area the day before, a fact that did not go unnoticed; Hani's bodyguards were (conveniently?) absent at the time - and this fact was known to the murderer; ANC leaders appeared on the scene of the murder within a very short time after it had occurred; and the murderer had not exactly hurried away from the scene, allowing a woman time to take down the number-plate of his car.

The right-wing stood to gain nothing from Hani's murder, but the ANC/SACP stood to gain much - and did. Did Communist agents plan and carry it out, to discredit the right-wing?

When we turn our attention to the reaction of the ANC-supporting "churches", their praise for, and adulation of, Chris Hani was absolutely nauseating. It knew no bounds.

By way of introduction to the "church" praise for the man, a little background information about him:

Chris Hani had been appointed chief of staff of the ANC's armed wing, MK, in 1987. When a bomb blast at Johannesburg's Ellis Park rugby stadium killed two and injured thirty in July 1988, Hani told the SA *Weekly Mail*: "We are prepared to see a wasteland if that is the price of freedom….the bombs were to tell Whites that we can creep and crawl next to you". In the mid-1980's, he openly called for the killing of black "collaborators": policemen, town councillors, etc. He called the killings "forceful persuasion to stop Blacks from collaborating….we warn them to do so at their own risk". Of the terrible "necklace" murder method, he said, "it was used for good reasons. I am not blaming those who used it". He openly called for intensified attacks on white suburbs, declaring white government officials, police, etc., "legitimate targets for attack or assassination".[500]

---

[500] *The Aida Parker Newsletter*, Issue No.134, First

This was the man who, after he was murdered, was eulogised by religious leaders as a Christian, a gentleman, a virtual "saint"!

Significantly Chris Hani had been a Roman Catholic! In Soweto, at a service for him, a French Roman Catholic priest, Emmanuel Lamont, led the huge crowd in prayers, expressing anger against God for Hani's murder! "Where were you [God] on Saturday;" he prayed, "when our leader was mowed down? Help us get a government of the people now."[501] On April 15, women from Roman Catholic, Methodist, Anglican, Lutheran, Zionist and Pentecostal "churches" held a memorial service for Hani in Pietermaritzburg. Prominent women activists, who had been dressed in ANC and SACP colours during the march in honour of Hani, now wore the religious attire of these "churches", showing how deeply revolutionaries were involved in religious organisations, and *vice versa*. At this meeting, the SACP regional treasurer said that there was no contradiction between Communism and the Church;[502] which prompted this author to write the following letter to the *Natal Witness,* Pietermaritzburg's daily newspaper, which was published on April 22:

"Leaving aside the Roman Catholic religion, which has long supported Marxist revolutions in Latin America and Africa, in full accordance with its bloodstained history, I challenge the `Protestant' ministers of those churches....represented at the memorial service, to justify, from Scripture, the praising of a violent revolutionary, responsible for the deaths of many, many people, and who passionately promoted Communism, which has been responsible for the deaths of untold numbers of Christians this century. You know such justification cannot be found; you are simply trying, with all your might, to hold on to your religious careers should the Communist forces ultimately take power in SA. While professing to serve Christ, you support the known enemies of Christ and his Gospel. If you truly believe that `there is no contradiction between Communism and the Church', speak up and back up your words with solid, factual evidence! You know that you cannot do it. I challenge those within these 'churches' who want nothing to do with the ANC/SACP: recognise your `church' for what it

---

Quarter 1990.
[501] *The Citizen,* April 15, 1993.
[502] *The Natal Witness,* April 16, 1993.

is - a tool in the hands of the revolutionaries - and leave it now! The Lord Jesus Christ is not present there. The true Christ of God is not on the side of killers."

A Jesuit priest, N. King, replied to this letter, and it was published in the *Witness* on April 30. He wrote: "In these difficult times for our country, almost the last thing we need, especially between Christians, is intemperate rhetoric. Therefore in response to the letter of Pastor Shaun Willcock, it seems proper to say that Catholics, and especially Pope John Paul II, might find themselves a little startled to be described as having a `blood-stained history' or as `supporting Marxist revolutions in Latin America and Africa'. Claims such as these ought really to be supported by evidence, as should the assertion that Chris Hani, a gentle and peaceable man, was `responsible for the deaths of many, many people'. I do not know of any such evidence, beyond gossip retailed in newspapers."

In reply, this author wrote the following, which was published in the *Witness* on May 31:

"N. King S.J. said that I used `intemperate rhetoric' when I wrote that the Roman Catholic institution has a bloodstained history, and has supported Marxist revolutions. Mr King's own Jesuit Order is up to its neck in revolution, and always has been. Letters to the paper have to be brief. Much evidence is available from Bible Based Ministries [the address was given]. Regarding Rome's bloodstained history, anyone who wants to can find all the evidence one needs in historical works. Rome cannot deny the historical evidence of centuries. Regarding Rome's support for revolutions, priests in Latin America fought alongside the Marxist terrorists. Christ was depicted as an armed revolutionary. Jesuit Luis Pellecor admitted that the Jesuits introduced a new, `bloodthirsty Jesus'. He also said that `every Jesuit in central America is actively serving not God, but Marxism and the revolution'. Again, evidence of priestly involvement in revolution is available from the address above. Regarding Chris Hani, a biographical sketch of his life, and quotations from his own mouth, are given in the *Aida Parker Newsletter,* issue No.134, 1990. Those who would deny the evidence must produce their own! The `difficult times for our country', to use Mr King's words, are to a large extent the result of the `intemperate rhetoric' of Red religious leaders. Once again, evidence is available from the address above."

No more was heard from the Jesuit. Meanwhile, however, another religious leader had responded to the author's first letter on the subject. This was the presiding bishop of the Methodist institution, M.S. Mogoba, one of SA's foremost liberation theologians, and his letter was published on May 5. In it, he said that it was recorded in the Bible of Jesus that he had welcomed outcasts, and that he ate with them; and he also quoted (from some modern Bible version) the words of Jesus regarding people who are sick needing a doctor, not those who are well, and that he had come to call outcasts, not respectable people. This author's reply, published on May 17, was short:

"In reply to Mr M.S. Mogoba of the Methodist denomination: ministering to those in need, and proclaiming the Gospel to unbelievers, is one thing; praising a Communist revolutionary is quite another. There is a world of difference between preaching to terrorists, and praising them. If your letter was an attempt to answer the issues I raised in mine, it failed miserably."

Chris Hani was given a Roman Catholic burial. In an interview, Romish bishop of Johannesburg, Reginald Orsmond, said that Hani had never given up his Roman Catholic faith. "People think," Orsmond said, "that when you become a Communist you give up your faith. He certainly never gave up his Christian [i.e. Roman Catholic] faith."[503] Orsmond, by this statement, revealed the very close ties between Rome and the Communist movement in South Africa. It was a plain admission that one could be both Papist and Communist at the same time, with the blessing of the "Church".

Orsmond's part in Hani's funeral deeply shocked and offended many Roman Catholics, large numbers of whom were still not reconciled to the fact that their "Church" supported the Communist movement. In fact, the outcry was so great that he had to attempt to justify his actions and words publicly. In a long letter to the *Citizen* newspaper, he made some very revealing remarks. "Chris Hani was a Catholic," he wrote, "and his family requested that he be buried with Catholic funeral rites". He went on: "From the first Sunday of Advent 1983 [the new code of canon law was published in 1983],

---

[503] *The Natal Witness*, April 19, 1993.

ecclesiastical penalties....are no longer incurred by those who are Communists or Marxists. Furthermore, in these times (and in Africa!) all Communists do not deny the existence of God, of a spiritual soul, of a life after death, of an absolute moral law."[504]

Orsmond thus gave the *official* position of Rome on the issue of Communism: to be a Communist was no longer a sin in the eyes of the Vatican! From the time of the pontificate of John XXIII (who became pope in 1958), the Vatican had realised the tremendous advantages to be gained by supporting Communism - by, in fact, *marrying* Communism to Romanism - and over the decades had worked tirelessly towards this goal. Consequently, a religious brand of Communism had developed in Africa and Latin America, through the diabolical doctrines of "liberation theology". Atheistic Communism was losing ground worldwide, but *religious* Communism was growing in strength.

Orsmond went on: "I got the impression that he was no atheist, that he was a Catholic and believed in Christ as his personal saviour, that, although he neglected to practise his faith fully, he was of the firm intention to return to the regular practise of this faith."

Chris Hani believed in Christ as his Saviour? No man, who has truly believed in the Lord Jesus Christ, will ever again be a terrorist, a Marxist guerrilla! His works will prove his faith (Jas.2:14-26). "By their fruits (works) ye shall know them," said Jesus (Matt.7:20).

Roman Catholic archbishop, Wilfred Napier, added to what Reginald Orsmond had written. He said that Hani was allowed a Roman Catholic burial because he did not belong to a party that worked against the "Church"! "The South African Communist Party," he said, "has no history of being against the churches and is no longer linked to the Communists of the former Soviet Union".[505] The SACP had certainly not worked against those so-called "churches" which supported it; but Communism is totally committed to the eradication of those which do *not* support it! Napier's words, like Orsmond's, revealed the very close ties between the Vatican and Communism. As for the SACP no longer being linked to the Communists of the old

---

[504] *The Citizen*, April 30, 1993.
[505] *The Southern Cross*, May 2, 1993.

USSR, where was the evidence to support this?

It seemed as if the Roman Catholic hierarchy in SA was doing everything in its power to convince the country in general, and SA's Roman Catholics in particular, that Chris Hani was a good man - a "Christian". The parish priest of Boksburg, Stan Brennan, said that Hani was a good friend of his, who was grateful for his Roman Catholic education and for what the "Church" was doing to educate the "oppressed masses". He was also (Brennan said) much influenced by fellow-revolutionary, Tokyo Sexwale, "a practising Catholic".[506] Indeed, the number of practising Romanists, as well as practising members of various Protestant denominations, within the ANC/SACP alliance was extremely large. Their religions, however, merely encouraged them in their terrorist activities, thereby revealing the absolutely unchristian nature of these religions claiming to be Christian.

Chris Hani's praises were sung by one liberation theologian after another. Desmond Tutu also jumped on the bandwagon, saying that Hani may have been a Communist, but Communists did not oppress black South Africans.[507] In a letter to the *Natal Witness* which was published on May 7, 1993, the present author wrote:

"The Red clergymen go on and on, heaping praises on Chris Hani's head and divine wrath upon their own. The tragedy is the number of people who follow these 'Religious Reds'. They are utter strangers to the Christ of Scripture, the Holy Son of God. First we had Roman Catholic bishop Reginald Orsmond saying that Hani never gave up his 'Christian faith', even though he became a Communist. Hani may never have given up his Roman Catholic faith; but he was never a true Christian. A man who planned sabotage and terror attacks, and who said that the gruesome, barbaric 'necklace' murder method was used for good reasons, as Hani did, can certainly not be called a Christian - not according to the Biblical definition of the word. But his 'church' has never had too many qualms about murdering people. Next we had Anglican archbishop Desmond Tutu saying that Hani may have been a Communist, but Communists did not oppress black South Africans. Not yet, Mr Tutu, not yet: for they're not quite in power yet. They

---

[506] *The Southern Cross*, May 2, 1993.
[507] *The Natal Witness*, April 20, 1993.

certainly kill and torture and maim non-Communist black South Africans, as you very well know - but they don't oppress them. Not yet."

Marxist-supporting theologians were quick to see the potential in equating Hani's murder with the crucifixion and resurrection of Christ! This was typical liberation theology, or what is called the "contextualisation" of Scripture. At Hani's funeral service, Desmond Tutu blasphemously equated his death with that of Christ (it was the time of the Easter festival when Hani was killed). Tutu said that, as from Christ's death a great victory came, so out of Hani's death the victory of liberation would come.[508] Christ died for the sins of his people, the just for the unjust, the spotless and holy for those defiled by sin; and yet Tutu, a man professing to be a servant of Christ, claimed that the death of a violent man, a man who advocated terrible means of murdering innocent people, could be equated with the death of the sinless Son of God! But he was not the only one. Frank Chikane, preaching at the memorial service for Hani at the Central Methodist "Church", Johannesburg, used Matt.27:45-54 - the account of Christ's crucifixion, when there was darkness over the earth, and the veil of the temple was torn in two when Jesus died. Chikane said in his sermon: "His death was no ordinary death. Even the timing of his death [during the Easter festival] was not without significance." He went on: "Darkness has come over the whole land. Our nation has been torn apart from top to bottom. For the whole world has been shaken by his death I cannot avoid seeing the similarities between the death of Chris Hani and that of Jesus Christ."[509] What vile wickedness! How utterly diabolical, that the death of a Communist guerrilla could be equated with the death of the Lord and Saviour; that the darkness that covered the land when Jesus hung on the cross could be equated with the (supposed) gloom and despair that the ANC/SACP claimed was hanging over SA ("supposed" because there were millions and millions of South Africans, of all races, who knew little or nothing about Hani before his murder, and who did not view him as a "beloved brother", as Chikane said *he* did); that the tearing in two of the veil in

---

[508] *Signposts*, Vol.12, No.3, 1993.
[509] *Challenge*, No.16, June/July 1993.

the temple, when Jesus died, could be equated with SA supposedly being "torn apart" when Hani died (presumably a reference to the grief that the entire nation felt - something that was a complete fallacy)!

The great God saw and heard it all, and great will be the judgement upon such religious wolves, who die in their sins.

The statements of Tutu and Chikane were echoed in a poem written by a priest, Seboka Mokete O.P. It contained such lines as these:

"The crucifixion of the comrade [Hani] is the last nail in the apartheid coffin."

"On the street he died. In the hearts of the people he is risen, he is alive, and will die no more."

"Death failed to destroy him, evil elevated him, fear favoured his victory and the grave grasped his glory, his blood proclaims: Victory is won!"[510]

The reader will easily note the overt comparison between the Lord Christ and Chris Hani, in these lines. As Christ was crucified by wicked men, so Hani was said to be "crucified". As Christ rose and lives in the hearts of his people, so Hani was said to rise and live in the hearts of "the people". As Christ's blood was shed for the redemption of his people, so Hani's blood was supposedly shed to redeem them from "oppression". This is liberation theology at its worst.

The poem also contained these blasphemous words: "There is no greater love than this, for Chris to lay down his life for peace." This was a distortion of Jesus' words in Jn.15:13, "Greater love hath no man than this, that a man lay down his life for his friends." Jesus laid down his life for his elect people, displaying his great love for them; and true Christians are called to lay down their lives for their friends, if need be, for they are to love one another as Christ has loved them (Jn.15:12). Hani, the poem said, laid down his life for peace. This was not true: he was a man of war. Suddenly, the Catholic-Communists had a new "saint"! Everywhere, his life was extolled in the highest possible terms, his praises were sung, and his death was viewed as the death of a Christian martyr. And the ANC/SACP alliance gained immense political mileage from his murder, while South Africa reeled as ANC thugs went on the rampage countrywide.

---

[510] *Challenge*, No.14, August/September 1993.

In addition to Hani's murder, top ANC leader Oliver Tambo, who during the years in which the ANC had been banned and Mandela had been imprisoned, had led the ANC from outside South Africa's borders, died. His death gave the organisation an excuse for further emotional propaganda, and the Red-supporting "churches" swung into action. Memorial services were held in many "church" buildings. Roman Catholic priest, Smangaliso Mkhatshwa, wrote that Tambo was "a man who took religion very seriously. He was an Anglican who had once thought of becoming a priest." And yet Mkhatshwa openly admitted that Tambo "was also commander in chief of MK and therefore in many ways the architect of the armed struggle".[511] In other words, a religious terrorist! Tambo's body lay in state in St Mary's Anglican cathedral in Johannesburg, following a requiem mass in his honour. Frank Chikane, at the funeral service, compared Tambo with Moses[512] (liberation theologians frequently made use of the account of the exodus of the Israelites from Egypt, comparing the exodus from Egyptian slavery with the "liberation" of the "oppressed blacks" from bondage to apartheid).

The terrible chant was being increasingly heard at ANC gatherings: "Kill the Boer, kill the Farmer!" Used by the ANC Youth League's fiery leader, Peter Mokaba, it drove South Africa's white farmers to prepare for war. Systematically, brutally, farmers and their wives were being murdered. In 1992, there were 369 attacks on elderly people on their farms. And yet Mokaba was not arrested for incitement to murder - and the killings continued to escalate. Platoons of men began patrolling farms, and other measures were taken,[513] reminiscent of Rhodesia in the 1970's.

Countrywide, the violence continued to escalate in 1993. Fifty-five people a day were being murdered, on average. On April 18, in Sebokeng, twenty-one people were killed in a series of random shootings. On April 21, a car bomb in Amanzimtoti injured nine people. In East London, five whites were killed and seven wounded by

---

[511] *Challenge*, No.16, June/July 1993.
[512] *Signposts*, Vol.12, No.3, 1993.
[513] *Roca Report*, No.53, May 1993.

gunmen armed with AK-47's. APLA claimed responsibility.

Far from calling a halt to the violence, Nelson Mandela urged youths, on April 22, to join MK, saying that they would be sent abroad for training. Quite plainly, various countries were still training MK guerrillas in terrorism.

Joe Slovo of the SA Communist Party proposed April 27, 1994, as the date for the first multiracial elections in SA. This date was accepted by the negotiating council, which was heavily biased in favour of the terrorist organisations.

Massive international pressure was exerted for the setting of the date, and for the installation of a "Transitional Executive Council" (TEC), long desired by the ANC, which would be the real ruling power in SA until the elections. Desmond Tutu said that he would urge the US to lift sanctions against SA once a transitional government was established. Mandela said that he would ask President Clinton of the US for "massive assistance" once "free elections" were held. He said that the ANC would call off sanctions once an election date was set and a TEC was installed. US Secretary of State Warren Christopher said that once the TEC was installed, and an election date set, the US and the so-called G7 countries would help SA re-enter the global economy. The World Bank said that it would loan SA a billion dollars - once the TEC was installed. It said that it was preparing projects with the ANC and PAC.[514]

Thus an election date, proposed by Communist Slovo and demanded by the internationalists desiring control over South Africa, was now a reality. The countdown had begun. It was the final lap of the race towards an ANC-controlled South Africa.

In May 1993, superiors of various Roman Catholic religious orders agreed to encourage their members to train as monitors to help in overseeing the election.[515] Given the blatant support for the ANC on the part of the Roman Catholic hierarchy in South Africa and internationally, these monitors would naturally work hard for an ANC victory. Just another reason why the elections would *not* be free and

---

[514] *Roca Report*, No.54, June 1993.
[515] *The Southern Cross*, June 13, 1993.

fair (and, indeed, *were* not).

In May, widespread intimidation accompanied school class boycotts, and education came to a halt in many major centres. Houses were burnt, shops were looted, and black children fought pitched battles with the police. Violent protests were organised by the ANC-aligned Congress of South African Students. Black schools were brought to a standstill countrywide by the ANC-aligned South African Democratic Teachers' Union. The protests were over a salary increase that was deemed too low, and over (ostensibly) the payment of pupils' matriculation examination fees. The government once again capitulated, and reduced the fees.[516] The students were nothing but pawns in the hands of the revolutionaries, as they had so often been in the past. While their education suffered as they became cannon fodder in a revolution they were hardly old enough to understand, the ANC scored another victory.

On May 25, at least 73 PAC/APLA members were arrested for murder, petrol bomb attacks on police and civilians, etc. The PAC, in protest, walked out of the negotiations process. The negotiating council called for the release of those arrested. The ANC demanded the dismissal of law and order minister Hernus Kriel. A few days later, in the face of local and international pressure, the government backed down and agreed to release three members of the PAC executive, and to return all confiscated PAC property.[517] Another government capitulation, another victory for the terrorists.

In June, the new Board of the South African Broadcasting Corporation (SABC) was appointed. Of the twenty-five names on the first list, sixteen had ANC connections! This was reduced to eleven on the second list, according to Chief Buthelezi.[518] Nevertheless, even this was a very significant number: almost half. The ANC's creeping takeover of all state bodies was proceeding apace.

On June 2, 1993, the Appeal Court ruled that Winnie Mandela, estranged wife of Nelson, was guilty of kidnapping in 1988; but it reduced her five-to-seven year jail term to a R15 000 fine, plus a two-year jail sentence, *suspended* for five years! It was now clear that even

---

[516] *Roca Report*, No.53, May 1993.
[517] *Roca Report*, No.54, June 1993.
[518] *Roca Report*, No.54, June 1993.

the courts were not prepared to severely punish highly-visible ANC leaders. That this woman could receive such a light sentence for such a serious crime was atrocious.

The Afrikaner Volksfront (AVF) was growing in popularity and strength among whites. This was an umbrella organisation for a number of white right-wing groups, such as the Conservative Party (CP). It was headed by General Constand Viljoen, and a few other top military generals. It was conservative, anti-Communist, and desired a *confederal* solution for South Africa, with each nation being given its own land and allowed to govern itself. On June 25, the radical Afrikaner right-wing organisation, the AWB (Afrikaner Resistance Movement), invaded and occupied the World Trade Centre while the negotiating council was in session. World reaction was hysterical, even though no-one was killed or even badly hurt (unlike ANC action!). The ANC demanded the arrest of all involved. The government hastily worked to arrest them (while, as the right-wing pointed out, ANC terrorists remained free). The AWB's action badly damaged the Afrikaner Volksfront's image, for the AWB was a member of the AVF.

The police did not stop the AWB invasion. Here some very significant facts emerge: firstly, the armoured car, used to smash the glass doors of the World Trade Centre, was abandoned inside; secondly, the driver was apparently not known to the AWB, and disappeared. The AWB, it was widely believed, had been heavily infiltrated by the security forces. Many believed the invasion was deliberately planned (by the security forces on orders from the NP/ANC) to *discredit the Afrikaner Volksfront.*[519] A deadly game was being played. The ANC planned to come to power at all costs, and the NP government was not standing in its way; in fact, there is ample evidence that the NP was actually assisting the ANC, by seeking to neutralise all opposition.

By now it was very clear to moderate, anti-Communist leaders in South Africa, that the National Party and the ANC were in *collusion,* and were manipulating the negotiating process behind the scenes, to

---

[519] *Roca Report,* No.55, July 1993.

their own advantage. Marxists have always understood that, for their plans to succeed, they must gain control of a country's security forces. In July 1993, the NP and the ANC approved proposals for forming a "peace army" drawn from the South African Defence Force (SADF), MK, APLA, and the black homeland armies. It was planned to place this united force under multi-party or "Transitional Executive Council" (TEC) control. Its purpose was to "monitor" the election. Of course, if the TEC controlled it, then the *ANC* would control it - which is just what the ANC desired.

How did the NP and ANC gain this victory?

All 26 parties at the negotiating council adopted a resolution providing for the establishment of a Peace/Youth Service Corps "to constructively channel the energies and anger of the youth....during the transition and thereafter". But in subsequent discussions, the "major parties" (presumably the NP and ANC) dropped reference to youth and turned the corps into a professional peace-keeping force! Some observers believed that this was deliberate: the NP and ANC tricked the other parties into accepting this merger of the SADF, MK and APLA by introducing it as a "youth" corps initially.[520]

In the black townships, the terrible killings continued to escalate. By mid-1993, the police were expressing concern over the rapidly increasing number of people being doused with petrol and set alight, in the Transvaal and Natal. On July 4, ANC supporters burnt alive three people accused of being IFP supporters in a black township of the East Rand, prompting a black reporter to say, "I have lived in the township of Katlehong for all my 36 years, but I have never seen such savagery as I witnessed on Monday night."[521]

Doubtless the plan was to so increase the level of violence that United Nations intervention would be invited. The ANC well knew the bias of that world body.

Within just a few months, 1993 had indeed become a "year of terror". But the year was far from over, and a massacre that would shock the world was yet to occur.

---

[520]*Roca Report*, No.55, July 1993.
[521]*Roca Report*, No.55, July 1993.

CHAPTER THIRTY-FIVE

1993: "KILL THE PASTOR, KILL THE CHURCH!"

At about 7.30 pm on Sunday, July 25, 1993, a group of gunmen burst into the St. James Church of England premises in Cape Town, where a service was in progress. They opened fire with automatic weapons. Two hand grenades were thrown into the centre of the building, and exploded.

A young man in the congregation drew his revolver and returned fire. A bullet wounded one of the gunmen, and the attackers fled. But the carnage inside the building can hardly be described in words. Blood was to be seen everywhere, bodies were lying on bloodstained carpets, pews were overturned, there was a hole in the floor, and even the ceiling was marked by shrapnel.

This savage, barbaric attack, which sent shock waves around the world, left eleven dead and over 50 wounded.

One man saw his wife murdered next to him. Another's wife died in his arms. A 17-year-old boy threw himself across two young girls to shield them, and died from a bullet through his head. A 21-year-old man died instantly as he dived on top of one of the grenades, thus saving the lives of many others. His 13-year-old brother also died in the attack. A woman died 30 minutes after arriving at the hospital. Four others who died were Russian sailors who were visiting the church for the first time. Another Russian sailor had both his legs ripped off when a grenade fell into his lap, and his right arm had to be amputated. Both of his eardrums burst. He was earning money as a sailor in order to pay for his wedding on his return to Russia.

Desmond Tutu barged into the church building and lied to the policemen on duty, according to a member of the church who wrote to the paper about it. He stated that Tutu claimed he was the head of the denomination in order to gain access to the site of the massacre and thereby to *exploit* the event for his own ends! But the Church of England in South Africa (CESA), the denomination to which the congregation of St. James Church belonged, was entirely separate from Tutu's Church of the Province of South Africa, as he well knew. He did this in order to exploit the situation for his image internationally - a truly disgusting act by this religious, unregenerate hypocrite.[522]

Other religious leaders involved in aiding the Marxist revolution suggested that the opportunity should be used for a "reconciliation" service. They sought to gain political mileage from the tragic event.

The ANC condemned the attack with its usual hypocrisy, itself having committed so many terrorist attacks over the years against innocent people.

APLA (the PAC's armed wing) claimed responsibility for the massacre, saying that the killings were part of "a widespread offensive against the settler regime"; and it also warned that more blood would be spilt. A man claiming to be an APLA spokesman said in a call to a Johannesburg newspaper on July 28 that the church had been selected because its congregation consisted of 99% whites. APLA had designated 1993 as "the year of great storm". He said that attacks against schools and crèches had already been planned on a countrywide basis.[523] Two people with PAC ties were arrested in connection with the attack and one formally charged with the murders on August 16 had documents linking APLA to the attack. These documents also detailed logistics and tactics for attacks on other churches, schools, restaurants and police stations.[524]

The Pan Africanist Student Association (PASO) and the Azanian National Youth Unity (AZANYU) declared that they were perplexed and shocked at the reaction to "the killing of only eleven European settlers"! They said that as churches were counter-revolutionary they were legitimate targets of war.[525]

What was the purpose behind this terrible attack? Why was this particular church chosen?

One reason could be that it had the largest Sunday evening congregation on the Cape peninsula, and therefore the terrorists knew that many would be killed. Another reason could be the fact that, although it was multiracial, most of the people attending were white because it was situated in a white area. But probably the most

---

[522] *Frontline Fellowship News*, 1993, Edition 4.
[523] *Signposts*, Vol.12, No.5, 1993.
[524] *Roca Report*, No.56, August 1993.
[525] *Frontline Fellowship News*, 1993, Edition 4.

important reason was that it was a very large and visible congregation that was *not* a member of the terrorist-supporting South African Council of Churches. It opposed liberation theology and Communism.[526] The message the terrorists doubtless wanted to convey was that those churches which did not support the revolution were "enemies of the people", and would be destroyed.

The blatant anti-Christian message the revolutionaries were sending came through loud and clear. The only "churches" that were considered legitimate were those which gave their support to the revolution. All others were illegitimate. The implications for true Christians in South Africa were horrifying.

On August 7, two weeks after the massacre, the Pentecostal Protestant Church premises in Newlands, Johannesburg, were set on fire and destroyed. This congregation, too, was not part of the SACC, and was predominantly white. Clearly, the terrorists were demonstrating their hatred of all religious groups which did not support them.

The massacre in Cape Town was to have a chilling sequel. On August 13, almost 1000 supporters of the PAC marched through Kenilworth, Cape Town. Called a "peace march", it was marked by terrible threats of murder. Posters declared, "APLA stick to your guns", "APLA kill a white a day", and "Kill Two Cops a Day". They demanded the release of the PAC members arrested in connection with the massacre. As they marched close by the St. James Church of England premises, they chanted, with a cold-blooded callousness and hatred that almost defies belief, "One Church, One Bomb!" Another chant heard during the march, and one which was increasingly being heard in the black townships, was, "Kill the Pastor, Kill the Church!" And in his speech at the police station where a petition was handed over, a PAC official demanded the expulsion of all missionaries from South Africa. Needless to say, none of these things received wide coverage in the media.[527]

---

[526] *Signposts*, Vol.12, No.5, 1993.
[527] *Natal Freedom Campaign Background Briefing*, No.1, September 1993. Published by the Natal Freedom Campaign, Durban, South Africa. See also *Roca*

South Africa, once so safe, such a haven for the Gospel, where freedom of religion was guaranteed, where churches could go about their business without interference, was a different country now. Communist killers had declared war on churches, on pastors, on missionaries. Literally hundreds of church buildings had, in fact, been attacked by firebombs, and either damaged or destroyed completely by arson.[528] The priests of the Roman Catholic institution, and the ministers of the SACC-affiliated "churches", were being lauded as heroes of the revolution, as comrades in the struggle; but those who stood against this tide of evil, who preached obedience to the government, and who warned of Communism's dangers, were now in grave, grave danger.

For white professing Christians, persecution had only just begun in 1993; for black professing Christians, however, it had been going on for years, and in 1993 their suffering was greater than ever. South Africa is a very religious country, with 75% of the population professing to be "Christians", and belonging to thousands of different religious denominations. The following account was reported without stating which church (or churches) those being persecuted belonged to, and so whether or not these people were *true* Christians is unknown. For this reason they are described here as *professing* Christians. But the terrorists were not interested in making distinctions: *all* who claimed to be Christians, but who refused to support the ANC, were targets. Communists persecute all religious groups that do not tow the line. For this reason, true Christians suffer at their hands alongside others who are not true Christians, but who profess to be. Similarly, the Roman Catholic institution has persecuted not only true Christians, but others who have claimed to be, as well as Jews, Muslims, etc. Satan, of course, seeks to destroy true believers in Christ; but it is of no concern to him if others die as well.

An 18-year-old black school pupil named Stanley, who attended the Mzokhanyayo School in KwaZulu, wanted to have nothing to do with the politics or the violence. He professed to be a Christian and he

---

Report, No.56, August 1993.
[528] Frontline Fellowship News, Special Report, September 1993.

and other professing Christians were determined to remain neutral. They were therefore denounced as collaborators. In May 1993, they were rounded up by ANC-supporting "comrades", and bussed to an IFP area. "We Christians were put together as prisoners in the front. We were marched off to Osizwemi location where we were forced to sing and chant. We were told, `You think you're clever, you Christians. You've taken the religion of the Boers into our land. You've taken the white man's Bible; they've taken our land.' Other groups of marchers converged from other schools, all with professing Christians in the front, and they were driven with wire whips. One large group was formed. They were forced to sing ANC songs, often to the tunes of hymns, with words such as "Go well Comrade Chris Hani. We will remain and kill the Afrikaner." The professing Christians were sent into shops to get food for the "comrades". If any of them refused, they were moved to the back ranks for punishment later. If the shopkeeper protested, petrol was poured around the shop, and a professing Christian was forced to light a match to burn down the shop. Three shops were burnt down in this way. When IFP supporters retaliated, they also rounded up the Christians who were again put in the front. And this time suspected ANC supporters were whipped and stoned. Again the professing Christians were forced to participate. Stanley eventually fled from that area.[529]

The Inkatha Freedom Party supporters who retaliated in like manner cannot be justified for doing so; but it must be remembered that, in the first place, the IFP officially did not support such methods, and in the second place, the war had not been started by the IFP, but so many IFP supporters had suffered so much at the hands of the ANC that, being unregenerate people, some of them retaliated in this cruel manner.

This was by no means an isolated incident. According to a British researcher for the Freedom Association, in a report entitled *Christians in the Crossfire,* in *Freedom Today,* August 1993, several incidents were documented of professing Christians in South Africa being singled out for whipping with barbed wire, stoning, and burning. It was noted that ANC radicals were prejudiced against Christians and were

---

[529]*Signposts,* Vol.12, No.5, 1993.

deliberately targeting them.[530] In the light of this, and of the known collusion between the ANC and the PAC, the ANC's condemnation of the St. James Church massacre was nauseatingly hypocritical. There is no reason to doubt that, although the PAC carried out the attack, the ANC (at the very least) approved of it.

With the rise in antichristian sentiment came a corresponding rise in the public role of *witchcraft* within the ranks of the ANC. Many men had shallow vertical cuts made on their chests into which *muti* (supposed magic potion) was rubbed, believing that this would make them invisible to the security forces and protect them from bullets. And on August 7, a *sangoma* (witch) led the ANC Women's League march in Pretoria.[531] Before the Europeans settled in South Africa, the black nations had been under the total power of witchcraft. Through the influence of the missionaries and also of the authorities, devotion to witchcraft was less visible. But only true Christians ever cast it off completely, and it continued to be practiced throughout the black territories. Millions of black people, who call themselves "Christians", and who attend "church" services every Sunday, immediately contact the witchdoctor when ill, or when they think that an enemy has placed a spell on them. Only the Gospel of Jesus Christ can set men and women free from the powers of darkness. As victory for the Communist forces seemed imminent, those devoted to the occult arts became more visible. For the two were united in their opposition to Christianity.

Three members of the Concerned South Africans Group - COSAG - withdrew from the negotiations. These were the Inkatha Freedom Party, the KwaZulu Government, and the Conservative Party. COSAG, an umbrella grouping of those parties opposed to Communism and the ANC/NP collusion, represented about half of the entire population of South Africa, but decisions were being taken on the basis of "sufficient consensus". COSAG leaders were overruled, ignored, and cut short every time they tried to put their case at the negotiations, according to Ben Ngubane, leader of the KwaZulu delegation. "Our presence at the World Trade Centre," he said, "is

---

[530] *Frontline Fellowship News*, 1993, Edition 4.
[531] *Roca Report*, No.56, August 1993.

required only to rubber-stamp what the ANC/SACP alliance and the government/NP have already decided."[532] He was right. The multi-party "negotiations" were being conducted merely to give an appearance of legitimacy to the entire takeover of power by the ANC. It had no intention of compromising at any point.

The Conservative Party (CP) said that it would not return to the talks unless the Afrikaners' right to self-determination was recognised, including their right to their own territorial area.

COSAG objected to the draft constitution because it meant that the ANC would have a free hand to draft a new constitution to suit itself following a heavily intimidated election. CP chief negotiator, Tom Langley, said on July 24 that the draft constitution was "clearly a Communist constitution drawn up by the godfather of the negotiation forum, Joe Slovo". COSAG wanted most power to be reserved for the states within a federal or confederal system (the only workable solution for South Africa's diverse society). On July 26, the CP leader, Ferdi Hartzenberg, said that none of the COSAG proposals had been accommodated in the draft constitution: the ANC/SACP proposals had been followed to the letter.[533]

He was right. The negotiators, under constant pressure to meet deadlines, repeatedly made concessions to the ANC/SACP alliance. Deliberately leaving the hardest questions till last, agreements on these were reached very hastily, and almost always in the ANC's favour. Through these negotiations, the ANC/SACP obtained the following successes: strong central government, with almost no real powers given to regional governments at all (and thus a resounding defeat for those advocating federalism); the boundaries of regions not to be finalised before the elections; South Africa to have *eleven* official languages; the reincorporation of the black homelands into South Africa, *even against the will of their governments if necessary* (yet this was called "democracy"!); a "government of national unity" for up to five years after the elections (which tied in well with the two-phase transition originally proposed by Joe Slovo); and the issuing of temporary voter cards for potential voters. The NP had insisted for a long time that only official identity documents should be used to

---

[532] *Roca Report*, No.56, August 1993.
[533] *Roca Report*, No.56, August 1993.

identify voters, in order to minimise fraud; but the ANC always advocated issuing voter cards, and this was approved, as was the use of identity documents issued by the homeland governments, which would enable homeland citizens to vote, *even if* their governments did not participate in the elections![534]

So much for free and fair elections!

Most crucial decisions depended on secret deals that were struck between the NP and the ANC. The NP was, in a word, surrendering to the ANC. The liberal *Weekly Mail* admitted these things, in its issue dated November 5, as well as stating that the main purpose for the smaller parties being present was merely to give the entire sordid process legitimacy.

The negotiating council also accepted the proposal submitted jointly by the ANC and NP that the judges of the constitutional court would be appointed by the State President, thereby, of course, destroying the independence of the judiciary. Even the liberal Democratic Party called this "total sell-out and capitulation" to the ANC. The negotiating council also accepted another proposal, also submitted jointly by the ANC and NP, that state pensions would be paid to non-civil servants "who had made sacrifices or who had served the public interests in the establishment of a democratic order". In other words, to members of MK! This would be nothing less than compensation to terrorist murderers![535]

Religious institutions in South Africa and abroad continued to give massive, enthusiastic support to Nelson Mandela and the ANC. In July, when Mandela visited the United States, leaders of Chicago's Roman Catholic, Protestant, Muslim, Jewish and Sikh communities attended a luncheon with him. He said, "The ANC is perfectly at home with religious leaders and the religious community. My generation is the product of missionary education Religion is in our blood because of what it has done for our community." It is true that the ANC was certainly at home with Romanism, and liberal Protestantism, and Islam, and other religions; but not with biblical Christianity. Satan, the great adversary of the Lord, his Church, and his Gospel, was behind

---

[534] *Roca Report*, No.59, November 1993.
[535] *Roca Report*, No.59, November 1993.

both the ANC and the religions which supported it.

The great majority of South Africans, and indeed the majority of people worldwide, have always believed that Marxists only advocate atheism; and therefore, when a Communist makes pro-religious statements, even (at times) what appear to be pro-*Christian* statements, many are completely fooled. They think to themselves, "How can this man be a Communist? How can the organisation he represents be Communist?" Most people have completely failed to understand that, especially in more recent times, Marxists came to view the "Church" as a useful organisation with which to influence the masses. This was particularly so in countries which were strongly religious, such as South Africa. Instead of waging outright war on religion, they sought to harness it, to make it work for them. Consider the words of Z. Berbeshkina, in a book entitled *What is Historical Materialism?* It was published by Progress Publishers in Moscow in 1985. "Marxist-Leninist parties," he wrote, "pay due attention to the role of religion in contemporary social development and to its influence on the masses. Marxists show deep regard for those who work for peace, whatever their religious belief....On the other hand, Marxists combat the alliance of reactionary clericals and the forces of imperialism and aggression....Marxism-Leninism provides the only correct scientific criticism of religion as a social phenomenon maintained and encouraged by the exploiter classes."[536]

Of particularly ominous significance in this quotation are the words, "Marxists combat the alliance of reactionary clericals and the forces of imperialism and aggression". By "reactionary clericals" the author meant of course those ministers who refuse to go along with Marxism, who oppose it and preach against it; and because such ministers generally preach that the government must be obeyed and not resisted, they are said to be in alliance with "the forces of imperialism and aggression"!

Famous American liberal religious leader, Jesse Jackson, cajoled and coaxed the crowd, at the Chicago gathering, to dig deep into their pockets, singling out people by name. "If he [Mandela] could give twenty-seven years of flesh and blood, could we not give some money?" he asked. A Roman Catholic priest called Mandela a "model

---

[536] *Signposts*, Vol.13, No.1, 1994.

of what it means to live the gospel"! Over R500 000 was raised for Mandela.[537]

From July 25 till August 1, a group of five religious personalities visited SA to further the mandates of EMPSA (the Ecumenical Monitoring Programme in South Africa). The team claimed that it was in the country to assist in creating a climate for free and fair elections. It consisted of three women and two men and it was called the Eminent Persons Group Delegation(!). It was led by Anglican archbishop, Sir Paul Reeves, who was the Anglican institution's observer at the United Nations, as well as being co-president of the World Conference on Religion and Peace. This group of meddling ecclesiastics met with de Klerk, as well as with the ANC, the IFP, the KwaZulu government, the PAC, President Mangope of Bophuthatswana, people connected with the National Peace Accord, the International Observer Missions, and people in ecclesiastical leadership positions. It stated that it saw policing as a major problem requiring urgent attention, particularly the control and role of the security forces before the election. In other words, this group, too, was calling for joint control of the security forces, and for their hands to be tied! Of course, once it is known who was behind EMPSA, the pieces of the puzzle come together: EMPSA was an initiative of the SACBC and the SACC, in conjunction with the WCC and the Vatican's Pontifical Commission on Justice and Peace. Its role, in its own opinion, was to "monitor" violence, political negotiations, and elections.[538]

In early August, the South African Council of Churches said in a statement that it was deeply disappointed and alarmed at the way in which the government had failed to take any effective action to stop the slaughter of people, expressing its horror at the fact that almost 700 people had been murdered since the announcement of a proposed election date;[539] and urged the involvement of international peace-keepers in SA if internal forces failed to halt the fighting, saying that police in troubled areas should be accompanied by international monitors. And retired Romish archbishop, Denis Hurley, said that it was "probably too late" for the police to build a "credible" image. He

---

[537] *The Southern Cross*, July 25, 1993.
[538] *The Southern Cross*, August 15, 1993.
[539] *The Southern Cross*, August 15, 1993.

said that the alternative was to create a police-keeping force drawn from within *and* without the country.[540] The Marxist plan was simple: increase the violence, then claim that as the police could not control it, international monitors and peace-keepers had to be brought in. And the "churches" were part of the plan, because religious leaders added credibility to the call for international interference. At all costs, control of the security forces had to be taken away from the government, and placed in the hands of ANC sympathisers.

On August 11, the Methodist bishops of Southern Africa called for a joint peace-keeping force to be deployed in violence-torn townships. They also said that, "wherever possible and appropriate, Methodist clergy should be released from normal pastoral duties, for one day a week, to be able to offer their services to Regional and Local Peace Accord structures and other peace-keeping initiatives."[541] These men were well aware of who had started the violence in the townships, and of who was primarily responsible for perpetuating it, but that made no difference: they, like so many other religious leaders in SA, were on the side of the revolutionaries.

Also on August 11, the SACC appealed to de Klerk to convene an emergency session of parliament to legislate the recommendations of "church" leaders. These included putting into place the transitional government mechanisms with authority to command and control the security forces, and the immediate establishment of a "peacekeeping force" under international command, to be deployed in flashpoint areas in the country. It also called for security forces to be accompanied by local and international monitors in all troubled areas.[542] Quite obviously the SACC was serving its ANC masters very well. At all costs the security forces had to be discredited and brought under ANC and international control, and the SACC was doing its utmost to bring this about. Yet it well knew that the problem was not the security forces, but ANC/SACP radicals who were causing the bloodshed and mayhem throughout the country.

On the same day, too, the SA Catholic Bishops Conference called for a nation-wide comprehensive campaign for "peace". They called

---

[540] *The Natal Witness*, August 7, 1993.
[541] *The Citizen*, August 12, 1993.
[542] *The Southern Cross*, August 29, 1993.

for Roman Catholics to undertake a campaign of prayer, fasting and alms-giving, to plead for "God's blessing" on SA during the months leading up to the election. The campaign, they said, should include a concerted drive to restore regard for the sacredness of human life and respect for the remains of those killed in violence.[543] This call sounded hollow indeed, given the SACBC's massive support for the Communist killers for many, many years.

Mandela himself, meanwhile, continued to depict himself as a religious man, thereby wooing gullible religious people to his cause. Like a chameleon, his colours changed according to his religious surroundings. He appeared equally at home with liberal Protestants (he was a Methodist), Charismatics, Roman Catholics, Hindus, Muslims, or witchdoctors. On August 15, at the Wanderers Stadium in Johannesburg, the Carmen Music for Peace Concert was held and Mandela was present. The concert was organised by the charismatic Rhema "Church" in Randburg. Frank Chikane, the general secretary of the SACC, led in prayer. Ray McCauley, the pastor of Rhema, was an enthusiastic supporter of Mandela. A photograph of Mandela with the McCauley family was published in the November 1993 issue of Rhema's mouthpiece, *Eagle News*.[544] On September 12, Mandela attended a service at St. Mary of the Angels Roman Catholic "Church" in Athlone, and was photographed giving the black power clenched-fist salute while members of the "church" sang "Nkosi Sikelel' iAfrika" ("God Bless Africa"), the anthem of the revolutionary movement in South Africa.[545] Another photograph, in the *Argus* newspaper on September 14, showed him with Muslims. And in November, he participated in the Hindu Dipawali festival.[546]

Then came the witchcraft ceremony in Durban on October 24, 1993, the purpose of which, according to the Johannesburg *Star* of October 26, was to call down the ancestors' blessings on Mandela and to cast away evil spirits. It was part of a cultural festival organised by the ANC, and 60 000 people attended. In a full-page advertisement for

---

[543] *The Citizen*, August 12, 1993.
[544] *Signposts*, Vol.13, No.1, 1994.
[545] *The Southern Cross*, September 26, 1993.
[546] *Signposts*, Vol.13, No.1, 1994.

the festival placed in the *Sunday Tribune* of October 17, it was stated: "Even your ancestors will be there"; and, "More than 100 Sangomas, from all parts of Southern Africa, will come together to call on the ancestors of our nation for guidance....If your ancestors will be there surely you can?" A Hindu guru, a Muslim imam, and a so-called "Christian" minister initiated the proceedings. During the ceremony, thirty-two witchdoctors called on the ancestral spirits to "bless" Mandela, who was present. This ceremony, however, was far, far more sinister than the *Star* made it out to be. It is a ceremony used by witchdoctors for anyone who wants power, riches, health or good luck. And for the ceremony to be valid, *human blood and human flesh is normally required!* For this reason, in many of the ritual murders which take place in South Africa, body parts are removed.[547]

Furthermore, the fact that Mandela was prayed for by witchdoctors, by spirit mediums, meant that he was now seen by many blacks, steeped as they were in their traditional beliefs, as a man too powerful to oppose. The effect of this was to intimidate blacks into supporting him.

This satanic festival was endorsed by the ANC, praised by the media, and supported by people claiming to be "Christians", even "ministers"! A religious Babel, an abomination in the sight of God, in which demons were invoked under the guise of ancestors, and in which (very probably) human blood and flesh played a part! Not even a whimper of protest was heard from the various religious leaders claiming to be "Christians" within the SACC, who were always so vocal in their praise of the ANC and Mandela. Not surprisingly, because these men were not true Christians, and the "churches" they represented were not true churches of Christ. They merely assumed the name of "Christians", and took the holy name of the Lord Jesus Christ into their wicked lips, but in truth they did not object to men following "other roads" to God (in direct violation of Matt.7:13,14, Jn.14:6, Acts 4:12, etc., because they themselves did not know the true way); they encouraged multi-faith worship, religious syncretism, for they knew not the God of the Bible.

Truly, the Charismatics, liberal Protestants, and Roman Catholics who praised Mandela, supported him, and supported and encouraged

---

[547] *Signposts*, Vol.13, No.1, 1994.

multi-faith worship, etc., were as spiritually blind, as dead in trespasses and sins, as any ancestor-worshipping witchdoctor! He who does not worship the true God worships devils, whether they are hidden behind the names of Mary, the so-called "saints", or even behind the name of Christ. For there is "another Jesus" as certainly as there is the true Jesus Christ, the Son of the living God (2 Cor.11:4): this "Jesus" is the Jesus of man's imagination, of man's invention, and he is worshipped by millions in many forms. But such worship is false worship, abominable to God. "There is a way which seemeth right unto a man, but the end thereof are the ways of death" (Prov.14:12); "wide is the gate, and broad is the way, that leadeth to destruction, and many there be which go in thereat" (Matt.7:13) - yes, and go in thinking that they are worshipping God, and are Christians! Few indeed find that narrow way which leads to life (Matt.7:14); and that way is Christ (Jn.14:6).

CHAPTER THIRTY-SIX

1993: THE ANC EFFECTIVELY IN POWER PRIOR TO THE ELECTION

Once Joe Slovo had proposed the election date and it had been accepted, it became very clear (even to liberals) that the NP and the ANC were colluding to hasten South Africa into a prearranged settlement by the time of the elections in April 1994. The liberal *Sunday Times* editor, Ken Owen, called the draft interim constitution an amalgam of "half formed thoughts and unfinished sentences", inviting civil war. He editorialised in the issue of August 1, 1993: "In the streets and churches, meanwhile, the slaughter continues....it is not difficult to understand the despair that seizes quite ordinary people and drives them to rage or emigration....serious doubts now arise as to the will, and even capacity, of the parties....to achieve an honourable constitution."[548]

Predictably, the country's Red religious leaders supported the interim constitution. The SA Catholic Bishops Conference was to declare, on November 18, that the interim constitution was cause for celebration and thanksgiving, and that it provided a framework for the transition to a new South Africa.[549]

The ANC had successfully infiltrated the South African Police. Large numbers of them were now carrying out its orders. On August 21, hundreds of members of the radical Police and Prisons Civil Rights Union (POPCRU), in uniform and armed, marched on the Johannesburg Police Headquarters, chanting, "Kill the Boer, Kill the Farmer", "One Settler, One Bullet", and "Let's Fight the Boers". They hailed Mandela, and at least one SACP flag was displayed. Uniformed MK members marched with them. The marchers demanded that white policemen be removed from black areas, and be replaced by a joint force, including members of MK and APLA.[550] In October, the conservative Afrikaner Volksfront declared that the Red revolution

---

[548] *Roca Report*, No.56, August 1993.
[549] *The Southern Cross*, November 28, 1993.
[550] *Roca Report*, No.57, September 1993.

had reached the core of the security forces through the Police and Prisons Civil Rights Union (POPCRU), and had split the SA Police; and law and order spokesman, Captain Craig Kotze, said on October 23 that the ANC had hijacked POPCRU. The evidence fully supported these statements.[551] When large numbers of a police force turn against the government and support its enemies, a country is in grave danger indeed.

The United States once again showed its support for the ANC in August, when a group of MK cadres flew to the US to be given special training by the State Department as bodyguards. It was believed that never before had people who were not in government service been given such training.[552]

A "Transitional Executive Council" (TEC) was what the ANC desired, which would effectively place it in power in South Africa, even before the elections; and in September 1993, the South African Parliament voted to *approve* the TEC. The very next day Nelson Mandela, addressing the United Nations, called for almost all sanctions to be lifted, and for massive investment in SA, saying that the "countdown to democracy" had begun; and his call was quickly heeded by the leading nations of the world. On September 26, ANC, SA government and business officials met at the World Bank in Washington to discuss the reconstruction of SA's economy. Of the International Monetary Fund, Mandela said, "they are prepared to fund us". On September 27, US President Clinton told the United Nations General Assembly that the fixing of the date for the elections was one of the New World miracles. On October 5, the Portuguese president decorated Mandela with the Order of Liberty - an award given only to heads of state! It was quite clear that the world's leaders considered him to *already* be the ruler of SA (or, at least, they believed that he *should* be)![553]

Mandela, when addressing the European Parliament, called on governments to bypass the SA government and deal directly with the TEC. As far as the ANC was concerned, the TEC would *be* the

---

[551]*Roca Report*, No.59, November 1993.
[552]*Roca Report*, No.57, September 1993.
[553]*Roca Report*, No.58, October 1993.

government henceforward, until the elections. The European Community had given over R986 million to "anti-apartheid" groups since 1985. In Glasgow, Scotland, Mandela received the freedom of nine British cities.

SA would not get the promised $850 million loan unless the "letter of intent" was signed by the TEC before the end of 1993. The EC was making it clear, in many ways, that the establishment of the TEC was essential before SA would receive money.[554] Thus the international community was continually pressurising SA into surrendering to the internationalists' plans.

The South African Council of Churches also urged its international partners to cease all campaigns for the international isolation of SA.[555] When the ANC was far from being in power, it had called for sanctions against SA; now, when it could sniff victory in the air, it called for the lifting of them. It did not want to inherit the economic problems that *it* had created! The SACC, by echoing Mandela's call, showed yet again its wholehearted support for the ANC. It had campaigned for sanctions when the ANC had wanted them, and was now calling for their lifting because the ANC had done so.

The leading nations of the world, by so swiftly heeding his call, showed that as far as they were concerned the ANC was the legitimate representative of SA's peoples. The internationalists wanted an ANC government, and were becoming blatant in their support for that organisation by this time. On the Board of Control of Mandela's international South African Free Election Fund were a number of leading New World Order proponents. One of them was former US Secretary of State, Cyrus Vance - who was also US Special Envoy to South Africa! How could he be an impartial Special Envoy when he was so deeply involved with the ANC? As for David Rockefeller, he was doing all he could to enable the ANC to raise the millions it wanted for its election campaign.[556]

The draft TEC Bill was adopted by "sufficient consensus" on

---

[554] *Roca Report*, No.58, October 1993.
[555] *The Los Angeles Times*, September 25, 1993.
[556] *The Aida Parker Newsletter*, Issue No.167, Spring 1993.

September 7, even though three COSAG members, representing millions of people, were not present, and two of the three that were (the independent homelands of Bophuthatswana and Ciskei) opposed it. The Bophuthatswana government declared that it was illegitimate, unrepresentative, undemocratic, and that the Bophuthatswana government would not be bound by the TEC's provisions. President Lucas Mangope said that his country would strongly repel campaigns by Communist elements in the ANC which sought to destroy Bophuthatswana.[557] A few short months later, as shall be seen, the ANC and SA government worked together to destroy Mangope's control of his country, and were successful, by means of a deliberately orchestrated campaign of lawlessness and terror.

The Inkatha Freedom Party totally rejected the TEC, as did the Afrikaner Volksfront. AVF leader, General Constand Viljoen, said that the talks had a "built-in slant favouring the ANC and SACP". He said that all the Afrikaner wanted, and it was a reasonable solution, was self-determination. The area he proposed for a *Volkstaat* (homeland) was that which historically belonged to the Boers, minus the rich mining and industrial areas. All they wanted were the farming parts. When CP leader Hartzenberg said that if the TEC came into being it would be regarded as a declaration of war, Mandela stated that the CP had no capacity to stop the TEC and that if it tried, it would be crushed.[558]

In September, an international consultation on elections in SA was held in Geneva, consisting of representatives of the SACBC, SACC, and WCC. These sponsored the Ecumenical Monitoring Programme in South Africa (EMPSA). The meeting called upon SA churches and those around the world to lobby for a new United Nations mandate to make it possible for the UN to monitor the elections.[559]

Meanwhile, the horrific violence continued unabated. Residents of the black areas in the Pretoria-Witwatersrand-Vereeniging (PWV) area, SA's political, economic and industrial centre, claimed that ANC

---

[557] *Roca Report*, No.57, September 1993.
[558] *Roca Report*, No.57, September 1993.
[559] *The Southern Cross*, October 24, 1993.

sympathisers were being brought in and settled systematically in squatter camps along main roads which could easily be closed at the right time. The huts were close together, enabling the members of ANC Self-Defence Units to move from one to another undetected by the security forces.

Between February 2, 1990 (when the ANC and other terror groups had been unbanned) and July 31, 1993, *over 52 000* people were killed in South Africa! This figure far exceeded the American soldiers killed in nearly ten years of fighting in Vietnam.[560] South Africa had become the world's most violent society, with a homicide rate of 46.5 per 100 000 men.[561]

Peter Mokaba, ANC Youth League leader, notorious for his "Kill the Boer, Kill the Farmer" chant, said at a meeting on August 12 that they must drive the police and the SADF out of the townships and take the war into "their areas". The ANC leadership fully supported him, as proved by his appointment by Mandela as chairman of the National Tourism Forum. At the same meeting, a PAC representative said, "Kill them. APLA forces, kill them"[562] - once again showing the collusion between the ANC and PAC. APLA continued to target whites.

As the world continued to sing Mandela's praises and throw its weight behind the ANC, that organisation stepped up its terror campaign to eliminate all opposition, particularly the Inkatha Freedom Party, the giant Zulu-based party of Chief Mangosuthu Buthelezi. On September 29, Brendan Willmer, chairman of the Natal Freedom Campaign, an organisation campaigning for a federal solution for the province of Natal (usually by now being called "KwaZulu/Natal"), revealed the following information, given to him by "an impeccable source within the intelligence community". Although the same information was given to the media as well, all major newspapers ignored it. The informant revealed that, between mid-January and mid-February 1994, MK was planning to launch a major assault on IFP strongholds in KwaZulu/Natal. Over 4000 MK members were to be involved. The purpose was to assassinate IFP leaders. 1358 IFP officials were targeted initially. It was believed that MK had between

---

[560] *Signposts*, Vol.12, No.5, 1993.
[561] *Roca Report*, No.57, September 1993.
[562] *Roca Report*, No.56, August 1993.

30-40 000 AK-47's cached in Natal, with vast quantities of ammunition, grenades, mines, etc. MK members had, for some months, been transferring into Natal, to prepare for this ethnic cleansing, codenamed "Operation Mbokodo" ("the stone that crushes"). They also planned to launch indiscriminate attacks into white and Indian areas, to terrorise the population into submitting to ANC control. The government was aware of these plans, but did nothing about them.

Brendan Willmer was contacted by the Goldstone Commission, and appeared before a hearing on October 4. He was told to reveal the source of this information, which he declined to do.[563]

Although, as it turned out, the planned *full-scale* "ethnic cleansing" did not begin in January 1994 (probably to a large extent because of the revelations made by Willmer), Zulus continued to be murdered, vast amounts of arms continued to be stockpiled, and MK guerrillas continued to pour into Natal. As the war raged between the ANC and IFP throughout the hills and valleys of the garden province, Natal became the focal point of the countrywide conflict, for it was there that the ANC came up against its greatest opposition. By October 1993, evidence was mounting that it was preparing for "ethnic cleansing" (i.e. the genocide of Zulus) in Natal. In the words of the *Aida Parker Newsletter:* "more and more evidence is accumulating that the ANC is preparing for outright war and `ethnic cleansing' in the beautiful but already blood-soaked garden province of Natal. Even as things stand now, Natal, heartland of Dr Mangosuthu Buthelezi's Inkatha movement, is drenched in some of the most vicious, intractable violence in the world today, a war pursued without mercy against women, children, the aged, the infirm, against animals and everything Zulu, often with a grotesque cruelty that would shame even the IRA."[564] According to the D.F. Malan Accord, which the government and the ANC signed on February 12, 1991, MK would not train inside SA. Yet they were blatantly violating the Accord. *Ilanga,* the Durban-based newspaper serving the Zulu community, confirmed that reports

---

[563] *Natal Freedom Campaign Background Briefing*, No.2, October 1993.
[564] *The Aida Parker Newsletter,* Issue No.168, October/November 1993.

were being received from all over Natal that the ANC was training military groups throughout the province. The IFP estimated that, in the black townships of Durban alone, 3000 ANC members were being trained militarily. In October, an IFP camera team filmed 300 trainees marching up the main street of KwaMashu, some of them holding AK-47's, R4 assault rifles, etc. Yet the ANC claimed the footage was faked, and that the whole thing had been stage-managed. ANC officials said that there was no training going on anywhere in South Africa; but an MK official, contradicting these statements, said that MK was training its members all over the country! Subsequent IFP investigations proved that military-style training was taking place at a number of places, including high schools, sports fields, and even primary schools. Although this training was, by this time, common knowledge in the townships, the IFP noted that the Goldstone Commission had not uttered a single word of condemnation, nor had any of the so-called "violence monitors".

Even before all these investigations, the KwaZulu government presented, to the SA government, documented evidence of revolutionary activities carried out by MK including the recruitment of almost 5000 cadres, particularly from Natal/KwaZulu and the PWV/East Rand areas, who had been flown to countries such as Uganda for military training. Cuban uniforms had been imported, as had arms and ammunition on a large scale. One IFP leader was being assassinated *every six days,* a total of almost 350 up until that time. The IFP declared that the ANC was obviously trying to dominate the Natal/KwaZulu region through intimidation, fear and violence, and by removing the power-base of Inkatha. Certainly it was planned to draft a very large number (perhaps as many as 40%) of MK members into Natal before the beginning of 1994; and huge supplies of weaponry were being shipped into the province.[565]

In October a major conservative political umbrella movement was formed, a powerful opponent of the ANC/SACP/PAC/NP alliance: the Freedom Alliance. It grew out of the old COSAG, and its leaders were Buthelezi (Inkatha), Mangope (Bophuthatswana), Gqozo (Ciskei),

---

[565] *The Aida Parker Newsletter,* Issue No.168, October/November 1993.

Hartzenberg (Conservative Party), and Viljoen (Afrikaner Volksfront). It stood for the right to self-determination of the various peoples of Southern Africa. It rejected a unitary state, racism, discrimination, and any form of totalitarianism or tyranny.[566]

It was an alliance of those who saw that the path the ANC and NP were leading SA down led only to disaster. The Afrikaners and the Zulus, the two most powerful nations in SA, had joined forces; and they were aided by the governments of two independent homelands, who wanted nothing to do with the ANC. It was a united front against the Communist onslaught, by conservative, generally moderate, freedom-loving men who believed in either a federal or confederal solution for South Africa, not a Communist unitary state. It posed an enormous threat to the ANC's plans, and we shall see how the ANC, assisted by the NP, sought to destroy it, and finally succeeded.

The world, meanwhile, continued to hail Mandela as the future president of South Africa, and to give him its wholehearted support.

On October 15, Mandela and de Klerk jointly received the Nobel Peace Prize. This prize had frequently been awarded to men who were anything but men of peace, and this time was no exception! But such is the gullibility of people the world over, that it was viewed as being a prize the two men richly deserved. Thanks to the world media cover-up, most were ignorant of the truth: that these two were dragging the country down the path to Communism, with tens of thousands of lives being lost in the process. The prize was their reward for their obedience to the orders of the internationalists. The president of the European Community said that South Africa was "returning to the world fold".[567] Yes it was - on conditions laid down by the New World Order advocates.

Also on October 15, two white men were sentenced to death for the murder of Chris Hani earlier in the year. They were Polish-born Januz Waluz, who had pulled the trigger, and Clive Derby-Lewis of the Conservative Party. There was no evidence that the latter was carrying out CP policy in any way. That same week, an ANC member who was

---

[566] *Roca Report,* No.58, October 1993.
[567] *Roca Report,* No.58, October 1993.

found guilty of killing *21* IFP supporters was given life sentences. It appeared that those found guilty of Hani's murders received harsher sentences because that was what the ANC wanted.

ANC supporters at the trial went absolutely wild with savage delight, screaming, whistling, and once again chanting the terrible chants, "Kill the Boer, Kill the Farmer", and "One Settler, One Bullet!" They wanted the two men to be dragged out for a public execution by the dreadful "necklace" method. Tokyo Sexwale of the ANC suggested that they be hanged in public, which was greeted by cheers from the crowd. He said that after the elections, the ANC government would decide what punishment would be applied to them. Derby-Lewis' wife, Gaye, was acquitted; but the mob, inflamed with hatred, shouted: "You will not survive, Gaye Derby-Lewis."[568] The death sentence is a punishment suitable to the crime of murder, as the Scriptures make clear; but this kind of hypocrisy was a foretaste of what kind of "justice" SA could expect under an ANC government: one standard for ANC members, another standard for those not allied to the ANC. The ANC always demanded the release of ANC killers - but demanded the public execution of the murderers of Chris Hani.

South Africa was spiralling down into complete anarchy; into mob rule. The utopia promised by the leaders of the ANC and SACP looked more and more like a terrifying nightmare. To make matters worse, by November the government and the ANC had agreed in principle to merge the SADF with MK. Senior SADF officers had come to accept the plan because MK had repeatedly stated that the officers would not be told to leave.[569]

So terrible was the performance of government negotiator Roelf Meyer and his assistants at the negotiations that in November, when the plenary session of the negotiating council concluded, Cyril Ramaphosa of the ANC labelled their performance a "complete collapse", and other ANC officials declared that they were "stunned by the ease" with which they had gained one concession after another from the government team.[570]

---

[568] *Roca Report*, No.58, October 1993.
[569] *Roca Report*, No.59, November 1993.
[570] *The Aida Parker Newsletter*, Issue No.169, December

The religious leaders who supported the ANC, and the institutions they represented, continued to prepare for the upcoming elections. Members of the Panel of Religious Leaders for Electoral Justice gathered in Johannesburg in November to discuss the monitoring of the election. These included Methodist bishop Stanley Mogoba, Anglican archbishop Desmond Tutu, Gerry Lubbe of the Dutch Reformed institution, and Jewish chief rabbi Harris. They declared that they would "stand above party political preferences" and that they would "guard" their "non-partisan image and role".[571] This statement was laughable. It was a well-known fact throughout South Africa and the world that Desmond Tutu and other liberation theologians were open supporters of the ANC. They certainly did *not* stand above party political preferences and they certainly had *no* image of being non-partisan!

The Pietermaritzburg Agency for Christian Social Awareness (PACSA) stated that churches, especially in Natal, could have a critical influence on those too afraid to vote, or who wrongly believed they were ineligible to vote. And the so-called Natal Church Leaders' Group promised to provide voter education programmes, and urged church members to become monitors, in order to create confidence that the elections would be free, fair and peaceful.[572] In truth, the presence of ANC-supporting religious leaders and their indoctrinated church members would play a major part in ensuring that the elections were *not* free or fair, for these people were not impartial monitors, and the voter education programmes they conducted were favourable to the ANC.

During 1993 the WCC's Special Fund to Combat Racism made US$100 000 (about R335 000) available "for liberation movements and other organisations to participate effectively in negotiation and electoral processes". According to the WCC, the aims of the groups which received grants were not to be in conflict with the general purposes of the WCC.[573] So once again the WCC demonstrated its full-fledged support for Marxist terrorists!

On November 20, ANC negotiators said that if the black

1993; also *Roca Report*, No.60, December 1993.
[571] *The Southern Cross*, November 21, 1993.
[572] *The Southern Cross*, January 2, 1994.
[573] *The Southern Cross*, December 5, 1993.

independent homelands resisted reincorporation into South Africa, the Transitional Executive Council would insist that laws be immediately passed to take away their powers. The day before, in fact, senior ANC official, Matthews Phosa, said that if the homelands or self-governing territories (such as KwaZulu) failed to cooperate in their own destruction, "if the only option left to us is to roll in the tanks, then that is what we will do."[574] And that *is* what they did, as shall be seen.

That the Communists had succeeded to a marked degree in achieving their objectives at the multi-party negotiations was made abundantly clear by Joe Slovo on November 20, whose words were quoted in *The African Communist,* No.136, Fourth Quarter 1993: "in the last few days .there was complete demoralisation in the ranks of the opposition"; "looking at the results as a whole, I can say....we got pretty much what we wanted"; "Our opponents wanted a `one stage process' Our approach was for a `two stage process' This we have won"; "our opponents hoped (for) federalism. We have won a united South Africa....In all critical areas....the future democratic state will have over-riding powers".[575]

On the 3rd December, three ANC members were appointed to senior positions in the SA Broadcasting Corporation. This gave the ANC immense power over the masses; and it lost no time in employing that power to its advantage. The SABC rapidly became even more pro-ANC than it had been before.

And then, on December 7, the Transitional Executive Council took effective control of South Africa, precisely according to ANC/SACP plans. No longer was the elected parliament in control of South Africa; instead, this self-appointed council controlled by the ANC/SACP alliance was.[576] Joe Slovo, chairman of the SACP, said, "We have achieved the seemingly impossible." There was rejoicing among Communist forces that day.

The TEC included senior government officials as well as members of eighteen other organisations that took part in the negotiations. But

---

[574]*Roca Report,* No.60, December 1993.
[575]*The Aida Parker Newsletter,* Issue No.170, January/February 1994.
[576]*Roca Report,* No.60, December 1993.

the dominant organisation was the ANC. The TEC was charged with supervising the pre-election period to ensure a "level playing field" so that supposedly no party had special campaign advantages (except the ANC, as the subsequent months made manifest!). Although the government would remain in office until the elections, the TEC would have a part to play in supervising decisions involving such key areas as finance, defence, intelligence gathering, broadcasting, police and foreign affairs. In essence, the government no longer ruled with complete power; it had surrendered vital aspects of its power into the hands of the TEC. De Klerk, predictably, said the "right" things to reassure the moderate, anti-Communist millions within South Africa. He said that "the TEC is not going to take over the government tomorrow. The TEC has a focus....to ensure that the government does not misuse the powers that it has." These were empty words. Cyril Ramaphosa of the ANC said, "We call on them [the government] to finally accept that the days of minority rule are over."[577] No government decision of any consequence could now be taken without the approval of the TEC or one of its sub-councils. It was given the power to monitor and the power to veto.

In December, Parliament overwhelmingly adopted the new interim constitution, thereby officially ending what remained of white rule in South Africa. The vote was 237 to 45 in a joint session of the three houses, consisting of whites, Coloureds and Indians. It was the beginning, *not* of black majority rule as the media was trumpeting and the world was believing, but of *de facto* Communist rule. In the words of the Conservative Party's Ferdi Hartzenberg, who called the new charter a "monster": "this is a transition to Communism, this is not a transition to freedom."

Roelf Meyer of the National Party, who had done so much to bring the country to this point, said, "It is the end of the old order, and the beginning of the new."[578] He was right, of course: a sinister new order had indeed begun - and at what dreadful cost in human misery and bloodshed!

And who could say how much more misery and bloodshed would follow in the days to come?

---

[577] *The Los Angeles Times,* December 8, 1993.
[578] *The Los Angeles Times,* December 23, 1993.

One final event, late in 1993, must be noted: a seemingly innocuous meeting to most people who read about it, but a meeting of immense significance in the light of biblical prophetic revelation. On December 13, President F.W. de Klerk met the Roman pontiff, John Paul II, in the Vatican. It is said in Scripture that the kings (rulers) of the earth commit fornication with the Papacy, the Great Whore, and that the city on seven hills is the very nerve centre of Satan's intrigues as he goes to and fro in the earth, and walks up and down in it (Rev.17:1-5; Job 1:7). On the very eve, as it were, of the dawn of a Marxist South Africa, President de Klerk visited the pope at his palace in the city on seven hills (Rev.17:3,9), "the habitation of devils, and the hold of every foul spirit" (Rev.18:2). A long-cherished goal of the Vatican was about to be fulfilled, and de Klerk had played his part well. He was there to receive his papal pat on the back.

John Paul II thanked him for his role in dismantling apartheid; and he in turn invited John Paul to visit South Africa - an invitation he accepted. At a press conference afterwards, de Klerk said that he had explained to the pope the steps being taken to bring peace to South Africa, and had expressed his desire to see diplomatic relations established soon between South Africa and the "Holy See".[579] It looked very much like a once-rebellious but now penitent son telling "papa" what he had done to make amends for his past naughty deeds! And de Klerk was not even a Papist. Just how extensive *was* Vatican/Jesuit influence over the National Party of F.W. de Klerk?

---

[579] *The Southern Cross*, December 26, 1993.

CHAPTER THIRTY-SEVEN

1994: ELIMINATING THE OPPONENTS OF ANC RULE

1994 was, without doubt, to be the most momentous year in South Africa's modern history, and one of the most momentous in *all* of its history. The election was set for April 27, and it was widely accepted, both in South Africa and the rest of the world, that Nelson Mandela would become the president. Decades of work by the ANC and its international supporters, from Washington to Moscow, from the Vatican to the frontline states of southern Africa, had paid off. South Africa was about to fall into the lap of the conspirators.

The World Council of Churches certainly knew it. In January, the WCC held its annual meeting in South Africa for the first time. It decided to do this in order to celebrate the beginning of the victory over "racism". The opening service was held at the Central Methodist premises in Johannesburg. SACC president Mgojo welcomed everyone by saying that this was "a historic day for us in South Africa". He said that the light was beginning to overcome the darkness, and that a special word of thanks for this was due to the WCC. And Stanley Mogoba, SA Methodist president and bishop, said that the WCC's Programme to Combat Racism had helped greatly to destroy racism.[580] Indeed, the WCC *had* played an extremely important role in bringing the country to this point - but it deserved no thanks whatsoever, for Communist rule was about to be implemented, and a river of blood had flowed as tens of thousands had been killed. Instead of being grateful to it, every true Christian viewed the WCC with loathing, knowing that the devil himself was its master.

On January 12, the United Nations secretary general, Boutros Boutros-Ghali, proposed that almost 1800 UN civilian observers should help monitor South Africa's first non-racial elections. These would form the largest contingent of an international observer group of over 2400, which would also include observers from the OAU, the EU, the Commonwealth, various countries and the diplomatic community. All would be coordinated by the UN. These, as well as

---

[580] *Challenge*, No.21, March 1994.

observers likely to be sent by foreign non-governmental organisations would probably total in excess of 5000, he said.[581] On January 25, the president of the EU said that 324 EU observers would be deployed as monitors.[582]

As the UN, the EU, the OAU, the Commonwealth, and the governments of most other countries supported the ANC and desired to see it installed as the next government, it was quite clear that the elections would not be fair.

An example of just how biased many monitors would be, in accordance with UN designs, was graphically given when it was decided that the Commonwealth division would be headed by Russell Marshall, a radical "clergyman", political activist and former New Zealand Minister of Foreign Affairs, known in New Zealand as "His Red Reverence".[583] With such men swarming over South Africa, the election results were a *fait accompli*. The election itself had become a mere formality, to give the entire sordid process of officially handing over power to the ANC a semblance of legitimacy.

The ANC declared in January that it planned to deploy about 40 000 people itself at polling booths during the elections to act as "peace-keepers". SA's Minister of Law and Order said that this was an outright threat of intimidation against voters and would be provocative in the extreme and a recipe for disaster.[584]

Within South Africa itself, the Freedom Alliance was gaining momentum. Although the ANC and the government made as if they really wanted the Freedom Alliance parties to participate in the elections (because this would give the entire process legitimacy), there was strong evidence that they were deliberately dragging out the negotiations with the Freedom Alliance to prevent it from becoming a serious contender and to divide its members. And indeed, on January 10, Brigadier Gqozo of the Ciskei said that his tiny country had been forced to join the TEC, and he was withdrawing from the Freedom Alliance, although he was still committed to the Alliance's position.

---

[581] *The Citizen*, January 13, 1994.
[582] *The Natal Witness*, January 26, 1994.
[583] *The Aida Parker Newsletter*, Issue No.170, January/February 1994.
[584] *The Citizen*, January 27, 1994.

The Alliance leaders said that they understood the tremendous pressure brought to bear upon Ciskei by the ANC and TEC.[585] It was just too small, too weak, to hold out.

Knowing that the TEC planned to put pressure on the KwaZulu government as well, and with the Xhosa-dominated ANC's war against the Zulu-based Inkatha Freedom Party continuing, the alliance between conservative whites and conservative Zulus strengthened. Zulus were being trained for self-defence units by white right-wingers in northern Natal and the Orange Free State, to protect themselves from ANC attacks. The ANC's so-called "Self-Defence Units" (SDU's), trained by MK members, had established a rule of fear in the East Rand townships, with residents living under ANC street committees run by teenaged activists. These SDU's were responsible for much of the violence. A senior member of the SDU in Katlehong said, "When we kill particular people, for me it is like I have killed a chicken, for I see no reason for him to live if he does not understand what the will of the people is and what we are fighting for."[586] Such was the mentality of so many within the Marxist African National Congress.

As for the Afrikaners' desire for self-determination in its own territory, Mandela had said that the ANC would never concede to the demand, by Afrikaners, for a separate Afrikaner *Volkstaat* (homeland for the Afrikaner people); but support for it was rapidly growing among whites, with at least 80% of Afrikaners wanting one, and 250 town councils indicating their support for it, according to the Conservative Party and the Afrikaner Volksfront.[587] The request was reasonable, it made sense in the multiracial mosaic of South Africa, but it went against the internationalist plans for a unitary state.

On January 16, the ANC was given a major boost by the *Sunday Times*, South Africa's biggest newspaper. The headline said: "ANC Heading for April 27 Landslide." In the editorial it was stated: "The

---

[585] *Roca Report*, No.61, January 1994.
[586] *Roca Report*, No.61, January 1994.
[587] *Roca Report*, No.60, December 1993, and No.61, January 1994.

ANC is in total command .and in permanent office." This was based on a Markinor poll which gave the ANC 64.6% of the votes, according to its estimates. It claimed that the IFP would hardly feature at all, which was an indication of how biased a survey it was, since the IFP enjoyed massive support in KwaZulu/Natal, and substantial support in other parts of the country as well.

This was blatant reader-manipulation, designed to make the populace give up and accept ANC rule. It also greatly influenced foreign investors and politicians. And it was followed by a Human Sciences Research Council claim that, according to its survey, the ANC would receive 70.3% of all votes.

The *Sunday Times* was owned by Times Media, and the giant Anglo American Corporation was the major shareholder. There can be little doubt that Anglo American was behind the newspaper's "revelations".[588] It was yet another example of the way the media seeks to influence the public. Polls are often notoriously incorrect, and can also be deliberately staged. Much depends on exactly who is polled. In South Africa, large percentages of the black population were not even aware that an election was to be held! Even mere days before the election, there were still large numbers of blacks, in various remote rural areas of South Africa, blissfully unaware of what was about to occur. As for the millions who were well aware of the upcoming election, significant numbers did not intend to vote at all for fear of violence and intimidation. Besides, when polls were conducted among blacks, many of them, afraid of intimidation, deliberately gave the wrong answers - but the answers they thought the pollsters wanted. In urban areas, where pollsters could reach blacks by phone, these were mainly ANC members. In rural areas, where most had no access to phones, the IFP had its strongest support. Yet another factor was that, in black areas, it was usually too dangerous for pollsters to conduct surveys at night, when the men would be home, and so women were the ones mainly polled.

A chilling aspect of the pre-election period was that ANC election agents were telling blacks, millions of whom were semi-literate or

---

[588] *The Aida Parker Newsletter,* Issue No.170, January/February 1994.

illiterate and deeply superstitious, that the ANC would know precisely how they voted, and would deal with those who did not vote for it.[589] This was widely believed throughout the country. It must also be remembered, as explained earlier, that after Mandela was prayed for by spirit mediums in October 1993, the message that this event sent to many black people was that he was now too powerful a man to oppose.

It was not just Mandela, however, who was "blessed" by spirit mediums. On February 20, 1994, at a ceremony in Soweto, Roelf Meyer, the Minister of Constitutional Development, was also "blessed" by *sangomas*. The ceremony began with him standing before the *sangomas* with a goat ready to be slaughtered. He stood in the yard outside the hall as the *sangomas*, who were from the "Amalgamated African Culture and Traditional Healers' Association", sang and went through their cleansing ceremony. They used a goat because it was considered the only animal through which communication with the ancestors could be established. Meyer was then sprinkled with the goat's bile to cleanse him. He took a sip of the traditional beer, and was declared to be "one of us" by a *sangoma*.[590]

This was nothing less than participation in blatant witchcraft and spiritualism by this leading member of the National Party. The worship of the goat has played an important part in witchcraft and in Satanist ceremonies through the ages, and around the world. The sacrifice of the goat is a sacrifice to devils (1 Cor.10:20). And what is alleged to be communication with dead ancestors is nothing less than communication with demons - as the Scriptures make abundantly clear. The dead are either in heaven or in hell, and are unable to return to earth (Lk.16:19-31). Any attempt to contact them (necromancy) is absolutely forbidden in God's Word (Deut.18:9-12; Isa.8:19,20).

Nor was Meyer the only government minister to dabble in occultic practices. When President F.W. de Klerk visited the royal kraal of Chief C.M. Dlamini near Badplaas on January 29, a Swazi praise singer "explained" to the ancestral spirits why he had done so; and he was then made an honorary Swazi on the assumption that the spirits

---

[589] *The Aida Parker Newsletter,* Issue No.170, January/February 1994.
[590] *Signposts,* Vol.13, No.2, 1994.

had accepted him.[591]

Doubtless these white National Party leaders, one of them the State President, participated in these occultic ceremonies in order to woo the black electorate. It matters not, however, what the motives were: such participation was a fellowshipping with devils. F.W. de Klerk, a member of a Protestant denomination that he was, had now, in addition to visiting the very *seat* of Satan, the Vatican, to be entertained by the Papal Antichrist, openly dabbled in African occultism.

With the birth of a Communist-controlled South Africa just around the corner, the great goal of the international Communist movement - control of the South African minerals treasure house - was soon, it appeared, to be realised. According to the British *Intelligence Digest*,[592] its Moscow contacts stated that Joe Slovo of the South African Communist Party was seeking, in early 1994, to establish a Russo-SA minerals cartel after the elections. The article, in the December 3, 1993 issue, stated: "A recurring nightmare of the Cold War for Western military strategists, was the possibility that a revolutionary government in SA could combine with the Soviet Union to deprive the West of vital raw materials. It may now surprise some to learn that the Russian Security Services have been discussing this very possibility with the ANC/SA Communist Party Alliance on the eve of its likely victory in the first all-race SA elections." In 1973, as pointed out earlier in this book, Soviet president Brezhnev had stated that it was their goal to gain control of the strategic oil reserves of the Middle East and the strategic minerals of South Africa, and then they would be able to dictate the terms of surrender to the United States and the West. The fulfilment of that goal was now in sight.

The article went on: "Russia and SA together possess over 90% of the world's strategic minerals. The Russian security forces believe that a Russian-SA metals and minerals cartel could wield enormous influence over the industrialised world and that this could be used to enable Russia to catch up with the West economically." Indeed, such a cartel could literally bring the West to its knees. And yet, while the

---

[591] *Signposts*, Vol.13, No.2, 1994.
[592] See *The Aida Parker Newsletter*, Issue No.170, January/February 1994.

US, Britain, and other Western powers had known this *would* occur if SA ever fell to Communism, they did nothing to save SA from a Communist fate, but actively supported its Communist enemies in their war against it, and also (since 1989) claimed that "Communism was dead" and that there was nothing to fear! This reveals, very plainly, that the governments of these countries were themselves controlled by the same forces that pulled the strings behind the scenes in Russia. Russia sought the destruction of the West, but the West's leaders were of course in the same camp as Russia's leaders: the camp of the New World Order. Behind both sets of leaders were even more powerful men, manipulating Russia's leaders to work for the downfall of the West, and the *West's* leaders to work for the same! And all roads lead to Rome.

The article continued: "Should such a cartel ever be established, the potential effect on the industrialised world cannot be exaggerated. SA is a geological freak of nature. It is the largest gold producer in the world; it also has the world's largest known deposits of chrome, manganese, vanadium, fluorspar, andalusite, and platinum."

In its issue of January 14, 1994, *Intelligence Digest* stated: "Slovo has also been conducting unofficial talks with representatives from North Korea, Iraq, Libya and Cuba about the possibility of SA supplying nuclear expertise following the expected triumph of the ANC/SACP alliance in the April 27 elections."[593] From being a powerful pro-Western country, South Africa was on the verge of becoming an ally of such Marxist dictatorships as the countries mentioned. It had been betrayed by those countries in the West that should have been its allies. The reason: the *governments* of those countries were the enemies of their own countries! They sought the destruction of their own countries, their surrender to Socialism, with as much zeal as the Russians did.

When the ANC released its election list, even the liberal press pointed out (in January) that thirteen of the top twenty people on the list were members of the South African Communist Party, Marxists, or members of the unions with close links to the Communists; and that

---

[593] *The Aida Parker Newsletter*, Issue No.170, January/February 1994.

twenty-seven of the first fifty people on the list were Communists, so that the SACP would certainly gain cabinet posts in the new government.[594] Without doubt the actual number of Communists on the list was far higher: many were secret ones. The SACP was coming to power on the back of the ANC, its puppet; an ANC victory would mean an SACP victory.

Some prominent *ecclesiastical activists* were also on the ANC's national election list. At number 25 was one Arnold Stofile; at number 43 was Roman Catholic priest, Smangaliso Mkhatshwa; and at number 68, Roman Catholic nun, Bernard Ncube.[595] Fiery liberation theologian, Allan Boesak, was to run for ANC premier of the Western Cape province.

The presence of Mkhatshwa's name on the list caused something of an outcry in Roman Catholic circles, because, according to Canon 287 of Rome's Code of Canon Law, "[Clerics] are not to play an active role in political parties or in directing trade unions unless, in the judgement of the competent ecclesiastical authority, this is required for the defence of the rights of the Church or to promote the common good."[596] Priest Mkhatshwa claimed that he had a specific "Christian input" to offer in the drawing up of the final constitution after the elections, and in March 1994 the Papal bishop of Witbank, an "appropriate ecclesiastical authority", gave him permission to *accept* nomination as an ANC candidate for the National Assembly in the election.[597]

Now, with the slide towards a Marxist SA being unstoppable, certain sinister facts began to surface. Of course, it was by this point too late to do anything about them. Early in 1994, on British TV's Channel Four in a documentary called *White Lies,* it was revealed that a clandestine organisation in London, called the International Defence and Aid Fund for Southern Africa (IDAF), had smuggled over 100 million British pounds in aid to revolutionary activists in South Africa.

---

[594] *The Sunday Tribune*, January 23, 1994.
[595] *The Sunday Tribune*, January 23, 1994.
[596] *The Code of Canon Law*, prepared by the Canon Law Society of Great Britain and Ireland, Canon 287, pg.49. Collins Liturgical Publications, London. 1983.
[597] *The Southern Cross*, March 13, 1994.

It was founded by Anglican priest, John Collins, in the 1950's. Banned in SA in 1966, it continued to pay the legal costs and support the families of "anti-apartheid" activists. From its London headquarters it set up many bogus trust funds to conceal the origins of funding destined for lawyers in SA. It paid for the defence of the accused in the famous Rivonia trial. Letters from SA confirming receipt of the money were never sent to IDAF offices, but to the home of an undercover agent, a Roman Catholic priest, who took a job as a road sweeper.[598] Once again we get a glimpse of just a small part of the global intrigue against South Africa, conducted by Roman Catholic, Anglican, and other "clergymen".

A very important newspaper purchase was announced in February. Ireland's Independent Newspapers Plc., headed by Heinz Corporation Chief Executive Tony O'Reilly, announced that it would be buying 31% of Argus Newspapers, giving it control of South Africa's biggest newspaper publishing group. But now for a very important aspect of this business:

A few short weeks before, in December 1993, Tony O'Reilly had hosted Nelson Mandela at his holiday home in the Bahamas! The two were good friends. Argus Newspapers had recently relinquished control of the *Sowetan* newspaper to a group of ANC members; and now, with control of Argus itself in the hands of Mandela's close friend, the major English dailies in South Africa were owned by interests either linked to, or sympathetic to, the ANC![599] This was a major victory for the ANC.

But the plot thickened still further. According to Nicholas Coleridge in his book, *Paper Tigers,* O'Reilly and Zimbabwean Marxist president, Robert Mugabe, were both taught by a *Jesuit,* a priest by the name of O'hAoah - a coincidence on which O'Reilly capitalised when he talked Mugabe into establishing Heinz' vast Zimbabwean baked bean and washing soda factories![600]

So the biggest newspaper publishing group in South Africa was now in the hands of an Irish Jesuit-trained friend of Nelson Mandela.

---

[598] *The Sunday Times,* January 23, 1994.
[599] *The Citizen,* February 10, 1994.
[600] *The Natal Witness,* February 11, 1994.

The net was tightening.

The leaders of the pro-Communist institutions calling themselves "churches" were up to their dog-collared necks, as usual, in directing the country along the path to Communism - a path which, they knew, culminated in April. On February 14, the Panel of Religious Leaders for Electoral Justice issued a statement to the effect that the negotiations process posed no threat to the survival of any of the peoples of South Africa - an attempt to allay the very real fears of Afrikaners, many English, Zulus, and others, to lull them to sleep.[601] From February 16-18, a conference conceived by the SACC ("Vision '94") was held in Johannesburg, attended by over 200 representatives from many different "churches", including the Dutch Reformed and Roman Catholic institutions, evangelical groups, and the charismatic Rhema institution. It issued a proclamation stating that South Africa's direction toward political democratization was in accordance with God's will for the country.[602] The Lord God Almighty, being absolutely sovereign in all his works, ordaining the powers that be (Rom.13:1), removing one ruler and setting up another (Dan.2:21), had obviously ordained that SA was to become a Communist "democracy"; but this is not what the SACC leaders meant. *They* meant that Communist "democracy" was the best form of government for South Africa: that God himself was on the side of the revolutionary killers who had brought such misery to the land. By issuing this proclamation, they once again sent a strong signal to the masses that the "churches" (to which the vast majority belonged) favoured the ANC.

A panel of "church" leaders answered questions at this conference: men such as Desmond Tutu, Peter Potgieter (Dutch Reformed moderator), a leader of the "African Indigenous Churches", Roman Catholic archbishop, Wilfred Napier, and Ray McCauley, pastor of Rhema. McCauley said, "If we are going to play a role in South Africa, unity and cooperation must be a top priority for the churches."[603] Not

---

[601] *The Southern Cross*, February 27, 1994.
[602] *The Southern Cross*, March 6, 1994; and *Challenge*, No.22, April 1994.
[603] *Challenge*, No.22, April 1994.

only, then, was this conference politically radical and pro-revolutionary, but religiously ecumenical as well.

And in early March, South Africa and the *Vatican* agreed to establish full diplomatic ties.[604] Another signal was sent to millions: the pope of Rome was fully in favour of the revolutionary changes underway. No longer an anti-Romanist country, its rulers were now committing open fornication with the Great Whore (Rev.17:1,2).

While the ANC was smiling benignly on the pro-Communist "churches" that had played such an important role in the revolution, there were ominous indications of what it planned for those churches and religious groups which did *not* support it, and which even opposed its revolutionary onslaught. At a meeting held on February 22 in Cape Town, to explain the ANC's position to "church" leaders, the main speaker, a Muslim, upheld "the right of the State to crack down on religious extremists". An ANC member spoke of the need to "clamp down on right-wing para-church organisations". He suggested that such "right-wing Christians be thrown in prison", and his comments were not challenged by the ANC panel.[605] These statements reveal that, although the ANC declared itself in favour of religious toleration, it despised, and sought the destruction of, any religious institution that wanted nothing to do with supporting it. It could very well be that persecution against true Christians and biblically-based local churches will break out in the not-too-distant future, with Christians, particularly pastors, being imprisoned ....or worse.

It was the plan of the SA Communist Party and its puppet, the ANC, to eliminate those independent black homelands (namely, Bophuthatswana and Ciskei) which were strongly anti-ANC, pro-Capitalist, etc., as well as the self-governing territory of KwaZulu: literally, to pick them off one by one, and reincorporate them into South Africa before the elections, so that the ANC would control them once it came to power. These were the only obstacles still standing in the way of a total ANC victory.

Zulu Chief Buthelezi, leader of Inkatha, was well aware of it. On

---

[604] *The Citizen*, March 7, 1994.
[605] *Signposts*, Vol.13, No.2, 1994.

February 13 he said to his people, "We Zulus must stand with our Tswana and Afrikaner brothers, and brothers of other ethnic groups, to fight for freedom, justice and democracy. We must resist the ANC and their Communist surrogates. We are the only thing that stands in the way of their quest for total power." He said that the IFP was not prepared to let the ANC/SACP alliance kill six million Zulus, "but if you look at the ethnic cleansing that is taking place on the East Rand, they seem to have started on this kind of genocide."[606] Indeed they had. All opposition to the ANC/SACP/NP plans had to be ruthlessly crushed.

Bophuthatswana (often called "Bop" for short), home of the Tswana people, was the first to come under assault, in March. President Lucas Mangope was the elected black president of the homeland, and he was fiercely anti-ANC. He refused to participate in SA's elections, saying (rightly!) that his country had been granted its independence by SA, and that therefore the elections had nothing to do with Bophuthatswana. The ANC/SACP determined to bring him down.

Prior to the anarchic conditions that erupted in Bophuthatswana in March, the Communist-supporting "churches" played an important role in stirring up the people. For example, in a sermon preached by a Bophuthatswana liberation theologian, S.R. Mudau, Moses was cited as an example of a man who caused civil chaos in Egypt - the very kind of chaos that occurred in Bop in March. Then, using Daniel chapter 6, when Daniel prayed to God despite the king's commandment forbidding it, he referred this to the situation in Bop, saying that "the people" were not allowed to pray and commemorate the falling of their heroes, men such as Chris Hani and Steve Biko, or to remember June 16 (Soweto Day) and other days. He also made use of Pharaoh's dream of the seven fat cows and the seven lean cows, recorded in Genesis 41, which Joseph interpreted to be foretelling seven prosperous years and seven years of famine. Mudau said, "This is exactly what Bishop Tutu did in the '80's when he was calling for sanctions. Elijah prayed for the rain not to fall. Was this not like calling for sanctions?"[607]

---

[606] *Roca Report*, No.62, February 1994.
[607] *Challenge*, No.22, April 1994.

The distorting of biblical truth to make it appear as if the Bible supports civil disobedience, Communism, etc., is what liberation theology is all about. It was *God* who brought the plagues on Egypt (Exod.3:20), the Israelites were passive spectators (not riotous mobs), and furthermore they were *his people* whom he was delivering from bondage as part of his specific redemptive purposes - he was not laying down a blueprint for revolutionary mass action and civil disobedience by other nations who do not enjoy (as nations) the special position which the Israelites enjoyed at that time; but what did any of this matter to this liberation theologian? Daniel prayed to God despite the king's commandment, because no ruler can forbid a believer to pray to God, and in this he obeyed God rather than man, but he did not rise up against the ruler and seek his downfall; but was Mudau going to allow the truth to interfere with his distorted usage of the biblical account? It was the Lord who sent the years of famine upon Egypt, Joseph did not call for them, and so the biblical account can in no honest way be used to justify Tutu's wicked call for world economic sanctions against South Africa; but so what? Mudau twisted the truth again, and "the people" were none the wiser. As for Elijah praying for the rain not to fall, he was a prophet of God, who prayed to God for this judgement to come upon the land, and whose prayer was answered; but this is a far cry from Tutu, a man neither a prophet nor even an ordinary minister called by God to preach his Word, but a false teacher, calling for the world's nations to impose sanctions upon South Africa, something nowhere commanded in Scripture. Israel was in a unique position, as the Old Testament Church or congregation of the Lord, to whom Elijah was sent; but no nation is in that unique position today, no entire nation can be called the congregation of the Lord, and consequently comparing Tutu's call for sanctions against SA with Elijah's prayer, was, for these reasons as well, utterly fanciful. But again, as far as this liberation theologian was concerned - so what? It was a "useful" biblical account for his purposes, and "the people", ignorant of the Scriptures, were not in a position to refute his false doctrine.

The problems in Bophuthatswana began when hospital workers went on strike - instigated by an affiliate of the giant ANC-aligned trade union organisation, COSATU. Postal and telecommunications workers joined the strike. They demanded the immediate payment of pension contributions. Next the focus was shifted to demands for reincorporation into SA and participation in the elections. Hundreds of employees of the Bop Broadcasting Corporation (BBC) also went on strike. Mangope fired all broadcasting workers who had been on strike for three days, and closed the BBC. There were clashes between police and striking civil servants in the main towns.[608]

On March 10, a delegation of 300 Bop policemen handed a memorandum to the SA embassy, demanding reincorporation. Policemen had been attacked, at least one had been killed, and it was clear that the security forces were switching loyalty from Mangope to the ANC. According to Pat Hlongwane, chairman of the Returned Exiles Committee, members of MK had infiltrated the Bop security forces months before.[609] They were successful in turning the security forces away from supporting Mangope.

General Constand Viljoen, leader of the Afrikaner Volksfront, said on March 11 that there was clear evidence that the ANC had brought in, from outside Bop, most of the people involved in the unrest in Mmabatho, the capital city. It was believed that 60 000 Zulu ANC supporters were at the heart of the violence in the Tswana homeland. Viljoen said that the ANC's action in Bop was "blatant terrorism aimed at destabilising the situation to the level of anarchy so that the SADF will be justified to intervene and force President Mangope, under intimidation, to submit to the TEC. If this action by the ANC/SACP alliance is allowed, the next will be KwaZulu and the Afrikaner people."[610] He was absolutely right, as subsequent events were to prove.

As Bop was a member of the conservative Freedom Alliance, Mangope requested the assistance of the Afrikaner Volksfront (AVF), one of its Freedom Alliance allies. 1500 AVF forces entered the capital to stabilise the situation, and another 2000 were held in reserve. They had their own weapons, and the Bop defence chief had promised them automatic weapons, armoured vehicles, and rations; but they never received these because the Bop Defence Force had switched

---

[608] *Roca Report*, No.63, March 1994.
[609] *The Citizen*, March 14, 1994.
[610] *Roca Report*, No.63, March 1994.

loyalty.

Only after General Viljoen had been assured by de Klerk that the SADF would *not* be used to depose Mangope, did the AVF agree to withdraw. But it was quite obvious that the SA government, under orders from the ANC-controlled TEC, planned to remove Mangope from power. And that is precisely what it did.

As soon as the AVF troops left the capital, thousands of people poured into the streets waving ANC and SACP placards. There was widespread rioting and looting which caused damage amounting to R150 million. The police did nothing to prevent it. By the end of the day at least sixty people had been killed and three hundred injured.

Unfortunately the radical ultra-right-wing Afrikaner group, the AWB (Afrikaner Resistance Movement), became involved as well, of its own accord. Three AWB men were shot dead in cold blood by a Bop policeman. The AWB's refusal to obey his orders in Bop led later to Viljoen's resignation from the Afrikaner Volksfront.

Colonel Jan Breytenbach, one of the most respected soldiers in SADF history, founder of 32 Battalion and of the 1st SA Special Services Unit, and commander of 44 Parachute Brigade, believed that the intervention of the AWB in the Bop crisis was orchestrated by SA's National Intelligence Service (NIS)! This belief was shared by General Viljoen. Breytenbach said: "This has the hallmarks of a very slick covert operation. They succeeded in placing the right wing in a very bad light, in placing General Viljoen in a situation where there was potentially a full-scale conflict with the BDF and the SADF, and they created the necessary chaos to get rid of Mangope."[611] He said that the NIS was so intertwined with the ANC's Department of Intelligence and Security as to be virtually indistinguishable. Since the secret agreements between the ANC and NP, the entire state apparatus was now supporting those agreements, setting the stage for the ANC and NP to run the country.

Pik Botha, SA's Minister of Foreign Affairs, and Mac Maharaj, an ANC member and leader in the TEC (which was now controlling SA), told Mangope that his presidency was no longer recognised by the SA

---

[611] *The Sunday Tribune*, April 3, 1994.

government, and that he could no longer be president.[612] He was placed under house arrest and Bop came under the joint administration of the TEC and the SA government. Mangope was correct when he said on March 14 that the SA government, the ANC and the SACP had looted political power.

The Freedom Alliance leaders called it a double-cross and a betrayal. It was perfectly clear that this was an ANC-orchestrated coup. The violence had been deliberately started by ANC instigators, and then the country was deliberately *allowed* to descend into anarchy so that the SA government would have the excuse it needed to send in SADF troops and remove Mangope from power. Mandela actually claimed that he had initiated Mangope's removal.[613] One of the joint administrators placed in control of Bop announced that he would be an ANC candidate for the National Assembly. Bophuthatswana, one of the very few real success stories in black Africa, was wiped off the map by a Communist coup, assisted every step of the way by the South African government, which had doubtless been encouraged by the internationalists abroad.

Herkules Booysen, professor in Constitutional and International Law at the University of South Africa, described SA's involvement in Bop as judicially and morally unacceptable. He said that Bop was a creation of the SA government and that even if the outside world did not recognise its independence, SA was judicially and morally bound to do so. He said that there is a maxim in law which reads that freedom once conferred can never be revoked, and added that in revoking it, the government had acted like thugs. This was even more so, since (as he put it) it appeared that SA had allowed Bop to be destabilised, and possibly played an active role in this.[614] Most definitely SA had actively assisted in Bop's destabilisation!

On March 13 Chief Buthelezi said that the TEC and the SA government had illegally removed Mangope from office, and that this showed that opposition to the interim constitution would be smashed by whatever means, including mob violence and anarchy. He added

---

[612] *The Citizen*, March 14, 1994.
[613] *The Citizen*, March 14, 1994.
[614] *The Citizen*, March 14, 1994.

that it was significant that at no stage during the week's turmoil in Bop did the ANC, SACP or the SA government deplore the criminal activities of those committing murder and mayhem. "I fear for the future," he said. "The right to disagree with the ANC/SACP/SA government/NP alliance is being ruthlessly snuffed out." He added that Mangope's removal was being applauded in SA and abroad as a triumph for democracy! He knew that the same strategy was being planned for KwaZulu/Natal.[615] His Inkatha Freedom Party allowed its registration for participation in the election to lapse.

"Democracy"! This word had now replaced Communism in the vocabulary of the Marxist world leaders! How could the overthrow of an elected leader of an independent country be called a triumph for democracy? Oh, but "democracy" was now merely another word for Communism. It was a triumph for the conspirators, a triumph for the Marxists, a triumph for the SACP and the ANC. To Communists, elections are only legitimate, they are only "free and fair", when they bring Communists to power! They will loudly praise democracy when they can use it to gain power; when they cannot do so, they will praise violence and anarchy (the *very opposite* of what democracy is supposed to be) *as* democracy!

The very word, "democracy", it must be borne in mind, means "government by the people". And who are meant by "the people" when Communists use the words? Why, they themselves, and them only!

Democracy is *not automatically* a better form of human government than any other. It can so easily be just another form of dictatorship.

The overthrow of Mangope's government was a major defeat for the conservative Freedom Alliance, dashing hopes of a confederation of anti-Communist Tswanas, Zulus and Afrikaners. The Tswanas' independent homeland was no more, the ANC had gained well over a million additional votes by the fall of Mangope, and the Afrikaners were now strongly divided over how to achieve a separate homeland for themselves. The Afrikaner Volksfront, led by the Conservative Party, wanted nothing to do with the elections. General Viljoen, on the

---

[615] *The Citizen*, March 14, 1994.

other hand, believed that the best way to achieve an Afrikaner homeland was by participating in the elections to show just how much support for a *Volkstaat* there really was, *and* to exhaust every non-violent avenue open to them. The Afrikaner nation was divided between these two positions, and many English-speaking whites were as well.

Thus, the ANC had succeeded in eliminating Tswana opposition, and dividing (and thereby terribly weakening) the Afrikaners. As for Ciskei, its anti-Communist leader, Brigadier Gqozo, had already been forced to join the TEC, in January. He still remained committed to opposing the ANC, however, and so was a prime target. "Next on the ANC's list is Ciskei," said Pat Hlongwane, chairman of the Returned Exiles Committee, which was monitoring MK's activities. He said that MK cadres had infiltrated the Ciskei Defence Force, and it was only a matter of time before they acted to overthrow Ciskei's government, as they had done in Bop.[616] And indeed, that is exactly what happened. 3000 policemen and a large number of soldiers mutinied over pay and pension benefits, demanding to be paid out before Ciskei was reincorporated into SA. This was extremely similar to the way the Bop crisis had begun.[617] It was designed to cause such chaotic conditions that Gqozo would be forced to resign. By March 22, Ciskei had collapsed and Gqozo stepped down, requesting the TEC to take control of the country. He resigned, he said, in order to save lives and prevent destruction of property, as had occurred in Bop.[618] Ciskei was just too small to put up an effective resistance.

And who was one of the two administrators appointed by the TEC to rule Ciskei until the elections? The (so-called) "Rev." Bongani Finca, regional leader of the South African Council of Churches![619] Quite obviously, the removal of Gqozo and the rule of the Communist-controlled TEC had the blessing and active cooperation of the SACC.

During all these terrible events in Bophuthatswana and Ciskei, where were the cries of outrage from the Roman Catholic bishops, the

---

[616] *The Citizen*, March 14, 1994.
[617] *The Citizen*, March 24, 1994.
[618] *The Natal Witness*, March 23, 1994.
[619] *Frontline Fellowship News*, Edition 2, 1994.

SA Council of Churches, and other religious institutions of their ilk when rioting, looting ANC mobs went on the rampage? Where were the cries of outrage when Lucas Mangope had to withdraw his party from the election on March 18, because a minister in the former Bop government was necklaced, along with his brother, and people were too afraid to stand for the party? There was only a deafening silence. Violence is only wrong when carried out by the security forces of a non-Communist country in order to stamp out anarchy and restore law and order, according to the teachings of liberation theology - *not* when it is carried out by Communist revolutionary forces bent on overthrowing the government. Then it is called "justifiable anger", "understandable anger"!

Only Zulu Chief Buthelezi and his Inkatha Freedom Party stood in the way of the ANC's plans now. He was the next target. The ANC declared that it was not attempting to topple the KwaZulu government in the way that the Bop government had been toppled, but warned that it could happen. The secretary of the ANC's southern Natal region said that his organisation was trying the peaceful way, but that it could embark on the "ghastly" alternative to "liberate" Natal, and that this would not be confined to black areas.[620] This was a dire threat of civil war in Natal. The ANC knew, however, that KwaZulu was a far more formidable foe than either Bop or Ciskei. It was treading carefully.

The IFP, meanwhile, brought an ANC/SACP document to the attention of the Goldstone Commission, entitled *Prepare the Anvil for the Coming Hammer*. This document outlined a plan to destabilise and overthrow the KwaZulu government. A statement by the TEC's Pravin Gordhan was, according to the IFP, in line with the document's strategy.[621] The Goldstone Commission, always so quick to investigate any ANC charges, was predictably slow in taking up *this* matter.

Events in KwaZulu/Natal in the weeks prior to the election closely paralleled the SACP blueprint. Calling the fall of Mangope of Bophuthatswana (which the document clearly showed was planned by the SACP) a serious reverse for the forces of "counter-revolution", it called Buthelezi and the IFP "the most significant outstanding

---

[620] *The Natal Witness*, March 23, 1994.
[621] *The Natal Witness*, March 23, 1994.

obstacle". The plan was to destroy KwaZulu and reincorporate it fully into SA. It stated that there were approximately 2000 MK members deployed in a "self-defence" capacity throughout Natal, as well as several thousand SDU members. It recognised that, in order to weaken Buthelezi, efforts had to be made to weaken the loyalty of KwaZulu civil servants, a strategy that had been used so successfully in Bophuthatswana; but that this had to have an appearance of spontaneity and popular support, and direct ANC involvement had to be played down.

ANC secretary general, Cyril Ramaphosa, threatened that the Transitional Executive Council could simply go into KwaZulu, tell Buthelezi he was no longer Chief Minister, and remove him. On March 25, the ANC began a campaign of mass action with a march of 50 000 through Durban, and demanding the deployment of SADF troops in KwaZulu/Natal. It well knew that the SADF could now be used to serve its own interests, for the government was in secret alliance with it. Significantly, as the IFP noted, by far the majority of the marchers were under eighteen (the voting age), and many were not Zulus at all, but Xhosas brought into Durban from the Transkei![622]

Then came the massacre of Zulus in central Johannesburg.

On March 28, 50 000 Zulus marched - peacefully, according to the police[623] - in support of their king in Johannesburg. The rally erupted into chaos when snipers began firing at them from the surrounding buildings. Zulu marchers were also fired on by ANC security guards brandishing automatic weapons outside the ANC headquarters at Shell House, and eight Zulus were killed. Bodies were strewn everywhere, and thousands of people ran for their lives. Altogether, fifty-three people were killed, and three hundred injured. Among the dead bodies only two handguns, neither of which had been fired, were found. The ANC gunmen had not been under any threat, nor were any of them injured. And yet Tokyo Sexwale, top ANC leader, said, "The Zulus deserved what they got."[624]

The IFP said that it had received information before the march that

---

[622] *Roca Report*, No.64, April 1994.
[623] *The Natal Witness*, March 30, 1994.
[624] *Roca Report*, No.64, April 1994.

the ANC meant to attack it, and that this information had been passed on to the police and the SADF. The IFP believed that the ANC was trying to create fear and hysteria in the country in order to justify a crackdown by the TEC. The ANC, of course, blamed the IFP and the police for the killings - and law and order minister, Hernus Kriel, also blamed the IFP! As for de Klerk himself, he said that insufficient care had been taken by the march organisers to prevent violence or to discipline participants.[625] In so saying, he laid the blame for the violence at the feet of the IFP, when in fact there was solid evidence that the ANC was to blame! It was quite evident that the NP government was deliberately siding with the ANC to make the IFP look like the guilty party, all the evidence to the contrary notwithstanding. It was all part of the plot to destroy the IFP. But worse was to come.

Police said that a warrant was issued for a raid on Shell House - but this was not carried out! The IFP's Transvaal director said that the raid was cancelled by the government, because a search could have had damaging repercussions on ANC/NP relations![626] The Conservative Party said that evidence was given under oath to the magistrate, according to the search warrant, that there were reasonable grounds to suspect that firearms, etc., in Shell House could have a bearing on the crimes of murder and assault. Reliable sources insisted that de Klerk himself intervened, at the request of Mandela, to prevent the search being carried out. According to the CP, reliable sources also said that the regional commissioner of police in the Witwatersrand had instructed police specifically not to shoot during the chaos in central Johannesburg, and threatened them with dismissal if they did so.[627]

On March 30, the commissioner of police said that he had asked the regional commissioner of the Witwatersrand to inform Mandela of the search warrant, and to ask for his *co-operation* in confiscating the weapons! He said that a search was not necessary because Mandela said that he would hand over the weapons. By April 17, police confirmed that the weapons had still not been handed over. The deputy minister of law and order defended the decision not to search by saying

---

[625] *The Natal Witness*, March 29, 1994.
[626] *The Natal Witness*, March 30, 1994.
[627] *The Citizen*, March 31, 1994.

that it might "interfere with the negotiating process".⁶²⁸ The IFP and CP had been right.

If anything should have alerted the South African public to the indisputable fact that the National Party government was in cahoots with the ANC, this was it. Tragically, the public, for the most part, continued to believe the propaganda and to trust the NP.

On March 30, Ramaphosa demanded a state of emergency to be declared in KwaZulu/Natal immediately, following a TEC decision in principle the day before to impose one. The state of emergency came into effect the very next day! This was just the latest capitulation to ANC demands by the government. Rightly, the IFP saw it as an attempt to topple the KwaZulu government. Thousands of SADF troops were deployed throughout the province. 10 000 citizen force part-time troops were also called up.⁶²⁹

It was, in fact, a *British* newspaper which told the truth about the NP and ANC. An editorial in the London *Sunday Times* after the Shell House massacre stated that Mandela and de Klerk were "perpetrating an enormous fraud on 40 million South Africans and the rest of the world." It went on: "Their propaganda machines insist the election will be substantially free and fair, and that once a popularly elected government is in place, peace will blossom. Neither will happen. There is no way that the elections are, by any standards, going to be free or fair. The campaign is a bloody mess." It said that the Shell House incident showed that "the ANC is determined to take power by riding roughshod over those who stand in its way. The movement's true nature was exposed when its gunmen mowed down Zulu traditionalists exercising their democratic right to demonstrate their opposition to the election and their support for their king's call for independence for KwaZulu/Natal." Of Buthelezi and King Goodwill, it said "all they are asking for are federal powers along the lines enjoyed by German, Canadian or American states or provinces. Is South Africa to be plunged into a bitter civil war for the sake of this?"⁶³⁰

It stated that the new constitution was certainly not a federal one, as

---

[628] *Roca Report*, No.64, April 1994.
[629] *Roca Report*, No.64, April 1994.
[630] Quoted in *The Natal Witness*, April 6, 1994.

scores of foreign experts had pointed out, but that de Klerk and Mandela persisted in claiming that it was; and that the ANC had won everything it wanted. Only Zulu royalists were now standing in its way. "At some point," it continued, "a solution to the Zulu question will have to be found. It is better to do it now rather than have a Bosnia raging on the southern tip of Africa with thousands more dead; around one million British passport holders clamouring to get to Heathrow; and a First World economy, Africa's best hope of salvation, lying in ruins."

The editorial also made the following important remarks: "the time has come to think about what the PC-brigade [politically-correct brigade] consider the unthinkable: whether South Africa is a viable state. The country is a tenuous entity, manhandled together by British imperial conquest just 90 years ago after British soldiers defeated the Zulus and then the Boers to get hold of the country's mineral riches, and kept together after independence by the authoritarian hand of Boer apartheid. It is a mish-mash of 11 tribes and lacks the typical requirements of a functional democracy." With these words, the present author concurs wholeheartedly. It is, in fact, a concise summary of one of the points he has sought to make in this book. Within the geographical boundaries of South Africa exist a number of radically diverse nations. It is not one nation, it is a mish-mash of a number of nations thrown into close proximity with one another by the turbulent events of centuries of history. By war and bloodshed, diverse nations *can,* over time, be forged into one nation. But why should they be? And why should there be such bloodshed and suffering in order to bring this about? Each nation governing a territory of its own is still the ideal, as history proves with countless examples. This author is not advocating the cruel humiliations of petty apartheid; he is merely contending for the fact (for fact it is) that, just as the British would not want to be governed by the Germans, or the French by the British, so the various nations of South Africa should be able to govern themselves in their own territory - while allowing others to live and work in that territory if they so desire, and if they are willing to submit themselves to the government of that place. But it will not be. The powerful forces working for a United World under a World Government will not permit it. It goes against their plans.

CHAPTER THIRTY-EIGHT

1994: THE "CHURCHES" PREPARE FOR THE ELECTION

The election was now barely weeks away. Millions of blacks were illiterate, and still had, moreover, little or no understanding of what to do when they entered a polling booth. Voter education was under way, but the Independent Forum for Electoral Education (IFEE) was *not* independent or neutral, but had close connections with the ANC, according to South Africa News Information Service, 27 January 1994. This meant that illiterate or semi-literate voters were being taught, not just *how* to vote, but *who to vote for*. The European Community, long a supporter of the ANC, and predominantly Roman Catholic, gave R20 million to the IFEE. And this was where the radical "churches" played an important role once again: funds for electoral training could not go directly to a political party, and so they were channelled through "church" organisations in SA sympathetic to the ANC. The Clinton Administration, for its part, decided to increase the funds it was giving to voter education, after the US helped to persuade the ANC to accept the double ballot system, one for the national and one for the regional governments. In order to compensate the ANC for the votes this would cost it, the US Agency for International Development gave $10 million for voter education, in addition to the $25 million already given to convince voters that they could vote for the same party both nationally and regionally. This would increase the number of ANC votes. The Agency declared that the extra money had reassured the ANC and the NP that they would not lose as a result of permitting the double ballot - something the IFP had wanted.[631] The ANC and NP, therefore, were receiving vast funds from the internationalists. Other parties, with very limited funds, could not hope to compete.

How could the election be free and fair? All opposition to the interim constitution and the transitional process was being destroyed by the ANC and the NP; only the ANC and NP had vast funds at their disposal for advertising and radio spots; voter education was totally inadequate, and such voter education as was being carried out was, for

---

[631] *Roca Report*, No.62, February 1994.

the most part, favourable to the ANC; the so-called Independent Electoral Commission (IEC) was not functioning properly, and it was certainly not independent or impartial, but extremely biased in favour of the ANC:[632] in fact, there was an unofficial ratio of three ANC appointees to every one NP official in the IEC, and it had been effectively nominated from the ANC/NP-dominated TEC, making it anything but independent;[633] massive intimidation of potential voters was being carried out by the ANC; UN, EU, and other observers were biased in favour of the ANC; religious observers were just as biased in its favour; and there was no way, nor any real desire, to control massive fraud and corruption over the election period.

Further facts were also coming to light about the major part played by the United States government in the South African revolution. The huge US embassy in Pretoria cost US taxpayers over $800 million. It was the world's most expensive diplomatic facility. At least sixty CIA agents were deployed there. It also reportedly had a communications satellite able to monitor all phone calls and fax messages that the US ambassador wanted to intercept. ANC and SACP leaders were welcome at the embassy and were often given money.[634]

Throughout South Africa, "churches" were preparing for the election by supporting voter education and urging their members to assist as observers, monitors, and electoral officials.

On April 13, the Natal Church Leaders Group asked members of its affiliated "churches" to pray for peaceful elections, and to participate as officials. Every "church" was asked to observe April 24 as a special day of reflection. In the Cape Town area, between 16 000 and 17 000 people were reached by the Roman Catholic institution with its voter education programme.[635] This all sounded harmless

---

[632] *Roca Report*, No.63, March 1994.
[633] *Roca Report*, No.64, April 1994.
[634] *Southern Africa Update*, Vol.2, No.2, February 1994, published by the editor, Robert L. Slimp, Columbia, South Carolina, USA; see also *The Insider*, No.3/94, 15 February 1994, Vol.5. Varama Publishers, Pretoria.
[635] *The Southern Cross*, April 24, 1994.

enough, indeed it sounded very helpful, to the millions of gullible, naïve, religious, churchgoing South Africans. But of course these various religious institutions were deeply involved in far more than teaching the voters how to vote: a great many of them were actively campaigning for the ANC at the same time.

Through the Ecumenical Monitoring Programme in South Africa (EMPSA), over 200 international observers observed the run-up to the elections, and 300 more monitors arrived to carry out monitoring duties till after the polls. They expressed the "solidarity and concern of the international Church" and "backed" the peacemaking efforts (!) of the "Church" in South Africa. And on April 20, the Panel of Religious Leaders for Electoral Justice convened interfaith services countrywide, demonstrating the unity of various religions in their alleged concern for the sanctity of life and in their alleged campaign for electoral justice.[636] This organisation consisted of leading Hindu, Muslim, Bahai, Buddhist, Jewish and so-called "Christian" leaders such as Tutu, Beyers Naudé, Romish bishops, the president of the World Conference on Religion and Peace in SA, the vice-moderator of the Dutch Reformed institution, Stanley Mogoba of the Methodist institution, and Ray McCauley, the pastor of the charismatic Rhema "Church". The liturgy consisted of quotations from various religions' sacred writings: the Old Testament, the New Testament, the Koran, Hindu writings, and many others.[637] The purpose of its interfaith service held at the Carlton Hotel in Johannesburg was to "emphasize the basic unity of South Africa's religious communities....in the light of current religious divisions fostered by political parties with different agendas. Religion should unify rather than divide the nation."[638]

In saying this, these wicked men attempted to convey the notion that the only reason for religious differences was because of divisions caused by political parties - which was absolute nonsense. Someone, moreover, who claimed that his religion was the only truth could be accused of having a political agenda, and he could be persecuted![639]

The SA Catholic Bishops Conference invited a group of forty

---

[636] *The Southern Cross*, April 24, 1994.
[637] *Signposts*, Vol.13, No.3, 1994.
[638] *Signposts*, Vol.13, No.3, 1994.
[639] *Signposts*, Vol.13, No.3, 1994.

international observers to SA, and they were deployed throughout the country to "observe" the elections. At least fourteen bishops and several priests arrived as representatives of their "churches".[640]

The World Council of Churches sent a high-level ecumenical delegation to "observe" the elections. The team was led by (of all people) Kenneth Kaunda, former Zambian president, and Anglican archbishop, Robert Runcie, the retired archbishop of Canterbury, a man notorious for his leftist views. Also on the team were the general secretary of the National Council of Churches in the US, the general secretary of the Philippines National Council of Churches, a former director of the WCC's Commission of the Churches on International Affairs, a former director of the WCC's Programme to Combat Racism, the chairman of the German Evangelical Mission for Southern Africa, and the general secretary of the London-based Catholic Institute for International Relations.[641] Hardly a neutral gang of ecclesiastical observers! There was probably not one who was not (at the very least) sympathetic to the ANC. Of that we can be certain.

The country, then, was literally crawling with Communist-supporting radical priests and pastors, all bent on ensuring that the ANC came to power. Religion played a far greater part in the entire electoral process than anyone could possibly accurately assess. It is no exaggeration to say that the ANC could not have hoped to win if it were not for the full support of the Roman Catholic institution, the World Council of Churches, and the latter's many affiliates.

Not only did the Papal institution, and the WCC and SACC, continue to give their wholehearted support to the ANC up until the last, but the ANC, for its part, continued to give its support to them. In April, Nelson Mandela addressed a memorial service for Chris Hani at a Roman Catholic "church" on the East Rand. He said that the service showed the importance of the "Church" in the struggle for change in South Africa. He added that the Roman Catholic religion should be commended for its vital role in fighting the "oppressive regime". ANC supporters formed a guard of honour outside.[642]

---

[640] *The Southern Cross*, May 8, 1994.
[641] *The Southern Cross*, April 3, 1994, and April 24, 1994.
[642] *The Citizen*, April 11, 1994; and *The Southern Cross*, May 1, 1994.

And yet, even as the ANC continued to work fully with the terrorist-supporting religious institutions to ensure its victory, members of religious institutions that refused to cooperate with the revolutionaries were being targeted. On April 1, three people were killed and eleven wounded in an attack on a black Zionist "church" near Estcourt, in Natal.[643] The Zionist religion, while calling itself "Christian", is certainly not a true Christian church, for it proclaims doctrines completely at variance with the Word of God; but traditionally the Zionists were often opposed to the ANC. And in a separate incident, the wife, mother, and six daughters of a black pastor were hacked and shot to death near Port Shepstone, in Natal.[644] These tragic events did not receive the coverage they deserved in the media. While the terrorists praised the "churches" which supported them in the revolution, they massacred those who did not. A horrifying portent of things in store for true Christians, perhaps, in the "New South Africa".

As South Africa rushed towards its first multiracial elections, witchcraft played an increasingly prominent role in the lives of millions of black people. Vast numbers believed that their lives were guided by ancestral spirits. They believed that witches could create and control zombies, and they feared the *tokoloshe,* a malicious spirit. And as the elections approached, many began to believe that these spirits would bewitch the polling booths. *Nyangas* (traditional healers) said that they had been approached for *muti* (potion) for protection during the elections. Some black people believed that spirits would see where they put their crosses on the ballot papers, leading to repercussions later, or that they could take control of their minds and make them vote for a party they did not support, according to a researcher at the Human Sciences Research Council.[645]

No Christian denies the awful reality of demon-possession, for the Scriptures contain abundant examples of it. Vast numbers of blacks are deeply involved in the worship of demons under the guise of "ancestral spirits". Such is the nature of black tribal religion in South Africa and

---

[643] *Frontline Fellowship News,* Edition 2, 1994.
[644] *Frontline Fellowship News,* Edition 2, 1994.
[645] *The Citizen,* April 15, 1994.

indeed the entire continent. It has already been shown, in this book, that as the Marxist revolution gained ground in South Africa, there was a corresponding rise in witchcraft in many parts of the country. Both Marxists and the practitioners of the occult arts loathe biblical Christianity, and in the kingdom of darkness the forces behind both were working in tandem to obliterate, from the hearts and minds of the blacks, any Christian influence.

According to the head of Witwatersrand University's Anthropology Department, Professor Robert Thornton, witchcraft had reached *epidemic proportions* in parts of rural Transvaal in the months leading up to the elections. He said that people were being killed, and witches were being burned. People superstitiously spoke of vampire-like bloodsuckers turning people into zombies or changing their blood into cash. As election-fever mounted, there were widespread reports from refugees in troubled areas of victims of politically-motivated killings having their skulls cut open. He said that this was because the brain was considered to be the strongest kind of *muti*. In 1993 there was an increase in *muti* killings, with parts of the victims' bodies being removed. And he added that many of the participants in the violence used *muti* which they believed could deflect bullets.[646]

Many parts of South Africa were again descending into the Dark Ages, from which they had partially emerged with the coming of Protestant missionaries and the subsequent dissemination of the Gospel of Christ, and of such civilising influences as inevitably follow in the wake of sound Protestant missionary activity.

On April 17, a mere ten days before the elections, six people were rescued by the police from the basement of the ANC's regional headquarters in Johannesburg. They had been abducted the day before, accused of being IFP supporters, held in a metal cage, tortured and threatened with death! All had been seriously assaulted, one having had his toes crushed, another having had his toenails pulled out. From the same building police confiscated 22 identity books, 4 passports, 100 passport photos, 26 birth certificates, 384 applications for identity documents, fingerprinting equipment and voters' lists![647] Yet did these

---

[646] *The Citizen*, April 15, 1994.
[647] *Roca Report*, No.65, May 1994.

shocking revelations alter the wholehearted support of the liberal "churches" for the ANC? Of course not. Nothing was going to stand in the way of an ANC victory now.

On April 19, the Romish archbishop of Johannesburg, Reginald Orsmond, urged the pope of Rome to make a "pastoral visit" to bless South Africa in its post-apartheid era. "Your Holiness, come to South Africa," he pleaded. "The situation has changed: now you can come and kiss the ground." This was a reference to John Paul II's unplanned landing in South Africa some years before, when he was on his way to Lesotho. He did not kiss the ground at that time. Orsmond said that an earlier papal visit had not been possible because of the "uncleanliness" of the country's racial policies, but "now we are cleaning up."[648]

Orsmond was right on this point: the situation in SA had most certainly changed. No longer were the country's leaders opposed to either Communism or Romanism. SA and the Vatican had even agreed to establish diplomatic ties. And the ANC, for so long supported by the Papacy, was about to come to power.

John Paul II said that a papal trip to SA was already under consideration. On April 27, the date of the elections, he said that he hoped the elections would "contribute to bringing peace and serenity in that country, thus ending the sad spiral of violence which, for much time, has caused death and destruction". He then exhorted "all, in particular Catholic South Africans, to seek with tenacity ways of peace and reconciliation, so as to assure for that great and dear country a future of harmony and authentic moral and civic growth".[649] Not a word did he speak against the real perpetrators of the "spiral of violence", the Marxists assisted by Rome itself to cause the very "death and destruction" he self-righteously lamented.

---

[648] *The Southern Cross*, May 8, 1994.
[649] *The Southern Cross*, May 8, 1994.

CHAPTER THIRTY-NINE

1994: AN ELECTION NEITHER FREE NOR FAIR

South Africa's first multiracial election was held from the 26th to the 29th April 1994.

Mere days before, the Inkatha Freedom Party decided to participate. It had previously declared that it would not do so unless certain demands were met. Millions of Zulus, intensely loyal to the IFP, would not have gone to the polls, and would have resisted any attempt by an ANC government after the election to impose its will on KwaZulu/Natal. The country was literally teetering on the very brink of anarchy and civil war. But at the eleventh hour, Buthelezi declared that his party would participate in the election. If Inkatha had only begun campaigning for the elections months before, it would have severely undermined both the ANC and the NP. Entering as late as it did, it still managed to do phenomenally well, sweeping to victory in the KwaZulu/Natal regional election, and on the national level emerging as at least one of the most successful parties.

General Constand Viljoen's Freedom Front entered the elections on behalf of Afrikaners (and English-speaking whites) who desired a *Volkstaat* and saw the election as a legitimate way to show their support for one. Tragically, the Afrikaner Volksfront refused to contest the election and called upon its supporters to boycott the polls, and hundreds of thousands heeded the call. As a result the Afrikaner cause suffered a very serious setback. The Afrikaners' influence in the future government was greatly weakened. The Freedom Front did exceptionally well under the circumstances, with hundreds of thousands of whites throughout the country voting for it. The actual number was far higher than the official final results, for reasons that shall be given later.

South Africans of all races turned up in their millions to vote. Each citizen over eighteen years of age was legally entitled to vote, and each was permitted to vote twice: once for the government at national level, and once for the government at regional level. The country had been divided into nine regions, or provinces: it was a small concession to the IFP and those who wanted a federal system, although the powers given to the regions were minimal, and certainly not truly federal.

At the end of it all, the African National Congress was declared to be the runaway winner, with over 60% of the votes nationally, and having won seven of the nine regions. The Inkatha Freedom Party swept to victory in the province of KwaZulu/Natal, and the National Party won the Western Cape province. The ANC took all the rest.

South Africa was now under Communist domination.

Yes, the ANC had come to power. But by what means? Answer: through massive fraud and deceit. Through what was probably the most rigged election in history, the ANC took control of this great land. This author, and others, had been warning for years that when elections were finally held, the ANC would not win by fair means, but by foul. And that is precisely what happened. Utter confusion prevailed across the country, in thousands of polling and counting stations. In order to advance Communism, Lenin had advocated "constructive chaos"; and this was certainly what there was. It was plainly obvious that the ANC/SACP *deliberately* created a situation of "constructive chaos" which they could manipulate to their own advantage - and did. What follows is just some of the overwhelming evidence. Where footnotes are not given, the information was generally obtained from SABC TV election coverage.

As one example of the Independent Electoral Commission's (IEC's) pro-ANC position, striking teachers and Edendale nurses (these were politically-inspired anti-IFP strikes) were employed in various capacities by the IEC.[650]

Most political parties recorded that IEC officials were mainly ANC sympathisers.[651] As pointed out in the London *Times,* the ANC managed to push its own supporters as presiding officers throughout KwaZulu/Natal; and as these people had the power to appoint other officers and agents, one polling station after another in the IFP's greatest stronghold was staffed with well-known ANC activists.[652]

At Mid-Rand on April 27, there were at least forty incidents reported of IEC officials "not acting democratically" at the polls. An

---

[650] *The Natal Witness,* April 29, 1994.
[651] *The Sunday Tribune,* May 1, 1994.
[652] *UCA News,* Edition 4/94.

untold number went unreported.

Significantly, the ANC allegedly rejected Jan Steyn, a judge with great administrative experience, as chairman of the IEC, and settled on Judge Kriegler, a man with none.[653]

For months before the election, much had been made in the media about voter education. Voter education, however, was totally inadequate, particularly in KwaZulu, but also elsewhere. Many, many people still had no idea what to do by voting day. Many could not read or write.

The South African Communist Party (SACP) participated *illegally* in the election. According to retired judge, Hector McDonald, by failing to register as a political party the SACP was in breach of the Electoral Act; and yet it admitted that it fielded thirty-four candidates on the ANC's list of their first hundred candidates! The judge noted that the ANC/SACP electoral alliance was unconstitutional and unlawful, there being no provision in the constitution "even remotely suggesting" that an alliance between a registered party (the ANC) and an unregistered party (the SACP) was permissible; and the continuation of this alliance at the time of the election legally rendered the entire election invalid.[654]

On the surface there *appeared* to be very little intimidation taking place during the election. Certainly the media gave the impression that there was almost none. But in reality there was *widespread* intimidation, especially in the very remote and rural areas. Large numbers of IFP supporters said that they were too afraid to vote, as their enemies controlled the election arrangements and could deal with them later.[655] There were reports of aged IFP supporters being threatened by armed ANC youths. There were allegations of armed men within polling stations threatening voters, and of voters being accompanied into booths.

In the Northern Transvaal, the United People's Front of Lebowa accused IEC officials of intimidating voters.[656] The Freedom Front

---

[653] *The Natal Witness*, May 7, 1994.
[654] Document (unnamed) reprinted from correspondence columns, Cape Times, and published by *The Aida Parker Newsletter*, 1994.
[655] *UCA News*, Edition 4/94.
[656] *The Natal Witness*, April 30, 1994.

documented cases where IEC officials *openly intimidated* voters to vote for the ANC.[657] The NP in Germiston claimed that voters had been induced to vote for the ANC at two high schools in Katlehong.[658] ANC officials were allegedly allowed to wear uniforms inside some polling stations (this was illegal, as it could intimidate the voters). Even the PAC accused the ANC and IEC of collaboration.

An election report by an observer in East London stated: "It was pandemonium! Some parties such as the PAC, ADM and ACDP who were allowed by law to have agents in each polling station, when they reported to their appointed places were told by the IEC officials that their services were no longer needed. As a result in some areas you found only ANC and NP officials appointed. In Mdantsane, ANC officials were actually in all the polling stations and flying their flags in front of the polling stations".[659] This was blatant intimidation!

It must also be borne in mind (as has been documented in this book) that *massive* intimidation had taken place over a period of many *years* before the election. ANC agents told people that they would know who they voted for, and would deal with them later if they did not vote ANC.

As just one example of the fear in the hearts of many blacks: at Tugela Ferry in KwaZulu/Natal, no-one answered reporters' questions about who they were going to vote for. They appeared to be scared, a reporter said.[660]

At the start of the campaign among blacks, 30% of voters were still undecided about which party to support. But such was the intimidation of parties other than the ANC, that their representatives had very little access to these millions. Indeed, there were many cases of other parties being literally driven away from certain areas. No other country holding to First World standards would ever have tolerated such a situation.[661] There were a few incidents where other parties did the same to ANC supporters, but these were a tiny percentage of all the cases: the vast majority were instances of ANC supporters intimidating and driving away supporters of other parties.

---

[657] *Roca Report*, No.65, May 1994.
[658] *UCA News*, Edition 4/94.
[659] *UCA News*, Edition 4/94.
[660] *The Natal Witness*, April 28, 1994.
[661] *The Natal Witness*, May 7, 1994.

As the IFP had entered the election after the ballot papers had been printed, stickers were printed with its details, to be affixed to all ballot papers. However, IFP stickers were deliberately *not* affixed to *many millions* of the ballot papers, thus making those papers invalid, not only in KwaZulu/Natal and the rest of South Africa, but also at South African embassies overseas (Britain, Portugal, the US, Greece, etc.), where South Africans were able to vote. The IFP said that 150 stations had problems with forms which did not bear the stickers. This meant that people who wanted to vote IFP had to *request* that a sticker be affixed, thereby exposing who they wanted to vote for, a violation of the secrecy of the ballot. In many places, people were simply too afraid to take that risk, and so they did not vote for the IFP at all.

Chief Buthelezi also pointed out, on April 27, that 60% of his people were illiterate or semi-literate, and as the IFP's sticker was to be affixed to the bottom of the papers, they had been told simply to put their mark next to the last name on the paper (being unable to read). But when the sticker was not affixed, these people would have voted NP, which was the name printed at the very bottom.

Many people were told that, if the sticker was not on the papers, they should simply scrawl "IFP" at the bottom. But in the first place, this was illegal, and in the second place, illiterate people would not have been able to do so even if it was legal.

By late on the 27th, Buthelezi said that countrywide, where stickers *had* been available, they were running out, or had already run out. On the 28th - the third day of the elections - there were *still* no IFP stickers on papers in at least seventeen areas in KwaZulu. And by the 29th, there were *still* no ballot papers in certain areas of KwaZulu!

When a close relative of the present author, who voted in East London in the Eastern Cape, complained to the official about the absence of the IFP sticker on his ballot paper, she *reluctantly* attached one. In Durban, too, many people found that there were no IFP stickers attached, and they were only attached *after* complaints were made, and then very reluctantly. The stickers were *in* the officials' possession, but they simply did not attach them until they were requested to do so by individuals! Even then they only placed them on those papers already in the hands of those who had complained - not on all of them!

The IFP said that there had been gross irregularities at the PWV counting station at Nasrec where papers without IFP stickers *were counted* in the provisional tallies, and IFP monitors were *chased away* by the ANC.[662]

In addition, huge numbers of ballot papers were declared "spoiled" because the IFP sticker was affixed so as to encroach upon the NP's space on the forms.[663]

In KwaZulu/Natal, officials arrived late at many polling stations. At the hospital in Mahlabatini, near Ulundi, there were *no* officials or materials on April 26.[664] At Mtubatuba and Richards Bay, among many other places, stations only started operating later in the day. On the 27th, the IEC said that stations would stay open as long as needed; but reports came in of doors being shut while people were still in line. Besides, voting was impossible after sunset in some rural areas because the IEC had failed to make arrangements for electricity. The IFP said it had documented proof of polling stations opening late, or not opening at all, on the 27th.[665]

By the end of the 28th, some stations in KwaZulu had *still* not opened - not since the election began on the 26th! Even as late as the 29th, some KwaZulu stations still did not open because IEC officials allegedly "did not know" that they were permitted to open on that day! If this was true, it shows astounding incompetence, regardless of how remote some places were; but more likely it was not true, but a deliberate attempt to reduce the number of IFP votes.

In the Northern Transvaal, about 160 polling stations failed to open, according to the Democratic Party.[666] And in Northwest Province, even the IEC admitted that about 35 000 people did not get to vote.

Altogether, *thousands* of polling stations failed to open on time on the 26th, and *hundreds* failed to open at all.[667]

---

[662] *The Citizen*, May 5, 1994.
[663] *UCA News*, Edition 4/94.
[664] *The Natal Witness*, April 27, 1994.
[665] *The Natal Witness*, April 29, 1994.
[666] *Roca Report*, No.65, May 1994.
[667] *UCA News*, Edition 4/94.

In many parts of KwaZulu/Natal, as well as other parts of the country, there were not enough ballot papers available, or the papers ran out. This was admitted by de Klerk on the 27th. At Newcastle, voting materials only arrived at 11.00 am on the 26th.[668] By 1.30 pm, papers meant for the Nqutu district were still in the IEC offices in Dundee, and the IFP stickers were lying in Ladysmith. By the 28th, there was *still* a lack of papers in KwaZulu (the third day of voting!), resulting in the closure of stations for periods.

The IEC admitted that ballot papers *never reached* the Jozini and Ingwavuma areas of northern KwaZulu/Natal, so that thousands never voted in this IFP stronghold.[669]

At Alberton, Transvaal, there were *no* materials on the 27th. On the 28th there were *still* none. The NP said that it had lost votes as a result. The Freedom Front rightly claimed that it was deliberate.

Altogether, *thousands* of polling stations reported having no ballot papers, no IFP stickers, no invisible ink, no stamps and no ballot boxes.[670]

There were also insufficient polling stations in the rural areas of KwaZulu. Buthelezi said that this was the case in some strong IFP areas. But there were reports, confirmed by various parties, that the ANC/SACP created *unauthorized* polling stations in a number of areas![671] At Menyexwayo in the Kranskop district of KwaZulu/Natal, an unauthorized polling station was set up close to the authorized one. The team brought no observers or security with them. When two observers did arrive, the presiding officer was very reluctant to receive them. The observers noticed that some IFP stickers were stuck on top of the NP area on the papers, thereby spoiling the papers. Some voting officers were also overheard telling voters to vote ANC. In the late afternoon, this unauthorized team left with their ballot box and no security.[672] In how many other places did this happen *without* being noticed?

---

[668] *The Natal Witness*, April 27, 1994.
[669] *Roca Report*, No.65, May 1994.
[670] *UCA News*, Edition 4/94.
[671] *UCA News*, Edition 4/94.
[672] *CFT Monitor Report*, April 27, as reported in *UCA News*, Edition 4/94.

In many places, IEC officials "assisted" the aged, infirm, and illiterate to make their crosses - and there was nothing to prevent them "assisting" them to vote ANC, even if they did not want to. Reports were received of officials covering up the IFP's name on the papers when they helped these people. There were instances where the ballot form was folded in such a way that the IFP's name was folded out of sight when given to the voters.[673] When IFP officials tried to intervene to prevent these things occurring, they were allegedly chased away in a number of cases.

In the Msinga district of KwaZulu/Natal, on April 26, at the Roman Catholic mission clinic, the people noticed that a monitor named Mr Khilmeet, who was "assisting" some of the elderly and sick people with their voting, was not putting the cross where they requested him to. In addition, he told voters to leave the voting station after giving them only one ballot paper (each voter was to receive two papers, enabling him to cast a national and regional vote). A row erupted, and he had to flee for his life.[674]

The ANC had wanted temporary voter identity cards to be issued to those without other identification, and this had been approved. The ANC knew that these cards made it easier to cheat. It was assisted by the US State Department which, through its front organisation, the SA Free Election Fund, persuaded the election authorities to issue temporary voters' cards to 3.5 million people before the election.[675] This SA Free Election Fund assisted with personnel and equipment for the issuing of these voter cards.

It is important to note that, because voters had been urged for months before the election to obtain proper identity documents, 97.5% of potential voters were in possession of current, proper identity documents by the time of the election! Only 500 000 were still without such documents. Yet even though this was the case, the ANC still insisted that a wide variety of obsolete documents be accepted, *and* also that temporary voter cards be issued! This greatly increased the

---

[673] *The Sunday Tribune*, May 1, 1994.
[674] *CFT Monitor Report*, April 26, as reported in *UCA News*, Edition 4/94.
[675] British *Intelligence Digest*, 13 May 1994, quoted in *The Aida Parker Newsletter*, No.173, May 1994.

potential for people to vote more than once. In addition, children under eighteen (the legal voting age), many as young as thirteen or fourteen, were given voter cards![676]

The SA government admitted that at least one of the computer systems used to produce these voter cards was *stolen* from the Department of Home Affairs office in Johannesburg in late February! Each machine was able to produce a voter card every three minutes.[677] How many cards could have been produced between late February and late April, when the elections were held?

On April 21, it was reported that the South African Police's Fraud Syndicate Unit had uncovered a huge fraud operation at Lancet House, Jeppe Street, Johannesburg - where the ANC's regional headquarters were housed. They found vast quantities of false identity documents, passports, birth certificates, application forms and receipts![678]

By the end of the 26th, thousands of *IFP* supporters still had not been issued voter cards.[679] But as the IFP pointed out, thousands of *underaged children* had been issued voter cards and were not challenged by IEC officers when they came to vote.[680] Vast numbers of the ANC's supporters, of course, were teenagers.

In Hillcrest, Natal, voter cards were issued without the Department of Home Affairs stamp on them. This was revealed on April 29.

104 *fake* voting cards were found in a car in Pietersburg that had been rented out to the IEC. The car was abandoned. All the cards had the same name and birth date on them. The SAP began an investigation. How many *other* fake cards were made, that were *not* discovered?

A Department of Justice official from Camperdown labelled the system of issuing temporary voter cards as "an absolute circus". She said that even if she did not think youngsters were eighteen years old, it was merely their word against hers: there was nothing she could do. She also said that she was sure some were applying twice.[681]

---

[676] *Roca Report*, No.65, May 1994.
[677] *UCA News*, Edition 4/94.
[678] *The Citizen*, April 21, 1994, as reported in *UCA News*, Edition 4/94.
[679] *The Natal Witness*, April 27, 1994.
[680] *The Sunday Tribune*, May 1, 1994.
[681] *The Natal Witness*, April 29, 1994.

The Democratic Party claimed, too, that voter cards were being issued to unaccompanied children without their ages being verified. The Freedom Front stated that children as young as fourteen were issued with voter cards.[682] And the NP estimated that *thousands* of underaged children were given cards.[683]

In Edendale, a number of under-aged youths were turned away for trying to get temporary voter cards, according to a Home Affairs official and an IEC presiding officer. The Home Affairs official said that without any proof of age, he had to exercise his discretion.[684] The question, of course (and one impossible to answer), is: in how many other cases were they *not* turned away?

A UN observer closed the Umzumbe station on the Natal south coast when he found temporary ID's handed out indiscriminately, allowing people to vote twice.[685] At least he was an honest UN observer! But how many got away with it in other places?

An IEC spokesman said that a case was under investigation at Ndwedwe, KwaZulu/Natal, where *dozens* of children, some barely older than *eight or nine,* arrived with temporary voter cards! In Tongaat, Natal, a man was arrested at a polling station after presenting a forged voting card.[686] But again, how many others got away with it?

In Lebowa, an ANC stronghold, temporary voter cards were sold for R50. The Department of Home Affairs there was unable to cope with the number of *false applications*, and fourteen-year-olds were caught applying. In some cases photographs were professionally tampered with. Reports of similar situations were received from the ANC strongholds of Transkei and Venda. Due to deadlines having to be met, as well as the huge demand for voter cards, the issuing officers in many cases were unable to check all applicants.[687]

In the Northern Cape, which was won by the ANC against all predictions, and with the highest percentage poll of all (92.7%),

---

[682] *The Citizen*, April 29, 1994, as reported in *UCA News*, Edition 4/94.
[683] *The Sunday Tribune*, May 1, 1994.
[684] *The Natal Witness*, April 29, 1994.
[685] *The Sunday Tribune*, May 1, 1994.
[686] *The Natal Witness*, April 30, 1994.
[687] *SA News Information Service*, April 22, 1994, as reported in *UCA News*, Edition 4/94.

thousands of temporary voter cards were issued as late as April 28.[688] Obviously the ANC did this in order to ensure its victory there.

A man claiming to be a church minister in Newcastle was arrested on the 28th for distributing false baptismal certificates. These stated that the bearer was baptized before he was actually born, "making" him old enough to acquire a voter card and vote! He sold almost 3500 at R10.00 each.

Another man claiming to be a priest was arrested at Ennerdale in northern Natal for allegedly issuing false birth certificates.[689] And in Frankfort in the Orange Free State, police arrested two people selling false birth certificates to people who used them to obtain voter cards.[690]

The question is: how many others went undiscovered?

The invisible ink placed on the hands of voters was meant to prevent them from trying to vote twice. It should have been a foolproof safeguard against electoral fraud; but it failed miserably. The ink ran out in some areas, the UV boxes used to check peoples' hands for the fluid were not delivered to other areas, and batteries were not available at still other stations.[691]

In certain places, such as Inanda, it was reported that IEC officials did not check hands for the ink.[692] IFP people complained, but were ignored. In how many other places was this the case?

The Freedom Front had evidence of voters arriving at polling stations with their hands *bleached white*. Even though these people *admitted* having placed their hands in chemicals, they were allowed to vote![693]

Some observers, having heard that the invisible ink could be neutralised with hair spray, tested it on themselves, and discovered that, by using VO5 hair spray, the ink could not be detected twenty-four hours later under the UV light![694] This meant that, with the

---

[688] *Roca Report*, No.65, May 1994.
[689] *The Natal Witness*, April 29, 1994.
[690] *The Natal Witness*, April 29, 1994.
[691] *Roca Report*, No.65, May 1994.
[692] *The Sunday Tribune*, May 1, 1994.
[693] *Roca Report*, No.65, May 1994.
[694] *UCA News*, Edition 4/94.

extended voting period, people could easily vote twice!

In many cases, dysfunctional UV lights which were battery-operated allowed streams of second-time voters through when the batteries ran out.[695]

ANC/SACP comrades actually broke into polling stations in some places and distributed voting papers to people, totally disregarding IEC officials![696]

On April 27, over thirty ballot boxes from sixteen voting stations in KwaZakhele, a black township near Port Elizabeth, were being taken to the official collection centre when the police, who were accompanying the IEC officials, were asked to stop at the K.K. Nkwanda Church hall after polling stations closed. The police were told to remain outside while the IEC officials carried the boxes into the hall. After half an hour they still had not emerged, and a senior policeman entered. He caught IEC officials opening the boxes.[697] They were literally caught red-handed, with their hands in the boxes! In how many other places did this occur, *without* being discovered?

There were reports in Soweto of ballot boxes being opened in a number of stations, and of IEC officials taking the IFP stickers off!

Many boxes were also found with the ballot papers *neatly stacked* - showing that they had been opened. When the IEC set twenty-four boxes aside pending an investigation, the counters went on strike, chanting, "ANC!" This clearly showed just how "impartial" the vote counters were!

In Newcastle on May 2, five boxes were found to contain neat stacks of ballots.[698]

At a voting station in East London, in the Eastern Cape, there were complaints that a ballot box used on April 26 was illegally opened and used again on the 27th.[699]

There were reports of unguarded trucks in KwaZulu filled with

---

[695] *The Sunday Tribune*, May 1, 1994.
[696] *UCA News*, Edition 4/94.
[697] *Roca Report*, No.65, May 1994; and *The Argus*, April 28, 1994, as reported in *UCA News*, Edition 4/94.
[698] *The Natal Witness*, May 3, 1994.
[699] *UCA News*, Edition 4/94.

ballot boxes (which then anyone could have tampered with); and of boxes without IEC markings on them (meaning they were not official, and yet were being used!). In Stanger, Natal, an IEC official said that police were not escorting them, and boxes were not sealed, making it possible for the boxes to be tampered with. This happened in many other places as well.

Boxes were noticed at times outside the "safe" area around stations, left unguarded, with people walking around who were not searched.

The NP Chief Organiser for Katlehong, Dan Volakazi, signed an affidavit that IEC officials were guilty of "fraudulent voting on a grand scale and voters' ballot papers were opened and checked before they were placed in the ballot boxes".[700]

When the boxes of ballots were sealed (and this was certainly not always done!), the sealing took place in front of observers. But these people were for the most part in favour of the ANC!

In Pretoria, it was admitted that some boxes were not as securely sealed as they should have been when they arrived at the counting stations. In Mmabatho, Northwest Province, boxes arrived which had damaged seals. At Hammersdale, Natal, broken seals actually lay openly on the ground outside the polling station; and the IFP leader was not allowed inside the station. He accused the IEC and ANC of foul play.

In a polling station in Duncan Village, East London, police arrested a suspected MK member after he allegedly carried a hand grenade into the polling station. He was one of six men who claimed to be ANC election monitors and attempted to gain access to a guarded building in which sealed ballot boxes were housed.[701]

At Mkhulisa Hall in the Ixopo district at Sandanezwa, KwaZulu/Natal, the ballot boxes were unsealed and had no serial numbers. In addition, the IEC officials handed out the *national* ballot paper for both the national and regional votes![702]

---

[700] *UCA News*, Edition 4/94.
[701] *The Natal Witness*, April 30, 1994.
[702] *CFT Monitor Report*, April 27, as reported in *UCA News*, Edition 4/94.

Many ballot boxes arrived at the Mapumulo strong-room (KwaZulu/Natal) either with broken seals, or completely unsealed. The district electoral officer sealed some of them just prior to putting them into a safe, instead of the boxes being sealed at the voting stations at the end of the day. At Mbitane, despite requests that the boxes be sealed, this was not done.[703] And at Efaye in the New Hanover district, ballot boxes could be opened on one side even though they had been sealed. These boxes arrived at Efaye with an IEC team from Mapumulo.[704]

In Uitenhage, residents cast their ballots into plastic bags - and yet three hundred unused ballot boxes stood empty at the IEC stores just a few kilometres away.[705] And in neighbouring Botswana, the ballot papers were being *photocopied,* and the used papers were put into plastic bags![706]

There were far more ballot papers printed than there were people (let alone voters) in the whole of South Africa! Originally 80 million ballot papers were printed (for security reasons) in Britain, for the estimated 21.7 million voters. This figure, in itself, was far too high. But there was such a *shortage* by the end of the 27th already - only the *second* day of voting - that SA printers printed an additional 16 million![707] IEC officials said that there were various possible reasons for this shortage, but they were not sure which was the correct one (in fact the real reason was blatantly obvious!). An official actually said on television on the 29th that security was *no longer* the priority, and that there was a definite drop in security standards with the additional printing done in SA. They needed them in a hurry, he said.

A member of the Freedom Front wrote that it was well known that half the black population was under the age of sixteen, and that the 1991 census revealed a *total* population of 37 million![708]

---

[703] *CFT Monitor Report,* April 27, as reported in *UCA News,* Edition 4/94.
[704] *CFT Monitor Report,* April 27, as reported in *UCA News,* Edition 4/94.
[705] *UCA News,* Edition 4/94.
[706] According to a Durban IFP official in a phone conversation with the author.
[707] *Roca Report,* No.65, May 1994.
[708] *The Natal Witness,* May 5, 1994.

Clearly the IEC had far more ballots printed than were necessary, either anticipating the massive, deliberate disappearance of millions of papers, or actually *planning* that millions would "mysteriously" disappear, and that millions would be illegally filled in!

How many ballot papers went missing? Perhaps as many as *twenty-two million*. The IFP charged that many of these were in the hands of the ANC, and said it had sufficient evidence.[709] Doubtless they were perfectly correct.

A Cape Town businessman revealed that *900 000* ballot papers had been dumped unattended at his storeroom near the airport the day before the election started. Two well-known transport companies brought the boxes. He was told that they contained IEC "material" and he was asked to store them. He reluctantly agreed, feeling very uneasy, and was astounded to discover what they contained. "I telephoned the police and the IEC telling them to come and remove them. Overseas ballot papers are guarded like gold in Fort Knox. The police and I counted the boxes and discovered there were 900 000 ballot papers in them," he said. The boxes were removed under police scrutiny to a second security company. The man said that he later received an anonymous death threat! IEC spokeswoman Ina van der Linde said on the 27th that they were "re-organising the distribution of ballot papers," and that "serious misplacement [of papers] had taken place." And Judge Kriegler, head of the IEC, admitted that there had been *massive* disappearances of *millions* of papers![710] No doubt it was intended that these "missing" papers were to be illegally filled in later. And these 900 000 were discovered: but millions were not!

In Empangeni, northern Natal, forty boxes of ballot papers found without any seals on them were a "mystery", it was admitted on the 30th. Their origin was unknown. At Ntuzuma, truckloads of boxes went missing on two consecutive nights.[711] And there were reports of private *ANC* cars carrying away ballot boxes, destination unknown. Boxes were often loaded into the private cars of IEC officials. This was admitted openly on SABC TV news on April 29.

---

[709] *The Natal Witness,* April 29, 1994.
[710] *The Cape Times,* April 28, 1994, as reported in *UCA News,* Edition 4/94.
[711] According to a Durban IFP official in a phone conversation with the author.

But this was just the tip of the iceberg.

Five IEC officials were under investigation for the concealment of large quantities of ballot papers and other materials, it was revealed on May 3.[712] One official was under investigation for "gross dereliction of duty at best", according to the chief director of IEC Monitoring. This official was in charge of 611 boxes containing *5 499 000* ballot slips. He gave conflicting accounts of his available material, and turned away electoral officers before a team of specialist monitors entered his warehouse on April 28.

In Pretoria a warehouse was found to contain 150 boxes (containing 9,000 ballot slips each) of PWV ballots, 100 boxes of Western Cape ones, 30 of Northern Cape, ten of national, 300 of OFS and ten of Northwest; as well as 100 boxes of IFP stickers, 200 UV lights and four boxes of ink. An investigation was also initiated concerning ballot papers and materials stashed on the West Rand. Many ballot boxes also originated from so-called "pirate stations" under dispute in northern Natal.[713]

The IFP said that there were millions of ballot papers stashed away at the Vosloorus civic centre. Ballot papers, claimed to have been missing or stolen, suddenly reappeared once voting had ended.[714] Boxes of ballots were found abandoned, or in taxis, or even in the homes of candidates![715]

The IFP found that many ballot papers already had the IEC stamp and ANC crosses on them, and that these were given to people in line to vote at KwaMashu, as well as in the PWV region (where police alerted the IFP to this).[716] There were reports of children in KwaMashu working throughout the night, putting crosses on ballot papers for the ANC!

It was decided, at the last moment, to declare April 28 a public holiday as well, to enable those who had not voted on the 27th to do so. But Buthelezi said that he had not been consulted; and many of his people went to work, unaware of the holiday; and this affected voting.

---

[712] *The Natal Witness*, May 3, 1994.
[713] *The Natal Witness*, May 3, 1994.
[714] *The Citizen*, May 5, 1994.
[715] *UCA News*, Edition 4/94.
[716] *The Natal Witness*, April 29, 1994.

Furthermore, by increasing the length of the voting period, the chances for fraud were also increased.[717]

The ANC accused IFP supporters in KwaZulu of violating the electoral act, and lodged a formal complaint with the IEC. They claimed that the IFP had removed ballot boxes, expelled ANC agents, and intimidated people into voting for the IFP.

There certainly could have been IFP supporters who also managed to do some of these illegal things. By no means is the present author attempting to convey the impression that the IFP was a perfectly virtuous party. But when one considers the massive bias of the IEC in favour of the ANC, not to mention the massive support for the ANC from foreign observers, as well as the facts of the ANC's sordid history, it is quite clear that such IFP irregularities as there may have been were far, far less than the *widespread, massive* ANC irregularities countrywide, and even overseas. Besides, as the IFP pointed out, the ANC allegations surfaced late in the electoral process, and therefore it was clear that these claims were a fall-back option should the ANC have failed to win a majority in KwaZulu/Natal (which it did, indeed, fail to do).

The IFP accused the IEC and ANC of colluding in alleging massive voting irregularities.[718] It said it was significant that IFP allegations against the ANC in the Johannesburg area had not been pursued with as much vigour as the ANC charges in KwaZulu/Natal.[719]

The ANC also claimed that there were pirate stations, not IEC-approved, set up under IFP control.[720] But the IFP pointed out that there was a state of emergency in KwaZulu/Natal, and such stations would immediately have been closed down. Indeed they would have, if the IFP had set such pirate stations up; but, as has been shown previously, unauthorized *ANC* stations were set up. The IEC, however, being so extremely pro-ANC, turned a blind eye towards these!

It was reported that number plates were stolen from KwaZulu government cars, and put on other cars to give the impression that the

---

[717] *Roca Report*, No.65, May 1994.
[718] *The Citizen*, May 5, 1994.
[719] *The Natal Witness*, May 5, 1994.
[720] *The Natal Witness*, April 29, 1994.

KwaZulu government was cheating. The IFP said that all that the ANC was accusing the IFP of doing, *it* was doing. Given the history of the ANC and the undoubted bias of the IEC in favour of the ANC, this was most certainly true.

Voting was extended until the end of the 29th in various ex-homelands. By extending it throughout most of them, and not just in KwaZulu, the appearance was given that *all* were having the same problems - even the ones which favoured the ANC. While in some places they were undoubtedly having problems, these were as nothing compared with what was going on in KwaZulu. Furthermore, it appeared *deliberate* that there were not enough materials in certain areas of the ANC stronghold of Transkei; because on the 28th it was said that there was just "no way" that everyone there could vote in time - so ANC supporters were transported into southern KwaZulu/Natal to vote![721] The ANC *admitted* doing this, saying it spent about R10 000 to do so; and perhaps as many as 250 000 people actually were taken there, because, while IEC officials had estimated that there would be about 400 000 voters in the region, about 650 000 cast their votes there.[722]

According to electoral officials, between 50 000 and 60 000 votes were cast in the Mount Currie district - an area with about 18 000 eligible voters![723]

The ANC could afford to lose some voters in the Transkei, as the Transkei was such an ANC stronghold, and bus them into IFP strongholds in order to sway the vote there. The head of the Department of Politics at Natal University said that it could be assumed that those who were brought *en masse* into KwaZulu/Natal were ANC supporters and that this would work against the IFP.[724]

The ANC was able to do this because it had insisted that there was to be no voters' roll in this election, nor any notice taken of the voters' places of residence.[725]

In the Ciskei on the 29th, very few voted (so why was an extra day

---

[721] *The Natal Witness*, April 28, 1994.
[722] *The Sunday Tribune*, May 1, 1994.
[723] *The Natal Witness*, April 30, 1994.
[724] *The Sunday Tribune*, May 1, 1994.
[725] *Roca Report*, No.65, May 1994.

needed there?); but in KwaZulu, large numbers voted on that day. Were they ferried into KwaZulu from Ciskei as well?

The ANC also transported tens of thousands of its supporters into the Western Cape, from the Transkei/Eastern Cape. In the Western Cape the NP was stronger than the ANC (and did, in fact, win there). Official Transkei government vehicles were used to do this, according to press reports.[726]

In Athens, Greece, voting at the SA embassy was chaotic. 10 000 people turned up to vote there on the 26th, and it was estimated that at least 3000 went home without voting after lining up for hours. IEC staff at the embassy allowed only two people at a time to take the lift to the polling station in the embassy.[727]

At least *four million* black refugees and migrant workers from neighbouring states were helped by the SACP to secure illegal SA passports, enabling them to vote in the election. Two million illegal immigrants from Mozambique voted,[728] as well as vast numbers of Batswana and Namibian refugees and migrant workers. False papers were printed for many of them.[729]

Ministers Johann Heynes (Dutch Reformed denomination) and Peter Storey (Methodist denomination) helped organise volunteers to assist with the counting of ballots. Storey was asked by the IEC to mobilise 600 people as special advisors in counting stations. He contacted churches in Johannesburg and surrounding areas, and by the 28th, 800 people had been mobilised. Storey was prominent in liberation theology circles.

In Johannesburg, over 1000 churchgoers went to the Rhema "Church" premises on the 29th to be trained as presiding officers in the counting of ballots, and were then deployed in about 700 counting stations countrywide. The volunteers included Roman Catholics, Anglicans, Methodists, Presbyterians, Lutherans, Dutch Reformed, and

---

[726] *UCA News*, Edition 4/94.
[727] *The Citizen*, April 30, 1994.
[728] British *Intelligence Digest*, May 13, 1994, quoted in *The Aida Parker Newsletter*, No.173, May 1994.
[729] *UCA News*, Edition 4/94.

Pentecostals.[730] Many of these people (as this book makes clear) would certainly not have been impartial!

By May 4th, vote counting was way behind in KwaZulu/Natal. The IFP said that it was being deliberately delayed in Durban by ANC party agents, who were disputing boxes from IFP strongholds to try to excise them from the count.[731]

On May 5 - *days* after the election was over - a post office bag filled with thousands of used, but uncounted, ballot papers was found under a pile of rubbish by NP officials at the Nasrec counting centre. Unused ballot papers lay around the floor, and on the pavement outside were strewn temporary voter cards and election documentation.[732]

The tally of an estimated 1.1 million votes was *lost* (!) in transmission between the Pretoria counting station and the IEC headquarters - despite verification that the tally had been received! The Pretoria counting station was one of the few to achieve a full reconciliation between votes cast and papers issued. A second tally was made. The Freedom Front claimed that this second one gave them 147 000 *fewer votes* than the first.[733] Pretoria was the stronghold of the Afrikaners and of the Freedom Front. It would appear that the ANC/IEC "lost" the original tally on purpose!

Already by the 29th April, various observers were saying that the election was "substantially" free and fair. Kriegler did the same. Yet all the evidence proves the contrary.

On the 30th, heads of the international observer missions to SA said the elections were free.[734]

"There were many opportunities for fraud," according to one top observer, "but these were not exploited." As documented here, they most certainly *were* exploited - and on a massive scale too!

On the 30th Judge Kriegler, in the face of the large-scale voting irregularities committed by IEC officials, admitted that *some*

---

[730] *The Citizen*, April 30, 1994.
[731] *The Natal Witness*, May 4, 1994.
[732] *Roca Report*, No.65, May 1994.
[733] *Roca Report*, No.65, May 1994.
[734] *The Natal Witness*, May 2, 1994.

irregularities had occurred. But he did not admit much. First, speaking at an IEC press conference, he said that in some places, when boxes were full, the electoral officers had opened them, poured their contents into containers, and started filling the boxes again. But far from condemning this illegal practice, he said that they displayed "commendable initiative"!

Next, he admitted that there were cases where people who claimed that they made mistakes on their ballot papers requested another one - and were given one! This, too, was illegal, of course.

On the 30th, Kriegler dropped his bombshell. Up until then, instructions were that the number of votes cast had to be reconciled with the number of ballot papers issued, before the counting of votes could begin. But on the 30th, Kriegler announced that the counting of ballots, and the releasing of figures, were more important than "reconciling procedures"; and the IEC had therefore decided to *drop* the reconciling procedures until *after* the votes had been counted! He admitted that this was a departure from the rules - but claimed that it was necessary.

He said that there was nothing in the process to prevent a corrupt presiding officer from stamping ballots and filling them in himself; and that reconciliation in such a case was of minimal value. He therefore told the counters: if you can reconcile, do so; if not, note the defects, the problems - but carry on counting!

"As far as we're concerned," he said, "the election is about national reconciliation, not ballot reconciliation. Let's forget about the formalities. Let's find out what the people said they want.".[735] Cheating, he admitted, was widespread, but (in his opinion!) probably not enough to distort the outcome seriously.[736] He added that they were not looking for efficiency only, or even primarily - but rather for a "people's election"!

What he was, in effect, saying, was that there *were* unscrupulous electoral officers; but that the reality of the situation must be accepted; that it was far more important to keep "the people" happy - even if it meant bending the rules. Efficiency and accuracy were not the priorities - this was Africa, it was an African election, and everyone

---

[735] *The Sunday Tribune*, May 1, 1994.
[736] *The Natal Witness*, May 6, 1994.

might as well accept that this was how the game was to be played from then on. In fact, the judge said as much in no uncertain terms: "It is an Africa-style election. It is not to be measured by European or North American standards. What we're trying to do is put together a credible test of the will of the people".[737]

In the end, he said, it was less important whether the election was really free and fair than whether people accepted the outcome as a national verdict on their future! He *openly admitted* that the rules were stretched - and that they *should* have been. "If it is manifest in a given situation that the rules ought to be stretched because that would do justice, yes, that's my approach. And I've applied it here".[738]

In the words of Hermann Giliomee, a teacher of politics at the University of Cape Town, responding to Kriegler's statement about national reconciliation and ballot reconciliation: "I find it hard to recall a statement which is politically more inane. If reconciliation means abandoning efficiency and simply resorting to the hope that no political fraud will occur, the entire project of nation-building rests on a false foundation".[739]

The DP told Kriegler that the decision to postpone ballot reconciliation until after counting would mean that fraud would go undetermined.[740] It was quite right. But that was exactly what the ANC and IEC wanted.

Later, Kriegler also decided that the *verification process* was to be dropped until after the figures were made known! This was the process whereby the IEC headquarters went through and checked everything before releasing the figures. It was dropped because it was holding up the results of the regional counts!

A senior official told the SABC's Mmabatho reporter on the 1st May that he doubted whether verification or reconciliation would *ever* occur.

Then, to solve the problem of disputed votes, the IEC adopted what it called "proportional adjustment". This meant that disputed

---

[737] *The Natal Witness*, May 6, 1994.
[738] *The Natal Witness*, May 6, 1994.
[739] *The Natal Witness*, May 7, 1994.
[740] *The Natal Witness*, May 2, 1994.

votes were either subtracted or allocated to parties in the same proportion as those which could be verified. In the Transkei, 50 000 votes from boxes that had been tampered with were subtracted from the parties proportionally. Ballots without IFP stickers, which, if they had been discarded as "technically" invalid, would have disenfranchised many, were also "adjusted".[741] As can readily be seen, this system was hardly fair!

The official election results were meant to have been announced by April 30. However, by May 2, this still had not been done, and there were such serious problems that the entire process was in danger of grinding to a halt. Only 25% of the votes had been counted - and yet de Klerk conceded defeat, and Mandela accepted victory! This clever move meant that the inauguration could now still go ahead as planned. The inaugural celebrations became the focal point for everyone, and the exact election results "became of academic interest only".[742] In this way attention was taken off the fraudulent results, and focused on the victory celebrations.

By May 1, there was growing suspicion within the IEC itself that there had been some "deliberate dirty play".[743]

On May 2, the IEC reported that three quarters of a million ballots had been spoiled in the PWV region. By the next day, this figure had been "revised" to 33 915.[744] Only 0.75% of all votes were finally declared spoiled. Considering that 70% of the electorate was illiterate, and that the vast majority had never voted before, this was far too good to be true![745] This was clear evidence of corruption.

On May 3, ballots counted nationally suddenly increased by 3 million votes - and then shrank by 2.75 million within twenty minutes![746]

On May 4, Kriegler said that sabotage lay behind the computer problems which stopped the IEC's delivery of results for over twenty-

---

[741] *The Natal Witness*, May 7, 1994.
[742] *Roca Report*, No.65, May 1994.
[743] *The Sunday Tribune*, May 1, 1994.
[744] *UCA News*, Edition 4/94.
[745] *Roca Report*, No.65, May 1994.
[746] *UCA News*, Edition 4/94.

seven hours; and he said that sabotage could also have been the reason for the distribution problems during the election itself. Admitting that a computer hacker had tampered with the IEC's computer programmes to progressively increase the number of votes for three parties at the expense of the others, Kriegler refused to say which parties had been favoured.[747] The IFP called for a police investigation into vote rigging at IEC headquarters. The IFP said, "There is mounting evidence that massive fraud has taken place to boost the ballot in favour of the ANC and that steps were taken to cover this up. Talk about alleged computer tampering appears to be a smokescreen to hide the real reason for the temporary freezing of publication of the results, which is electoral fraud on a grand scale".[748] It stated, "We have been given information by IEC officials that IEC head office officials had been rigging the results to the advantage of the ANC for an extended period, and that this electoral fraud was only halted after other IEC officials could no longer stomach the fraud".[749]

Kriegler *actually admitted* that the results were being "manipulated to resolve political disputes and irregularities". And an IEC official said, "We have vast powers .to make some adjustments". Yet another admitted that it had been decided, despite all the fraud and irregularities, that free and fair elections *had to* be declared, come what may.[750]

On May 4, with three-quarters of the votes counted, the ANC had 65.2%, and was moving towards the 67% it needed to give it the right to re-write the constitution on its own. Mandela, however, felt that it would be better if the ANC did not get 67%, because this would alarm people too much. So the next figures released by the IEC showed a *drop* in the ANC's percentage to 64.7%! It finally totalled 62.65%.[751] Here was clear evidence of the ability of the IEC to manipulate the results to suit the ANC!

---

[747] *The Natal Witness*, May 5, 1994; and *UCA News*, Edition 4/94.
[748] *The Natal Witness*, May 6, 1994.
[749] *Roca Report*, No.65, May 1994; and *UCA News*, Edition 4/94.
[750] *Business Day*, May 5, 1994, as reported in *UCA News*, Edition 4/94.
[751] *Roca Report*, No.65, May 1994.

The ANC, by its massive rigging of the elections, actually exceeded the expectations of political analysts. Around 53% was what most expected the ANC to get, although some expected it to do much worse. In addition, the other parties all did far *worse* than analysts had expected.[752] Further evidence of just how extensive the rigging was!

On May 27 - a month after the election - Kriegler, addressing a Press Club lunch, revealed that, when he went on the air to announce the final result of the election, he did not yet have the final data in hand! He said that, because the provincial legislatures had to be constituted the next day, and because Inauguration Day had been set for the following Tuesday, "we simply had to go public on the available data at that stage."[753]

Despite the widespread, massive fraud, the irregularities, the large-scale intimidation, etc., Kriegler called the election "an outstanding success", and pronounced it "substantially free and fair". Predictably, so did almost all foreign observers. They were working for governments and organisations that were bent on seeing to it that the ANC came to power in South Africa. The evidence given above, however, reveals that the election was anything *but* free or fair. The Freedom Front claimed that it was free and fair at only 20% of the polling stations.[754] The general secretary of the Freedom Front said, "This election made a farce of democracy and will go down in history as the Kriegler fiasco".[755] A premier candidate for the African Democratic Movement said, "This election has been an exercise in futility. This election was not free and fair. It's the biggest confidence trick in history ever played against an unsuspecting and gullible public."[756]

The British *Intelligence Digest* put it very well when it stated that in the final analysis the ANC/SACP "polled less than 50% of the vote, so the obvious Black joy at witnessing the end of apartheid should not

---

[752] *Roca Report*, No.65, May 1994.
[753] *The Natal Witness*, May 28, 1994.
[754] *UCA News*, Edition 4/94.
[755] *The Citizen*, April 29, as reported in *UCA News*, Edition 4/94.
[756] *The Sunday Tribune*, May 1, 1994.

be mistaken for unqualified support for the ANC. Its official tally of 62.5% was only arrived at by massive fraud. Furthermore, we are told, it was a fraud that was prepared according to a plan drawn up by the former Soviet KGB."[757]

The present author wrote the following soon after the election:
"It has finally happened.
"Following the April 26-29 election in South Africa, the Marxist-controlled African National Congress of Nelson Mandela has come to power. It is the culmination of decades of revolution, conspiracy, murder and mayhem: decades which have seen this once-great land reduced from a First World giant to what promises to be a Third World disaster; decades which have seen literally tens of thousands of lives lost in one of the most brutal, most savage guerrilla revolutions the world has ever known.

"The Communist forces have been victorious. They have won. In the face of unprecedented international pressure, betrayed by its `friends' in Washington and London and by its own weak, infiltrated government, besieged by Moscow-financed terrorists who bombed civilians, murdered farmers and township residents, burned to death so-called `collaborators', and undermined by evil, scheming, Communistic `clergymen' who preached fiery revolutionary sermons and stirred up the masses to hate and kill and to think that they were doing God's will all the while, South Africa has caved in. And on its ashes `the New South Africa', a `People's Democracy', a Marxist state, will now arise.

"From politicians in halls of government to the pope of Rome in the Vatican, from the dirty streets of Soweto to the manicured lawns of the White House, an ecstatic cry of victory has ascended. `Free at last!' said Mandela in his victory speech, echoing the words of Martin Luther King. `Power to the People!' screamed the headlines. `A triumph for democracy!' blubbered the journalists. The masses, both here and around the world, are for the most part blissfully ignorant of the stark truth: *that South Africa has just become the world's youngest*

---

[757]The British *Intelligence Digest*, May 13, 1994, quoted in *The Aida Parker Newsletter*, No.170, May 1994.

Communist state. It is not freedom that has come to the black people of South Africa, but rather a worse form of tyranny than any they have ever known. 'Equality' of a sort has come, yes: they will be equally poor, equally miserable, equally oppressed.

"The election is over, and the ANC has won. But if anyone pays any heed to the cries which we are hearing from all quarters now, that the election was 'free and fair', he is naive in the extreme. That this election has been 'free and fair' will surely rank as one of the greatest lies of the twentieth century, a lie perpetrated by newsmen, 'churchmen', politicians, observer missions; a lie that they planned to tell, long before the election was even held. No matter what happened, there was no way this election was ever going to be declared anything but 'free and fair'. The internationalists wanted this election; the United Nations wanted it; the United States wanted it; Britain wanted it; the European Union wanted it; the Organisation of African Unity wanted it; the World Council of Churches wanted it; the Vatican wanted it. And all of them wanted the ANC to win, and by fair means or foul, they were going to see to it that it did."[758]

It did; and the world rejoiced. But if the world had cared to notice, there were those whose hearts were broken, and whose eyes were full of tears. They knew that this was not a time for rejoicing.

---

[758] *The Bible Based Ministries Magazine*, April-May 1994, No.71. Article: 'South Africa Now Under Communist Domination!' Published by Bible Based Ministries, Pietermaritzburg, South Africa.

SOUTH AFRICA'S ELECTION: 1994

Don't ask the politicians if the vote was free and fair,
And foreign observations count for nought;
Ask the simple village people who will tell you - if they dare -
Whose lives have been with so much danger fraught.

Ask the old man sitting silently upon a log of wood,
With nothing but the clothes upon his back;
Only ashes mark the spot where once his little house had stood:
They came in dead of night and torched his shack.

Ask the woman rocking to and fro with eyes so tightly shut -
So recently the nightmares came to life:
Her husband had been pulled from bed and dragged outside the hut,
And killers made a widow of the wife.

Ask the parents who had seen their pride and joy, their only son,
Butchered before their eyes, and heard, "Beware!"
If they'd "exercised their franchise" at the cold point of a gun,
Their vote would have been just as "free" and "fair".

For the warning had been given and was as plain as could be:
"Vote for us or you will meet the selfsame fate!"
And faces on election day hid hearts in agony -
The thousands who'd been targets of the hate.

And as upon the mounds of dead the new land came to birth -
"A victory for democracy!" they said -
It seemed, when all across the land the flag was lowered to earth,
The hammer and the sickle rose instead.

Shaun Willcock
3 May 1994

CHAPTER FORTY

1994: INAUGURATION DAY

"For promotion cometh neither from the east, nor from the west, nor from the south. But God is the judge: he putteth down one, and setteth up another" (Psalm 75:6,7).
"And he [God] changeth the times and the seasons: he removeth kings, and setteth up kings" (Daniel 2:21).

The life story of Nelson Mandela illustrates so well the truth of the two texts given above. From childhood obscurity in the rolling hills of the Eastern Cape/Transkei, to the practice of law, to active involvement in the Communist revolution, to imprisonment for twenty-seven years, to release in his old age from that life behind bars, to globetrotting hero of the conspiratorial forces and the blinded masses, to exaltation to the highest political office in the land, that of President of South Africa. Truly, it would be hard to *invent* a story more astounding! His is a true-life story stranger than fiction indeed, a story of a rise to power and worldwide fame that, as he grew to manhood, he could never have imagined, not in his wildest dreams. A story so bizarre, so full of surprises, so unique, that it defies all logic, all rational explanation, and must be attributed to the hand of God in the affairs of men.

His is not a good story, but it is an astounding one. His rise to power was not without terrible bloodshed, cruelty that defies description, and almost unbelievable deception and intrigue; but nevertheless his inauguration as President of South Africa on May 10, 1994, would never have come to pass if God Almighty had not ordained it. This is by no means to say that the Lord approved of the terrible events that transpired whereby Mandela came to power, and truly there is a day of judgement coming; but it is absolutely certain that all things that occur in this world, do so by the decree of God. "He doeth according to his will in the army of heaven, and among the inhabitants of the earth" (Dan.4:35); and "the powers that be are ordained of God" (Rom.13:1), whether they be good or evil, benevolent or tyrannical, for the performance of his purposes

(Isa.10:12).

On May 6, Mandela attended religious services at a Muslim mosque; on May 7, he attended religious services at a Jewish synagogue;[759] and then on May 8, two days before the inauguration, he was the guest of honour at a "National Service of Thanksgiving" at the FNB Stadium, Johannesburg, organised by the South African Council of Churches. He was escorted to the podium by prominent religious leaders. The purpose of the service was to give thanks for "the attainment of a democratic dispensation in South Africa" and to "express the commitment of the Christian community towards the transformation of South Africa".[760]

The religious leaders associated with the vile SACC had much to crow over: their objective had been attained. They were ecstatic. They could not suppress their glee. The revolution, which they had baptized and blessed, had been successful. It had cost the lives of tens of thousands of people; but what did they care? All that mattered was that they had won. And they had gathered to celebrate.

But true Christians did not participate in this ecumenical Babel. They did not unite in prayer with these wicked people.

Addressing the service, Mandela said that South Africans should forget the past, hold hands, and begin the task of building a new country. From then on South Africans would constantly hear this theme, whereas in fact it was the ANC and its cohorts who had destroyed the country in the first place. Now that they were in power, they called on everyone to rebuild what they had destroyed! Mandela thanked the "Church" (meaning, of course, those institutions, falsely calling themselves "churches", that had done so much to assist the ANC to power), as well as Muslim, Hindu and Jewish leaders for the role they had played in the "struggle" for "liberation".[761]

Local and international religious leaders were present. Romish archbishop, Denis Hurley, led the crowd in a prayer for forgiveness and reconciliation for the "long history of oppression and discrimination in our country....and for those responsible for the

---

[759] *Signposts*, Vol.13, No.3, 1994.
[760] *Signposts*, Vol.13, No.3, 1994.
[761] *The Natal Witness*, May 9, 1994.

imposition of apartheid with all its cruel consequences."[762] Desmond Tutu, Frank Chikane, and Dutch Reformed moderator Pieter Potgieter conducted a symbolic act of "reconciliation" at a wooden cross. Tutu said: "We have emerged from a history of strife and death to seek a future of life and health. We are the rainbow people, we are free, all of us, black and white together, we are free."[763]

Nothing could be further from the truth.

Inauguration day, May 10, 1994: South Africa had never seen a spectacle like it. It was more like a coronation than an inauguration. In front of thousands - among them royal personages, presidents, vice-presidents, dictators, tyrants, and terrorist leaders - and watched by millions of television viewers around the world, Nelson Mandela was inaugurated as South Africa's president. He ended his speech with the words, "God bless Africa"; but which god did he mean? Certainly not the true and living God, the God of the Bible, for he was a stranger to the true God. After he took the oath as president, prayers and readings by a Hindu priest, a Jewish rabbi, an Islamic sheikh, and Anglican archbishop Desmond Tutu followed.[764] None of these men knew the true God. This religious syncretism was an abomination to the Lord.

The world's leaders had come to celebrate the entry of South Africa into the World Order. And what an assembly of wicked people it was! Among many others, there was arch-Socialist Hillary Clinton, wife of United States President Bill Clinton, along with US vice-president, Al Gore; there was President Robert Mugabe of neighbouring Zimbabwe, a Marxist dictator with the blood of thousands on his hands; there was the leader of the Palestine Liberation Organisation, Yasser Arafat, that vile terrorist organisation, smiling and speaking of Mandela as his "brother"; there was the Marxist President dos Santos of Angola; the UN secretary general, Boutros Boutros-Ghali; US Senator Ted Kennedy; US leftist religious leader Jesse Jackson; and there was Cuban Marxist dictator, Fidel Castro, the man whose forces had been engaged in a bloody and protracted battle with South African forces, as Cuba had done all it

---

[762] *The Natal Witness*, May 9, 1994.
[763] *The Natal Witness*, May 9, 1994.
[764] *The Natal Witness*, May 11, 1994.

could to promote the Marxist cause in southern Africa, a man with the blood of hundreds of South African soldiers on his hands. "Welcome to South Africa," said the now deputy-president, F.W. de Klerk, warmly shaking Castro's hand.[765] Castro had reason to be pleased: South Africa had finally caved in to the forces which Cuba had so long assisted, not by being beaten on the field of battle, but by betrayal. Here he was, one of South Africa's arch-foes, shaking hands with de Klerk on South African soil.

A very interesting fact about the inauguration was that, while foreign guests turned up in great numbers, South Africans themselves did not! In addition to the 5000 VIP's, 150 000 free tickets were issued to the South African people. Yet thousands of tickets were not distributed, and of the thousands who did receive them, there were only 40 000 who attended. Most of the tickets were to have been distributed through ANC channels, and this indicates that the ANC certainly did not have as much support as the polls had suggested![766]

But it was a day of celebration around the world, for South Africa had been conquered. A Communist was in power, the immense wealth of the country was available to the internationalist forces, and one of the last remaining pieces of the jigsaw was now in place. Piece by piece, the world map was taking shape according to the plans of the Jesuit/Illuminati forces at work behind the scenes. Another domino had fallen, a vitally important one.

Never had the world united around a single cause - the fall of South Africa to Communism - as it had around this one. Deceptively, the *end* of the freedom which it once enjoyed was proclaimed jubilantly as the *beginning* of its freedom. Its diverse peoples were now under Marxist rule, and the country itself in bondage to the powerful masters who had orchestrated its fall.

And behind May 10, 1994, stretching back into the years that had passed, was a river of blood and tears that no celebrations on that day could ever dry up.

---

[765] *The Natal Witness*, May 11, 1994.
[766] *Roca Report*, No.65, May 1994.

CHAPTER FORTY-ONE

WHAT HAS THIS BOOK SHOWN?

In this chapter we must consider some of the truths that it has been the purpose of this book to demonstrate; and then we must answer the question: Why did the Lord God allow South Africa to fall to Communism?

What, then, has this book shown? It has been something of a history of South Africa, certainly; but its purpose has not simply been to record various historical facts. There are a number of important truths that stand out as we peruse the history of this country.

The first one is this: that *God is sovereign over the affairs of men and nations.* This has been a constantly recurring theme in this book. As the events of centuries have been set before our view - the discoveries, the adventures, the wars, the political intrigues, the drama, the terror, the deceit, as well as the coming of Christianity and the diffusion of the Gospel - the sovereignty of God has stood out in bold relief. Above the shouts of sailors rounding the Cape of Good Hope, above the creaking sounds of trek-wagons crossing the open grasslands or being dragged up mighty mountain ranges, above the noise of gunfire and the clashing of spears and shields, and above the arrogant claims of men in high places, can be heard the voice of a proud ruler of old, who was brought to acknowledge a truth which is proclaimed throughout the Word of God and throughout the pages of history: the voice of the great king, Nebuchadnezzar, can be heard saying, "I blessed the most High, and I praised and honoured him that liveth for ever, whose dominion is an everlasting dominion, and his kingdom is from generation to generation: and all the inhabitants of the earth are reputed as nothing: and he doeth according to his will in the army of heaven, and among the inhabitants of the earth: and none can stay his hand, or say unto him, What doest thou?" (Dan.4:34,35). Reader, can you hear that voice speaking? Though Nebuchadnezzar is long dead, his testimony to the sovereignty of God lives on in Holy Scripture, and finds an answering echo in the pages of history.

Behind the many scenes which have unfolded in these pages, can be discerned the hand of God in the affairs of men. For God is not a mere spectator of all that occurs on this earth which he has made. He governs all things which occur in heaven and on earth, for he has decreed from all eternity whatsoever takes place throughout his mighty universe. "Whatsoever the Lord pleased, that did he in heaven, and in earth, in the seas, and all deep places" (Psa.135:6). The movement of mighty armies (Isa.10:5,6; 46:9-11), and the flight and fall of tiny sparrows (Matt.10:29), are both governed by his sovereignty.

Reader, do you see it? Is the God you worship a God of your own imagination, weak, helpless, unable to do anything unless man helps him? Or is he the sovereign, omnipotent God of the Bible? Has the Lord opened your eyes to see and understand that all that is occurring on this earth is occurring because God has decreed it? Have you been enabled to see that his prophetic Word is being fulfilled; that nations, no less than individuals, are in his hands, and he does with them what he wills?

The unregenerate man is of the earth, and sees only the things of earth. His eyes can rise no higher. But the child of God, born from above, looks *up;* and there he sees God, the Almighty God, the sovereign God, sitting on his throne. "The Lord is in his holy temple, the Lord's throne is in heaven: his eyes behold, his eyelids try, the children of men" (Psa.11:4). In his sight "the nations are as a drop of a bucket, and are counted as the small dust of the balance: behold, he taketh up the isles as a very little thing" (Isa.40:15). Indeed, "all nations before him are as nothing; and they are counted to him less than nothing, and vanity" (vs.17). The child of God sees more than a seemingly random series of historical events. He sees, behind them all, a divine *plan.* And he is awed, he is humbled, and....he is content. "For yet a little while, and the wicked shall not be: yea, thou shalt diligently consider his place, and it shall not be" (Psa.37:10). The wicked certainly "plotteth against the just, and gnasheth upon him with his teeth"; but "the Lord shall laugh at him: for he seeth that his day is coming" (vss.12,13).

You, dear reader, are in the hands of this God. "In [his] hand is the soul of every living thing, and the breath of all mankind" (Job 12:10). He "giveth to all life, and breath, and all things", and "in him we live, and move, and have our being" (Acts 17:25,28). He can extinguish your life in a moment. Your very existence, right now, is by his goodness and mercy alone. Fall down before him! Repent, and call upon the name of the Lord Jesus Christ! Cry out to him for mercy and salvation, if you have never done so, trusting in the merits of the Son of God, Jesus Christ, alone, and not in your own works. He alone is the Saviour, and through him alone men and women can come to God. For God gave him to be the Redeemer of his elect: he died on the cross for their sins, and rose again from the dead for their justification (Rom.4:25).

Another important truth which this book demonstrates, is that *the Roman Catholic institution is not a Christian church.* Compare the deeds of this institution with the Word of God: do you see it walking in the steps of Christ (1 Pet.2:21)? Its leaders condoned all kinds of crimes, justified all kinds of atrocities. They praised murderers and terrorists, supported the barbaric revolution in South Africa, and perverted the Holy Scripture so as to make the Word of the living God *appear* to support revolution and terrorism. *Are these the servants of God?* And bear in mind that this book focuses on one particular country, and what the Papal priesthood has done here. Around the world, however, they have been, and are, active in the same kinds of abominations, as modern history testifies, and for which there is ample evidence, from Europe, Latin America, other parts of Africa, North America, Asia. And not only modern history. Search the records! Study the history of nations! The horrifying facts are all there. Centuries of wickedness cannot be obliterated from the records of mankind. No organisation on the face of the earth has ever been so deeply involved in murders, assassinations, wars, revolutions, and a thousand other crimes as has the Roman Catholic system. So says the Word of God, in Revelation 17, 18, and elsewhere, and history testifies to the truth of every sentence of the prophetic Word. The Papal system, and no other, is "that great whore that sitteth upon many waters: with whom the kings of the earth have committed fornication, and the inhabitants of the earth have been made drunk with the wine of her fornication" (Rev.17:1,2); sitting on seven mountains, manipulating political powers, reigning over the nations of the world, immensely wealthy, heathenism professing to be Christianity, drunk with the blood of the saints and martyrs of Jesus (vss.3-18).

Look at her! She is not in any sense a Christian church! And the vile part she played in the downfall of South Africa is yet another piece of evidence against her. Where and when, in all the centuries since she rose among the nations (Dan.7:8,19-22,24,25), has she displayed the marks of a Christian church? Nowhere. Not once. She is the Great Whore, not the spotless bride of Christ (compare Rev.17:1 with Rev.21:9); mystical Babylon, not mystical Zion (compare Rev.17:5 with Psa.87); the religion of Antichrist, not the Church of Christ.

And, as certainly as the Papal system is not a Christian church, but "the Mother of Harlots and Abominations of the earth" (Rev.17:5), this book also shows that, just as certainly, the so-called "Protestant" institutions which are members of the World Council of Churches, and/or in fellowship with the Great Whore, are *the harlot daughters of Rome, and not Christian churches!* Compare the deeds of these institutions with the Word of God: do you see *them* walking in the steps of Christ? Their leaders, too, have condoned all kinds of wickedness, and distorted the true meaning of Holy Scripture, in order to promote the Marxist revolution in South Africa. Can such men possibly be the servants of the most high God, the ambassadors of Christ? And again, bear in mind that this book focuses on one particular country, and what they have done here. Around the world, however, the story is the same.

Nor will it do for anyone to put forward the names of this man, and that man, who are allegedly exceptions to the rule. That is not the point. Within these institutions there can be found men who are *not* Communists, supporters of killers, revolutionaries, etc. Of course there can! There are, within them, men who are, no doubt, good men, according to the world's judgement of goodness. There are, within these systems, sincere men, kind men, loving men, gentle men (and gentlemen). But the fact remains that the institutions themselves are abominations, not Christian churches, any decent men within them notwithstanding; and *all* those within them are participating in their sins, directly or indirectly.

Is this to say that there are no true Christians within these institutions? Within the Roman Catholic institution, it can be said with absolute certainty that there are none. No Roman Catholic is a true

Christian. No-one who prays and trusts in Mary and so-called "saints", elevates human tradition to an equality with the Word of God, trusts in such human works as the sacraments of Rome, views his "baptism" as the moment when he was "born again", believes he "receives Christ" every time he eats the wafer in the mass, and confesses his sins to a priest and not to the Lord alone - no-one who holds to these lies can possibly be a Christian. And no-one who says he is a Roman Catholic, but rejects these things, is a Roman Catholic. For these are the doctrines of Roman Catholicism.

When the Lord, in his sovereign mercy, saves the soul of a Romanist, that person leaves the religion of Rome. It has never been otherwise, and never will be (Rev.18:4,5).

Within certain "Protestant" institutions that are harlot daughters of Rome, however, there may yet be a small number of true Christians. The reason for this is that some of them are still sound doctrinally, at least on those doctrines necessary to be known and believed for salvation - such things as the person and work of Christ, and salvation by grace through faith alone. They cannot be called true Christian churches, however, because they do not live according to what they profess to believe, they harbour wicked men in their ranks, they condone (or at the least, overlook) evil deeds in their members, they flirt with the Great Whore and other ungodly institutions, etc. Within them, there are Christian men and women who, out of ignorance regarding either the doings of these institutions, or out of ignorance regarding their duty to leave, remain within them. They are, however, sinning against the Lord, for separation from such wicked institutions is commanded in Scripture (2 Cor.6:14-18).

To illustrate: here is a man within a particular Protestant denomination. He has been saved by the grace of God. He trusts in Jesus Christ alone. But his denomination is fellowshipping with various kinds of heretics and ungodly men and institutions. *He* does not do so, but either out of ignorance as to what, precisely, his denomination is doing, or out of a mistaken belief that it would somehow be wrong just to separate entirely from it, he remains within it. There is a great dearth of sound preaching (and preachers) in our day, and much ignorance on such matters abounds.

Here, on the other hand, is a man who, having been a Roman

Catholic, has now been converted. Even if no fellow-Christian ever told him that he must leave the Papal system, it will not take him long to realise that this *is,* without question, his duty. He is trusting in Christ, but every week Papists address prayers to Mary for salvation and mercy and assistance. He has confessed his sins to the Lord, but every day Papists are confessing to a man. He knows that salvation is by faith alone, but blinded Papists are trusting in baptism, and penances, and the mass, and a whole host of other things. The errors, the blasphemies, are too blatant. The quickened child of God will soon see them, and forsake that heathen religion.

Reader, are *you* a Roman Catholic? If so, you are an idolater, trusting in various works of your own to earn heaven. You are not a Christian. Repent, and believe on the Lord Jesus Christ for salvation! Flee from mystical Babylon and all its wickedness.

Or are you, perhaps, a member of some so-called "Protestant" institution that, at least on paper, appears sound, but is in reality a false religious system, as evidenced by its works? Perhaps you never knew what the leaders of your denomination were doing. Perhaps you knew little, or nothing, about the World Council of Churches, to which your denomination belongs; or about Romanism, with which, you now realise, your denomination is flirting. Have you called upon the Lord, by faith? Are you a child of God by faith in Jesus Christ? If so, then forsake your denomination! For to remain is to participate, however indirectly, in its sin. And if you have never been saved by the grace of God, but now realise that you are lost, and that you have been deceiving yourself as to your own spiritual state, then fall before the Lord and cry out for mercy; and he *will* save you.

Other facts which this book reveals are: that Communism is still very much alive and well, as much a danger to true Christians as ever; that there *are* diabolical plots to place the nations and peoples of the world under a single government; but that, behind them, unnoticed by most of the world and even by many of the plotters, stands the Papacy.

South Africa has fallen to Communism. Communism persecutes the saints of God, and strives to destroy the true Christian Church. It is a terrible danger to all true believers in Christ, and for this reason its plots and intrigues must be exposed. The watchmen of Zion are to warn the flocks of Christ about the dangers they face. But in addition, the present author has sought to demonstrate in this book that Communism - that diabolical ideology, responsible for the deaths of millions upon millions of people, including an untold number of Christians - is in fact a daughter of Rome. And it is being manipulated by, and furthering the interests of, the Vatican.

That the Papal system is the very centre of all conspiracies is what the prophetic Word of God informs us, in the prophecies of Daniel, Revelation, 2 Thessalonians, etc. And this is what the facts confirm. The woman, the harlot, sits on seven mountains; and truly, all roads *do* lead to Rome, "that great city, which reigneth over the kings of the earth" (Rev.17:9,18). Some of the roads are clearly visible, and some are not. There is much evidence showing the connection between Rome and some of the conspiracies and plotters, and little evidence showing its connections with some of the others. This is to be expected. It is in the nature of such things to be deliberately very secretive. But whether we have every single shred of evidence or not, we have God's prophetic Word: and *it* tells us to look to Rome! Every so often, the curtain is drawn aside just a little, and we see a piece of evidence proving the connection; and all the pieces form a great picture. Some of the evidence is given in this book.

And this makes the exposure of Communism all the more necessary! For not only is it a monstrous persecuting system, a terrible danger to true Christians everywhere, which would be reason enough to expose it; but *in addition,* in exposing Communism, *Romanism* is exposed. As the horrifying nature of Communism is made known, along with the evidence of its connections with Popery, this information is yet another nail in the coffin of the Papal system's claim to be a Church of Jesus Christ - *the* Church of Jesus Christ, in fact. For no true Church of Christ would ever throw its weight behind such evil.

Popery never had a leg to stand on, anyway, in making such a claim. By both its doctrines and its centuries of evil deeds, it has always shown itself to be nothing more than heathenism masquerading as Christianity. But why should we stop accumulating the evidence? Why should we only refer to its dark deeds in the past? We must expose its *present* crimes as well! God's prophetic Word declares that the Roman Catholic institution will continue to persecute the saints of God, and commit its other abominable deeds, until the very return of the Lord Jesus Christ! See, for example, Dan.7:21,22, 2 Thess.2:8, and Rev.18. It did not cease to persecute, or to belch out its blasphemies, at the time of the Reformation, or the French Revolution, or at the beginning of the twentieth century! We *must* continue to expose the sins it committed in centuries gone by - but it is *still* committing them today, and these must be exposed too!

The twentieth century has experienced two world wars, and a vast number of other regional wars, conflicts, revolutions, etc. (such as the revolution in South Africa). How many, today, know just how deeply the Vatican was involved in the first and second world wars,[767] or in many of the regional wars worldwide?[768] Rome has been very successful in covering its tracks, suppressing the truth about itself; but the evidence *is* still there, and it is truly overwhelming! The Great Whore has *not* changed since the Second Vatican Council in the early 1960's, as she would like the world to believe. She remains what she ever has been, and she will remain so until the end of the world and the return of Christ. Exposing her deep involvement with Communism is simply hammering another nail into the coffin. It is yet another piece of evidence, added to the accumulated mounds of centuries, demonstrating that she is not a Christian Church, and that her adherents are not Christians.

The Papacy seeks world control, a Roman Catholic world. All countries are targets, but in particular those which are predominantly

---

[767] See, for example, the following by Edmond Paris: *The Vatican Against Europe* (The Wycliffe Press, 1988); *The Secret History of the Jesuits* (Chick Publications, undated); and *Convert….or Die!* (Chick Publications, undated). See also the following by Avro Manhattan: *The Vatican in World Politics* (Horizon Press, Inc., 1949), and *The Vatican's Holocaust* (Ozark Books, 1988); as well as *Ratlines*, by Mark Aarons and John Loftus (William Heinemann Ltd., 1991).

[768] See, for example, the following by Avro Manhattan: *The Vatican Moscow Washington Alliance* (1986); *Catholic Terror in Ireland* (1988); and *Vietnam: Why Did We Go?* (1984); all published by Chick Publications.

Protestant, or which are governed by Protestants. This is not to say that, being predominantly Protestant, they are predominantly Christian, or that, being governed by Protestants, they are governed by Christians! By no means! Certainly biblical Christianity is Protestant, but by no means can all that is termed Protestant be equated with biblical Christianity (as this book has shown)! Nevertheless, so-called "Protestant" countries have generally been havens for the true Gospel, and their citizens less inclined towards Popery than the citizens of other countries. They have generally permitted freedom of worship, freedom to print Bibles, literature, etc., and freedom to propagate the Gospel. And for these reasons, such countries are, in particular, targets of the Great Whore. South Africa was one of the chief prizes, and it finally fell. As of April/May 1994, it had a Marxist-dominated government which looked with favour upon the Vatican.

May this book, even as it documents the Communist assault on South Africa over the decades, go some way in making up the deficiency in the published documentation regarding the abominable deeds of the Roman Catholic institution in modern times.

Finally in this chapter, we must seek an answer to this question: *Why* did the Lord permit South Africa to fall to the forces of Communism?

We have seen, in this book, why the string-pullers behind the scenes wanted it to fall; but why did the Lord permit it? Let us consider the reasons.

The first is that South Africa, like all the countries of the world, inexorably follows the path that the Lord God has decreed for it. Nothing is by chance. Of all the nations of men, God's Word says that he "hath determined the times before appointed, and the bounds of their habitation" (Acts 17:26). And not only where they will dwell, but who will govern them, and when (Dan.2:21), and what their state and condition will be from one year to the next, from one century to the next. The rise and fall of the empires of Babylon, Greece, Medo-Persia, and Rome, occurred at precisely such times in history as God had ordained (Dan.2:31-45). Many lands around the world were once colonised by Great Britain; but where is its glory today? The United States of America is at present a world power; but this great power, too, will wane. Indeed, the decline is already well-advanced.

The Lord is sovereignly controlling the movement of all nations, and all countries, along a predestined path. Events on the world stage fulfil prophecy. For this to be so, every single nation must be in precisely the place that the sovereign Lord wants it to be, at any given time. And before the return of the Lord Jesus Christ, all the nations of the earth will be in precisely the state they are meant to be in, before that blessed event occurs.

Seen in this context, then, the fall of South Africa to Communism was not an accident: it was permitted by God. It was predestined by God. One important reason for the change of government in a country, then, is simply the sovereign, predestined will of God.

Another reason is this: that as the iniquity of all nations, all countries, increases, sooner or later they fall under divine judgement. On this the Scriptures are very clear:

The Lord promised Abraham that he would give the land of Canaan to his descendants. But first, the Lord told him, they would dwell in Egypt, and in the fourth generation they would come into the promised land; "for the iniquity of the Amorites is not yet full" (Gen.15:16). The Amorites dwelt in that land. They were a wicked nation, but when God spoke these words to Abraham, their sins had not yet reached the very brim of the cup, so to speak: going on in their wickedness, they would add iniquity to iniquity, until the cup was so full that the Lord would punish them by using the Israelites as his instrument against them. In Scripture we find that the Lord often used one nation to punish another for its wickedness, once the iniquity of that nation was full. In Isaiah 10, God calls the Assyrian "the rod of mine anger", and says, "I will send him against an hypocritical nation" (vss.5,6), the nation of Israel. He used the Assyrians to punish Israel for its wickedness. In Dan.8:23, we read, "And in the latter time of their kingdom, when the transgressors are come to the full, a king of fierce countenance, and understanding dark sentences, shall stand up." Without going into the full meaning of the verse, let it be noted that, when the sins of the people reached the limit decreed by God, they were to be punished. And consider the words of the Lord Jesus to the Jews, in Matt.23:32: "Fill ye up then the measure of your fathers"; that is to say, their fathers had been filling the cup over many, many years, but now they were to fill it to the brim, by adding their iniquities to their fathers' iniquities.

Nations and countries are made up of sinful individuals; and the heart of man being as desperately wicked as it is, nations and countries do not generally improve, morally, as one generation succeeds another: they grow worse. Biblical history, as well as general world history seen in the light of the Bible, confirms this. And sooner or later, every nation, and every country, comes under the wrath of God. And he afflicts it with severe wars, or famines, or pestilences, or other calamities.

Now, if this is true of any nation or country, even one without the Scriptures, or sound preachers of righteousness, or any knowledge of the truth, how much more so of one in which the majority of inhabitants falsely profess to be Christians! For their iniquity is that much greater. Jesus, in pronouncing woe upon the cities of Chorazin, Bethsaida, and Capernaum, said that their eternal punishment would be greater than that of Tyre, Sidon, and Sodom (Matt.11:20-24). For Tyre, Sidon, and Sodom did not witness the mighty works of Christ which Chorazin, Bethsaida and Capernaum witnessed. Christ did not walk the streets of the former three cities, as he did the streets of the latter three. And a land which has enjoyed much Gospel light; a land which has had an open Bible, readily available, and preachers of righteousness; a land, the vast majority of whose inhabitants profess to be Christians; and yet which heaps iniquity upon iniquity, year after year - such a land will come under the wrath of God.

Take South Africa. The great majority of South Africans profess to be Christians. They are *not,* of course; but they profess to be. They *claim* to see; and Jesus once said to those who claimed not to be spiritually blind, "If ye were blind, ye should have no sin: but now ye say, We see; therefore your sin remaineth" (Jn.9:41). All across the land, week after week after week, millions upon millions of South Africans stream to their various places of worship, claiming to be Christians, claiming to worship the true God and his Son Jesus Christ. All across the land, in multiplied millions of homes, the Bible is prominently displayed, and they profess to order their lives according to its holy teachings. *And yet.....*

South Africans, professing to be Christians, are *idolaters*, worshipping the modern idols of sport, television, and a whole host of other worldly pleasures; they indulge in drunkenness, revelries, sexual sins of all types; their bookstores and libraries flooded with pornographic filth, their homes awash in alcohol, their nights filled with erotic "entertainment", their days spent in pursuing the idol of wealth and the idol of luxury; their marriages ending in divorce, their children seen as mere nuisances and dispatched with enough money to entertain themselves as they see fit, while their parents indulge their own brands of sin. Whites despise blacks, and blacks hate whites. And yet they profess to be Christians, the vast majority of them!

Is it any wonder that South Africa has been suffered to endure such a terrible revolution? The Bible says, "Righteousness exalteth a nation: but sin is a reproach to any people" (Prov.14:34). This again is not to say that any particular nation is a *Christian* nation, or that any ever has been; for that is not the case. But certainly it is true that there have been times, in history, when certain nations have been (in one sense) righteous nations, for the most part; their governments and most of the people doing what is externally right, at least in their relationships with one another; and this has been the case when a large section of the population has been greatly influenced by biblical truth, with many being truly regenerate. Such nations have risen above the nations around them, and reached heights which their neighbours were not even able to dream of.

The various nations inhabiting the borders of the country of South Africa, with all their privileges, with all their divine favours, with their readily-available Bibles, with their preachers and Gospel literature, have nevertheless rejected the Gospel which once many of their forefathers embraced heartily, and have rejected the moral law of God which in the past was such a restraining influence on so many of their leaders and people, even though the majority of them were not true Christians. They have become "lovers of their own selves, covetous, boasters, proud, blasphemers, disobedient to parents, unthankful, unholy, without natural affection, trucebreakers, false accusers, incontinent, fierce, despisers of those that are good, traitors, heady, high-minded, lovers of pleasures more than lovers of God; having a form of godliness, but denying the power thereof" (2 Tim.3:2-5). Is it any wonder that they have been suffered to go through such a revolution, or that they are now ruled by such wicked men?

The Lord said, "But Jeshurun [Israel] waxed fat, and kicked" (Deut.32:15); that is, he rebelled against God, he kicked against him. In prosperity he lightly esteemed the Lord. And so it can be said of South Africa. Fat and prosperous, its people kicked against God. Having spiritual blessings above many of the lands of the earth, they lightly esteemed them. And judgement finally fell.

But what has been said of South Africa can also be said of the other lands of the earth which have enjoyed such blessings from God, sometimes even more than South Africa ever did. What of thou, O Great Britain? Or of thou, the United States of America? All that has been said above about the sins which South Africans are wallowing in, can be applied with equal force to the peoples of Great Britain, the United States, and the other Western lands. The US, for example, is a moral cesspool and a land of bloodshed. Sexual perversion of all types is rampant. Homosexual parades, with tens of thousands of participants, are held in many cities, with this wickedness being openly and defiantly flaunted, and with the blessing of those in top government positions. Hollywood continues to spew out its filth, and its heroes and heroines are those who can sink the lowest in human depravity. Tens of millions of human beings have been killed in abortion clinics around the land. Violent crime in the major cities is almost epidemic. And in addition, the US is committing increasingly open fornication with the Great Whore. Can divine judgement be too far away? As for what was once "Great" Britain, that once-blessed isle is filled with the same abominations, and crying out for the judgement of God. Indeed, has not divine wrath *already* begun to be poured out on the US and Britain and other Western lands? Surely it has, and it will increase more and more as the days go by. No country can tolerate within its borders the kind of wickedness that now characterises the Western lands, and escape the wrath of the Almighty God; much less can those do so, which in the past enjoyed so many divine favours.

It may also be that the Lord has permitted the Marxist takeover of this country, with all the misery that could follow, in order to use these things to awaken many to their spiritual emptiness, and to their need of him. South Africa has been prosperous for so long that most of the population is utterly indifferent to spiritual truth. A time of want, of suffering, of hopelessness, could be used, in the hands of the sovereign God, to cause people to seek after the Lord, as happened in Russia in recent times, and in other parts of the world during different periods of history.

And finally, yet another reason why the Lord may have permitted South Africa to fall to Marxism is to *try his Church* in this land. To all true believers the Word of God says that "we must through much tribulation enter into the kingdom of God" (Acts 14:22); that "all that will live godly in Christ Jesus shall suffer persecution" (2 Tim.3:12). South African Christians have enjoyed a long period of freedom from any form of persecution. That time may now be over. Should persecution break out against the Church, many, who for years have *professed* to follow the Lord, will be offended, and wither away (Matt.13:5,6,20,21). Then it shall be made manifest who the *true* followers of the Lamb are. This is an extremely religious country. The overwhelming majority of the population professes to be Christian. As has been pointed out in this book, the truth is very different. The plain fact is that the vast majority of professing "Christians" in this country (as in all other Western lands today) are *not true Christians.* A time of persecution would prove to be a time of purging, as it did in Israel of old (Dan.11:33-35). This will, in one sense, be beneficial to the Church of Christ. The professing "Church" in South Africa is filled to the brim with worldly, prosperous, pleasure-loving people. They would be purged out in the fiery trial.

To those who are the Lord's little flock in this land, this question must be posed: are you ready for what you may be called upon to endure?

And to those in other, safer lands who are true believers, a question must be posed as well: are you praying for your brethren in South Africa and other places where they are being, or could soon be, persecuted? And are you preparing for the trials that could soon come *your* way too?

CHAPTER FORTY-TWO

THE CHRISTIAN'S DUTIES

What are the duties of Christians under a Marxist government? How are they to live?

Let it be clearly understood from the outset, that regarding the worship and service of the Lord their duties under a Marxist government are precisely the same as their duties under any other government. They are to go on meeting for worship, even if forbidden to do so (Heb.10:25); they are to go on preaching the Gospel to the lost, even if forbidden to do so (Acts 5:27-29); they are to go on living as Christians in the midst of a crooked and perverse nation (Phil.2:15). God must be obeyed. It is right to obey earthly governments in all lawful matters (Rom.13:1-7), but not if they command that which is sinful (Acts 5:29).

In May 1994 Nelson Mandela became the new President of South Africa. Regardless of how he came to that exalted position, regardless of the terrible deeds that took place over many years in order to bring him to power, the fact remains that in May 1994 he became president. He became the supreme ruler of the land.

It was the will of God. And however much Christians abhor the method whereby he came to power, and although such abominable deeds can never be condoned, brushed aside or forgotten, as of May 1994 Christians in South Africa were duty-bound to submit to him and to his government as the highest power in the land. Caesar plundered and fought and killed in order to become ruler of virtually the entire known world of his time, including the land of the Jews, but the Lord Jesus still said to those Jews who objected paying tribute to this heathen tyrant, "Render therefore unto Caesar the things which are Caesar's; and unto God the things that are God's" (Matt.22:21). And it was while bloodthirsty Caesar ruled the known world that Paul wrote, "Let every soul be subject unto the higher powers. For there is no power but of God: the powers that be are ordained of God. Whosoever therefore resisteth the power, resisteth the ordinance of God: and they that resist shall receive to themselves damnation" (Rom.13:1,2). It was while bloodthirsty Caesar ruled, too, that Peter wrote, "Submit yourselves to every ordinance of man for the Lord's sake: whether it be to the king, as supreme; or unto governors" (1 Pet.2:13,14).

True Christians rightly abhor the wicked deeds of the liberal, leftist "church" leaders who resisted the National Party government, and called it illegal, and sought its violent downfall so that the ANC could take power. Once the ANC came to power, however, no true Christian could resist the legitimate laws of the new government. To do so would be to commit the very same sin that the Marxist-supporting "churches" had committed when they resisted the previous government. The Bible does not command Christians to submit only to good governments, but to bad ones as well; to Communist as well as non-Communist ones, to dictatorships as much as to republican or monarchical forms of government. It is God who removes and sets up rulers.

When Nelson Mandela became president, Christians became duty-bound to submit to him in all lawful matters, obeying the laws laid down, paying their taxes (Rom.13:6), etc.; and thereby rendering that honour due to him, as the one holding the highest position in the land, which Christians are commanded to render, regardless of the personal character of the man occupying that position (vs.7; also 1 Pet.2:17). Furthermore, they became duty-bound to *pray* for him, and for his government (1 Tim.2:1,2): praying for the conversion of members of the government; praying for them to rule wisely; and praying that the Christian Church would be left alone to go about its business, and that Christians would be able to "lead a quiet and peaceable life in all godliness and honesty" (1 Tim.2:2).

Christians may not oppose a government with violence, or campaigns of disobedience. When elections are held, however, they may certainly oppose a government legally. For if a government grants its citizens the right to vote it out of office, they may certainly make use of the privilege.

Of course, having rigged one election, the ANC could easily rig another; but such things are in the hands of the Lord.

And Christians may readily become involved in politics, and even run for public office, if they can do so without sinning against the Lord and his Word. Joseph in Egypt, and Daniel in Babylon, are examples of two godly men who held high positions in powerful governments, and were able to do much good there. As certainly as there are Christians in business and commerce and industry, so there can be Christians in politics. History contains examples of Christian believers who served their Lord faithfully in high positions, and brought about changes for the better. No earthly government lasts forever. Rulers come and go; governments rise and fall. The years roll on, and only the Lord remains the same, yesterday, today and forever.

And so, dear Christian reader, look up! "If ye then be risen with Christ, seek those things which are above, where Christ sitteth on the right hand of God. Set your affection on things above, not on things on the earth. For ye are dead, and your life is hid with Christ in God" (Col.3:1-3). This world, and the kingdoms of it, and the puny empires which ungodly men seek to build, shall all pass away in God's appointed time. Do not be dismayed, nor fearful. The Lord God omnipotent reigns! Men shake their fists at him, but he laughs at them. And the day is coming when the Lord Jesus Christ, the Son of the living God, will return to the earth in power and great glory, to gather his elect to himself, and to destroy this wicked world. And then time shall be no more, and the righteous shall shine forth as the sun in the kingdom of their Father, for ever and ever.

Be about the Father's business! Love God above all, worship him, study his Word, be much in prayer, live godly in Christ Jesus, preach his Gospel to the lost. "Let love be without dissimulation. Abhor that which is evil; cleave to that which is good. Be kindly affectioned one to another with brotherly love; in honour preferring one another; not slothful in business; fervent in spirit; serving the Lord; rejoicing in hope; patient in tribulation; continuing instant in prayer; distributing to the necessity of saints; given to hospitality. Bless them which persecute you; bless, and curse not" (Rom.12:9-14).

Oh, this continent of Africa! This war-ravaged, disease-ridden, poverty-stricken, yet beautiful continent. In the north, Islam holds sway, and is advancing southward, assisted by international

Communism. In the centre, Romanism holds sway, and is both assisted by, and assisting, Communism and tyranny and dictatorial rule. And in the south, South Africa came under Communist rule, assisted by Romanism and the World Council of Churches. "The harvest truly is plenteous, but the labourers are few; pray ye therefore the Lord of the harvest, that he will send forth labourers into his harvest" (Matt.9:37,38). Where are the labourers for Africa? Where are those who will weep, and pray, and go? "He that goeth forth and weepeth, bearing precious seed, shall doubtless come again with rejoicing, bringing his sheaves with him" (Psa.126:6). May many be found who will weep, and pray, and go forth with the precious seed of the Gospel.

And oh! this country of South Africa! This land of breathtaking natural beauty, and yet of such horrifying savagery. Infested with "churches" and "ministers" that hold to, and proclaim, a false "gospel", its peoples desperately need to hear the *true* Gospel of the grace of God. Here and there a preacher of righteousness may be found, here and there a faithful church. But that is all. And the day may come when the few that there are may be forced into exile, or called to lay down their lives for Christ and his Gospel. It may not happen, but the signs are all there. Let the saints of God weep, and pray, and go forth with the precious seed of the everlasting Gospel. The Papal Antichrist must be opposed, and the Lord Jesus Christ must be exalted. The Great Whore and her "Protestant" daughters must be exposed for what they are: the enemies of Christ, his Gospel and his Church. And this must be done by lifting up the Word of God, the Bible, and saying with a loud and certain voice, "Thus saith the Lord!" There is "another Jesus" being preached, and "another gospel" being accepted, by millions in South Africa, in Africa, and around the world. Let the saints of God arise and say, "Lies! They speak lies in the name of the Lord! They are false teachers proclaiming damnable heresies! What they say is *not* what the Scriptures say! Hear, all you people, the Word of the living God!"

It is the prayer of the author that this book goes some way towards asserting biblical truth, and exposing the devilish lies of wicked men claiming to be servants of Christ, in these days of great darkness.

ABOUT THE AUTHOR:

Shaun Willcock was born in the southern African country known then as Rhodesia (now Marxist-ruled Zimbabwe), but apart from a few years spent there during his childhood, he has lived all his life in South Africa, a country he dearly loves. A minister of the Gospel, he operates Bible Based Ministries, the purpose of which is to teach the Word of God, and to expose and biblically refute Roman Catholicism, its "daughter" institutions, its assaults upon the Christian faith and the Christian Church, and the various Popish trappings to be found even amongst true Christians.

For information about available books, tapes, pamphlets and tracts, please write to Bible Based Ministries' U.S. distributor:

**Contending for the Faith Ministries
42055 Crestland Drive
Lancaster, CA 93536
United States of America**